D1547449

The 'Red Years'

EUROPEAN SOCIALISM VERSUS
BOLSHEVISM, 1919–1921

The 'Red Years'

EUROPEAN SOCIALISM VERSUS
BOLSHEVISM, 1919-1921

Albert S. Lindemann

UNIVERSITY OF CALIFORNIA PRESS
Berkeley, Los Angeles, London
1974

University of California Press
Berkeley and Los Angeles, California

University of California Press, Ltd.
London, England

ISBN: 0–520–02511–3
Library of Congress Catalog Card Number: 73–80834
Copyright © 1974 by The Regents of the University of California

Printed in the United States of America

We dreamt of taking part in a harmonious synthesis of the broad humanism of Jaurès and the revolutionary audacity of Lenin.

L.-O. Frossard

I cannot agree with those confused workers and intellectuals who have made a fetish out of the Russian example.

Ernst Däumig

It is easy to destroy but difficult to rebuild.

G. M. Serrati

Either one is a menshevik or a bolshevik; there is no third way.

Gregory Zinoviev

Acknowledgments

I have incurred relatively few debts in preparing this work, and rather than offer the traditional list of pro-forma acknowledgements, I would like to devote a few lines to those for whose help I feel a special gratitude. First, to Agnes Peterson, curator of the western European collection of the Hoover Institution, whose efficiency, helpfulness, and broad knowledge were of inestimable help in the opening stage of my research. Second, to professors Peter Kenez and William Rosenberg, friends who offered valuable advice when the work was in a difficult stage of composition. Finally, and most of all, to my wife, Barbara, who took much time—more than I had any right to ask of her—from her own historical research to help me; nearly every page of this work has been influenced by her clarity of mind and solid sense of literary style.

A. S. L.

Santa Barbara

Contents

Introduction

As the machines of war were stilled in the late autumn of 1918, virtually all observers agreed that the old Europe was dead. The fifty-two month nightmare had come to an end, but what would now follow? The smoking ruins, the dizzying row upon row of graveyard crosses, the hobbling and mutilated veterans of the trenches constituted a searing indictment of those who had been in positions of power during the past generation. To many it seemed inevitable that the socialists, the political pariahs of pre-1914 Europe, would move toward the center of the political stage in most countries. Indeed, the first major political upheaval growing out of the war, the revolution in Russia, saw a steady swing leftward until even moderate socialists lost all control, and leadership of Russia fell to the most extreme of all Russian socialist factions, the bolsheviks, who within a year adopted the name "communist." Thereafter, the specter of communism haunted Europe far more than when, seventy years before, Marx had made it dance before the eyes of an anxious ruling class. By the time of the signing of the Armistice in November 1918, socialists had assumed political leadership of Germany, and by the summer of 1919 pro-bolshevik communist regimes were in power in Hungary and Bavaria. In the two decisive years following the end of the war, succinctly termed the *biennio rosso* (the red two years) by the Italians, most of Europe was shaken to its roots by strikes, uprisings, mutinies, factory occupations, and other challenges to existing authority.

A climax to these developments came in the late summer of 1920. The Red Army, having driven back an attack by the Poles, was triumphantly marching into central Europe, and in the halls of the Kremlin high hopes were entertained that the proletariat of western Europe would rise up to join hands with the advancing Russian forces. Gathered in Moscow at the same time was perhaps the greatest meeting of revolutionaries ever to assemble: men from nearly every country of the world had come to the Second Congress of the Communist International, to learn from the bolsheviks and to speed the progress of world revolution. The most important of these delegations, from the standpoint of the bolsheviks' hopes to break out of their isolation, were those from Germany, France, and Italy. It was to these three countries that the bolsheviks gave special attention in planning revolution and in establishing communist parties. It was in these three countries as well that revolutionaries especially admired the success of the bolsheviks and hoped to work together with them to assure the success of revolution throughout Europe.

The *biennio rosso* was a period remarkable for the richness of ideological debate between those western socialists who were favorably impressed by the Bolshevik Revolution and those who were suspicious of or even hostile to it. The prewar doyens of Marxian orthodoxy, such men as Karl Kautsky, Filippo Turati, and Jules Guesde, were vigorously challenged by the first successful Marxian revolutionary, V. I. Lenin. These champions of scientific socialism were forced to reformulate carefully what they believed to be the fundamental theoretical verities of Marxism against what seemed to them an eastern, anarchist corruption of Marx's thought. From Moscow the bolsheviks in turn cited chapter and verse to support their accusation that the prewar leaders of socialism had betrayed the revolutionary essence of Marxism. Younger voices in the West, such men as Antonio Gramsci, Ernst Däumig, and Ferdinand Loriot, struggled with the problem of making revolution in western Europe and sought to glean something from the Russian experience while struggling to preserve their own particular additions to or reinterpretations of Marxian writ. Thus to follow the polemics of these years constitutes a wide-ranging exploration of the many possible varieties of Marxism, Leninist and non-Leninist.

The concrete revolutionary experiences of the *biennio rosso* were equally rich. The Spartacist Uprising of January 1919, the Hungarian and Bavarian soviet regimes of the summer of 1919, the French general strike of the spring of 1920, the factory occupations in Italy in the autumn of that year, the German March Uprising of 1921—these are only some of the more important revolutionary experiences of this period. The spring of 1921 marked a more or less definite exhaustion of this revolutionary thrust, except for a belated spasm in Germany in 1923, but the general period stretching from the end of the war to the early months of 1921 constituted undoubtedly the richest period of revolutionary activity in western Europe after 1848.

The interplay between bolshevism and western socialism in the *biennio rosso* falls into remarkably neat and logically divided stages, as if a historical dramatist had set them down to be observed as acts of a play. In the course of each act the protagonists gain new insights that push them, often against their wills, to ineluctable strife. The final act is one of tragic triumph: Lenin emerges victorious over his western socialist opponents, but his victory is gnawed by a cancerous paradox, since bolshevik ascendancy over western revolutionary socialists was facilitated by the failure of revolution in the West, the very revolution that was necessary if the Bolshevik Revolution was to have a more profound Marxian significance as the first stage of world socialist revolution.

The first act opens with the establishment of rival internationals, one led by western socialists who hoped to restore the much discredited prewar international, and one led by the bolsheviks who looked to a radically new international (March to August 1919). The following act sees an attempt by certain western socialists to work out a compromise or "reconstructed" international, which ultimately fails (August to April 1920). Subsequently, the "reconstructionist" socialists journey to revolutionary Russia, hoping to negotiate favorable terms for their entry into the Communist International (April to August 1920). From these negotiations emerges the impossibility of compromise and thus an ardent campaign in the West for and against communism, climaxing in a series of schisms in the leading socialist parties of the West (October 1920 to January 1921). The left factions of each of these schisms then establish communist parties, tightly bound to the Moscow international.

The most dramatic and revealing confrontation of western and Russian varieties of Marxism was at the Second Congress of the Communist International in the summer of 1920. (This was the first genuinely international congress. The first official congress, in

March 1919, was a token affair, organized while Russia was still blockaded, and thus very few westerners were present.) After a series of confusing and inconclusive contacts with Moscow across the Allied blockade in 1919 and early 1920, delegations from France, Germany, and Italy, as well as from many other nations, made it into the promised land of the revolution. This was their first chance to have a sustained dialogue with the bolsheviks and to observe the revolution directly. Many surprises were in store for them. To the outrage of some of the westerners, the Russians proved themselves masters in the art of factional intrigue and manipulation. The western delegations were also surprised and disappointed to discover that the leaders of the Communist International were less tolerant of the peculiarities of western socialism than had been hoped. The Twenty-one Conditions for admission into the new international, worked out at the Second Congress, reflected bolshevik principles, narrowly interpreted, with few or ambiguous concessions to the more liberal-democratic aspects of western socialist tradition.

Yet at the same time the experiences of war and the high hopes awakened by the Bolshevik Revolution spelled an end to the prewar unity of western socialist parties with a decisiveness that exceeded anything the bolsheviks could accomplish through direct intervention in the affairs of western socialists. In fact, rather than mindlessly seeking to shatter western socialist unity, the bolsheviks worked for the broadest possible unity in the new communist parties, at least a broader unity than was desired by many western revolutionaries.

The splits that developed failed to serve the positive function—that of liberating revolutionary energies by providing revolutionary leadership—which both the bolsheviks and leading western revolutionaries hoped for. The disastrous communist uprising in March 1921 in Germany and the Kronstadt Revolt in Russia in the same month marked the end of an era. The reins of bolshevik despotism in Russia were tightened, and the bolsheviks began to insist on an even more dogmatic and imitative operation of communist parties in the West. The high hopes and ardent optimism of the *biennio rosso* would not return.

The fascinating period following World War I, when Europe's socialist parties split and when communist parties were established, has drawn the attention of many writers, both scholarly and popular. With a few exceptions, these writers have focused on a single country. The following pages attempt to bring together the findings of the many scholarly monographs on Russia, Germany, France, Italy, and the Communist International, and to blend them into a broader yet integrated picture of western socialism following the war. It is hoped that this more comprehensive, comparative approach will merit the attention not only of the scholarly expert but also of the intelligent layman who is interested in socialism and communism but who does not have the time or inclination to delve into the vast monographic literature.

At the same time this aspires to be more than a work of synthesis, for the author has dug thoroughly into the firsthand accounts and other primary sources of the period in Germany, France, Italy, and Russia, and has attempted to make use of the new perspectives opened up by abandoning the confines of national history. This effort has born fruit in a number of ways. For example, it was possible to discover new information pertaining to developments in one socialist or communist party in the sources of another, as in the case of notes taken by a German communist at an important meeting between the bolsheviks and French socialists in Moscow—notes that escaped the scrutiny of even the most thorough scholars of French socialism and communism in this period. On a different level, it was possible to gain insights into the forces working on men like G. M. Serrati and Paul Levi—ostensibly very different men, but men who responded to the bolsheviks in quite similar ways for quite similar reasons—insights that scholars concentrating on Italy or Germany alone missed or failed to explore because of their more narrow focus. From yet another perspective the international approach opened up interesting and instructive comparisons among the thoughts of such revolutionary figures as Antonio Gramsci, Ernst Däumig, and Alfred Rosmer (all associated with syndicalist perspectives), figures almost never mentioned together in accounts dealing with individual socialist or communist movements.

Leninism also has been exhaustively described and analyzed by scholars and popularizers. The following account attempts to add something to the historical understanding of Leninism by examining Lenin's thought in the context both of his polemics and of his more friendly exchanges with western socialists in 1919 and 1920. By following these exchanges and by exploring the ways in which he and his lieutenants worked out tactically separate policies in dealing with the socialists of France, Germany, and Italy, it is possible to gain a new awareness of the important transformations of Leninism in these years, as well as—and perhaps more significantly —of its lasting ambiguities.

None of the existing monographs has given much attention to the colorful sequence of events surrounding the Second Congress of the Communist International in the summer of 1920 in Russia. This lapse may exist because the accounts of visitors from individual countries do not provide adequate information for a rounded account. Here again the international approach has proved fruitful, for the various reports and memoirs composed by foreign visitors to Russia complement one another in many ways. By weaving together the accounts of the French, German, and Italian visitors, a much more complete picture is possible than if only Russian sources or the sources of one other country were used. The experiences of most delegates to Russia were decisive, either in making them decide to abandon certain of their earlier beliefs or in making them take up a firmly anti-bolshevik position. It is hoped that the reader will find this account of western socialists in Russia one of the more engaging, instructive, and even amusing aspects of the complex story of the split among western socialists and the birth of communist parties in the West.

Before the *Biennio Rosso*: The Deeper Roots of the Socialist-Communist Conflict

The struggle between communist and socialist parties, and the splits within the latter, was directly tied to the world crisis of 1914 to 1918, to World War I and the Bolshevik Revolution. Yet the appeal of Lenin's theories was not exclusively dependent upon his success as a revolutionary or upon the inadequacies of western socialist leadership. Prior to 1917 many non-Russian socialists had entertained ideas similar to those which would later be called Leninist. On the other hand, Lenin was thoroughly schooled in the writings of the great western socialists, and these writings constituted the basic texts from which he formulated his particular adaptations to Russian conditions. Thus in order better to understand the postwar divisions between socialists and communists, it is important to gain some sense of prewar socialism in Russia and the West, the ways in which western socialists responded to World War I and to the Bolshevik Revolution.

The SPD, SFIO, and PSI in the generation before the war

The generation before World War I has often been termed the "classic age" of European socialist parties. From modest beginnings in the 1890s they grew steadily, becoming on the eve of the war a major political force in many countries, although nowhere in the majority or even sharing power with other parties. In a number of countries, most notably in Germany, the socialist party was the largest party, and where not the largest it was the most disciplined and determined, eliciting a sense of commitment on the part of its membership which was unequaled in other parties. The Socialist International, an organization of the world's socialist and labor organizations, convoked regular congresses of increasingly impressive dimensions, where the great issues of theory and practical politics were debated and where it was confidently predicted that the future belonged to socialism.

The German Social Democratic party, or SPD (*Sozialdemokratische Partei Deutschlands*), was the paragon of prewar international socialism. Just as the German Reich enjoyed a degree of economic, diplomatic, and cultural hegemony in continental Europe during the late nineteenth and early twentieth century, so the SPD stood as the most admired and imitated by other socialist parties. Indeed, the SPD's position in international socialism was intimately linked with Germany's power as a nation state, and the particular character of the SPD was in many ways a reflection of the character of the German nation. Germany's rapid industrialization, following her dramatic national unification in 1871, created the basic social and economic conditions for a powerful socialist party. The expansion of industry entailed a concomitant growth of the working class, and the harsh dynamics of industrialization spawned a hostile working population, yoked to an unfamiliar factory discipline, separated from ownership of the means of production, overworked, and underpaid. The SPD offered a natural channel for these resentments, and it grew by leaps and bounds: emerging from an outlawed status in 1890, the party by 1906 had attracted approximately 385,000 members; by 1914 this figure had shot up to over one million, which was well over ten times the membership of the French and Italian socialist parties.[1]

But the SPD's growth was not paralleled by a growing participation in Germany's political institutions. In the Reichstag the SPD deputies stood as a body apart, refusing to join in most of the formalities and rituals of parliamentary life and shunned by the representatives of the bourgeois parties. In the world outside parliament the situation was similar. The German worker, especially one of socialist fidelities, experienced a strong sense of social ostracism and exclusion from his country's ruling circles. Even if the SPD could have obtained a majority in the Reichstag, the constitution of the Reich effectively precluded the possibility of a socialist exercise of power because the chancellor was not responsible to the Reichstag and other institutional arrangements preserved real political and military power for a clique of Prussian Junkers and Rhenish-Westphalian industrial magnates. Faced with such a constitutional bulwark, German socialists found much relevance in revolutionary Marxism; legal reform through majority rule was not a real alternative, at least not before constitutional reforms, the likelihood of which seemed extremely remote.

In terms of prestige and overall eminence the French Socialist party, or SFIO (*Section Française de l'Internationale Ouvrière*), was the second party of the International, and like the SPD it bore unmistakable signs of the country of its birth. France experienced a slower rate of industrial growth, which did not suddenly or seriously undermine the stability of her social and economic structures. The SFIO never grew to the impressive dimensions of the SPD, in part because France did not possess the masses of proletarians who might have been attracted to a socialist party. She remained a country of small enterprise and luxury production, of independent peasants, shopkeepers, and artisans. And since the fruits of her smoothly expanding productivity went to a relatively static population, real wages rose roughly 50 percent between 1870 and 1914.[2] Life for much of France's popular classes was less harsh than for Germany's industrial workers. In France, one sees some of the material realities underlying the rosy hues of the *belle époque*.

French socialists did not suffer quite the same sense of isolation or ostracism as did the German socialists. This was in part because France was a democratic republic, whose institutions many socialists found more compatible with a steady development toward a socialist victory. Moreover, left-wing or revolutionary sentiments were far more familiar and respectable to Frenchmen, who thought of France as *le pays de la révolution*, the country of revolution. But an equally important consideration in explaining the SFIO's relative integration into French political and social life is the social origin of her leadership and membership. The SFIO, unlike the SPD, received a considerable proportion of its support from non-proletarian elements of society, most notably from intellectuals. On the other hand, it had difficulty in eliciting active participation from France's working population, at least in comparison to the SPD. Similarly, the SFIO, being composed in large part of highly individual bourgeois intellectuals, was not as sternly organized or monolithic in appearance as the SPD, with its working-class leaders and members and their sense of strength through unity and discipline. To be sure, the pronouncements of the SFIO were often full of revolutionary rhetoric, but the actual sense of class conflict was inevitably diminished in a party whose leaders were themselves overwhelmingly of bourgeois origin.

Rather than give their allegiance to a political party, France's revolutionary workers tended to identify with the CGT (*Confédération Générale du Travail*), an anarchosyndicalist or revolutionary trade-union organization (*syndicat* means, roughly, "trade union" in French), which shunned participation in parliamentary struggles and was in particular deeply suspicious of the bourgeois intellectuals at the head of the SFIO. This degree of separation and suspicion was not the norm in most other countries, where socialist parties and trade unions cooperated actively. Equally, the aggressive revolutionaries at the head of the CGT were unlike the trade union officials in other countries. The leaders of the German "free" trade unions ("free" of the influence of the church or of management), for example, represented a voice of caution and moderation in relation to the SPD, and union officials were generally in favor of reformist rather than revolutionary socialism. Insofar as the anarchosyndicalists mixed elements of Marxism and anarchism in their beliefs, they shared some characteristics with the extreme left—sometimes called "anarcho-Marxist"—of the Socialist International. The anarchosyndicalists and the left of the SFIO would come together at the end of the war as constituent parts of the French Communist party.

The Italian Socialist party, or PSI (*Partito Socialista Italiano*), grew up in a country much less developed economically than either Germany or France, a country of severely limited natural wealth, with remarkable disparities in industrial advancement between north and south. Italy lacked adequate supplies of iron and coal to support heavy industry, and her arable land was limited and often poor. Even the land that was under cultivation was much less evenly distributed than in France: nine-tenths of Italy's five million land-holders possessed less than an hectare of land—not enough to sustain a family.[3] Italy, unlike France, still had a land-hungry peasantry, pressed at times to desperation and prone to violent, anarchic up-risings.

Modern, heavy industry in Italy existed almost exclusively in the north, where a number of very large and quite advanced indus-trial concentrations had developed, especially in the three cities of the so-called "industrial triangle," Milan, Turin, and Genoa. The PSI recruited almost exclusively from the northern urban centers, and in these limited areas the organizations of the proletariat were in many ways comparable to those in Germany. Moreover, strong support for the ideals of socialism existed in the north not only among factory proletarians but also among the agricultural prole-tariat, the *braccianti* or landless day laborers of the Po valley, who worked the large farms of that area and whose conditions of work and social position made them ready recruits to socialism.

The harshness of the social and economic experience of the Ital-ian masses helps to explain why in the generation before the war a number of dramatic and bloody confrontations occurred between the government and the working class. Inevitably the PSI became involved in them, although the leadership of the party was by no means consistently revolutionary; from one year to the next party leadership shifted between ardent revolutionaries and moderate reformists. Significantly, however, the party experienced unprece-dented growth and became increasingly militant between 1911 and 1914 under the leadership of Benito Mussolini, who at the time was an ardent socialist revolutionary of more or less anarcho-Marxist complexion. When World War I broke out, the PSI stood far to the left in the International, a circumstance that would have pro-found implications for the relationship of the PSI to antiwar ac-tivity and to the creation of the Communist International at the end of the war.

Trends of the prewar socialist parties

The PSI's move to the left in the few years before the war was an exception to the trend of the most important parties of the International. The leadership of both the SPD and the SFIO tended to fall increasingly under the sway of the parties' more conservative wings, while the counterparts to Mussolini's wing, the radical revolutionaries in the French and German parties, lost influence in the higher party councils. This was an ironic development, since the opening years of the century had seen a coalition of the center and left of the SPD leading the struggle in the International against Revisionism, that is, the revision of revolutionary Marxism in favor of gradualism. Similarly, the divided and warring factions of French socialism finally came together in 1905 to form the SFIO with a program that represented a victory of the orthodox Marxists in France over the parliamentary reformists.

The growing preeminence of more cautious figures in the SPD was in a paradoxical way related to the party's remarkable success since 1890. The SPD's growing numbers and the multiplication of its functions entailed the proliferation of professional party functionaries, since the complexities of such matters as party finance and the organization of national electoral campaigns became more than the old-style volunteer party workers could manage. But party bureaucrats are reluctant revolutionaries because illegal actions of any sort run the risk of governmental repression, which can in turn mean the loss of party funds and property—and the end of jobs for party bureaucrats. Similarly, the SPD's growing strength at the polls tended to justify those who believed that constitutional reforms would eventually be attained and who thus advocated the parliamentary road of "peaceful attrition" of capitalism. In 1912 the SPD won four and one-half million votes, nearly twice as many as its nearest rival, the Catholic Center party.[4]

It was obvious that the SPD could not continue to grow as it had since 1890 and still remain isolated from political power in Germany. Of course the left wing of the party predicted a violent confrontation between the state and the socialist working class, but the more cautious members of the SPD and the trade unions—and they constituted a solid majority of each—contemplated less dramatic and less risky alternatives. They were yearly more concerned with this dilemma: as long as the SPD refused to enter left-wing parliamentary coalitions, the governing coalitions would unavoidably be pushed further to the right because the great size of the SPD made its presence in any coalition of the left a virtual necessity. Such considerations, among others, impelled many in the SPD to reconsider the orthodox Marxist notions of the bourgeois state and of the irreconcilability of class conflict under capitalism. The yearnings of many moderate leaders of the SPD to make their party a *Volkspartei*, a democratic party of all the people rather than a class party, were already apparent at this time, although there was no forthright and open expression in the higher organs of the party or in its congress resolutions until the Weimar years, after the left wing had split off. The war would act as a catalyst in these matters, forcing German socialists to make the decision they had so long postponed: whether to try to work within the existing social and economic system for piecemeal and "realistic" reforms, or to wage an uncompromising struggle culminating in revolution.

The SFIO's drift to the right from 1905 to 1914 was less distinct, in part because the French party was far less successful than the SPD in recruiting members and winning votes and thus did not have to deal with the many dilemmas facing a large party. Moreover, it was easier for the moderate members of the SFIO to put up with fierce-sounding revolutionary rhetoric than it was for their counterparts in Germany, since a kind of verbal revolutionary conformism existed among the leaders of the SFIO which gave a quite false impression of genuine revolutionary commitment. But a fundamental shift in factional alliances occurred in the SFIO in the nine years before the war: Jean Jaurès, the former leader of the parliamentary reformist Independent Socialists, who had bowed to Jules Guesde and the revolutionary left in 1905, emerged in the following years as the unquestioned leader of the SFIO. He gave the party its direction and its image and was usually supported by Guesde against the noisy, antipatriotic extreme left of Gustave Hervé. In other words, there was a fundamental shift to the right in the factional alliances of the party, similar to the shift in the SPD against the left radicals around Rosa Luxemburg. Thus cracks existed in the SFIO before the war which presaged the postwar schism in the party, although Hervé and his faction were not as isolated or as superciliously dealt with as were Luxemburg and the German revolutionary left.

Although the question was not posed with the same immediacy in France as in Germany, many in the SFIO looked forward to a reform of French society based on cooperation in parliament between the French bourgeois democratic radicals and the SFIO. Had the war not intervened, this might have been a realistic perspective, although in the immediate prewar period the Radical party, the socialists' nearest neighbor in the French political spectrum, moved to the right, away from the socialists, partly in response to their greater verbal militancy. At any rate, the war would drastically intensify the factional hostilities within the SFIO and would postpone until the mid-1930s the question of left-wing parliamentary alliances for social reform.

As remarked previously, it is more appropriate to term the left-wing thrust of the PSI after 1911 an episode rather than a trend, for between 1900 to 1914 the peculiar tergiversations of Italian politics and foreign policy encouraged first one and then another of the wings of the PSI to assume leadership. This alternation was made all the easier by the relatively small number of party members in the PSI and the concomitant delicate balance between the factions. In the SPD a rapid assumption of power by one faction was impeded by the inherent difficulties of organizing mass support and bucking established bureaucrats; in the PSI the contending factions did not have to deal with the many problems of pulling hundreds of thousands of members in new directions. Thus the anarcho-revolutionary factions that came to the forefront periodically in the PSI remained permanently minority trends in the French and German parties.

Mussolini's rise to leadership of the PSI was directly related to Italy's blatantly imperialistic campaign in 1911 into Tripoli and Cyrenaica. Most socialists violently opposed this adventure, but Lionida Bissolati, a leader of the reformist faction of the party, supported the campaign on the grounds that expansion was the proper concern of a young state and that colonies would help to alleviate the poverty of Italy's south. Within a year Bissolati and many of his followers were expelled from the PSI, and Mussolini's "intransigent revolutionary" faction assumed control.

This sharp move to the left troubled not only the remaining reformists but many of the older members of the party, who voiced concern about what they believed were Mussolini's Bakuninist tendencies and about the drift of the PSI away from solid Marxian principles. But Mussolini's threat to resign was enough to silence these critics; he had become far too valuable to the party and seemed in large part responsible for its remarkable growth after the expulsion of Bissolati. By the time of the congress of Ancona in 1914 the PSI's membership had mushroomed to 58,000, almost double what it had been two years before,[5] and close to the membership of the SFIO (70,000) in 1914.

Thus the campaign into Libya precluded a right-wing trend in the PSI, parallel to that in the SPD and SFIO. The sense of *malaise* and *Verdrossenheit*, of unease and disillusionment, which more and more were topics of discussion in the SPD and SFIO in the immediate prewar period, could hardly bother the PSI while it waged an ardent campaign, sparked by the charismatic Mussolini, against Italy's imperialist war. Italian socialists found a sense of direction, while the French and German socialists were plagued by uncertainty.

Prewar socialism in Russia

The suggestion that Russian socialists would one day assume leadership over a major part of the socialist movement in western Europe would have seemed laughable to most observers of the prewar scene, for the Russians had traditionally borrowed from and relied upon westerners, both intellectually and materially. For example, Russia's extremely rapid industrial expansion between 1890 and 1914 was of a peculiarly "imported" nature; Russian industry was in large part brought from the West, both in terms of capital investment and technological ability. Only the brawn of the laboring masses was Russia's own, and most of these masses were freshly torn from the countryside, thus lacking the more deeply rooted traditions and institutions of the contemporary working class in the West. In short, in nearly all areas of concern to socialists, Russia was a backward country.

There were, however, certain surprising aspects to Russia's social and economic development. Although by 1905 most of Russia's nonagricultural labor force was still employed in small shops, the percentage of workers (though of course not the total number) in factories of one thousand or more workers was three times as great as that in Germany.[6] Of course the total production of Germany was enormously greater than that of Russia, but backward Russia had *relatively* more industrial concentration than did highly industrialized Germany. Russia thus had areas of intense proletarian concentrations, and these proletarians were easily attracted to socialism. And insofar as Marx's theories focused on the implications of industrial concentration, a socialist in Russia could find much of relevance in them.

Lenin himself was not only attracted to Marxism as a scientific description of the trends of industrial society but also to the organizational model of the leading Marxist party, the SPD. It may seem paradoxical that an ardent revolutionary like Lenin should admire the party machine that became a bulwark of reformism and that was responsible for isolating and emasculating the SPD's radicals. But the dangers of bureaucratization in the SPD were not so patent when Lenin began to forge his own ideas of party organization in the first few years of the twentieth century. And, more important, in the context of Russia's state and society the dangers of a self-serving bureaucracy at the head of a socialist party hardly existed. Living outside the law, usually in exile, and animated by a spirit of self-sacrifice verging on fanaticism, the members of the Russian Social Democratic Workers' party could hardly be compared to the SPD *Bonzen* or bureaucrats-on-high.

Lenin welded the Russian populist or narodnik notion of professional revolutionaries, an elite corps of "pures" and "hards" (also seen in the theories of the French socialist Blanqui), to the German socialist notion of a bureaucratic machine designed to lead and manipulate the proletarian masses; and he infused into the amalgam his own remarkably assertive personality. His unshakeable

faith in the infallibility of his own judgment made the actual operation of the Bolshevik party even less democratic than it was in theory. At the same time, his realistic approach to the problems of
working-class consciousness—that workers needed firm, constant
guidance and could not develop a mature revolutionary mentality
without being taught it by the party—saved him the inconveniences
and obstacles to action with which revolutionaries like Rosa Luxemburg (who looked to a more spontaneous development of socialist consciousness among the working class) had to deal.

Before the war Lenin did not devise his theories with an eye
primarily to western socialism. Yet, while his theories were not
known in the West at this time, he did offer, without directly so
intending, some rather interesting if draconian solutions to the
problems that were of growing concern in the West: the loss of *élan*
through bureaucratization and parliamentarization, a growing
sense of frustration on the left because of the apparent incompati-
bilities between democracy and social revolution, and the failure
of even the most highly industrialized countries to produce a prole-
tarianized and rebellious majority according to Marx's predictions.
Lenin stipulated that party leaders, and even party members, were
to be professional revolutionaries of tested revolutionary courage
and commitment; anyone who showed weakness in the direction of
reformism, careerism, or parliamentarism was to be ruthlessly cast
aside. If necessary, the revolutionary minority of a socialist party,
unable to effect the necessary purging of the ranks of its party,
should break away and form a new party that *would* be faithful to
revolutionary principles. Professional revolutionaries could not
concern themselves about the "false consciousness" of the formal
majority of the population—or even the majority of the proletariat
—since only an intellectual and moral elite could be expected to
achieve a true socialist consciousness before the actual victory of
socialist revolution.

Actually, each of these notions and many others central to Lenin's thought can be found as individual propositions in the writings of western socialists. But gathered together and presented in
Lenin's forceful style—and of course with the authority of revolutionary victory behind them—they exercised an understandable at-

traction to many revolutionaries who were still searching for ways out of the dilemmas mentioned above, which merely became intensified in the immediate postwar period. There is a certain irony to all of this because in the prewar international socialist community Russians were normally shrugged off as hopeless sectarians, and any sympathy western socialists showed tended to be condescending. The Russians' odd ideas and unending quarrels were regarded as an unhappy consequence of their economic and cultural backwardness. This condescension was most blatant on the part of the leaders of the SPD; but even in France, where one might have expected a more genuine comprehension of socialist sectarianism, there was little interest in the affairs of Russian socialists. Jaurès himself ordered the staff of *L'Humanité*, the newspaper of the SFIO, to avoid accepting articles or letters from them in order not to become involved in their interminable quarrels.[7] And when G. M. Serrati, a leader of the left wing of the PSI, received admiring letters from Lenin in late 1914 he did not even bother to answer them.[8]

The trauma of war

The war marked a dramatic turning point for European socialism. It forced the leaders of each party to make the choices they had so often avoided: between patriotism and internationalism, reformism and revolution, commitment to the ideals of the International or commitment to the interests of the nation. The pressures of war introduced into party life a sense of stringent necessity which often threw former comrades at each others' throats. Thus the war meant an ultimate schism in the International and in the individual parties that made it up.

The unanimous support given first by the SPD and then the SFIO parliamentary delegates for war credits in early August 1914 dramatically demonstrated the impracticality of the earlier resolutions of the International to oppose the threat of war. The outbreak of World War I was a failure of working-class internationalism, not only because workingmen were killing one another, but also because most of the leading parties of the International had lost the ability, and even the desire, to communicate with one another. The leaders of the SFIO rigidly insisted that the SPD had sold out to German militarism, while the German socialist leaders felt that the initial mobilization of military forces by tsarist Russia, France's ally, against Germany was the decisive consideration. But all socialist leaders were bewildered by the rapid march of events, and soon nearly all were caught up in the intoxication of national defense.

So also were the masses. In spite of the crowds that rallied to the socialist antiwar demonstrations in each country in late July, once the declarations of war had been delivered, the working classes in all the belligerent countries yielded to a paroxysm of patriotic frenzy. The mood was caught poignantly by a French anarchosyndicalist: "On the second of August, disgusted and morally reduced to dust, I left in a cattle car jammed with men who were bellowing 'to Berlin!' "[9] Under such circumstances a call for a general strike or other revolutionary action would have been quixotic, if not suicidal. A leading German socialist later remarked that the SPD Reichstag deputies voted for war credits to avoid being beaten to death by their followers in front of the Brandenburg Gate.[10]

The question of which country was guilty of initiating the war was not finally of decisive importance. With German troops crashing into the north of their country, French socialists could hardly pause to ask themselves if Russia were responsible for the whole mess. And even if the German socialists had recognized that their country was at fault, they could hardly have stood with their arms crossed as the Cossack hordes streamed into Germany. All were forced to recognize the impracticality of internationalist ideals in the context of rival nation-states and power politics.

Socialist leaders who had previously acquiesced in the official Marxian orthodoxy but who at heart doubted the concept of the obstinate iniquity of the bourgeoisie and dreamed of class cooperation for the gradual reform of capitalism found in the war a most welcome opportunity to put their repressed beliefs to the test, to leave behind their political and social ostracism. For men like Friedrich Ebert in Germany or Albert Thomas in France the class cooperation forged by the shock of war represented an escape from the growing dilemmas of prewar socialism. On the other hand, the war convinced many left radicals, especially in Germany, that continued unity with the right-wing socialists was no longer viable. They could not accept the end of class conflict; they could only turn away in disgust from what was for them the stinking corpse of capitalist society. For them cooperation with the class enemy and acquiescence in the inequities and murderous irrationalities of capitalism were inconceivable. The war merely intensified their feeling that revolution was an absolute necessity. In between these two extremes stood a large number of socialists who could only wring their hands at the turn of events and hope for better days.

World War I was an industrial war of mass participation, which required close cooperation between state and people, bourgeois and proletarian, army and civilian populations; it demanded levels of social cohesion, nationalist passion, and industrial output best achieved in such advanced industrial nations as Germany, England, and France. This was one of the reasons why the leaders of these countries welcomed the active participation of socialist and union leaders in the war effort. This was also a reason why socialist opposition to the war was first taken up by those socialists whose countries were incompletely engaged by the dynamics of mass industrial warfare. The socialists of Italy and Russia were at the forefront of antiwar activities, although the socialists of other small countries that had not entered the war, such as Switzerland and the Scandinavian countries, also played a role.

By 1914 a large part of the Italian population was still rural—illiterate, backward, politically passive, and little concerned with national affairs. Mobilizing such a population into active and ardent support of the war was far more difficult than in France or Germany, and Italy's leaders made little effort to do so. When Italy entered the conflict, ten months after it had begun, its entry was obviously the work of a small clique of politicians and demagogues whose motives were grossly opportunistic and who cared little about the lack of enthusiasm for war among the population at large. Moreover, Italy was not invaded; no fearsome troops advanced into the Italian *patria*, spreading terror and panic. The Italian people were thus not exposed to the raging passions that swept over Frenchmen and Germans who feared for their homeland and loved ones. And when Italy was finally maneuvered into war by her leaders, it was after the Italian masses had spent ten months observing the horrors of trench warfare—horrors they believed were now in store for them.

These fundamental aspects of Italy's involvement in the war greatly help to explain the relative ease with which the leaders of the PSI were able to avoid the contradictions and reversals of their French and German counterparts. As previously noted, Italian socialists had already been forced to make concrete decisions in opposition to the Libyan war three years before. After August 1914 they had a number of months during which to consider the problem of World War I in relative calm. Opposition to this war remained an extremely popular option, even after Italy's entry; the leaders of the PSI were joined in opposing it by former prime minister Giolitti and the pope.

Yet many influential Italians were attracted to the advantages Italy might reap, in spite of its treaty with the Central powers, as in ally of the Entente—for one, the acquisition of those lands still held by Austria which Italians felt were naturally part of the Italian homeland. Even within the PSI such notions were attractive, although masked in the rhetoric of a fight for Right, Justice, and Democracy against Teutonic militarism. It was primarily the right wing of the party that thought in such terms. But in the autumn and winter of 1914–1915 Mussolini, the party's revolutionary antimilitarist and the fiery editor of *Avanti!*, gradually revealed his conversion to the cause of intervention on the side of the French, English, and Russians. For the other leaders of the party Mussolini's change of mind seemed an astonishing betrayal, a deeply upsetting *rifiuto* by the party's most promising young orator and revolutionary leader. The exertions and emotions required to force Mussolini's resignation from the editorship of *Avanti!*, followed by his expulsion from the party itself, tended to stamp even more forcefully in the minds of the party leaders a lasting opposition to any kind of participation in the war. Later, after the Russian Revolution and the entry of the United States into the war, when the temptations increased to interpret the war as a campaign for Democracy and

Justice, Mussolini's apostasy continued to exert its influence. Such older party leaders as Serrati, Lazzari, and Bacci were not likely to admit that the young Mussolini had been correct all along.[11]

Much of what has been said concerning the lack of fundamental conditions facilitating mass enthusiasm for war in Italy was true *a fortiori* in Russia, where history and geography combined to create an unusual distance between state and people, and where the present tsar, Nicholas II, no longer enjoyed even the distant veneration in which the tsar had traditionally been held by the rural masses of Russia. Although opposition to the war was by no means unanimous among Russian socialists—Plekhanov, for one, the patriarch of Russian Marxists, supported it—nothing like the tidal wave of patriotic emotion that overwhelmed the SPD and SFIO swept over them. Fidelity to the resolutions of the Socialist International remained strong in both the bolshevik and menshevik wings of the Russian Social Democratic Workers' party.

According to these resolutions socialists were to do all in their power to prevent the outbreak of war; if war broke out nevertheless, they were to direct their efforts to ending it quickly. It left ambiguous, however, whether these efforts were to be of an exclusively revolutionary nature or whether they could take the less audacious form of working for a simple negotiated peace. After the war broke out, and even after it became clear that the conflict was destined to be long and bloody, the leaders of the International took no initiative either to foment revolutionary opposition or to work for a negotiated peace. In the face of this complete abdication of responsibility, the Italian socialists themselves took steps to reestablish relations between the parties of the International with a view to putting the prewar resolutions into effect.

The meetings that the Italians set into motion, the first at Zimmerwald, Switzerland, in September 1915, and the second at Kienthal, Switzerland, in April 1916 (often collectively called the Zimmerwald conferences, part of the Zimmerwald "movement"), were rather disappointing affairs for most of those who attended. The deep divisions that existed in the left factions of the parties of the International and their overall isolation became distressingly obvious. At the first meeting very few indeed were willing to commit themselves to revolutionary action against the war; thus the discussions tended to focus on the problem of how to bring the leaders of the International around to reason, and more generally how to exert pressures for a negotiated peace without victors or vanquished. The experiences of the PSI constituted strong evidence that violent antiwar activity at this time was futile. In Turin on May 15 an antiwar general strike had taken place. The military took over the city, occupied the strike centers, shot down demonstrating workers, and left no doubt that public order would be maintained. Further bloodshed seemed pointless, and the PSI retired into a position of *"nè aderire nè sabotare"* (neither aid nor sabotage) for the rest of the war. It was abundantly clear to other antiwar socialists in the major countries of the West that their governments were even more capable of repressing revolutionary opposition should the need arise. Thus even at the Kienthal conference, where a distinct shift to the left was apparent and where the participants affirmed that no acceptable peace could be made without a revolution, the appeal to revolutionary action remained rhetorical and without specific recommendations.

Lenin and the problem of war

Lenin remained a rather isolated and disruptive figure at the antiwar conferences. He and Georg Ledebour, a leader of the German revolutionary left, engaged in fiery verbal duels.[12] Alfred Merrheim, a French anarchosyndicalist, expressed utter astonishment at his demands,[13] and even Serrati, a leader of the extreme left of the PSI, became so angry with Lenin at one point that he seemed ready to provoke a fist-fight.[14] Socialists in the West tended to regard the war as a terrible disaster, and even the patriotic socialists usually took little pleasure in the splendors of war. Lenin too considered the war a disaster of sorts; yet he did not indulge in teeth-gnashing theatrics, he did not share the grief over the destruction that so afflicted many western revolutionaries. Lenin remained "hard." If anything he gloated. He was convinced that the war had sharply advanced the date of social revolution. Moreover, he began to talk with obvious satisfaction of revolution breaking out first in Russia, the weakest link of European capitalism, and then spreading to the West.[15] The bloodshed, the senseless and seemingly endless destruction did not seem to grip Lenin's inner emotions. He observed the mad spectacle with remarkable detachment and even felt a degree of sardonic satisfaction that the capitalists were making such a mess of things.

While Lenin remained in certain ways detached from the simple human pathos of the war, he did not remain completely unmoved. His detestation of the leading figures of the International who had surrendered to patriotism knew no bounds. He spewed insults at them and soon invariably referred to them with the fixed epithets "social-patriot," "social-chauvinist," and, in moments of particular rage or frustration, "social-cretins."

Lenin's theoretical analysis of the war remained part and parcel of his prewar theories, although the war spurred him on to an even more harshly single-minded revolutionary internationalism. He was, for example, more consistent and thoroughgoing than other socialists in insisting that *all* imperialism alike—German, French, Russian, Austro-Hungarian—was responsible for the war. In the same vein, in his evaluation of the effects of imperialism on European socialism, he went beyond other socialists, proclaiming that imperialism was not only the underlying cause of the war but also the reason for patriotism among socialists. As he saw it, the extraordinary profits that imperialistic capitalism was able to reap allowed it to "buy off" a section of the working class with higher salaries and a generally nonproletarian existence. This "workers' aristocracy," which was composed of highly skilled workers and the high functionaries of socialist parties and trade unions, had lost all desire for revolution and in fact worked to dampen the natural revolutionary passions of the masses. Moreover, the profits made possible by monopoly capitalism and imperialism allowed the capitalists of the advanced West to feel so firmly entrenched and secure in their rule that they could easily afford to extend the blessings of formal political democracy—civil rights, freedom of the press, universal manhood suffrage—as an effective means of pacifying the masses without worrying that these formal rights would be turned against such real sources of economic and political power as private property and the market economy.

The workers' aristocracy had rallied to the trumpet calls of imperialistic war instead of leading the working masses to socialist revolution in opposition to the war. In the same way, these traitors to their class now vehemently opposed any efforts to bring the war to an end and sought to stifle any movements of social unrest within their countries. Little better were the centrists or "social-pacifists," who were interested only in peace, not revolution, and who were perfectly willing to return to the capitalist *status quo ante bellum.* Both social-patriots and social-pacifists were in fact afraid of revolution and thus "objectively" little different.

The only course for truly revolutionary leaders was to break away from the grips of these traitors, to denounce them ruthlessly before the masses, and to agitate among the workers in the factories and the men in the armed forces in favor of strikes, work stoppages, economic sabotage, antiwar demonstrations, mutiny and, finally, general insurrection. Lenin's most striking slogan of the period was "turn the national war into civil war!"[16]

Although Lenin's analysis of the war and his prescription for action seem at first extraordinarily unequivocal, a number of significant and characteristic ambiguities lurk behind the imposing polemical façade. Implicit in his analysis is the assumption of the *naturally* revolutionary instinct of the broad masses of the working class, a natural instinct that was smothered by the devices of monopoly capitalism. Yet this view of working-class mentality is contrary in tendency to Lenin's earlier views, as developed in his best known work, *What is to be done?* In this pamphlet Lenin put forth the view that the working class naturally assumes a "trade-union consciousness"; only with the aid of a revolutionary elite can the proletariat attain a truly revolutionary perception of its condition.

The question of working-class consciousness is one of the more subtle and elusive of the many fine distinctions so dear to Russian Marxists. To some extent the apparent contradiction in Lenin's thought can be resolved by a more careful scrutiny of the Russian terms for "consciousness" (*soznanie*) and "spontaneity" (*stikhinost'*). These terms in Russian imply an antithesis between rational control and brute energy, the first being associated in Lenin's mind with the revolutionary elite and the second with the proletariat. The spontaneous rebellion of the proletarian against his condition progresses no further than a desire for immediate gains in terms of wages and factory conditions. Moreover, the brute energy (*stikhinost'*) of this rebellion, since it was irrational, might be channeled even into nonrevolutionary directions, if the revolutionary elite did not provide a proper consciousness (*soznanie*). Lenin explicitly recognized the great danger of the spontaneous "anarchy" of the masses, which tended to be ". . . non-rational and hence purely destructive. . . ."[17] Thus the rational direction provided by the revolutionary elite was enormously important, and the need for firm direction constituted a prime rationale for the totalitarian party developed by Lenin.

Yet other problems immediately suggest themselves. If even the lowest ranks of the working class are not in any full sense naturally revolutionary, and if monopoly capitalism is capable of developing elaborate and powerful tools to deceive and manipulate the masses, does this not mean that capitalism can remain in firm control for a more or less indefinite period? How can revolutionaries possibly match their meagre forces of propaganda with those of monopoly capitalism? Clearly it would seem that in most of the countries of the West the ideological forces of capitalism were incomparably stronger than those of revolutionary Marxism, since the masses marched enthusiastically to war. In other words, does Lenin's analysis not imply a lasting impotence of revolutionaries?

Obviously, Lenin did not think so. Much in his analysis depends upon the *internal* disintegration of capitalism along more traditional Marxian lines, on a development, in other words, more related to the objective evolution of capitalism than to the initiatives of revolutionaries. But this was not the main thrust of his wartime writings. In them we can observe a characteristically Leninist stance: a high-powered polemical façade behind which lurked many doctrinal obscurities.

War's end and the radicalization of western socialist parties

The year 1917 was a year of decision not only in Russia but also in the West. War weariness in western Europe as in Russia reached desperate levels, but while it brought on the collapse of the tsarist state and then that of the Provisional Government, western states survived. Moreover, Soviet Russia's departure from the war, Germany's decision to resume unrestricted submarine warfare, and the entry of the United States turned the stalemated war into one of movement. Russia's departure and America's growing aid allowed the leaders of the Axis and the Entente to turn a deaf ear to appeals for a negotiated settlement; instead they moved forcefully against the strikes, demonstrations, and mutinies that broke out in 1917 and early 1918. But these repressions brought deep and lasting rancor. By the summer of 1918 the socialist antiwar minorities in each country had grown so much that they expected shortly to become majorities.

Early 1917 saw the final break-up of the SPD and the formation of the USPD or Independent (*Unabhängig*) Social Democratic party of Germany, the party that attempted to preserve the mother party's internationalist and revolutionary traditions. Until early 1917 the growing division within the SPD over the question of socialist support for the war had been kept on a parliamentary level by separate caucuses, but the party leaders' harassment of the antiwar minority forced the latter to consider ways of protecting itself. Mainly with this end in view a special conference of dissenting socialists was held in Berlin, in January 1917. After much heated debate, the conference unanimously issued a statement that recalled the resolutions of the prewar International and supported a peace without victors or vanquished.[18]

The leaders of the SPD thereafter announced that they considered the conference a disloyal and provocative act; support of its resolutions was thus incompatible with membership in the party. They then moved rapidly and vigorously: in the local branches where the opposition was a minority, they formally expelled all those associated with it; where the oppositionists were in a majority (the situation in a number of important industrial areas), the leaders of the SPD outlawed the entire branch and established a new one.[19]

The oppositionists were thus virtually forced into establishing a new party, which they did in April, meeting at Gotha. It was obvious that many conceived of the USPD as a temporary affair and that after the war there would be a reconciliation. The membership of the new party came almost entirely from the left and center of the old party. That Eduard Bernstein, the Revisionist leader, joined it was a reflection more of his own sense of moral obligation to struggle for peace than of any general trend within the right wing of the SPD.

The liberalized and highly decentralized organization of the new party reflected the long-standing belief of most of its members that bureaucratization was at the heart of the difficulties in the old party. The painful experiences of the oppositionists at the hands of the party *Bonzen* during the war deeply reinforced the conviction that something had to be done to prevent such autocratic action in the future. Thus while the Gotha conference basically patterned the organization of the new party around the old party statutes of 1912, these statutes were amended to remove the possibility of new bureaucratic abuses. The new executive body, or *Zentrale*, had no authority to appoint paid secretaries, and its own salaried officials, who could never consist of more than one-third of the total membership of the *Zentrale*, were appointed by the local branches. In a number of other ways the local branches maintained considerable leverage in relation to the central bodies of the party, a very different situation from that which existed in the SPD, and certainly a far cry from bolshevik practices.

The USPD was established under the most difficult of circumstances; it had to fend off not only police persecution but the relentless and ruthless hostility of the old party leaders. In the nineteen-month period between the Gotha meeting and the November 1918 revolution in Germany the USPD grew from perhaps 50,000 members to about 100,000. Given the conditions under which the party had to operate, this was a very impressive rate of growth, especially when it is realized that the membership of the SPD had fallen from one million in 1914 to about 250,000 at the time of the split.

The year 1917 in France has been dubbed *"l'année trouble,"* a time of declining national morale and increasing doubts among Socialists concerning the viability of the *Union sacrée,* the sacred union of all parties in defense of France. The year saw mutinies following the spring Nivelle offensive, a series of politically oriented strikes in May and June, and ended with Clemenceau's stern repressions of any who suggested that the war not be carried to a victorious end. In the spring of 1918 *Le Tigre* called out the cavalry to repress the metal workers in the Loire valley, although in general he preferred to work through the leaders of the unions, who did all they could to control their followers.

In the late summer of 1917 both the pope and former prime minister Giolitti made public denunciations of the war, describing it as a tragic waste, a useless slaughter, and the cause of innumerable domestic injustices—terms that strikingly resembled those used by the leaders of the PSI since Italy's entry. The PSI itself began to step up its agitation against the war, and in late August a general strike and bloody confrontations with the forces of order occurred in Turin—once again, and not for the last time, the center of revolutionary action in Italy. Scores were killed, hundreds wounded, and thousands arrested before order was restored.

Two months later Italy's armies at Caporetto suffered a humiliating defeat and rout, which for the first time threatened to open the nation's borders to invasion. Opposition to the war now became truly unpopular. Moreover, the so-called Sacchi decrees of October 1917 gave the government wide-ranging authority to move against the "defeatists." Many of the leading figures of the PSI, including Serrati and Lazzari, were arrested and sentenced to stiff jail terms. Reeling under these shocks, the party for a time lost a certain amount of its combativeness. Many leading figures, especially in the right wing, expressed doubts about the policy of *nè aderire nè sabotare.* Some went so far as to advocate a policy of national defense.[20]

In July 1918, after the Germans and Clemenceau had done their worst, the SFIO's national council (or *conseil national,* a gathering of leading officials and parliamentary deputies) approved a resolution demanding from the government a declaration of peace terms based on socialist and Wilsonian principles, condemned the intervention initiated by the Entente against the Soviets, and required the SFIO's parliamentary deputies to vote against war credits if the government would not grant them passports to attend international socialist gatherings (such passports had been refused in 1917). At the full party congress in October, a complete change of leadership took place, with L. -O. Frossard becoming general secretary of the party and Marcel Cachin taking over as political director of *L'Humanité*. (Both of these men would go to Moscow in 1920.) The proportion of former *Minoritaires*, as the previous antiwar minority was called, in the party's central executive body, the CAP (*Commission Administrative Permanente*), was strengthened, although the old right wing, the previous *Majoritaires*, and the revolutionary Zimmerwaldian left were also represented in proportion to their strength at the congress. Thus the left took over the SFIO, averting the kind of split that had occurred within the SPD.

The PSI's last wartime congress, meeting in Rome in September 1918, after Austria's offensive had been blocked and Italy was about to launch a counteroffensive, also saw a victory of the left. The so-called intransigent or Maximalist faction of the PSI won a stunning 70 percent of the votes cast, and was thus able to assume virtually uncontested control of the party; this faction espoused a more active antiwar policy than the passive *nè aderire nè sabotare* (although as in France these questions had less relevance with the end of the war in sight). Turati and the right wing of the party, by associating themselves with a policy of national defense after Caporetto, had failed to follow the party line, and now constituted a small and isolated minority. There was even talk of expelling Turati and other right-wing figures,[21] a topic that would repeatedly trouble the party during the next three years and would become a central point of controversy with the bolsheviks in 1920. In addressing the congress, Turati was penitent; he promised to abide more faithfully in the future to the directives of the party *Direzione*. Serrati, still in prison, was reelected by acclamation to the editorship of *Avanti!* (the *de facto* presidency of the party), the post Mussolini had earlier held. Serrati emerged as the hero of the controlling Maximalist faction and would lead the PSI throughout the *biennio rosso*.

In Germany, January, 1918 saw a large-scale strike to protest the German government's imperialistic demands in the Brest-Litovsk peace negotiations. The driving force behind this strike was the freshly organized *revolutionäre Obleute* (revolutionary shop stewards), who had banded together out of common disgust for the lack of revolutionary leadership in the higher echelons of the unions. They were workers from the bench, particularly strong in Berlin and in the metal workers' union, and were itching for revolutionary action. On January 28, 400,000 workers in Berlin laid down their tools, demanding peace without annexations or indemnities, and a democratization of Germany's institutions, and appealing to the workers of other countries to join the strike in order to put an end to the war. German authorities replied with a declaration of martial law and ruthless repression, crushing the strike but instilling smouldering hatreds. Under the later blows of military defeat these sentiments would flare into revolution.

By the autumn of 1918 the left of the socialist parties of France, Germany, and Italy had come to the forefront. In Germany military collapse and blockade would accent the swing to the left. In France victory would tend to assuage some of the bitterness following upon Clemenceau's repressions. In Italy a less than satisfactory victory would further justify the PSI's opposition to the war and would contribute powerfully to the revolutionary unrest that was to sweep across Italy.

Chapter II

The Russian "Spark"

The bolsheviks' success in seizing power in November 1917—and even more in holding it—transformed their party from an insignificant sect, ignored or denigrated by western socialists, into a powerful force in world affairs, inordinately admired or deeply detested. The bolsheviks' advance to proletarian socialist revolution was in part based upon the expectation of the imminent approach of socialist revolution in the West, particularly in Germany and in those other industrial areas of central Europe that were largely German in language and culture. A revolution in Russia that could link itself to these industrial centers could exercise a tremendous influence on the rest of continental Europe, presumably inducing a further spread of socialist revolution.

Yet revolution was slow in coming to Germany. The strikes of the German working class in protest over the terms of Brest-Litovsk were easily crushed by the German military authorities, and, thereafter, while the bolsheviks scrambled to establish control over the vast territories of Russia, Germany launched another offensive in the West. Only after this last great effort of the German war machine had failed did the expected collapse of the institutions of the Reich occur. Yet the German revolution of November, 1918 was not a proletarian socialist revolution, and its leaders had no intention of linking their efforts with those of the bolsheviks toward the goal of world revolution. Thus the bolsheviks awaited a second wave of revolution in Germany, similar to the second wave in Russia that had deposed the Provisional Government.

The extent to which Russian revolutionaries could or should help western revolutionaries remained a moot point, although up to this time it was widely assumed, both in Russia and in western

Europe, that backward Russia could offer only a modicum of aid and that ultimately western revolutionaries would take over leadership of the communist movement. But the weaknesses of western revolutionary leadership and the repeated failures of socialist revolution in the West impelled the bolsheviks to take an increasingly active role—an attitude natural to Lenin, in any case. Moreover, the resources available to the bolsheviks as heads of state and their relative security compared to western revolutionaries permitted them a special role. Thus the bolsheviks took the initiative to establish a new international in early 1919, the Communist International (variously termed "Comintern" or "Third International"), which thereafter remained entirely under their leadership and inspiration. Increasingly, bolshevik advice and criticism was offered to western revolutionaries; and increasingly westerners interested themselves in this advice. Yet the first year of the Comintern's existence was one of many confusions and ambiguities which would not be remedied until mid-1920.

Revolution in Russia

For most Marxists the collapse of the tsarist state in March 1917 could only mean the advent of bourgeois revolution in Russia, similar in nature to the revolution in France nearly a century and a half before. Russian political and legal institutions that were no longer historically relevant were being cast off and replaced by institutions that would provide the most favorable environment for the expansion of capitalism and a new leading role for the bourgeoisie. Starting from such premises as a Marxist, Lenin arrived at some extraordinarily imaginative applications to the Russian situation. The passive determinism implied in the orderly stages of the orthodox Marxist revolutionary scenario was not compatible with Lenin's own psychological makeup. His analysis of the bourgeois stage of development was pervaded by a hungry yearning after the final goal of socialist revolution. These yearnings found a certain outlet in the obvious fact that there were many gradations of bourgeois-capitalist regimes, varying as widely, to use two examples employed by Lenin himself, as the American and Prussian forms.

Therefore, a revolutionary living under a predominantly precapitalist or "feudal" regime could feel a certain range of possibilities concerning how thorough the bourgeois revolution in his country would be: would it sweep away all remnants of feudalism, as in the American model, or would it allow many to remain, as in the German? Lenin's preference was for the American model, for the simple reason that it would permit the most unimpeded development of capitalism and thus the more rapid advent of socialist revolution.

What form then would the Russian March revolution assume, the American or the Prussian? Prior to 1917 Lenin had worked out, giving full sway to the peculiarities of Russia's development, an elaborate and tortuous conception of the proper form of Russian bourgeois revolution. His reasoning centered around two particularly important idiosyncrasies of the Russian situation: Russia's lack of an assertive, numerous, and historically rooted urban bourgeoisie; and her superabundant, land-hungry peasantry, which was among the most backward, exploited, and potentially rebellious in all of Europe. Russia's lack of a significant native bourgeoisie meant that a very large part of her remarkable industrial growth in the two generations before World War I relied on foreign capital and foreign management. Politically and ideologically, Russia's lack of bourgeois, urban centers meant a tardy and feeble appearance of liberalism, the political and ideological expression of capitalism. Lenin came to believe that because of its weakness the Russian bourgeoisie would not be capable of pushing forward vigorously its own revolution; it would be tempted to sell out to tsarism before the archaic framework of the old regime was completely destroyed. Lenin found confirmation of this analysis in the actions of the bourgeoisie during the abortive revolution of 1905. Thus he was driven to the awkward conclusion that in order to accomplish a complete casting-off of the old regime in Russia it would be necessary for the working masses themselves to take the lead and force the bourgeoisie to make its own revolution. If necessary, in the face of a complete lack of will on the part of the bourgeoisie, the proletariat, with Russia's restive peasantry as an ally, should make the bourgeois revolution *for* the bourgeoisie. The twisted formula that Lenin used to describe the kind of regime that would realize this twisted conception was "the revolutionary democratic dictatorship of the proletariat and peasantry." This would be, to repeat, *not* a dictatorship of the proletariat which would initiate socialism but a special form of dictatorship, adapted to Russian conditions, which would open the way to the American or most complete variety of bourgeois-democratic capitalism.

Lenin further distinguished two "special" developments that would alter the quality and pace of revolution in Russia in 1917. First, the Russian masses and their revolutionary leaders had already been through a "dress rehearsal" in the revolution of 1905. Now it would be possible to proceed rapidly with few hesitations, uncertainties, and errors. Second, the war had effected an enormous acceleration and intensification of historical trends, further preparing a rapid advance of revolutionary development in 1917. Thus by 1917 Lenin had an even stronger sense of the peculiarity of Russian development and of the resulting indeterminacy of the situation.

He did well to cultivate this sense, because the forms that the revolution had taken by the time Lenin arrived in Petrograd were somewhat different from what he or any other revolutionary theorist had foreseen. In particular the so-called "dual power" surprised and dismayed Lenin. He did not expect that the soviets, the institutions of the revolutionary masses that he expected would take the lead in pushing forward a radical-democratic bourgeois regime, would have such blind faith in the bourgeois ministers of the Provisional Government, who were obviously fearful of a radical democracy and did what they could to prevent its advent. He urged the soviets to push the hesitant bourgeois ministers into a more radical direction, into something more like his revolutionary democratic dictatorship of the proletariat and peasantry. This would be a state more consistent with the needs and desires of the working masses behind the soviets, and would be directly controlled by them, not by the Provisional Government or by an eventual parliamentary democracy.

However, Lenin obviously did not conceive of this stage in the orthodox Marxian sense, with the manifold economic, social, and cultural implications of the bourgeois-democratic stage in the West. Rather—and here one sees the tug of Lenin's will to socialist revolution—he saw it in narrow political terms, in terms of revolutionary dynamics: he urged that the revolutionary democratic dictatorship of the proletariat and peasantry begin immediately with such measures as the establishment of a workers' and peasants' militia to replace the old forces of police and army, the dissolution of the bureaucratic structures of the old state, and the abolition of all political privileges based on ownership of property. Such measures, by strongly underlining problems of class interest and power, would intensify class conflict to fever pitch and pave the way to socialist revolution. In other words, Lenin's famous April Theses, in urging that the soviets take all power in their hands, did not technically propose proletarian revolution. Yet he was narrowing down in the most extreme fashion the duration of the bourgeois-democratic stage of development; he was suggesting that the revolutionary democratic dictatorship of the proletariat and peasantry would easily merge into proletarian dictatorship pure and simple.

Lenin predicted that the concrete experiences of the revolution would cause the masses to withdraw their support from the Provisional Government and transfer it to the bolsheviks. These were hardly unrealistic predictions. In deciding to continue the war and to launch a new offensive in July, the Provisional Government provided one of the many such concrete experiences, alienating many previous supporters. The popular uprising of July, which was not in the strictest sense led by the bolsheviks but in which they acquiesced, was a striking manifestation of popular antipathy to the Provisional Government. The policy of stern repression then carried out by the Provisional Government and accepted by the moderate socialists in the soviets (a number of whom had now joined the Provisional Government) further added to the alienation between the government and the radical masses, and further contributed to the image of the bolsheviks as the only true revolutionaries.

Lenin now declared that since the mensheviks and socialist-revolutionaries had supported the measures of repression, they had in effect gone over to the counterrevolution. This gave the entire revolution a new turn, and after the July uprising Lenin began to call for the immediate establishment of the dictatorship of the proletariat, a dictatorship that was no longer to be promulgated by the peaceful road of propaganda among the masses that Lenin had so far advocated, but by an armed uprising. At this point Lenin seemed to abandon Marxism, even his very special variety of it, for something resembling narodnik anarchism or Blanquism. Throughout this period he resisted relating his plans for action to clear or previously established theoretical standards, insisting that the situation in Russia was so fluid that theory might become a hindrance to flexible and courageous revolutionary action. This was a puzzling, even an astonishing attitude for a man who had spent the better part of his life developing theory and who gave Marxian theory the value of rigorous science.

If Lenin had not been a Marxist, then a pragmatic justification for a proletarian dictatorship could have been plausibly advanced. The industrial proletariat and the party of the proletariat (that is, the bolsheviks), in spite of their relatively limited numbers, were the only coherent, disciplined, and determined force left in Russia in late 1917. The parties of the rural petty bourgeoisie and misguided workers (that is, the socialist-revolutionaries and mensheviks) had already demonstrated their inner contradictions and inability to rule, to say nothing of the kadets (the bourgeois liberals). If the very poorest agricultural proletarians could be induced to join hands with the urban proletariat, while the bulk of the wealthier peasantry was neutralized by the offer of land, a proletarian dictatorship would be possible, at least for a limited period of time.

Such is in fact what occurred in late 1917. Yet a dictatorship along these lines is narrowly political or even military, and has little apparent relationship to the Marxian conception of the dictatorship of the proletariat which would introduce socialism. But Lenin maintained a semblance of Marxian orthodoxy by reasoning that socialism could come to Russia as soon as the industrial proletariat of the West had joined its great numbers and powerful resources to those of the Russian proletariat. The party of the proletariat could come to power first in Russia, not because Russia was itself ready for socialism but because Russia constituted the "weakest link" in world imperialism. A dictatorship of the proletariat in Russia thus served the important function of a "spark," an impetus, an inspiration to revolutionaries in the West. Yet it was a spark that provided more than the ethereal force of an ideal or an example, since it also broke the economic chain of imperalism, thus further accelerating the dissolution of European capitalism, already in an advanced state of decay because of the world war. With the final collapse of capitalism in the West, the proletariat of the West and that of Russia could build socialism together.

By early September the bolsheviks were beginning to win majorities in the soviets of the main urban areas and had made dramatic progress toward controlling or at least neutralizing military garrisons and other power centers. Lenin's main problem by this time was not in convincing the masses—important numbers of whom were armed and rearing to go—that it was necessary for the soviets to take all power into their hands, but rather to convince many leading figures in his own party. Zinoviev and Kamenev, as well as a number of other prominent bolsheviks, were not convinced that the western proletariat would come to the aid of the Russian proletariat once the latter had come to power. This wing of the party feared that a proletarian revolution in Russia would remain isolated and would thus inevitably be crushed by the antisocialist forces inside and outside Russia. In fact Lenin's own earlier position, in his debates with Trotsky, had been very close to that of the now cautious wing of the party. Only with the events of July did Lenin come around to a more optimistic appraisal of the likelihood of a proximate proletarian revolution in the West.

Whatever the debates inside the party, in a very real sense the bolsheviks had little choice left but to assume power. Since their energies had been devoted to exposing the inadequacies of the Provisional Government and the other soviet parties while at the same time articulating in the minds of the masses the deep desires for land, bread, and peace, they could hardly now refuse to take power and to attempt to give leadership to the furies of those masses.

In viewing the final success of the bolsheviks in taking power, it is difficult to accept without strong reservations the reason for this success most often put forth by the bolsheviks themselves, especially in their contacts in 1920 and 1921 with western revolutionaries.

According to this view it was the discipline and centralization of the Bolshevik party machine, the revolutionary skill of its leaders, and the essential "correctness" of their interpretation of Marxism which permitted the party to seize and hold power. The corollary of this view was of course that by carefully studying and copying the Bolshevik party—its organizational principles, its doctrine, the qualities of its leaders—other revolutionaries could succeed elsewhere. Yet, with due recognition of the importance of the organization of the Bolshevik party, it seems abundantly clear that the bolsheviks benefited from any number of very special conditions and particular turns of events that had little to do with their own proficiencies and which did not and could not hold in the West. In particular, the disintegration of the older institutions of rule was so pervasive and the thrust from below was so strong that it seems more appropriate to assert that the bolsheviks "caught" the revolution than to say that they "made" it. Obviously the organization of the party had relatively little to do with creating the revolutionary conditions at the end of the summer of 1917; these conditions were created by the double collapse of the tsarist regime and of the Provisional Government under the pressures of war. The special talents of the bolsheviks and the organization of their party allowed them to mount and to a limited degree steer—but certainly not cause—the mass upheaval stimulated by this dual collapse.

After the intoxication of victory a hard fact remained: the bolsheviks had not made proletarian socialist revolution in any full or Marxian sense of the term. The only plausible rationale for their takeover in Russia was that they were starting something that necessarily had to be completed in the highly industrialized West, where the material conditions existed upon which to build socialism. Until revolution in the West came to their aid, the bolsheviks would remain in an anomalous position, having come to power primarily through opportunistic appeals to the yearnings for peace and land. They were able to hold power not so much because of the strength of their proletarian backing but because opposition to them was divided. Russian society was so atomized that a ruthless and terroristic minority could maintain power over it. This was not an auspicious beginning to world socialist revolution.

The spread of revolution to Germany

The concept of a spark from Russia acting both as an inspiration and as a concrete aid to revolution in the West was one that offered a wide variety of possible interpretations. The political strikes in Germany in January, 1918 might be considered one of the earliest manifestations of the revolutionary impact on Germany of the Bolshevik Revolution. Yet at the same time many of those Germans who were ardently opposed to the punitive clauses of the Brest-Litovsk treaty were not deeply inspired or even favorably impressed by the bolshevik victory. Moreover, the year 1918, after the heady triumphs of late 1917, was a time when the bolsheviks found themselves compelled to take many harsh measures. These measures had an unavoidably negative impact in the West.

The bolsheviks' final assent to the Brest-Litovsk peace was one of the first of these. In signing it they lost vast stretches of rich territory but gained an essential breathing spell, at the expense of releasing Germany's military forces to concentrate on the western front. Prior to the negotiations at Brest-Litovsk nearly all bolsheviks, Lenin included, had maintained that revolutionary Russia could not accept a punitive peace; if the Germans demanded such a peace, then Soviet Russia would be forced to wage a "revolutionary war" against them. This war would have the impact of further spurring western revolutionaries into action. Such a view was consistent with Lenin's reasoning that a proletarian revolution in Russia could survive because the Russian proletariat would find its indispensable ally in the proletariat of western Europe. It was a view also consistent with Lenin's and Trotsky's general attitude of revolutionary audacity, of *révolution à outrance*, that had borne fruit in the autumn of 1917. However, once faced with the real possibility that the Germans might crush the bolshevik regime, Lenin rapidly changed his mind and returned to a position that in some ways resembled his pre-1917 views or those of Kamenev and Zinoviev on the eve of the revolution: now he affirmed that the precise timing of the revolution in Germany was completely incalculable, and thus the bolsheviks could not rely upon the immediate aid of the German proletariat. Lenin had much difficulty in convincing the rest of the party leadership and was able to get his views accepted only under the threat of resignation.

Because the German revolution did not come to the aid of the bolsheviks in early 1918, they were forced to come to grips with the fact that they were a small minority ruling over a vast, increasingly hostile population. Symbolic of the dangers faced by the bolsheviks was the attempt on Lenin's life in August. Bolshevik leaders reasoned that if they were to maintain themselves in power they themselves would have to resort to terror, to exemplary and retaliatory violence. Thus the year 1918 saw the initiation of the so-called Red Terror, the establishment of an active secret police uncontrolled by law (the Cheka), and the first steps in the creation of significant military organizations—in short a whole range of measures designed to terrorize and subdue the anti-bolshevik part of the Russian population.

However necessary these measures (once one accepts the unavoidability of bolshevik minority rule), they had a distinctly unfavorable impact in the West. Even the revolutionary wing of the working-class movement in Germany, the wing that enthusiastically greeted the Bolshevik Revolution and that tended to discount the atrocity stories that filled the bourgeois press, found this aspect of bolshevik rule awkward and perplexing. Most German revolutionaries insisted that proletarian revolution in Germany would of necessity base itself on a proletarian majority or at least on a very significant proportion of the population, and would thus not be obliged to resort to such devices.

By the eve of the German revolution, the spark of revolution from Russia exercised not only favorable but also unfavorable influence on revolution in Germany. As a model for making revolution the bolshevik example was not widely admired and was in fact little understood in Germany at this time.[1] Indeed, the methods the bolsheviks were forced to use in order to catch and hold power in Russia tended to discredit the idea of proletarian dictatorship for large parts of the working class in the West and turned nonproletarian classes even more vehemently against the idea of social revolution. There was thus a strong impetus for German revolutionaries to insist upon the uniqueness of the bolshevik example.

The German revolution began in early November 1918 with a naval mutiny in the port of Kiel, from where it spread to other cities, meeting spontaneous working-class support. Revolutionary workers' and soldiers' councils (*Arbeiter- und Soldatenräte*) sprang up throughout Germany within a few days of the Kiel mutiny. Before long the Kaiser had abdicated and Germany was declared a republic. For socialist revolutionaries these developments, especially the appearance and rapid spread of *Räte*, or soviets,[2] was a most exciting development. The bolsheviks were equally jubilant, and the pages of *Pravda* and *Izvestia* were full of glowing predictions that the Russian soviet regime would soon be rescued by revolution in Germany.[3] However, for the leaders of the SPD and the trade unions, both of whom had concerned themselves during the war with "controlling" the working class in the interests of Germany's war effort, the appearance of *Räte* was a most threatening phenomenon. The German revolutionary councils had obviously taken their lead from the Russian soviets and were potentially unruly institutions which could be expected to make "unrealistic" demands without consulting the more experienced leaders of the working class.[4]

The threat of uncontrolled mass radicalism seemed all the more disturbing to the union and SPD leaders because early in the revolution they felt that their goals had been attained, that the ad hoc economic arrangements and the promises for constitutional reform made by Germany's leaders during the war had now taken on permanent form. Before the war the army and the leaders of heavy industry had been the mainstays of Germany's authoritarian political and social system. The pressures of war had worked a transformation in the system, a transformation that solidified in the initial months of the revolution. Behind the plans for a new democratic-republican constitution in Germany, a new social and political balance came into being: the SPD and officer corps formed an alliance, and the industrialists joined hands with the unions. This new balance of forces not only excluded the German *Mittelstand*, or middle class, but also was a way of heading off the demands of the more radical elements of the German working class for a thoroughgoing revolution. Part of the working class was appeased, at least temporarily, by these new alliances. At the same time the alliances perpetuated and intensified the divisions within the working class.

When it became clear by early October that defeat in war had fatally weakened imperial Germany's authoritarian state, the industrialists recognized that the strongest ally they could find in their struggle to preserve the existing economic system was in organized labor, with its limited and "reasonable" demands. In order to avoid social revolution the industrialists were willing to pay a price, as long as that price left them with the substance of their former power. On November 12 an agreement, the so-called Stinnes-Legien Agreement, was drawn up in which they recognized the unions as the proper representatives of labor (and thus agreed to stop financial support of the yellow unions), accepted collective bargaining and factory councils, and approved an eight-hour working day (although a secret protocol made this invalid if other countries failed to introduce the eight-hour day also).[5]

If on the whole the industrialists were able to get off lightly, Germany's officer corps emerged from the months of crisis immediately following the war even more miraculously unscathed, in spite of the enormous discredit of the military in October and November. The *Räte* were virtually unanimous in their belief that the backbone of Junker militarism must be broken. Yet Germany's military leaders played their cards in a manner that permitted them to retain a position of eminence in the new German state. The army agreed with the leadership of the SPD to support the new German republic in return for the republic's support of social discipline and military *Ordnung*. This alliance was entirely to the liking of the SPD leadership, especially since it seemed the only effective way to control working-class radicalism.

These new alliances took shape in the background, while an interim cabinet attempted to establish itself at the head of the revolution. This cabinet, calling itself the "Council of People's Representatives" (*Rat der Volksbeauftragten*, or RdV), was composed of six members, three from the SPD and three from the USPD. The RdV recognized the *Räte* as the source of its authority, although the exact nature of the relationship was left unclear. As could be imagined, cooperation between these two parties was difficult because of their wartime antipathies. Moreover, they did not agree on basic issues concerning what the RdV was to accomplish. Of the six only Emil Barth of the USPD could be described as a radical revolutionary who desired an immediate social revolution in Germany. Friedrich Ebert, the head of the SPD, thought that the RdV should function only as an interim body until a democratically elected constituent assembly could take over. Somewhere in between these two positions were the USPD representatives Hugo Haase and Wilhelm Dittmann, whose views were expressed in their party's manifesto of November 12, which looked to continued rule by the *Räte* at least until the "necessary work" of revolution had been accomplished, even if this entailed taking measures which lacked the clear or formal backing of the majority of the population. This necessary work included purging and democratizing the German state bureaucracy and the military, and instituting wide-ranging economic and social reforms, although stopping short of a dictatorship of the proletariat on the Russian model or wholesale socialization of the means of production.[6]

The first national congress of all the *Räte* in Germany, which met in mid-December, saw a serious setback for those who hoped that just as the Russian soviets had constituted the popular institutions that underpinned the dictatorship of the proletariat, so would the *Räte* play a similar role in Germany. The arguments of the SPD delegates that the *Räte* should exercise limited economic and not political functions and that a constituent assembly should be called as soon as possible won the overwhelming support of the congress. The SPD's resolution won 400 votes as opposed to fifty for a resolution presented by the left-USPD delegate, Ernst Däumig, favoring rule by the *Räte* alone.[7]

Yet, initial appearances to the contrary, this vote did not reflect an acceptance by the congress of the overall policies of Ebert and the SPD (that is, to cooperate with and preserve the older authorities as long as those authorities recognized the need for a democratically elected constituent assembly). Even though the delegates to the *Räte* congress were generally repelled by the idea of a proletarian dictatorship with its overtones of further bloodshed and civil war, later debates at the congress made it clear that they were still enthusiastically committed to democratizing the army and socializing the economy (in other words, a program substantially the same as that outlined in the USPD's November 12 manifesto). The congress approved the quite radical "Hamburg Points," so called because they were introduced by the soldiers' councils in Hamburg, without opposition. The Points stipulated that the RdV, not the High Command, should be the highest authority in the army; that all marks of rank should be done away with; that the *Soldatenräte* should take charge of military discipline; that officers should be elected by their men; and that a national militia should replace the standing army. These were measures that very much resembled those taken by the soldiers' soviets in Russia in 1917, and Ebert, who was present at the congress, knew that the Points were absolutely unacceptable to the High Command. Yet he dared not oppose them openly; he could more effectively undermine them behind the scenes through his position as Representative for Military Affairs in the RdV.[8]

The debates at the congress also established that the great majority of the delegates were enthusiastically in favor of socialization, even though the economic experts of both the SPD and USPD emphasized the great practical obstacles to socialization at this time. The congress passed, against a small minority, a resolution calling for socialization in all industries which were "ripe" for it.[9] Thus the overwhelming consensus at the congress was that demilitarization and socialization were necessary; yet at the same time the congress gave the SPD overwhelming support for its program of immediate elections. The *Räte* delegates were not clear-sighted enough to understand that their support of the constituent assembly doomed the measures of demilitarization and socialization that were probably more important to them than democratic elections.

The coalition between the SPD and USPD did not survive the year. Their relationship, in spite of the equal number of Representatives, was not one of equality, partly because Ebert was able to exercise a kind of *de facto* leadership, a role facilitated by the obvious partiality of nearly all government officials for the SPD over the USPD. The USPD members felt, with good reason, that they were not being properly consulted on important issues, and they were deeply disturbed by Ebert's obsequious attitude to the military. They did not know of his secret agreements with General Groener, but they suspected something of the sort, especially after Ebert sanctioned brutal and indiscriminate measures by the military in late 1918 in and around Berlin. The events of the following months would more than confirm these suspicions.

The breakup of the USPD-SPD coalition inevitably caused the USPD to move more sharply to the left and released some of the restraints on the SPD's own move to the right. The USPD's present moderate leadership had increasing difficulty in resisting the left's urgings to push on to a "second revolution," as the bolsheviks had done. Yet the reluctance of the *Räte* congress to endorse a proletarian dictatorship put those on the left in the position of advocating violent action not only in the name of the proletarian minority of the total population in Germany but even in the name of the minority of the working class itself that favored proletarian dictatorship. This was actually not a path that many revolutionaries were yet ready to follow. The alternative was to wait, with the expectation that the masses were in a process of rapid radicalization and would soon support a violent seizure of power in the name of social revolution.

The failures of revolutionary socialists in Germany

In observing the march of revolution in Russia in 1917, one is led almost to the conclusion that events conspired to favor the bolsheviks, that they enjoyed some kind of special favor from the Muse of History. One could easily be led to the opposite conclusion in observing the revolutionary events in Germany in late 1918 and early 1919. German revolutionaries had to deal with a vast array of conditions hostile to socialist revolution, and they were in no way able to duplicate the achievements of the bolsheviks. Indeed, they staggered from disaster to disaster.

In 1917 and 1918 little united the USPD beyond a hostility to the policies of the leaders of the SPD. The highly decentralized nature of the new party allowed great diversity to flower within its ranks. At the left of the USPD, the *Spartakusbund*, led by Rosa Luxemburg and Karl Liebknecht, frankly viewed its presence in the party as a tactical measure: the USPD could be used as a protecting umbrella and as a vehicle through which to establish working-class contacts; at some future, more auspicious time, the Spartacists fully expected to form a separate party. This would be a new kind of party, based on much greater mass participation than had been the case in the prewar SPD. Indeed, they desired an even more decentralized party than the present USPD. Their ideal was a party with the barest minimum of permanent organizational structures and paid officials; some of them even recommended that there should be no paid officials whatsoever. It hardly need be observed that such views were worlds away from Lenin's belief in the necessity of a party *apparat* to lead and educate the masses.

Other left-wing factions existed in the USPD, quite distinct from the Spartacists but certainly no less revolutionary than they. The *revolutionäre Obleute* were workers from the bench, and they maintained extensive and effective organizational contacts with certain radical elements of the German working class. The *Obleute* generally understood little and cared less about Luxemburgism versus Leninism or other aspects of Marxian theory in its more elevated forms. They distrusted the numerous intellectuals of the *Spartakusbund*, whom they accused of being mere café revolutionaries, playing with pointless street tactics or "revolutionary gymnastics." The Spartacists in turn accused the *Obleute*, because of their emphasis on the organizational aspects of preparation for revolution in the factories, of having an overly "mechanical" view of revolution.[10]

The Spartacists' assertion that revolution should find its base in the streets of Germany's urban centers implicitly looked to the unorganized masses, the unemployed and unskilled workers, the rebellious soldiery, the down-and-out slum dwellers. These were the elements of Germany's working population over which the established socialist party and union officials exercised the least control. And, significantly, it was comparable elements of the Russian population that rallied in great numbers to the bolsheviks in 1917. The *revolu-*

tionäre Obleute thought more in terms of the disciplined and well-integrated factory proletarian, especially those in the large, advanced industries, such as the metal industry. Spanning both of these approaches were those in the USPD who put their main hopes for revolution in the *Räte*. A particularly interesting figure in this respect was Ernst Däumig, one of the few leading USPD officials who had the confidence of the *Obleute* and who had friendships among the Spartacists.[11] Däumig went so far as to argue, in the early stages of the revolution in Germany, that the hostile Socialist parties should dissolve themselves in favor of the *Räte* alone, as a way of reuniting the German proletariat and providing for a solid organizational foundation for revolutionary socialism. (He would remain a leader of the USPD left wing for the following two years and would go to Moscow in 1920 as one of the four official delegates of his party to the Comintern's Second World Congress.)

In other ways as well Däumig consciously tried to work out positions that would bridge the many gaps between German socialists. His attitude to the bolshevik regime was thus a combination of admiration and friendly criticism, moderated by a frank recognition that information about Russia was not yet adequate or reliable enough to make firm judgments.[12] On the one hand he emphasized the enormous importance of the revolution in Russia, but on the other he termed it a "fundamental error" (*Riesenfehler*) of the bolsheviks to have based their rule exclusively on the lowest ranks of the working class. He felt that it was of the utmost importance to unite the intellectual and manual workers (*Kopf- und Handarbeiter*) in the socialist *Rätesystem*.[13] Moreover, he explicitly rejected the idea that the Russian model was one that German revolutionaries should follow dogmatically, and he disassociated himself from those "confused workers and intellectuals who have made a fetish out of the Russian example."[14]

In spite of the differing emphases of these left-wing factions of the USPD, they all shared a vague admiration for the Bolshevik Revolution—although many, like Däumig retained a degree of critical reserve about it—and a determination to push the revolution in Germany beyond the point at which it had been blocked by the SPD. Moreover, they all tended to suspect the USPD's controlling moderate wing of being inadequately committed to revolutionary action. Such being the case it seemed natural that these factions should unite into a single party, similar to the way in which various leftwing mensheviks, left socialist-revolutionaries, and Trotsky's *Mezhrayontsi* (members of the "Inter-borough Organization") had swallowed their differences and joined Lenin's bolsheviks in the summer and autumn of 1917. In late December the Spartacists took the initiative to form such a party, to be called the German Communist party or KPD (*Kommunistische Partei Deutschlands*), using the same name that the bolsheviks had adopted at their October 1918 party congress and which since the time of Marx had been used primarily by the anarchists in western Europe.

However, the only other organized group finally to join the Spartacists in the new KPD was the so-called "Bremen Left," a semi-anarchist body that had previously remained outside both the SPD and USPD. The leaders of the *Spartakusbund* made a serious tactical error in allying themselves with the Bremen group before making every effort to come to an agreement with the *revolutionäre Obleute*, for the Bremen Left personified in an even more extreme form those very qualities of revolutionary irresponsibility which the *Obleute* already distrusted in the Spartacists. Thus the Spartacist–Bremen Left KPD was doubly repellent to the *Obleute*, and they refused to join the new party.

Leo Jogiches, the Spartacists' organizational leader, voiced suspicion from the very beginning of the Bremen group, but his suspicions and those of other Spartacists were allayed by Karl Radek, who had been sent to Germany by the bolsheviks and who favored the alliance.[15] Here the ironies abound, for prior to the Bolshevik Revolution Radek had been a pariah among many who would later become Spartacists—Rosa Luxemburg had been instrumental in having him hounded from the Polish Social Democratic Party on charges of embezzling party funds.[16] However, Radek's association with the bolsheviks gave him a new mantle of authority.

The alliance with the Bremen Left compounded the organizational inadequacies of the *Spartakusbund*. Its glorification of mass spontaneity came in practice to mean that the leadership of the new KPD had a very imperfect grip on the rank and file. This problem was embarrassingly obvious at the founding congress, since the recommendations of the party leadership were repeatedly voted down by the congress delegates. Certainly the young KPD resembled the Bolshevik party in little more than name, and one can easily agree with the judgment that the German communists were far more a "syndicalist-anarchist-utopian" band of young enthusiasts than a solid Marxist or Leninist party.[17]

In January 1919 the KPD, only a few days after its founding congress, had to face a crisis similar to that which the Bolshevik party had faced in July 1917—an uncontrolled and unplanned mass uprising. The January Uprising in Germany began as a conflict over the dismissal of Emil Eichhorn, the USPD chief of police in Berlin. On Sunday, the fifth of January, a huge pro-Eichhorn demonstration filled the central squares and streets of Berlin. Perhaps 700,000 demonstrators turned out, surprising nearly everyone, and constituting the largest political gathering ever recorded in Berlin.[18] It seemed clear that a large part of Berlin's working-class population was intent on violent action.

The leaders of the KPD, or at least of its Luxemburgist wing, had actually been more hesitant than the *Obleute* and USPD leadership in supporting the Eichhorn demonstrations. Luxemburg and Jogiches understood that their party was not ready for a showdown with the Ebert government. But they had little control over the masses, and they submitted to the pressures from below, much as the bolsheviks had been obliged to do in July 1917. But the former had far less ability to cope with the implications of this decision than had the latter.

When a hurriedly assembled "Revolutionary Committee" issued a manifesto calling for the much awaited "second revolution" through a general strike and the violent overthrow of the SPD-controlled RdV,[19] Ebert felt the need to respond decisively. His deepest fears were stirred that he would become the German Kerensky. Now his earlier agreements with the High Command took on real meaning: a leading figure of the right wing of the SPD, Gustav Noske, was given the task of organizing the government's resistance to the revolutionaries; Noske pinned his hopes primarily on the new military detachments, soon familiar by the name *Freikorps*, which officers of the demobilizing imperial army had begun to organize under their own initiative. Noske gave them official government encouragement in this enterprise, and coordinated these actions with the High Command. Unlike the troops that now took part in the *Räte* organizations, these troops were disciplined, loyal to their commanders, and fiercely hostile to the "foreign" doctrines of revolutionary socialism. The *Freikorps* experienced little difficulty in putting down the uprising. In the process Liebknecht and Luxemburg were caught, brutally beaten, and put to death. The following months saw armed conflicts in most major cities of Germany. The *Räte* attempted to reassert their waning power, but against the *Freikorps* they repeatedly made a poor showing. At a great price in blood, order was reestablished in Germany.

These months saw a move by the leadership of the SPD from covert opposition to the demands of the *Räte* to the sanction of all out armed force against them. While this further move to the right was a logical culmination of the SPD's wartime policies and the November Ebert-Groener agreements, it also reflected the new power base the SPD had established in the January elections to the constituent assembly: the SPD won 11.5 million votes and 163 seats (out of a total of 421).[20] It was clear that a good number of these votes came from nonproletarian or semiproletarian voters who had not voted for socialists before and who supported the SPD's firm stand against revolutionary radicalism. In many ways the SPD thus came to have much in common with bourgeois parties.

The USPD won only twenty-two seats in the assembly, and the KPD none at all, since it boycotted the elections. Significantly, the SPD and USPD together still did not represent a majority of the total vote; the non-socialist parties, although sharply divided among themselves, could conceivably have taken over the affairs of the new republic. This failure of socialism, even in its mildest form, to win a majority was a bitter disappointment to many. Understandably, the enthusiasm of socialists in Germany for formal majority rule and parliamentary democracy tended to cool.[21] In any case, the only way that the SPD could now continue to rule, even if the USPD would once again consent to a coalition with it—a highly unlikely eventuality—and remain consistent with its majoritarian-democratic principles was to form a coalition with non-socialist parties, which it proceeded to do. This entry into bourgeois coalition politics constituted a further large step for the SPD away from its prewar Marxian origins. For nearly all socialists who considered themselves Marxian revolutionaries, the SPD now stood beyond the pale.

The failures of the KPD, especially when compared to the relative successes of the USPD, which continued a remarkable growth in 1919, was to have an important influence on the peculiar relationships of German revolutionaries to the bolsheviks. It was obvious that the KPD required important corrections if it was to aspire to leadership of proletarian revolution in Germany. On the other hand, the leaders of the USPD groped about for some sense of direction and some way in which the party's many factions could continue to work together. The growing mass base of radicalized workers behind the USPD inevitably attracted Comintern attention to it, while the bolsheviks' own continued revolutionary success attracted the attention of many in the USPD who felt increasingly frustrated and disoriented.

The Bern Conference

The *gran rifiuto* of the majority socialists during the war, their failure to live up to the ideals of internationalism, meant the end of the Socialist International for many western socialists, though by no means all of them. By the war's end many hoped to reconstitute the International and thus revive the solidarity of the prewar years. To do this seemed particularly desirable to those socialists who felt it important that the forthcoming peace negotiations in Paris be presented with an official international socialist position concerning a just and lasting peace.

In response to the invitations of a committee which acted in conjunction with Camille Huysmans, the Secretary of the prewar International Socialist Bureau (the executive body of the Socialist International), delegates from the socialist parties and labor organizations of twenty-six countries assembled at Bern, Switzerland, on February 3. Both the USPD and the SPD sent delegations, just as the SFIO sent representatives of both the *Majoritaires* and *Minori-*

taires. Conspicuously absent were delegations from nearly all the parties or groups which had been associated with the Zimmerwald left during the war—the bolsheviks, the Spartacists, the PSI, and the Swiss Socialist party.

The delegates immediately tackled the most vexing questions for socialists at that time—"war guilt" and democracy versus dictatorship in the struggle for socialism. The first proved a veritable hornets' nest, and after an impassioned but rather fruitless debate lasting two days, the delegates decided to postpone a full discussion of the problem until a later meeting. For the time being a declaration by the SPD delegation strongly disassociating itself from the imperial regime had to suffice. The second question proved no easier to resolve, and the conference finally referred the matter to a special committee which produced two rival resolutions. The "Branting resolution," which gained the support of a majority of the committee, represented the views of the right of the conference and implicitly condemned the bolshevik regime by declaring emphatically that socialism and democracy were inseparable. The "Adler-Longuet resolution" shied away from criticism of the bolsheviks and declared that not enough was yet securely known about Soviet Russia to allow a fair judgment; a hostile statement at this time would only make more difficult the eventual reestablishment of a united international.[22]

The USPD delegation surprisingly voted with the SPD for the Branting resolution, a vote which reflected the right-wing character of the delegates sent by the USPD. Two of them, Karl Kautsky and Eduard Bernstein, attacked the bolsheviks at Bern at least as bitterly as did the representatives of the SPD. Actually this right-wing cast to the USPD delegation was rather fortuitous, but it would not be forgotten when the party leaders sought to make contact with the new Communist International.

Once these preliminary questions had been dealt with, the conference turned to the task of preparing a socialist case for presentation to the Paris Peace conference. The proposals worked out were for a powerful international organization of nations, based on the principle of democratic self-determination of peoples, with a permanent international commission to oversee labor legislation. The proposals, in other words, while going considerably beyond what would later be decided in Paris, restricted themselves to "realistic," reformist measures within the context of capitalism.

The final concern of the Bern conference was to try to reestablish the International. But it was obvious from the first days that because of the profound divisions among the delegates this would be an extremely difficult task and certainly one which the conference could not accomplish at this first meeting. Consequently, an attempt was made simply to lay the foundations for a new international by choosing a permanent commission, made up of two representatives from each country, which would take on the double task of presenting the Bern conference's final recommendations to the Peace Conference and of arranging for a further meeting where the reestablishment of the international would be the principal concern.[23]

The First Congress of the Communist International

In the meantime the bolsheviks themselves were hurriedly making plans for a new revolutionary international. Although Lenin had called for the establishment of a new international since August 1914, he had hesitated to take specific measures to organize it. This hesitation was due in part to the practical difficulties caused by the war, in part to the fear that the creation of a revolutionary international organization might anger the Allies, giving them further pretext for action against the Soviet regime, and in part to the simple fact that few independent revolutionary parties of the sort that Lenin envisaged as members had yet been established in western or central Europe.[24] The lack of such a party in Germany had been especially important, since the bolsheviks considered a German communist party absolutely necessary for a strong revolutionary international.

The events of the last two months of 1918 drastically changed these conditions. Revolution erupted in Germany and in the rest of central Europe, the war finally came to an end, and a communist party was established in Germany. As previously noted, the news of the collapse of the Reich and the establishment of a regime based on workers' and soldiers' councils revived in Lenin and the bolsheviks an intense belief that world revolution was imminent. The jubilation in Petrograd and Moscow knew no bounds,[25] and Lenin announced "our predictions have come true, our sacrifices are justified. Never have we been so close to an international proletarian revolution as we are at this moment."[26]

Yet contacts between the West and Russia continued to be extremely uncertain. And except for Germany there were as yet only communist tendencies or groups within the larger socialist parties. But the news of the proposed meeting at Bern dissolved whatever hesitations the bolsheviks may have had. Lenin was particularly concerned that the patriotic socialists, by taking the lead in the restoration of the international, might attract the "confused and undecided elements of the proletariat."[27] He thus decided that no matter how difficult the task a new international must be established that would hold high the banners of revolution and that could at least offer an alternative to the Bern organization.

Therefore the bolsheviks forged ahead, although in a fashion that was necessarily haphazard and lacking in adequate preparation. On January 24 invitations were sent out by wireless for a meeting of revolutionary socialists in Moscow. However, this was hardly an effective way to arrange a world congress: the wireless messages were not even received by many of those invited, and many others that did receive them were not able to get into Russia because of the troubled conditions on her borders. Moreover, the bolsheviks had to issue such vague and ludicrous invitations as the following: "to the groups and organizations within the French socialist and syndicalist movement which agree by and large with Loriot."[28]

Given these circumstances there were a number of important socialist leaders in the West who still considered it premature to set up a new international. Notable among these was Rosa Luxemburg. She had developed some private doubts concerning the wisdom of the bolshevik seizure of power,[29] and she further worried that the creation of a new international in early 1919, before the masses were ready and before revolutionary parties had been firmly established in the West, would mean overwhelming bolshevik predominance in it, an unhealthy state of affairs, in her opinion. Therefore, when

confronted with the invitation to the Moscow conference, she in-
structed the KPD delegate, Hugo Eberlein, to oppose any move to
set up a new international.[30]

As it turned out, Eberlein was the only delegate from a western
party or organization of any significance who made it into Russia.
Aside from the bolsheviks, only four of the fifty-two persons that
finally assembled in Moscow on March 2 could be considered bona
fide spokesmen for active and independent parties. These were
Eberlein, Strange of the Norwegian social democrats, Steinhardt of
the Austrian Communist party, and Grimlund of the Left Social
Democratic party of Sweden. The latter three represented organizations of considerably less significance than the KPD, and of these
three only Grimlund had specific directives from his party to attend
the Moscow congress and vote for a new international.[31]

Of the other delegates eight were bolsheviks, and a large number
were representatives of revolutionary parties of former parts of the
Russian Empire—Poland, Finland, the Ukraine, Latvia, Estonia,
and the German colonies in Russia—each of which was awarded full
voting powers. The remaining delegates were either former prisoners of war who were still in Russia or random revolutionaries who
for one reason or another found themselves in or able to reach Russia at this time. One of these, Henri Guilbeaux, was awarded five
votes, the maximum possible for any delegation, on the grounds
that he represented France, one of the most important countries.
Yet he was practically unknown in socialist or anarchosyndicalist
circles in France, and certainly had no formal mandate from the
SFIO, CGT, or any other organization in France. He was apparently accepted because Lenin had known him in Switzerland and
because Loriot had recently described him as one of those who were
in basic agreement with the Zimmerwaldian left in France.[32] Similarly, Boris Reinstein, a Russian-born citizen of the United States,
was awarded five votes as a spokesman for the American Socialist
Labor party, although he had not been in the United States for two
years and had lost contact with the American party.

In short, it is obvious that while the bolsheviks allowed themselves only five votes, their influence was immense, since the overwhelming majority of the delegates were handpicked by them, and

since they were the representatives of the only party that had successfully taken power. Bolshevik speakers completely dominated
the proceedings, and the bolsheviks were the sole authors of the various official pronouncements finally issued by the congress.

However, Eberlein's influence was also great, since he represented the country most important in revolutionary potential. Thus
his objections to the formation of a new international, even though
he could have been easily outvoted, caused the bolsheviks to retract
—very reluctantly—their original proposal that this meeting be officially proclaimed the first meeting of the Communist International.

But this was not the end of the matter. On March 4 the conference was thrown into great excitement by the breathless arrival of
Steinhardt, the delegate from the Austrian Communist party, who
had completed a harrowing seventeen-day trip through the war
zone. An ungainly and shaggily bearded worker, Steinhardt excitedly announced the imminent outbreak of revolution throughout
the West. His appearance seems to have changed the mood of the
meeting: one by one the delegates rose to argue for the immediate
establishment of a new international. When the question was put
to a vote, Eberlein abstained but let it be known that he personally
approved of the decision.[33]

Leninism and the First Congress of the Comintern

The revolutionary excitement that spurred the bolsheviks on to an immediate establishment of the Comintern was obvious in their speeches at the congress and in the final declarations of
the congress. Zinoviev went so far as to predict that within the year
there would be soviet regimes in power throughout Europe and
that the next congress of the Comintern would be in some western
European capital.[34] A similar tone could be seen in the new "Communist Manifesto," proclaimed to be the successor of the Manifesto
of 1848. The pen of Trotsky can be discerned in the biting and
grandiloquent style of this document. The ideas expressed also be-
long to what might be called the "Trotskyite" emphasis of bolshevism at this time. Most striking in this respect was the Manifesto's

lack of any explicit reference to the decisive role of the party in making revolution or guiding the dictatorship of the proletariat.

More surprising was that Lenin's own "Theses on Bourgeois Democracy and Proletarian Dictatorship" also neglected the role of the party and the importance of a militarily disciplined revolutionary elite. Lenin seemed to ignore his more characteristic emphases on control and organization, and instead displayed relative confidence in the spontaneous push from below. Only in his strictures against the turncoat social-patriots and the unreliable, treacherous social-pacifists could one detect a more familiar Lenin, since he recommended that the revolutionary wings of western socialist parties separate immediately from their larger parties and set up pure communist parties. This at least implicitly looked to disciplined, elitist parties, but Lenin offered no explicit advice in these directions.

Part of the reason for this curious lapse may well have been his hope to attract western anarchists to the Comintern. Significantly, his Theses recognized two basic kinds of revolutionaries: mature Marxian revolutionaries or communists, and immature anarchistic or syndicalist revolutionaries; and he urged communists to work with the anarchists and syndicalists in order to win them over to Marxian principles. Unlike the social-patriots and social-pacifists this "immature left" at least had revolutionary commitment and courage, and could be depended upon not to sell out in a revolutionary crisis.

On the other hand, Lenin's Theses and the other documents of the First Congress must be considered primarily as revolutionary propaganda, not a fully considered and elaborated program. Throughout a kind of "heroic" tone can be sensed, a tone appropriate to men who had undergone tremendous sacrifices in the past year. The unguarded optimism, the faith in the spontaneous revolutionary will of the proletariat and the inevitable collapse of capitalism can be seen as aspects of an unrestrained psychological release. After months of constant tension and the ever-present prospect of failure, it seemed that revolution in the West was coming to the rescue.

Similarly, given the basically propagandistic purposes of the
First Congress, many of the appurtenances of a normal founding
congress were lacking. No statutes were voted upon, and the details
of organization were almost totally ignored. An Executive Committee of the Communist International (ECCI) was set up almost as an
afterthought, without clearly designating who its members would
be. Procedures after the First Congress were in fact largely *ad hoc*,
and quite naturally the bolsheviks assumed complete control of the
ECCI and of the smaller bureau which came to do most of its daily
work. Zinoviev later became the chairman of the ECCI, again with
little consideration for normal procedures, largely because such
procedures were hardly practical in 1919.[35]

The PSI and the Comintern

Just as the history of the PSI during the war differed in
important ways from that of the French and German parties, so the
relationship of the PSI to the Communist International was rather
special. Important questions were taken up by the Italian party
which did not become central concerns for the SFIO and the USPD
until 1920.

Admiration for the Bolshevik Revolution within the PSI was so
unqualified that there was little polemic about it within the party,
at least not in comparison to the debates within other western socialist parties. Turati and his wing did assert that the Bolshevik Revolution was premature and perhaps a serious mistake, but he avoided
the harsh and aggressive tone typical of such leaders as Karl Kautsky
and Jules Guesde. He believed that soviets or revolutionary councils had no relevance in the West, where firmly established working-
class institutions already existed, and he termed the Communist
International a "dream," which, like the bolshevik regime, would
probably not last.[36] But, significantly, Turati defended the Soviet
regime in the Italian parliament and did not oppose the initiative
taken by the party leadership in mid-March, 1919, to leave the Socialist International officially and to join the Communist International. In fact, no one in the PSI seriously opposed this initiative,

whereas in the SFIO and USPD the issue of whether or not to join the Comintern was long and hotly debated throughout 1919 and 1920.

Even before Lenin's Theses attacking the right and center socialists reached Italy, there had been repeated talk of excluding Turati and other members of the parliamentary right wing. It will be recalled that Turati's conduct after Caporetto very nearly earned him the expulsion that had been demanded by the left wing on several occasions earlier in the war, and that Turati himself considered leaving the party.[37] In early 1919, without any prompting from Moscow, a young engineer from Naples named Amadeo Bordiga repeated in strong terms the demand for Turati's expulsion from the PSI.

Bordiga's variety of Marxian socialism bore a remarkable resemblance to that of Lenin, although he was in no substantial way influenced by Lenin before 1919, and he may not have even heard of the leader of bolshevism before 1917. With the outbreak of the war Bordiga wrote a series of articles in *Avanti!* analyzing the war as the last stage of imperialism, similar in broad outline to Lenin's well-known book, *Imperialism, the Highest Stage of Capitalism.* Bordiga was critical of the PSI's policy of *nè aderire nè sabotare*; his own views were quite close to Lenin's "turn the imperialist war into civil war."[38] Moreover, Bordiga's whole mental framework resembled that of Lenin in his tireless tenacity and iron will to revolution, his supreme confidence in the correctness of his views, his sense of the extreme importance of "purity" or orthodoxy in ideological questions. Bordiga, like Lenin, conceived of a revolutionary party of professional revolutionaries, an elite which would direct the uncomprehending masses.

Even after the documents of the First Congress of the Comintern began to arrive in Italy, Bordiga's demands for the exclusion of Turati did not win wide backing. The leaders of the controlling Maximalist faction of the PSI were deeply concerned to preserve the party's unity, and they were thus inclined to accept Turati's penitence at the Rome congress. Equally they felt that Lenin's strictures against the right-wing socialists in western Europe did not apply to the PSI, which had expelled its right wing in 1912, or to

Turati since he had not supported the war and now defended the bolsheviks in parliament. Of course Lenin had attacked not only the right wing but also the social-pacifist centrists—and in fact Turati by name—but on these points the party leaders preferred to turn a deaf ear.

The issue of whether socialist or communist parties should participate in bourgeois parliamentary elections was not clearly spelled out in the pronouncements of the First Congress, aside from a passing and obscure reference to the "revolutionary use of bourgeois parliament."[39] However, these pronouncements did make clear the belief of the Comintern that no substantial transformation of society could occur through parliament and that social revolution could succeed only through a dictatorship of the proletariat based on soviets. Moreover, since the bolsheviks had dispersed the Russian Constituent Assembly, it was often believed in the West that the bolsheviks rejected communist participation in parliamentary elections. The leading western party of the Comintern, the KPD, had abstained from the parliamentary elections in Germany in early 1919, which further strengthened the impression among left-wing socialists in the West that communism was abstentionist or anti-parliamentarian.

Bordiga strongly argued that such was the case, but again the controlling faction of the PSI chose to ignore the evidence. Serrati expressed the prevailing opinion among the Maximalists in asserting that the party should enter the elections not because its leaders believed in the possibility of reform through parliament but rather for the purposes of general propaganda against the capitalist regime during the electoral campaign. Once in parliament the deputies of the PSI should use the parliamentary platform to denounce parliament as a sham and a device of the bourgeois ruling classes. As a matter of fact, although Serrati and the Maximalists came to this position without prompting from the bolsheviks, it resembled Lenin's own attitude—in spite of what seemed evidence to the contrary —which he would articulate for westerners in a less ambiguous fashion in late 1919 and early 1920.

The issue that evoked the most profound and lasting perplexity in the PSI concerned the nature and functioning of soviets. As noted previously, the tendency in the West was to perceive the October Revolution, however indistinctly, as a *soviet* revolution rather than a revolution of the Bolshevik party. Certainly the pronouncements of the First Congress reinforced this impression. But here it was Bordiga who resisted what seemed to be the lessons of the Russian model. Yet, again paradoxically, it was Bordiga who was closest to the real bolshevik point of view, although he did not perceive it.

For Bordiga the soviets, the revolutionary councils of workers, soldiers, and peasants, were potentially dangerous institutions because they threatened the authority and effectiveness of the sole dependable revolutionary force, the revolutionary party. It is likely that Bordiga's suspicion of the soviets stemmed from his observation of the experience of revolutionary councils in Germany, concerning which he possessed much fuller information than was the case for Russia. He knew that the *Räte* in Germany, through their hesitations and confusion, had acted as an impediment to the accomplishment of a socialist program. Thus he insisted that revolutionary councils be created in Italy only *after* the revolutionary party had accomplished the seizure of political power.

Since Bordiga knew that in Russia soviets had already existed before the Bolshevik Revolution, he was implicitly proposing for Italy a course of action that differed from what he understood the Russian model to be. Yet his attitude was not actually so very different from that of Lenin, who had also been very suspicious of the soviets, seeing in them a manifestation of the dangerously anarchic and insufficiently conscious spirit of the masses. Lenin continued throughout 1917 to see the Bolshevik party as the only reliable focus of revolutionary action, and on several occasions—in particular during the July–August repression—he termed the soviets institutions of reaction, no longer valuable to the revolution.

Bordiga's distrust of revolutionary councils was shared by a large part of the leaders of the PSI, although usually for different reasons and in spite of much verbal enthusiasm for the councils.[40] For Turati the soviets were a mere fad that could not last because they had no roots in Italian national tradition. The parliamentary deputies and the trade-union officials in the PSI were suspicious of them because they threatened the authority of existing working-class institutions in Italy. Throughout the party it was possible to sense a kind of caution in dealing with these unfamiliar institutions.

Only one group within the PSI was strongly attached to the idea of the immediate creation of soviets in Italy. Again paradoxically, it was this group that was the most thoroughly misinformed concerning the functioning of the soviets in Russia. In Turin the weekly newspaper *L'Ordine Nuovo* (The New Order) was created in May 1919 by a group of young intellectuals, prominent among whom were Antonio Gramsci, Angela Tasca, and Palmiro Togliatti. The members of the *Ordine Nuovo* group were ardent admirers of the Bolshevik Revolution and put great hopes in the revolutionary potential of the *consigli* (or *comitati*) *di fabbrica* (factory councils), which had already begun to establish themselves in the huge industrial concentrations of Turin. These councils were rooted in the prewar *commissioni interni* (shop councils), which had served a rather limited and purely administrative function within the context of capitalist factory discipline. The Turin group hoped to transform them on a wide scale into revolutionary councils which would challenge management and which would form the institutional base for the dictatorship of the proletariat.

The Turin group viewed the *consigli di fabbrica* not really so much as organs of a "seizure" of power but of a gradually consolidated workers' control over production. In this way the councils would replace the traditional and increasingly nonrevolutionary proletarian organizations, such as trade union, political party, and cooperative, which lacked adequate and direct contact with the factory proletariat.[41]

It should be noted both how little this conception of soviets corresponded to the soviets which had become the mass instruments of revolution in Russia, and how different the conceptions of the *Ordine Nuovo* were from those of Bordiga—to say nothing of how utterly un-Leninist was the conception of doing away with the political party as an organization of revolution. Soviets similar to the *consigli di fabbrica* did in fact exist in Russia, but they had little importance in the bolsheviks' seizure or retention of political power. If anything they became something of an obstacle to the revolution, and as such the bolsheviks soon found it necessary to bring them under such severe control that they lost most of their earlier significance as organs of control over production. In any case they were never more than organs of control over production; they did not assume the *political* role of such organizations as the Petrograd Soviet or the All-Russian Congress of Soviets.

These latter did not concern themselves directly with work in the factories. Moreover, they were organized according to geographical rather than industrial or factory divisions. In this sense Bordiga's notion of the kind of soviets that should eventually be established in Italy was much closer to the Russian model, although it should again be emphasized that neither Bordiga nor the *Ordine Nuovo* group derived their ideas from a study of the situation in Russia.

(It might be noted in passing that the ideas of Gramsci and his colleagues in many ways resembled those of Ernst Däumig in Germany, who also believed that councils should become the sole instruments of revolution, replacing the political party and restoring working-class unity. However, Däumig made a clear distinction between factory councils as elements of control over production and soviets as instruments of political power.[42] It seems that the German experience with revolutionary councils had little influence on the Turin group; at least little evidence of such influence is to be found in the pages of *L'Ordine Nuovo*.)

Bordiga, writing in his journal, *Il Soviet*, subjected the ideas of the Turin group to a searching criticism.[43] He described the factory council idea as little more than a new form of syndicalism and insisted that these councils would be too limited in their membership, since they would not include unemployed workers or agricultural proletarians, and would be too likely to evolve into reformist rather than revolutionary institutions. He further emphasized that soviets in Italy should be composed of *all* laboring and exploited peoples, elected along geographical lines, but that they were to be created as governing institutions only after the communist party had assumed power.

Bordiga's articles made clear his central concern with seizing political power rather than with holding power or with building socialism—again an emphasis that reminds one of Lenin. The Turin intellectuals, on the other hand, were primarily concerned with the problems of making socialism work once capitalism had been defeated. Gramsci tended to put much more emphasis on the importance of lifting the intellectual level of the workers *before* the actual seizure of power, in order that they be prepared for the tasks of building socialism. Bordiga maintained that the decisive changes in proletarian consciousness could not occur until *after* the power of the bourgeoisie had been destroyed.

The PSI's full party congress in Bologna, in early October, 1919, provided an opportunity for these various viewpoints to be presented in a more formal fashion and to determine with greater clarity the appeals of each. The congress also adopted a new party program, one which differed in important ways from the former program, adopted in 1892, and one which would direct the party's political action throughout late 1919 and early 1920.

The congress proceedings made clear the overwhelming popularity of Serrati and his wing, which at Bologna organized itself formally as the Maximalist Electionists. In the final voting Serrati's followers (who included the *Ordine Nuovo* group) received 48,500 votes, compared to 3,500 for Bordiga's Abstentionist faction, and 15,000 for the right-center coalition (Turati-Lazzari), which opposed the Maximalists' new party program and favored retaining the old one.[44]

One of the most interesting debates at the congress and one that revealed much about the various wings revolved around the question of the possibility of revolution in Italy. Bordiga argued that the war and the Bolshevik Revolution had initiated a stage of world revolution. Thus proletarian revolution was imminent in Italy as in the rest of Europe. Similar viewpoints had been expressed at the First Congress of the Comintern and had become nearly an article of faith among revolutionaries in most countries. Yet in Bordiga's hands the concept of imminent revolution remained curiously general. He failed almost completely to discuss the concrete, objective factors that weighed for and against revolution in Italy. Even when discussing the Bolshevik Revolution he seemed to believe that the really important factor in Russia had been the existence of a party with a "precise, exclusive, and secure method"[45] rather than the collapse of the central institutions of the state.

Bordiga's curiously unexamined assumption that revolution was to be expected in the immediate future was especially significant because his own belief in abstention from parliament rested upon it. That is, his assertion that participation in parliamentary elections was a waste of time was based on his conviction that in the present context all the energies of a revolutionary party should be devoted to preparing for revolution. The Abstentionist speakers at Bologna backed up their own belief in the appropriateness of boycotting parliament by asserting that the bolsheviks in the revolutionary crisis of 1905 had also advocated abstentionism because parliamentary activity in a revolutionary situation was a waste of time.[46] Bordiga argued in *Il Soviet* that the Maximalist Electionists had involved themselves in a serious contradiction by arguing both in favor of joining the Comintern and in favor of participating in the elections coming up in November, since the Comintern was officially an abstentionist organization.[47]

The right wing of the congress strongly challenged the belief that Italy was on the verge of revolution. Claudio Treves noted how the collective security measures of the League of Nations gave new powers to the Italian bourgeoisie, since internal disorders in one country could now be put down by collective intervention. Moreover, the ignominious failure of the international general strike of July 1919 in favor of the Russian and Hungarian revolutions had demonstrated that the international unity of the proletariat was still not much greater than it had been in August 1914. Turati stressed that the majority of the working class in Italy was not revolutionary or even socialist. Thus any revolution in Italy at the present time would entail not only a dictatorship of a proletarian minority of the total population but even more a dictatorship *over* the proletariat itself. Turati equally stressed Italy's lack of preparation for socialism because of her unusual dependence on other nations for grain, iron, and coal.[48]

Turati and his friends emphasized that socialist revolution in a poor country was inconceivable without revolution in other, more industrially advanced nations. Actually, such reasoning was very close to that of the bolsheviks, but the Italian socialist right wing added the qualification that revolution would have to come *first* to other countries before it could possibly come to Italy. Ironically, this was the very point made by many *German* socialists—representatives of the very country which poor countries like Italy and Russia were expecting to take the decisive revolutionary step. German revolutionaries at this time pointed to Germany's vulnerability to blockade and invasion by the Allies, especially after her defeat in war. Most socialists seemed to believe that if revolution was to succeed in their country, some other country would have to start things rolling.

On the question of revolution the Maximalist Electionists tended to assume a middle position between Bordiga and Turati. Serrati's followers did not directly deny that revolution was at hand; yet they implied that it was farther away than Bordiga believed. The Maximalists resorted to such fine distinctions as the "revolutionary moment" as opposed to the "revolutionary period," which had the advantage of allowing them to continue to predict revolution without drawing any practical conclusions about those predictions. This would be a central problem for the Maximalists throughout 1919 and 1920.

The new party program differed from that of 1892 in ways that were obviously influenced by the Bolshevik Revolution and the pronouncements of the First Congress of the Communist International. In a more palpable fashion the program seems to have been affected by a letter from the ECCI, dated September 22, to the Bologna congress. In it the leaders of the Comintern profusely thanked the Italian proletariat for its sympathy toward the bolshevik regime but added that now more than sympathy was necessary. The PSI needed to incorporate into its party program a clear commitment to the dictatorship of the proletariat, to a soviet regime, to the abolition of Italy's parliament, and to the creation of a red army.[49]

The PSI program of 1892 had spoken of the need to "transform the organizations of the oppressive bourgeois state into organizations of proletarian liberation." This strongly implied working for a majority in parliament, a right-wing socialist concept, specifically condemned by the bolsheviks and no longer acceptable to either the Maximalists or the Abstentionists. Serrati's wing now explicitly adopted the bolshevik view that the institutions of bourgeois power had to be destroyed, not transformed, and replaced by revolutionary councils.

The pronouncements of the First Congress had not been very explicit concerning how bourgeois power was to be conquered. A similar area of ambiguity remained in the new program of the PSI, an ambiguity complemented by the lack of agreement at the congress concerning precisely what soviets were and what form they should assume in Italy. The new program observed that soviets should be the organs of proletarian power "in general," but the congress finally accepted neither Bordiga's ideas nor those of the Turin group concerning their nature and origin. A resolution was passed instructing the *Direzione* (that is, the executive committee of the party) to work out the details for the creation of soviets in Italy within the next three months. Yet, in spite of a number of elaborate projects worked out after the Bologna congress, the *Direzione* took no concrete action for the creation of soviets within the time limit stipulated.

The question of the relationship of the revolution in Italy to that in Russia, that is, whether the Italians would follow the model established by the bolsheviks, was not clarified at the Bologna congress and remained vague during the following six to eight months. For Bordiga's wing and for many left Maximalists, it seemed sufficient simply to affirm that Italian revolutionaries would do "as the Russians had done," without really exploring in any depth what the Russians had in fact done. Other Maximalists, such as Antonio Graziadei, were less impressed with the Russian model and emphasized that Russia was too different from Italy to provide many useful lessons,[50] but Graziadei and other speakers were uncertain as to how the Italian experience would differ.

Generally uncritical attitudes prevailed on the question of the Communist International. The congress not only ratified the earlier initiative of the *Direzione* to enter the Moscow international, but it did so without discussion, without any analysis of the documents of the First Congress, without asking what would be the practical obligations of membership, and even without waiting for the report of the fact-finding committee which had been set up to report to the congress concerning the Comintern.

In all of these matters it is tempting to find fault with the Italians and to speak of a typically Italian lack of discretion and a Latin attachment to revolutionary posturing. Yet it should be kept in mind that in 1919 any openly articulated differences of opinion with the bolsheviks inevitably appeared to be a criticism of the revolution, something the traitors of the Socialist International men like Kautsky, Guesde, and Plekhanov, had endlessly engaged in, but which the Italians wished to avoid. It would have been considered a slap in the face for the bolsheviks if the PSI, the leading party of the Zimmerwald movement, had rejected the Communist International or had hesitated to join it. It is indicative that even Turati favored joining the Moscow organization, simply because he did not believe in the possibility of working with the patriotic socialists who headed the Bern organization.

Comintern policy in 1919

The confusion that existed within the PSI concerning the nature of the new international can be partly excused by the vagueness of the pronouncements of the First Congress and by the lack of coherence on the part of the Executive Committee of the Comintern in its first year of activity. This lack of consistent leadership was understandable and was even later acknowledged by the bolsheviks, but it was to have a number of unfortunate repercussions, since it would contribute to the general and growing confusion in the West in late 1919 and early 1920 about the Moscow international. Although this confusion may have for a time served certain tactical goals of the Comintern—and indeed may be seen in part as another example of the deliberate elusiveness of Leninism—by early 1920 the leaders of the Comintern found it imperative to clarify their positions and to devote great energies to compensating for their initial vagaries of leadership.

One of the first examples of this equivocal leadership was the ardent welcome extended to the PSI. The denunciations made of

Turati at the First Congress and the earlier description of him as one of those who could never be accepted into a true communist party were now carefully avoided. As soon as the Italian *Direzione* applied for membership, Turati's name was noticeably missing in most of the ECCI's tirades against the right-wing socialists in the West. And not only was Turati's presence in the party ignored, but the unity of the Italian party was praised.[51]

There were a number of good reasons for this equivocation. In order to establish itself as a serious competitor to the Bern organization, the Communist International needed to attract the western European parties that were so conspicuously absent at the First Congress. Otherwise, it seemed entirely possible that western revolutionaries, surveying the rather meagre membership and "eastern" orientation of the Comintern, would decide to throw in their lot with the socialists at Bern. The leaders of the Moscow international obviously very much feared this turn of events, and were thus willing to make a few useful compromises with the formal pronouncements of the First Congress.

Another important factor was the genuine esteem that Lenin and the bolsheviks felt for the conduct of the PSI during the war. At that time Lenin had sent admiring letters to Serrati, even though on a few occasions he had disagreed with the Italian leader.[52] The PSI was the only united western socialist party to be invited to the First Congress; in all other cases only the left wings of the unified parties were invited. In the above-mentioned letter from the ECCI to the Bologna congress an unmistakeably sentimental tone emerged, in spite of its gentle chiding to establish greater clarity in the party program. For example, in speaking of the PSI's fidelity to internationalism during the war and of the Italian socialists' struggle against Allied intervention in Russia, the first paragraph ended with the promise that "the Third International will never forget the heroic aid and fidelity of the Italian socialists." The end of the letter proclaimed "one of the leading places in the Third International belongs to you comrades!"[53]

In the context of such statements it was hardly appropriate for the ECCI to launch into a polemic against Turati and the treacherous right wing. The letter thus limited itself to veiled and general criticisms of the Italian reformists and parliamentarians. Since there had already been much talk within the PSI about expelling Turati, perhaps the Comintern leaders hoped that the *Direzione*, now controlled completely by the Maximalists, would expel him and other right wingers on its own initiative. In 1920 the bolsheviks would regret not having pushed harder at this time for Turati's expulsion, for this question would become a central one in the eventual estrangement of the Comintern from Serrati's Maximalists. As it was, the discipline imposed on the Italians in 1919 was so minimal that Modigliani, a prominent figure of the right of the PSI (and brother of the painter), wrote some French friends that the only thing one needed to do as a member of the Comintern was to send off a postcard to Moscow from time to time.[54]

The ECCI was equally tolerant toward the Scandinavian members of the Comintern. They had within their ranks, as did the Italians, a wide range of socialist opinion, and they were certainly not organized according to bolshevik principles. Yet throughout 1919 the ECCI made no effort to discipline them. It insisted neither on greater centralization nor on the expulsion of those judged inadequately revolutionary. This was all the more remarkable because Otto Grimlund, the leader of the Swedish Left Social Democrats (who had been at the First Congress), made it very clear that the Swedish party had no intention of closely following the directives of the Moscow congress. The Swedes were concerned above all to show sympathy for the bolshevik regime and were tolerating what seemed to them a strident radicalism on the part of the bolsheviks merely because they felt sure that the latter would soon be outnumbered and Russian influence in the new international would be curbed by new western members.[55]

This initial tolerance of diversity and lack of discipline within the Comintern was also due to the situation in Russia in 1919: the Soviet Republic was blockaded and in the midst of a raging civil war. It was obviously difficult to devote the amount of attention to the new international that was necessary to give it firm leadership. Contact between the PSI and the ECCI in 1919 was, for example, highly uncertain. In the few messages from Moscow that did reach Italy, the bolsheviks stressed their lack of information about conditions in Italy, and because of their isolation they were hesitant to offer any strong advice.[56]

Similarly, the bolsheviks had not yet become accustomed to the idea of their lasting preeminence in the Communist International. Like the Scandinavians they expected that revolution in the West would transfer the center of communist power to the parties of the highly industrialized countries, which would then naturally play the most important role in the international communist movement. And although the pronouncements of the First Congress were unmistakably imbued with a narrowly bolshevik point of view, they also implied that the bolshevik model was not necessarily to be followed by others.[57]

This view of bolshevik expectations is confirmed by Lenin's response to the advent of a communist regime in Hungary in late March 1919. The Hungarian communists assumed control on the basis of an alliance with the Hungarian social democrats—in other words, in clear contradiction to the admonitions of the First Congress concerning such an alliance. Yet as soon as it appeared that this alliance was successfully holding power, Lenin refrained from warning about social-democratic treachery. He even went so far as to speculate that the Hungarian proletariat was giving the world a *better* model of revolution than had Russia, because in Hungary all socialists were showing themselves able to unite on a platform of true proletarian dictatorship.[58] Lenin assumed a similarly undogmatic attitude to the Polish communists. He himself related how, after he had told a Polish revolutionary, "you will do it [make revolution] in a different way," the latter replied, "no, we will do the same thing, but better than you." Lenin remarked, "to such an argument I had absolutely nothing to object."[59]

Perhaps these incidents show not so much that Lenin genuinely expected revolution in the West to be better than in Russia but merely that he was always ready to respond undogmatically to any situation that seemed to have revolutionary potential. His growing tendency to insist on the universal validity of the Russian model will be analysed in Chapter Four. At any rate, by the late summer of 1919 he had cause to feel that his initial warnings about working with social democrats was correct. In August the Hungarian regime collapsed, and the western sympathy strike that was planned for July in favor of both the Hungarian and Russian revolutions itself petered out, providing little aid for either revolution. The factors behind both of these failures were complex, but the bolsheviks emphasized, in public at least, the treachery of the right and center socialists in both Hungary and the West. For the rest of the year and throughout 1920 the ECCI hammered away at the theme: the social democrats would inevitably betray the revolution.

Actually it is clear that the leaders of the Comintern themselves did not believe that social-democratic treachery was the only factor in the Hungarian collapse, since before the fall of the Hungarian regime Lenin had analysed the unfavorable situation in Hungary with his usual realism. He cited in particular Hungary's vulnerable geographical position, which made it much more difficult to defend her frontiers than was the case for Russia with her vast plains. However, as propaganda these oversimplified denunciations had distinct tactical goals. If the communists could "expose" the centrists and right-wing socialists by showing that they, in several revolutionary situations, had undermined the course of revolutionary development, then presumably the revolutionary workers would gravitate more rapidly to the communist sphere. More truthful—and more complicated—interpretations did not fulfill this vital propagandistic function and thus were ignored in public statements.

While Lenin's official propaganda blamed the cowardice of the social democrats for the failure of the revolution, he himself emphasized the dangers of premature attempts to seize power. For example, in a letter to Serrati and the PSI in October he congratulated the party leadership for its prudence and discipline in not being provoked into ill-considered revolutionary efforts.[60] In tone at least this was noticeably different from the revolutionary exaltations of the first part of the year.

As will be discussed more fully in Chapter Four, by the late summer of 1919 Lenin was moving away from his untypical, semi-anarchistic confidence in the spontaneous revolutionary inclinations of the masses, and he was soon speaking in more typically cautious terms of the difficulties of making revolution and of what he would call the "infantile disorder" of anarchic leftism. In short, the revolutionary failures of 1919 not only impelled Lenin to a reaffirmation of his fundamental hostility to the socialist right and center, but also to a reaffirmation of his longstanding caution in dealing with the anarchic left.

Chapter III

Between Socialist and Communist Internationals

Because of the obstacles of the Russian Civil War and the Allied blockade of Russia, western socialist parties were unable to establish regular contacts with the leaders of the Communist International. The pronouncements of the First Congress still left doubt concerning the nature of the new international, especially since it was impossible to question the Moscow leaders about the general implications and exact application of their theses. But the polemics within western socialist parties between pro- and anti-Comintern forces continued to rage—without solid evidence and often in ways that betrayed a fundamental misunderstanding of bolshevism.

The great debates within the USPD and SFIO reached a decisive stage at the party congresses of Leipzig, in December 1919, and Strasbourg, in February 1920. At both congresses the controlling factions hoped to guide their parties toward yet another kind of international, which would be a compromise between the old Socialist International, judged inadequately revolutionary, and the new Communist International, which seemed too narrowly bolshevik in orientation. But the leaders of both parties found themselves inexorably pushed toward joining the Moscow international directly.

The response of the USPD and SFIO to bolshevik doctrine in early 1919

The attitudes of the USPD in 1919 to the Communist International and to the doctrines of bolshevism were more com-

plex and divided than was the case for the PSI. The debates within
the party were more acrimonious and searching, and a large part of
the party leadership remained very cautious throughout 1919 and
1920 in their attitudes to the meaning of bolshevism and to the possibility of joining the Comintern.

The first postwar congress of the USPD, which convened from
March 2 to 6 (that is, at the same time as the First Congress of the
Communist International), met in the context of the intense internal divisions and factionalism provoked by the party's ill-fated
participation in the RdV. The questions of democracy or dictatorship quickly assumed a central position in the congress debates,
just as they had at the international conference at Bern a month
before. The party chairman, Hugo Haase, insisted on the orthodox
Marxist view: revolutionary action in Germany could be justified
only when a majority of the population had been won to the banners of social revolution; he thus launched an attack on the notion
that revolution could be carried out by a narrow elite.

Ernst Däumig, speaking for the left of the party, was less concerned about formal majorities, and tried again, as he had at the
congresses of the *Räte*, to win support for his ideas that the *Räte*
should constitute the sole instrument of proletarian power. Since
the *Räte* themselves had already rejected his notions and had favored the immediate convocation of the Constituent Assembly, he
now argued that the task at hand was to educate the workers to accept their revolutionary role.[1]

The program finally adopted was a combination of Däumig's
and Haase's ideas, and in many ways resembled the program the
PSI would later adopt at Bologna. It spoke favorably of revolutionary councils which would be the foundation of proletarian power—
obviously with a far more concrete sense of what they were than the
Italians possessed even eight months later—but also said that revolutionaries should make full use of *all* economic and social institutions (unions, cooperatives, and other such organizations) in struggling for the liberation of the proletariat. The party for the first
time explicitly committed itself to the notion of the "dictatorship
of the proletariat," but defined it by describing the proletariat,
somewhat ambiguously, as the "representative of the great majority

of the nation." In speaking favorably of the use of parliament and in condemning "planless acts of violence," the party underlined its differences with the KPD.

Consistent with the compromise nature of the party program, Haase and Däumig were elected to be party cochairmen. But since Däumig had refused in December to permit his name to be placed beside that of Haase in the USPD electoral list for the January elections, now Haase refused to serve as cochairman with Däumig. After long negotiations, Arthur Crispien replaced Däumig as co-chairman.[2]

The USPD emerged from its first postwar congress, rather surprisingly, more united than it had been since before the upheaval in November. This is not to say that all was harmony within the party, as Haase's refusal to share leadership with Däumig clearly showed. Still, the left, feeling that the new program was a victory for its point of view, seemed to reconcile itself, at least more than it had in the months before, to working with the right. And the other factions of the party seemed also to have hopes for united action in the months ahead. These adjustments made it possible for the USPD to continue to attract the growing numbers of workers who were repelled by both the SPD and the KPD.

The attitudes of the SFIO to the doctrines of the Communist International were as complex and ambiguous as they were in the USPD. At the same time the internal factionalism of the SFIO was less intense and the unity of the party more secure, even though within the ranks of the French party there remained social-patriots, social-pacifists, and a pro-Leninist left—the three tendencies which had already split into three separate parties in Germany.

In late April 1919, the SFIO met in Paris for its first postwar congress. Although this congress met in the background of considerable unrest—including working-class demonstrations to protest the acquittal of Vilain, Jaurès' assassin, and a revolt in the French squadron sent to the Black Sea against the bolsheviks—the delegates that met in Paris seemed to bring with them little sense of revolutionary emergency, certainly much less than the USPD delegates the month before. Thus the debates at the congress centered not so much on revolutionary dictatorship versus democracy, as they did in the USPD March congress and the PSI's Bologna congress, but on parliamentary action and electoral policies. The new party program approved by the congress was more moderate than either the USPD or PSI programs and spoke in quite traditional terms of a proletarian revolution that could come only at the proper historical moment, when the proletariat was fully educated to the task of social responsibility and when the objective conditions of industrialization were ripe for socialization. The dictatorship of the proletariat was hesitantly described as the form that the revolution "probably" would take, but before that, "the pressure of universal suffrage" would have established the proletariat's position of power.[3]

In the course of the congress debates the moderate tone of this program was denounced by Fernand Loriot and the extreme left of the party. Loriot especially objected to the hesitation of the authors of the program to proclaim that present conditions in France were revolutionary, and he ridiculed the program's language of reform rather than revolution. But Loriot and his wing found far less support at this time than Däumig's wing and scarcely more than Bordiga's Abstentionists at the Bologna congress. Thus the centrists and moderate right wingers that backed the new program felt no need to work out a compromise program in order to placate the revolutionary left.

News of the First Congress of the Communist International reached France in time for the Paris congress, and Loriot's wing presented a resolution proposing withdrawal from the Bern organization and immediate affiliation to the new international. This resolution won only 270 votes, compared to 890 votes for conditional acceptance of the Bern organization and 790 votes for unconditional acceptance of it. The former *Minoritaires*, now in control of the party, were behind the resolution for conditional acceptance, which proposed that the SFIO send delegates to the next meeting organized by the Bern Permanent Committee in order to fight for a "revolutionary" program and to give the Bern organization a chance to reform itself—which meant formal condemnation of those socialists guilty of "un-socialist" action during the war.[4]

The debates of the congress made clear that not only the right of the party but also its center (that is, the former *Minoritaires*) had scant sympathy for the Moscow international. The center, however, avoided aggressive criticism of the Bolshevik Revolution and expressed hope that the Second International could be revitalized and that the bolsheviks could find a place in it. The right was openly hostile to both the revolution and the Comintern and obviously preferred not to invite the bolsheviks to any restored international. Given these attitudes, the news, which arrived just before the Paris congress, that the Italian *Direzione* had decided to join the Comintern, caused great consternation in both wings. *L'Humanité*, which was in the hands of the center and right, deplored the Italian move and expressed the hope that the Italians would reconsider.[5]

Loriot's wing, on the other hand, set to work to encourage the French party to follow the example of the PSI. In early May, Loriot helped to organize the *Comité de la Troisième Internationale* (hereafter referred to as the "Committee for the Comintern"), from the nucleus of the wartime Zimmerwaldian *Comité pour la reprise des relations internationales*. The Committee included the extreme left of the SFIO and those members of the anarchosyndicalist left who had participated in the Zimmerwald movement,[6] thus forming in fact the kind of alliance recommended by the First Congress of the Communist International. The Committee for the Comintern began a campaign to spread the ideas of bolshevism in France, insofar as they were known or understood, and to drum up enthusiasm for the immediate affiliation of the SFIO to the new international.

In spite of the work of the Committee, contacts between it and Moscow were as uncertain and irregular as they were with the PSI. The anarchosyndicalist newspaper, *La Vie Ouvrière*, which became the voice of the Committee, complained at the end of July that there was a "total absence of communication" with Russia.[7] None of the Committee's members had been present at the founding congress of the Comintern, and they had only a general and uncertain understanding of its goals and doctrinal positions. Loriot and those around him, like the Italians, made no concerted effort to model their actions on the pronouncements of the First Congress. The former spoke much of the need to do in France "as the bolsheviks had done in Russia," which seemed to them to mean struggling against parliamentary democracy and establishing a revolutionary dictatorship of the proletariat based on soviets. Yet throughout 1919 these remained vague concepts and slogans which were not searchingly analysed, and no serious efforts were made to plan a seizure of power. Even more than was the case for the Italian Maximalists, the exact meaning of the word "soviet" remained extremely unclear among the pro-Leninists in France. In fact, quite contrary to national stereotypes, one has the impression in reading the socialist press of each country that the French revolutionaries were considerably more superficial than the Italians. The pages of *L'Ordine Nuovo* or *Il Soviet* were generally far more sophisticated in tone and penetrating in analysis than were those of *L'Humanité, Le Populaire,* and *La Vie Ouvrière.*

Impasse at Lucerne: The USPD in search of a new international

While the loose lines thrown out by the founding congress of the Communist International were being slowly drawn in, the Permanent Commission established at the Bern conference had speedily set to work, first to make the attitude of international labor known to the Paris Peace Conference, and second, to try to arrange the reestablishment of the International on a more definite schedule. In its meeting in August at Lucerne, Switzerland, the Commission agreed on a detailed criticism of the Allied peace terms, but the left and right wings of the commission were further from an agreement on the question of a new international than they had been in February. The left still insisted on a more inclusive international and resisted any moves that would condemn the bolshevik regime, explicitly or implicitly.

A principal reason that agreement on the question of the International was even more difficult was that the SFIO and USPD had moved to the left since March, and the USPD had now sent representatives who were more attentive to the pro-bolshevik wing of the party. After acrimonious debate with the right-wing representatives on the Commission, both the representatives of the USPD and SFIO returned home deeply disillusioned with the Bern organization.

Since the Lucerne meeting had failed to come to a satisfactory position on the question of a new international, a majority of the leaders of the USPD and the SFIO gave up their attempts to change or win over the Bern organization. The controlling centrist majorities of each party affirmed that their only purpose in sending delegates to Lucerne had been to win control of it from the right-wing socialists. The leaders of the USPD wanted to "expose" the SPD and to prevent any "lies" from going unchallenged.[8] Besides, the USPD March congress, which had of course met before anything certain was known about the bolshevik international, had committed the party to an international along the lines of the Zimmerwald and Kienthal conferences—something which the Bern organization would obviously never become. The prevailing wing of the SFIO considered its presence at Lucerne to be necessary in order to oppose the "bad shepherds" of the Second International.[9] The SFIO's April congress had given the CAP only a provisory mandate to stay in the Bern organization—and then only for the expressed purpose of pulling it to the left, hoping eventually to merge it with the Comintern into one powerful revolutionary organization, freed of the stigma of war socialism.[10]

But since it had proved impossible to wrench the Bern organization away from the control of the right-wing socialists, the leaders of the USPD and SFIO had to try a new tack. The simplest course in the face of rival internationals was simply to apply directly for membership in the Comintern. This was the course of action already advocated by the left in each party. However, it was not a course that elicited much enthusiasm from the rest of either party, for a variety of reasons.

The situation within each party was complicated and made more unstable by the ground swell of new recruits to socialism, usually young men whose inspiration was the Bolshevik Revolution and who were swamping the parties' organizational structures, giving powerful impetus to the left's demand for immediate and unconditional affiliation with the Comintern. Yet the right wing of each party made no secret of its deep hostility to the Moscow international and to bolshevism in general. In turn, on several occasions Moscow had indicated that it would not accept any party that permitted men like Kautsky or Renaudel to remain in its ranks.

The center of both the USPD and SFIO was caught between these two extremes. It was firmly opposed to expelling the right wing; yet it was sharply conscious of the growing power of the pro-bolshevik left. The left wing of each party shared with the center a distaste for forced exclusions, largely because it knew that the exclusion of prominent right-wing figures would result in a major schism, and at this time in neither party was the idea of such a schism widely acceptable. Such was the prevailing attitude in the PSI as well. The pro-bolshevik factions of all three parties, with the exception of Bordiga's Abstentionists, refused to believe that joining the Third International would entail forced exclusions. (Of course the PSI's membership had *not* entailed exclusions.) The center of the USPD and SFIO, largely composed of older, more experienced men who had not been so caught up in the mystique of the Russian Revolution, urged caution on the question of the Comintern until more solid information was available.

After the return of the party's delegates from Lucerne, debate within the USPD about the Comintern took on particular intensity, especially between the party's anti-bolshevik extreme right wing and its pro-bolshevik extreme left wing. The right wing insisted that it was quite simply a waste of time to discuss joining the Comintern, because Moscow would not accept the USPD into its ranks. Kautsky, who through his writings had already established himself as the leading theoretical opponent of the bolsheviks, cited a recently arrived letter of the ECCI which vehemently attacked the USPD and *all* its leadership, right, left, and center. The right wing further pointed to the Comintern's instructions to its member party, the KPD, to encourage a split in the USPD by attacking its leaders.[11]

At the other end of the party spectrum, the advocates of immediate affiliation to the Comintern tended to avoid mention of the attacks by the ECCI and to disdain refuting the points made by the right. Instead they concentrated their energies on one central and monotonously repeated theme: to join the Comintern immediately and without reservations, in order to give support to the beleaguered Soviet Republic. At the same time, membership in the new international would advance revolutionary socialism in the West.

When the left did bother to turn its attention to the criticisms made of the Comintern by the right, it often revealed its own state of confusion and wishful thinking concerning the nature of bolshevism and the new international. For example, Walter Stoecker, speaking at the party's *Reichskonferenz* on the ninth and tenth of September, maintained that it would not be necessary for the USPD to adopt what he termed "pure bolshevik tactics" in order to join the Comintern. He particularly emphasized that membership in the Comintern would not necessarily entail abandoning parliamentary activity.[12] (Since the KPD had boycotted the elections of early 1919 it was widely assumed in the USPD that the bolsheviks were also abstentionists—an incorrect conclusion.)

The left's attempts to explain away the Comintern's virulent attacks on the USPD were hardly more satisfactory. Paul Schwenk affirmed that these were merely "chance utterances" that need not be taken too seriously; they had been directed at the USPD as constituted before March, and now that the party had adopted its new, more revolutionary program, the old criticisms no longer held.[13] This was certainly wishful thinking and could have been easily disproved by attention to the dates of the latest messages from Moscow. Not surprisingly these rationalizations did little to allay the suspicions of the rest of the party.

The reconstructionist movement

As previously remarked, the ready acceptance of the PSI into the Third International in 1919 contributed to the confusion and uncertainty about the new international. This already blurred image was further confused by the actions in the summer of 1919 of the other leading party of the Zimmerwald movement, the Swiss Socialist party. At the same time, the Swiss seemed to offer the USPD and SFIO a way out of their uncertainties concerning the Comintern.

At their August congress at Basel the Swiss socialists voted by large majorities to leave the "Second International" (as the Bern organization was now informally called, although it was not technically the same organization as the prewar International) and to join the Third. Yet there was considerably more doubt within the Swiss party about the wisdom of this move than there would be two months later at the PSI's Bologna congress. The Graber-Huggler wing of the party argued that the Moscow international was too narrowly an eastern organization to be a true international.[14] The rest of the delegates to the congress were so uncertain that they decided to put the question of affiliation with the Comintern to a full party referendum. The referendum was held in September, and although fewer than half of the party membership voted, those that did vote defeated the proposition for affiliation by a decisive majority.[15]

The Swiss were now in the strange position of having voted themselves out of both internationals. While at first puzzled by these developments, the centrists of the USPD and SFIO came to realize that the Swiss, by working themselves into a position that posed the dilemma of the rival internationals in the sharpest conceivable manner, would now have to either split into two parties or show the way to some compromise, third possibility. And indeed the Swiss leaders themselves now decided to follow the course previously urged by the Graber-Huggler wing at Basel: to contact other parties who had not yet joined the Comintern and work for a broader, more western international than that which existed in Russia, but one which would be more revolutionary than the Bern organization.[16]

While keeping an eye on the Swiss party for a possible indication of new directions, the leaders of the center of the USPD also began to work on the possibility of a western "centrist bloc," which came to be called the "reconstructionist movement." At the aforementioned *Reichskonferenz* on the ninth and tenth of September, the party leadership reported that it had already taken the initiative to establish contact with various other parties "on the basis of Zimmerwald and Kienthal."[17] Arthur Crispien later reported that by the time of the *Reichskonferenz* he and others had established contact, either personally or by letter, with interested parties in France, England, Italy, Switzerland, Austria, Hungary, Rumania, and the Scandinavian countries.[18] In France, *Le Populaire*, noted on September 20 a letter sent by the USPD asking for support in common action for a new, broader international. The French CAP sent off an enthusiastic response.[19] The Italians apparently showed less interest, but the Swedes continued to encourage these initiatives.[20] However, since the energies of the French were taken up with their November elections, they did not take any real initiative at this time. The USPD, in any case, felt that as the largest centrist party it should be the natural leader of the new reconstructionist effort.

What the USPD leadership meant by "on the basis of Zimmerwald and Kienthal" remained imprecise. The USPD leaders apparently hoped to oversee the construction of an international which would be a compromise between the Second International and the Third, free of the stigma of patriotic socialism, with the concomitant rejection of all bourgeois governmental alliances, yet equally unencumbered by what appeared to most of the USPD leaders to be the bolsheviks' rigid dogmatism and narrowly Russian view of things. This would be an international that would be democratic in the western sense, yet "hard"—*aktionsfähig*, capable of action, was the term repeatedly used—in a revolutionary crisis.

One might say that the centrist leaders of the USPD were hoping to work out the kind of *via media* in the international sphere which they had failed to achieve in Germany with the breakup of the RdV coalition. The principal area of uncertainty lay in the highly important question of the role the bolsheviks would be allowed to play in this new international. All seemed to agree that the bolsheviks should be encouraged to join, but everyone also concurred that the Russians should not be allowed to exercise the kind of overwhelming leadership that they so obviously did in the Third International.

The practical problem of how to approach the bolsheviks thus posed itself, and it was here that the reconstructionists were at their most ambiguous. To those who might be called "left-wing reconstructionists"—that is, those who felt most strongly the necessity of an agreement with the bolsheviks—the reconstructionist movement was a maneuver, a temporary grouping outside the discredited Second International, formed in order to have a strong bargaining position with Moscow for an eventual merger. These men hoped to attract the parties in the West that rejected patriotic socialism and that wished to remain true to revolutionary ideals but that had so far hesitated to join the Comintern. They seemed also to hope that certain key Comintern members, especially the Italians and the Scandinavians, would join them. The Swiss would of course play a central role as mediator in these plans. If the reconstructionists could constitute such a broad coalition then presumably the bolsheviks could not afford to be hostile and would be forced to compromise. For those who might be called "right-wing reconstructionists," the vision of a new, western-oriented yet revolutionary international was a powerful one, and they intended to persist in their efforts to form it no matter what the attitude of the bolsheviks to it.[21]

For the time being these ambiguities of the reconstructionist movement remained below the surface. In the following months, they were to be brought to the surface and dealt with, but only slowly, and only as the ambiguities and uncertainties of the Comintern itself were resolved. The first important step in the process was the USPD congress at Leipzig.

The Leipzig Congress

The Leipzig Congress, which lasted from November 30 to December 6, provided a fuller airing of the problem of the international and a more distinct mandate to the USPD party leadership, which had been able so far to take only tentative action on the question of the international. In light of the rapid growth of the party since the last congress (from 300,000 to 750,000)[22] and because of the frequent accusations by Moscow, by the KPD, and within the USPD itself, that the party leadership was failing to carry out the desires of the masses, it was especially important to get the explicit and formal backing of a full congress before more resolute action was taken.

All three of the initial competing resolutions offered at Leipzig favored retiring from the Second International and forming a new, larger revolutionary organization. All factions had bitter criticisms for the Second International, especially for the role played in it by the SPD. The differences in the resolutions lay largely in the attitude taken toward the Third International.

The right-wing resolution, composed by Rudolf Hilferding,

professed equal scorn for both the Second and Third Internationals, and insisted that neither of the existing internationals could serve as the nucleus of a new one. Thus any hope for international unity would have to be deferred to the distant future. However, Hilferding's wing was hesitant to cut all ties with the Bern organization, since it still had within its ranks a significant portion of the western proletariat; thus Hilferding's resolution proposed to make one last attempt at the forthcoming Geneva conference to secure a condemnation of the SPD and other patriotic socialists.[23]

In the course of his speech at Leipzig Hilferding read to the congress a series of crude attacks on western socialists by Lenin and the Comintern leadership, one of the bitterest of which, ironically, assailed Ernst Däumig, a leader of the pro-Comintern faction in the USPD.[24] Hilferding affirmed that it would be impossible for the USPD to work with men capable of such fanatical and indiscriminate broadsides. It was thus inconceivable that Moscow could be the nucleus of a new international of any significance: joining the Comintern would destroy the USPD as it had contributed to the weakness of the KPD.

Walter Stoecker, speaking for the resolution that proposed immediately joining the Comintern, departed somewhat from the attitude the left had taken in the precongress debates. He recognized, as he was hesitant to do before, that many of the criticisms made of the Comintern by Hilferding and others were well founded, and he insisted that he and his followers were neither blind to the faults of the bolsheviks nor incapable of criticizing them. He agreed with Hilferding that the Comintern had been founded too hastily, and he recognized that the First Congress had been dominated entirely by the Russians, whose decisions were too often determined by uniquely Russian conditions. Finally, he agreed that too much emphasis had been put by the bolsheviks on harsh discipline, and the "purely military" aspects of revolutionary action—apparently alluding to the bolshevik use of terror.[25] But Stoecker reasoned that the USPD must learn from Russia's mistakes and not lose sight of the fact that nothing "essential" separated the Comintern from the USPD.

Stoecker, however, still had several illusions about Moscow's current attitude to the USPD and what would be demanded of it before it could be accepted into the Comintern. He maintained, as he had at the September *Reichskonferenz*, that Moscow's attacks on the USPD were based on the latter's pre-March stance and did not apply any longer now that the party had moved clearly away from the influence of Kautsky. Further, Stoecker emphasized that there could be "no question of splitting the party" to join the Comintern.[26] He noted, plausibly enough, that the Italians and Swedes were members and that they were obviously not threatened with schism. He urged the USPD to give the Russians the same support that the Italians and Swedes had given by immediately and unconditionally affiliating with the Comintern.

The third resolution presented at Leipzig, composed by Georg Ledebour and representing the center of the party, resembled the Hilferding resolution in many respects but was far less negative in its attitude to the Comintern. Although it did stress that the premature creation of the Third International had made the organization of a new, more significant international much more difficult, it did not rule out the possibility of working with the Comintern.

While expressing hope for a rapid settlement of the problem of the international, Ledebour's resolution very clearly opposed the idea of immediate and unconditional affiliation with the Comintern, and in the debates at the congress it was evident that he and the rest of the center were little impressed with Stoecker's arguments. For them, common work with the bolsheviks would be possible only if the USPD could count on the company of other important western parties and only if the bolsheviks were induced, through negotiation, to make compromises on essential questions—for example, the continued unity of the USPD, retention of right-wing members, and internal autonomy in doctrinal and administrative matters.[27]

On December 4, with two more days left for the congress, it became obvious that none of the resolutions could gain a decisive majority, and thus negotiations were opened between the left and center for a compromise resolution. (Such negotiations had already been proposed by Ledebour before the congress convened, but had been rejected by the left.)[28] While the rest of the congress waited, the leaders of the two factions negotiated through the evening of the fourth and morning of the fifth.[29] The negotiations remained fruitless, however, since Stoecker's group, and especially the left of it led by Däumig, stubbornly resisted any alternative to immediate and unconditional affiliation with the Comintern.

Although it is difficult to reconstruct developments from the stenographic account, this stalemate seems to have opened the door to a right-center agreement. The backers of the Ledebour resolution got together with Hilferding and his followers, and both agreed to withdraw their resolutions in favor of a new resolution. However, the text of this new resolution did not really make concessions to the right wing; it was merely a shorter, less explicit statement that skirted areas of friction or controversy. While affirming the necessity of leaving the Second International, it made no concession to the right wing's hostility to the Third International or its desire to attend the Geneva conference. On the contrary the resolution tried to stress points of agreement with the Comintern by criticizing the idea of socialist alliances with bourgeois parties and by recognizing the necessity for a dictatorship of the proletariat based on revolutionary councils.

The resolution further looked to the future merger "with the Third International *and* the social revolutionary parties of other lands" and gave the USPD *Zentrale* an explicit mandate to work for agreements "with all these parties."[30] In other words, in spite of its friendly attitude toward the Comintern the resolution remained a "reconstructionist" document, although it skipped over Ledebour's explicit insistence on a *negotiated* settlement in Moscow.

A plausible explanation of this new move is that, in the first place, Hilferding and the right wing realized that support for their resolution was embarrassingly small, and they thus decided to ally with the center. Secondly, during the course of the left-center negotiations, the representatives of the center had observed that not all of Stoecker's backers were equally opposed to compromise. Thus the new resolution, with its favorable but cautious attitude to the Comintern, was composed in order to divide and pull over part of Stoecker's wing. Certainly the centrist leader Arthur Crispien, in introducing and defending the new resolution, made an obvious effort to give it a strongly leftist color, more so than a simple reading of the resolution itself would justify—and so much so that he made statements ultimately detrimental to the reconstructionist goals that he intended to forward. Especially significant in this respect was his assurance—not specifically expressed in the new resolution —that if other western parties were not willing to go along with the initiative of the USPD to form a new international, then the USPD would join the Comintern alone. The resolution, backed with this assurance, succeeded in convincing a significant portion of the left of the congress that Crispien and the other centrists were ultimately committed to the Comintern and its revolutionary goals, and that they merely wanted to try to bring in some of the other western revolutionary parties with them. This was in fact a questionable assumption, because most of the centrists were concerned to form a basically *western* international and were not at all certain that they wanted to join the Moscow international if no other western parties were inclined to go along with them.

To be fair to Crispien, it should be noted that he had qualified his statement by saying that the USPD would join the Comintern alone "if we, on the basis of our party program, are in agreement with Moscow."[31] This was an important qualification, but one that did not seem so important to the left at the time, since it assumed that the USPD and Moscow *were* in agreement. Thus Crispien's speech and the text of the new resolution seemed to the left a significant conversion or at least concession to the pro-Comintern point of view.

That Crispien's efforts achieved the desired results was made evident in a speech following soon after his. Kurt Rosenfeld, who had earlier been one of the signers of the Stoecker resolution, announced that the discussions concerning the new resolution had helped him and many others to see the issues more clearly.[32] He noted that both Hilferding and Ledebour had withdrawn their resolution in favor of the new one and observed that the wording of the new resolution was far less divisive than Stoecker's; the unity of the party would thus not be threatened by voting for it. But Rosenfeld insisted, rather convincingly, that there was in any event little difference between the Stoecker resolution and the new one;

both expressed support for the Russian Revolution and both provided for an eventual agreement with the Moscow International. Crispien nodded and shouted, *"sehr richtig!"*[33]

Futilely, Däumig and other members of the extreme left insisted that it was important to give immediate and unequivocal support to the Bolshevik Revolution by acclaiming immediate and *unconditional* adhesion to the Comintern, but they were unable to prevent large-scale desertions to the new resolution. However, Däumig's wing was not at the end of its resources. In a last-minute attempt to counter what now seemed like certain defeat, the pro-Comintern forces tried to "pack" the new resolution by proposing amendments to it. The second of these amendments, dealing with the seizure of power, was rejected by the congress, but the first was less easy to dispose of because it merely repeated the assertions that Crispien and Rosenfeld had made to the congress: if the USPD could find no support in the West for its idea of a new international, it would join Moscow anyway.

Again, from the stenographic account it is difficult to determine if either faction realized the full significance of this amendment. Crispien objected to what he termed *"Resolutionssabotage"* and advised the Stoecker-Däumig forces to concern themselves with their own resolution and "not try to pack ours";[34] yet at the same time he asserted that the amendment was "completely superfluous" and did not alter the meaning of his resolution in the slightest. Again he repeated, "if the other parties will not go with us, then we will go without them, if we are agreed [with Moscow] on program and tactics,"[35] but neither he nor his followers seemed to realize that the left's amendment failed to include the important qualifying clause; it merely asserted that the USPD would join the Comintern eventually—ignoring the phrase "if we are agreed on program and tactics."[36]

It is tempting to see in this amendment a clever maneuver by the extreme left to undermine the bargaining position of the center in any future negotiations with Moscow. Since the USPD had now publicly asserted that it planned to join the Comintern in any case (or so it seemed, although this was not entirely clear),[37] the bolsheviks had scarcely to worry about making concessions or meeting the conditions that most of the centrists considered necessary to an understanding with Moscow. Further, Moscow was certain to do everything in its power to block the USPD's efforts to gather western parties around it. Once the reconstructionist movement was blocked, Moscow could simply insist that the USPD carry out the mandate of Leipzig by coming to Russia to negotiate alone. If the center of the party tried to resist, then the bolsheviks, the KPD, and the left of the USPD could denounce the resistance as a betrayal of the Leipzig mandate.

On the final day of voting, it was decided that the Stoecker resolution should be voted upon first, so that those whose second choice was the new resolution could vote for it if the Stoecker resolution failed to win a majority. Stoecker's resolution received 114 "yes" votes and 169 "no" votes.[38] The new resolution, carrying the left's amendment, won 227 "yes" votes and 54 "no" votes.

It seems from these figures that the Ledebour center could have won a majority by a simple alliance with the Hilferding right wing but not a particularly decisive one. Given the precarious unity of the party, it no doubt seemed better to seek a broader, less divisive mandate, even at the price of vagueness and equivocation.

Most party members at the time of Leipzig were obviously unaware of the dangers inherent in this vague resolution. In fact, one gains the impression of general satisfaction with the compromise arrived at and confidence in the future of the party. In spite of continuing intraparty strife, most members of the USPD, including those of the extreme left, rejected out of hand the idea of a party split and were proud that they had been able to avoid the divisive sectarianism of the KPD while remaining committed to revolutionary goals. They were now taking a positive, forceful step in a new direction by leaving the Second International and working for a truly revolutionary international. The idea that the USPD might eventually rejoin the SPD, something which some of the USPD leadership had considered possible and even desirable shortly after the revolution,[39] was now generally abandoned—no doubt more because of the left's vehement opposition than because of any strong feeling by the right wing of the party that an eventual union was undesirable. Equally the left, certain members of which had earlier contemplated joining the KPD,[40] now reasoned that the more sensible elements of the KPD should join the USPD.

The Leipzig congress' decided turn to the left on the question of the international was complemented by a more pro-bolshevik party program. Although the left had argued that the March program had established the USPD as sufficiently revolutionary to be accepted by the Communist International, a new, even more radical program was proposed, and the congress accepted it unanimously. Most members of the USPD seemed to agree that, since the forces of reaction were much stronger than in March, the party needed to take a tougher stand. It was clear also that the party's leaders felt that negotiation with Moscow would be easier if the party had a more revolutionary program. Thus the concern for democratic niceties contained in the March program disappeared, and more emphasis was put on the necessity of a forceful seizure of power and the establishment of a proletarian dictatorship, even if the revolutionary proletariat did not have the backing of the majority of the population.[41]

If the significance of the extreme left's amendment to the new resolution on the international had not been perceived at Leipzig, in the days following the congress it became increasingly clear to many of the leaders of the center. Ledebour, writing in *Die Freiheit* a short time after the congress, angrily accused the left of "trickery" (*Schiebertaktik*).[42] He affirmed that the resolution adopted by the congress, with the exception of the last-minute amendment, was a total victory for his own position, and that he had withdrawn his particular resolution merely to do away with any questions of personal prestige. The amendment, on the other hand, was flatly contradictory to the intent of the resolution and had been accepted because the delegates failed to understand the significance of this "surprise move," which Ledebour complained was "contrary to parliamentary procedure" (*geschäftsordnungwidrig*) and thus "completely invalid."[43]

In spite of Ledebour's angry protests, the amendment remained —and with it the ambiguity of the Leipzig mandate—throughout the opening phases of the negotiations initiated by the USPD. But since most of the party's leadership was centrist, at first the import of the amendment was ignored. In the first part of 1920 the mandate of Leipzig was interpreted in an entirely centrist and reconstructionist manner.

November elections in France and Italy

The French socialists were unwilling to devote much attention to the question of joining the Comintern or of rebuilding the international because most of their energies in the fall of 1919 were directed to what the party leaders considered to be a highly important matter: the parliamentary elections in November. At its September party congress the SFIO had decided, in the form of the so-called Bracke Amendment, to reject all electoral alliances and campaign on a purely socialist ticket. This meant abandoning the party's earlier inclination to soften its position at times for the sake of its bourgeois electoral allies. Moreover, the SFIO concentrated its campaign on the issue of the defense of the Soviet regime. Jacques Sadoul, who had been condemned to death *in absentia* for his aid to the bolsheviks while still in French uniform, was provocatively placed at the head of one of the lists of SFIO candidates.

The right-wing parties eagerly accepted the socialist challenge; they concentrated their campaign on the theme of protecting western Europe from the uncivilized bolshevik hordes, and plastered the walls of France's cities with the famous posters of the hirsute and grisly *homme au couteau entre les dents* (man with a knife between his teeth). Probably more effective, however, was the right's use of a complicated new electoral law, which gave an incentive to party coalitions by awarding *all* the seats of a particular electoral district to any list of candidates that obtained an absolute majority on the first round of voting. The *Bloc national*, which in many districts was able to gather in coalition every party to the right of the SFIO, was able to trounce the unallied socialists at the polls, leaving them with a meagre 68 seats in the Chamber, compared with their 101 before the war.

The members of the right wing of the party had the bitter satisfaction of seeing in November a fulfillment of their direst predictions. The right, which won most of the socialist parliamentary seats that were salvaged, had opposed the Bracke Amendment because its members did not believe that the SFIO, running without electoral allies, could possibly hope for an absolute majority in many electoral districts; and without such victories the new electoral law would assure the party's ruin. Thus after November the right of the party tended to assume an attitude of aggressive rancor.

The November defeat merely confirmed the antiparliamentary tendencies of Loriot's wing and of the members of the Committee for the Comintern (a number of whom, it will be remembered, were anarchosyndicalists and thus particularly antipolitical in any case). For the extreme left, and particularly the anarchosyndicalists who were now cooperating with Loriot, the new electoral law was a forceful demonstration of what it had long proclaimed: the French parliament was a corrupt sham, controlled subtly by the bourgeoisie; and thus parliamentary democracy could never be the vehicle for social revolution, an attitude which found reinforcement in various pronouncements from Moscow. However, the whole question of the "revolutionary" exploitation of parliament was not clearly posed, and abstentionism did not become such a clear point of contention and division among French revolutionaries at this time as it had already in Italy.

The experience of the PSI in its November elections provides some interesting contrasts to the experience of the SFIO. Italy also had a new electoral law, equally complicated in conception, but far more favorable to the socialists in its effect. The new law removed the few remaining restrictions on male suffrage of the 1912 law (thus adding many younger and many illiterate voters) and replaced the single-member constituencies with larger units, lists of candidates, and proportional representation. Whereas the former electoral arrangement tended to favor individuals, the new one was highly favorable to organized parties. Since the only two organized mass parties of postwar Italy were the PSI and the *Partito Popolare*, both were great winners in the elections.[44]

It was of course not only the new electoral law that accounted for the victory of the socialists. The PSI had been the only party forcefully opposed to the war. By November 1919 the bitter fruits of war were ever more apparent to most Italians, and many of them were inclined to vote for the PSI not so much out of socialist convictions as out of resentment over the war. The party's parliamentary candidates exploited these resentments to the full: instead of concentrating on revolutionary, antiparliamentary propaganda, as the victorious Maximalist resolution at Bologna had advocated, the PSI's candidates simply went after votes by playing up the question of the war. Thus, just as Bordiga had feared, the PSI did not engage in "revolutionary parliamentarism," did not seek to dispel "parliamentary illusions," and did not even attempt a very searching or vigorous defense of the bolshevik regime. The main concern of the November electoral campaign was clearly to appeal to as wide as possible a variety of resentments and frustrations in Italian society in order to get as many votes as possible.[45]

In figures the results were impressive. The PSI became the largest party in Italy, with 156 seats in parliament (out of 508 total), which represented a doubling of the prewar vote and a tripling of the number of socialist deputies in parliament.[46] This represented a particular success for the PSI's right wing, which could more than ever emphasize that it spoke for great numbers of voters (1,800,000) while the Maximalist *Direzione* spoke for a relatively few party members (ca. 80,000). Unavoidably the prestige and influence of the parliamentary wing of the PSI increased, something which Bordiga had also feared, and he now saw his worst predictions confirmed.

While the socialist victory was impressive, it was hardly unqualified. The socialists remained a party of the north and center of Italy. Even though a few rural areas went over massively to the PSI,[47] most of its majorities and pluralities occurred in urban and industrial areas. The South and the Islands gave the party only 7 percent and 2 percent, respectively, of its total vote.[48] Moreover, the increase in the socialist vote was almost always at the expense of the other parties of the left. A redivision of the left's votes occurred, but there was no massive leftward shift of Italy's voters. The socialists grew, but the radicals and republicans shrank. Thus the PSI's victory at the polls was by no means a "revolutionary" victory, as many enthusiasts liked to call it. It was not even a victory for revolutionary principles. Parliamentary seats were reshuffled, but socialist revolution was not thereby brought closer. In short, rhetoric aside, both the PSI and the SFIO were still substantially parliamentary parties by early 1920, parties whose avid attention to the autumn parliamentary campaigns far exceeded their attention to or real interest in preparing for revolution. All of this would be strongly underlined in 1920 when both parties proved themselves utterly unequipped to deal with revolutionary crises.

The advance of the reconstructionist movement

After the Leipzig congress the first step taken by the USPD leadership to forward the reconstructionist movement was to arrange a preliminary meeting in Berlin on December 9, with revolutionary socialists of Sweden, Denmark, Norway, and Rumania, and with the Jewish Bund of Russia to discuss the possibility of some kind of international gathering which would consider the formation of a new, reconstructed international. The Scandinavians at Leipzig had promised to use their good offices with the Russians and had assured their hosts that they agreed that the attacks on the USPD by the ECCI were not justified.[49] Now at the meeting in Berlin, the Scandinavians proposed that a general meeting, including the bolsheviks, take place in Scandinavia in the near future. All present apparently accepted the idea.[50] (It will be recalled that the Swedish socialist Grimlund hoped that substantial numbers of western socialists would join the new international in order to overcome Moscow's predominance in it).

As the initiatives arranged on the ninth were getting under way, the USPD leadership had the opportunity of meeting with Karl Radek, who was just then preparing to return to Russia. Radek had spent the past year in Germany as bolshevik adviser to the KPD. In February 1919 he had been captured and put in jail. Since then he had used his time behind bars to meet with many of the leading political figures in Germany.[51] He had encouraging words for the USPD leaders, affirming that the decisions made at Leipzig were a very good foundation for negotiations with the Comintern. He further promised that he personally would forward such negotiations when he arrived in Moscow. However, he was not enthusiastic about the initiative the Scandinavians had undertaken; he felt that they had no authority to arrange an international meeting and suggested that the initiative for such a meeting be left up to the ECCI—from which, he promised, the USPD would hear in the very near future.[52]

Probably because they felt Radek's opposition would impede the progress of the meeting the Scandinavians were to arrange, the leaders of the USPD took the initiative themselves soon after they had met with the bolshevik leader. On the fifteenth of December they sent out letters to nineteen parties and groups, including the bolsheviks, suggesting that a meeting to discuss the problem of the international be held either in Germany or in Austria sometime in February.[53] This suggestion was implicitly contrary to Radek's advice to let the ECCI take the initiative for such a meeting,[54] but the USPD leaders obviously felt little bound by what Radek had told them would be pleasing to the Comintern. Moreover, in spite of what Radek had promised, it was some time before the USPD heard directly from Moscow about the proposed meeting and negotiations. While they waited, the USPD leaders were not shy about taking initiatives themselves.

After November, the question of international affiliations was once again brought to life in the French party. The results of the Leipzig congress, coming just after the defeat of the November elections in France, were something of a shock and a setback for the French centrists—a second defeat, in a sense, because the center of the SFIO had been largely responsible for the Bracke Amendment. Now it seemed that the USPD, in breaking cleanly with the Second International and looking toward the Third, was making a decisive turn to the left, inevitably strengthening the hand of the left in the SFIO.

From September to early December, *L'Humanité* and *Le Populaire* had carried virtually no news or opinion on the question of the international, even though an article in *Le Populaire* on September 20 had stressed the need for rapid action.[55] But after early December, articles about the international appeared regularly, mostly in *Le Populaire*, under the signatures of Paul Louis and "Istina" (a

Russian word for "truth"—probably a pseudonym for Boris Souva-rine). Both these writers stressed that the question of the international had become of central importance for the future of the SFIO. They also concluded that without the USPD, PSI, and Swiss socialists the Second International was dead as a revolutionary organization. Other important articles appeared from the pens of Paul Faure and Daniel Renoult, influential leaders of the center. They agreed that a new period in international socialist development was at hand, and they strongly backed the ideas of the reconstructionist movement. Faure, probably in reply to the USPD's letter of December 15, urged that the Swiss (rather than the Germans) call a general meeting of all parties concerned as soon as possible.[56]

At the same time, the French center, in response to the threat to its position within the party posed both by the November results and by the Leipzig congress, began to maneuver to reestablish firm control of the SFIO. The first move in this direction was to establish the *Comité pour la reconstruction de l'Internationale* (hereafter referred to as the Reconstruction Committee).[57] The leaders of the Reconstruction Committee stressed their sympathy for all revolutions in progress, their decision to leave the Second International, and their hope to rebuild a new international, with none of the faults of either the Bern organization or the Comintern. The Committee's founders appealed to the "left and extreme left" to join them and made overtures to the Committee for the Comintern to form one united committee[58]—a rather obvious attempt to "swallow" the extreme left. It is hardly surprising that the leaders of the latter would have nothing to do with the offer.

The Reconstruction Committee followed up the initiatives taken by the USPD by arranging a small information gathering meeting with it and the Swiss socialists in late January in Switzerland. The French particularly hoped to determine the precise significance of the ambiguous Leipzig resolution and the meaning of the Swiss socialists' contradictory record on the question of the Comintern.[59]

The Party Secretary, L. -O Frossard, was selected to represent the SFIO at the meeting in Switzerland, and Arthur Crispien, the

President of the USPD, was sent by the USPD. They met with all
the members of the Swiss Directing Committee. Frossard opened
the meeting by asking why the Swiss party referendum had rejected
joining the Comintern.[60] The Secretary of the Swiss party, Graber,
answered that a change of opinion in the Swiss party had taken
place after the defeat of the general strike at the end of 1919. Presumably the Swiss workers were tired of revolutionary tactics and
had rejected the Comintern for that reason. Graber asserted that if
another referendum were called, the Swiss rank and file would reject the Comintern even more decisively.[61] The Swiss Directing
Committee affirmed that an international could not be rebuilt without long and arduous efforts, but that a beginning should be made
immediately, especially now that the blockade of Russia was being
lifted. The Swiss party, because of the unique position it had taken,
could serve as a useful center for future developments.

In response to Frossard's questions about the meaning of Leipzig, Crispien stressed that the USPD now considered the Second
International to be "liquidated,"[62] but that his party hesitated to
join the Comintern while the latter remained a predominantly eastern organization. The USPD preferred to work for an international
that could "ally itself with Moscow, but not without conditions."[63]
Crispien supplemented this tendentious interpretation of the Leipzig resolution by a false account of developments at the congress
itself: he described the final resolution as merely a compromise between two slightly differing points of view—his and Ledebour's—
and made no reference at all to the manner in which the resolution
had been reformulated to attract Stoecker's followers.[64]

Frossard questioned Crispien about the meaning of the amendment tacked onto his resolution at the last minute. The latter said
nothing about his own indignation at the congress concerning this
amendment and was generally evasive. Frossard asked him an obvious question: what if Moscow and the other parties in the Comintern refused to have anything to do with the proposed reconstructionist conference? From the tone of his questions it seems that
Frossard was aware of the very poor bargaining position the USPD
had created for itself vis-à-vis the Comintern, because of the great

power the latter would have to disrupt the conference if it so desired. Crispien vaguely replied that if Moscow did in fact refuse to have anything to do with the proposed conference, then a "new situation" would be created which "we will examine when it comes up."[65]

The meeting with the USPD and Swiss socialists was no doubt comforting to the centrist leaders of the SFIO, particularly since shortly before Frossard's departure they had received similarly comforting information from a leading figure of the PSI, Antonio Graziadei. The latter had spent several days in Paris on a "courtesy visit" to the SFIO, and in the course of a dinner in his honor, he was asked about his party's membership in the Comintern. The description he gave of the PSI's role in the new international was very similar to that given by the Swede Grimlund to the Leipzig congress. Graziadei stressed that the bolsheviks were not to be copied in a servile manner by other Comintern members and that each member party should have wide latitude to deal with the special problems that concerned its internal affairs. He assured his French friends that he sympathized entirely with their desire to obtain clear guarantees from the ECCI that the SFIO would not be forced to split if it joined the Comintern. Finally, he agreed with them that the Communist International should not be a narrow "*internationale de tendance*" but should seek to attract all proletarians into its ranks.[66]

Yet Graziadei's assurances were strangely inconsonant with the few direct communications from Moscow which had arrived in France. The most recent was a telegram, dated February 6, 1920 and published in *Vie Ouvrière*. It urged Loriot's wing to split from the SFIO and establish a separate communist party. Frossard was particularly upset to see his friend and factional ally, Jean Longuet, described in the telegram as a "refined opportunist" and to read that the leaders of right and center of the SFIO were "agents of the capitalist class."[67] He publicly worried in an article in *L'Humanité* that Moscow would require not only the exclusion of the party's right wing but also such figures as Longuet, Cachin, and Paul Faure.[68] Moreover, a few weeks after Graziadei's visit, which was personal and unofficial, word came directly from the *Direzione* of the PSI that the Italians would have nothing to do with the reconstructionist movement.[69] Graziadei had obviously been talking too freely, and his opinions were not shared by Serrati and the Maximalists.

The Strasbourg congress

The SFIO's Strasbourg congress was in many ways similar to the USPD's Leipzig congress. The question of what attitude to assume toward the Comintern had become decisive for both, and in both parties the controlling centrist faction was concerned about the rapidly growing left wing, which was ardently in favor of immediate and unconditional affiliation with the Moscow international. However, the French centrists enjoyed stronger popular support than their counterparts in Germany. Some of the leaders of the SFIO center subjected the bolshevik regime to a more damning criticism—without becoming explicitly anti-bolshevik—than the centrists of the USPD either cared or dared to do. At the same time the left of the SFIO was relatively unsophisticated and even incompetent when compared to the left of the USPD or PSI. These differences would take on considerable importance later in the year.

At Strasbourg as at Leipzig, there were three competing resolutions, corresponding to the three main organized factions in the party—right, center, and left. The right composed a long and wordy resolution which, in the finest parliamentary tradition, said little in a great many words but basically made the same points as had Hilferding's resolution at Leipzig.[70] The SFIO right wing further insisted that the SPD must be made to recognize its "guilt" for its wartime actions and proposed that the SFIO work with the Belgian socialists to secure the "necessary condemnations" of the German socialists. On the other hand, the right wing for obvious reasons wanted nothing to do with any conferences designed to prepare an international free of the stigma of patriotic socialism. The right was still fiercely opposed to abandoning the idea of national defense.

Pierre Renaudel, one of the main speakers for the right-wing resolution, did his best, as had Kautsky and Hilferding in the USPD, to ridicule the bolsheviks' revolutionary accomplishments and the international they had created. Also like the USPD right wing, he paid particular attention to the bolsheviks' attacks on the centrists and played on the party leaders' fear that Moscow planned to split the SFIO. He singled out Longuet, Cachin, and Bracke as those who, according to the messages from Russia, must be "pitilessly criticized" as "softs" and "traitors to the working class." Renaudel summed up by warning "then it will be Loriot who will rise over the ruins of our party." [71]

The resolution of the Reconstruction Committee[72] reiterated its by now familiar ideas but carefully avoided the ambiguity of the Leipzig resolution: it explicitly stressed the need for a *negotiated* settlement with Moscow which would be worked out *in alliance* with other western socialist parties. The rest of the resolution cautiously sought to underline areas of agreement with the Comintern. It asserted that there were no "essential differences" between the SFIO and the Communist International, although certainly many of the signers of the resolution were aware of some rather important differences between their conception of socialism and that of the bolsheviks, as the debates at the congress would make clear.

The resolution was frequently evasive on important points. For example, it termed the workers' and peasants' councils or soviets "one of the forms which the exercise of proletarian power can take," but it made no suggestion that soviets should be created in France, and the next paragraph stressed the importance of working with those organizations already in existence in western Europe, especially the *syndicats* and cooperatives. This particular formulation was interesting because it underlined a concern the French centrists shared with the Italian Maximalists: soviets might easily constitute a challenge to existing working-class institutions. For the same reasons the SPD leadership had been hostile to the *Räte*. There were certainly important differences between these three parties, but their common attachment to the institutions of the old working-class order underlined a similarity of the most diverse socialist parties in the West in comparison to the bolsheviks, for whom these institutions represented an obstacle to revolution.

The Reconstructionists strongly emphasized the significance of the decisions made at Leipzig to leave the old international and to approach the new in order to negotiate for a broader international.

Thus they were disturbed when Loriot, in the course of his speech attacking the Reconstructionist resolution, asserted that he had been told by a qualified representative of the USPD that the German party had never stipulated that special conditions be met before it would enter the Third International. Loriot noted that certain orators at Leipzig had voiced their *personal* belief in the necessity for conditions, but the final resolution made no mention at all of conditions, and in fact said that the USPD would enter the Comintern alone if it could find no other parties who wished to enter with it. Further, Loriot pointed out that Crispien's assertion in Switzerland that the USPD would not enter the Comintern without previous conditions had subsequently provoked strong protests within the USPD.[73]

In making these points, Loriot was interrupted on several occasions by delegates who contested the truth of what he was saying. Finally Frossard himself recognized that in fact, as he had been told that very morning by the same USPD representative,[74] the left wing of the USPD very much objected to Crispien's interpretation of the Leipzig congress at the meeting in Switzerland; he acknowledged that there was nothing in the Leipzig resolution that mentioned preconditions to joining the Comintern. However, Frossard asserted that the USPD leaders would insist that the USPD not enter the Comintern without conditions.[75] To this Loriot readily agreed; but he added that the USPD leadership therefore was acting on its own initiative, beyond the mandate of Leipzig, and against the majority of the revolutionary mass of the party.

The resolution composed by the Committee for the Comintern proclaimed profound admiration for the Russian Revolution and bolshevik principles in general[76] and predicted imminent revolution in France. The French bourgeoisie's control over parliament had been "perfected" in the November elections because the bourgeoisie had now begun seriously to fear losing power; class conflict inevitably was growing more intense. Class lines were being drawn with portentous clarity, and soon the "decisive stage" would be reached. In preparing for this rapidly approaching moment, the duty of the French proletariat was to break with the reformist Second International and to join immediately the revolutionary Third International. When the revolution came to France, it would follow the lines of the Russian Revolution—destroying all bourgeois institutions and erecting soviets or "similar organizations" to preside over the dictatorship of the proletariat.

The debates at Strasbourg proved colorful and tumultuous. Repeatedly the congress disintegrated into chaotic packs of shouting delegates, hurling charges and countercharges, often drowning out the main speakers. In spite of the passion and confusion, however, there were frequent moments of clarity and insight. The speakers for the Committee for the Comintern were not those that usually provided the moments of clarity. Significantly, they failed throughout the entire congress to cite a single Comintern document or bolshevik text to back up their statements.[77] The center and right, on the other hand, cited material recently received from Moscow to substantiate their carefully aimed attacks. In attempting to defend themselves and the Moscow international against these attacks, the leaders of the left repeatedly made statements which were wholly inaccurate and which they soon had to retract.

The uncertainty and incoherence of the speeches of Fernand Loriot, generally recognized as the leading figure of the extreme left in France, was typical of his entire wing. In his speech defending the pro-Comintern resolution, for example, he agreed that Moscow should not pose any conditions for affiliation that would require any member of the SFIO to be excluded, and he cited Turati's continued presence in the Italian Socialist party as evidence of Moscow's toleration in this respect. Yet at the same time he admitted that Albert Thomas, a leading figure of the right of the SFIO, would have to be excluded if the French party were to be acceptable to Moscow.[78] A few days before the congress Loriot had asserted that the French socialist party could never be accepted with all its present membership—only to insist shortly after, in response to the uproar this assertion provoked, that he had been totally misunderstood. Yet he could not make clear the basis of the misunderstanding.[79] He simply appeared ridiculous, and the congress was greatly amused when it was revealed that he had failed to read the Reconstructionist resolution in its entirety, and had thus missed many of its essential passages, passages that countered clearly the very points upon which he based his criticism of the resolution.[80]

Loriot was able to offset this humiliation shortly afterward with a *beau geste* in the course of a speech by Renaudel. The latter, having read the passages from Lenin and Zinoviev's *Against the Current*, which called for "revolutionary defeatism," demanded dramatically, "I ask to stand up, here and now, any French socialist, no matter to what faction he belongs, who is ready to say that it was necessary to work for the defeat of France! (shouts of '*très bien*' from the delegates, applause, noise)." After a pause, the eyes of the delegates turned to the tall, gaunt figure with a patriarchal beard who was rising to his feet. "Yes, I will stand," Loriot announced. (Applause on the left). "I declare . . . that I accept entirely that point of view; and if, in the course of the war, we hesitated . . . it was not because we were against defeat but rather because the proletarian revolution which would have resulted . . . seemed to us too costly— the price of the blood of twenty million [*sic*] workers!"[81]

It was a splendid moment, but its effect was soon destroyed. In the uproar that followed Loriot awkwardly reversed himself and explained that Lenin's revolutionary defeatism "might have been acceptable for Russia, but was not for France." And even more feebly: "When Lenin wrote those lines . . . he did not write them in the name of any national group or any international; he wrote them under his own personal responsibility, and they thus affect him only."[82] Not long after this, Paul Faure read to the congress an article written by Loriot early in the war titled "Appeal to arms," which in its patriotic fervor could hardly be distinguished from the work of any of the social patriots. Loriot at first denied writing the article, but Faure seemed to have incontrovertible proof, and Loriot did not persist in his denials.[83]

The mediocre performance of Loriot and the left at Strasbourg —Charles Rappoport, another left-wing leader was similarly humiliated[84]—revealed that Leninism for them was more a powerful symbol, a revolutionary mystique, than a carefully formulated or fully understood program of action. Thus when confronted with evidence that the Comintern would require the exclusion of right-wing and centrist leaders, a split in the party, rigid control by the ECCI, "revolutionary defeatism"—measures that most of the left clearly opposed—Loriot's wing reacted with plain incredulity. A good example of this came when Solomon Grumbach, a leader of the right wing of the party, read to the congress excerpts from the ECCI's letter (which will be discussed in the next chapter), answering the invitation of the USPD to attend a reconstructionist conference. The letter attacked in harshly critical language the actions of the USPD since the German November Revolution, rejected the idea of a reconstructionist conference, and asserted the impossibility of working with the right of the USPD or the Longuettists in France.[85] The unbelieving response of the pro-Comintern delegates to this letter can be seen in the following excerpt from the stenographic account of the congress:

A VOICE: (from the congress floor): Where does it [the letter] come from?
GRUMBACH: It was sent by the official bureau of the Communist Party of Christiania[86] to the bureau of our congress of Strasbourg . . . (noise on the congress floor). Comrades, I just the same ought . . . —Well, what are you blaming me for? I read you a text by Lenin sent to the congress.
A VOICE: It's just a joke! [*C'est de la blague, tout simplement!*]
GRUMBACH: A joke! . . . You will be excommunicated . . .
A VOICE: It's only a telegram written for a special case, and, anyway, it's not signed "Lenin." [*C'est un télégramme de circonstance, qui n'est pas signé 'Lénine.'*][87]

To the generally feeble objections of the left, the right and center proceeded to portray bolshevism as a dogmatic, bigoted, and "Blanquist" perversion of Marxism which had gained success in Russia largely through an opportunistic exploitation of the war and through the extreme weakness of its opponents; it was now sustained only by the use of terror and the good fortune of having vast expanses of land between Moscow and a hostile, capitalist West.[88] In short, the right and center asserted forcefully that there was no basis for deifying the bolsheviks: their accomplishments offered no guidelines for France in the making of revolution, in the organization of a socialist party, in the operation of soviets or any other organizations of proletarian power. Yet, in spite of this thoroughgoing criticism, the Reconstructionists, in their resolution, vowed support for the Russian Revolution and asserted that nothing "essential" separated the SFIO from the Comintern, though "lack of information" made judgments difficult.[89]

In the final vote, the right-wing faction decided at the last minute to support the Reconstructionists, and thus it was decided by an overwhelming majority ((4,330 votes to 337) to leave the Second International, since all three major factions were united on the question. The right-center coalition also provided a healthy, though not so overwhelming majority (3,031 to 1,621) in rejecting immediate affiliation with the Comintern.[90] Thus at Strasbourg the right and center made the kind of alliance that would have been possible at Leipzig, but which had been bypassed in order to assure a larger and less divisive majority.

The implications of the right-center alliance, however, were hardly less disturbing for the SFIO than they would have been for the USPD. For within the left of the party were important elements that wanted to break away from the SFIO and form a separate French Communist party in conformity with the proclamations of the First Congress of the Communist International.[91] On the right also it was hoped in some quarters that the center-right coalition of Strasbourg could be continued and the disruptive elements on the left be excluded.[92] In short, the price of greater clarity at Strasbourg was to exaggerate the divisive tendencies in the party. This was not what the center desired, and in the months following its leaders would do their best to overcome the ominous divisions encouraged at Strasbourg.

Chapter IV

Paths to Moscow

The first six months of 1920 was a time of important adjustments and rectifications on the part of both the bolsheviks and western socialists. Emerging victorious over their internal enemies and at last finding relatively easy access to the West, the leaders of the Comintern began to compensate for many of the difficulties created by the hurried foundation of the Communist International and the inadequate leadership given it during the rest of the year. This entailed on the one hand efforts to control and discipline the excesses of the ultra-left, and on the other hand, a far more flexible and imaginative approach to the socialists of the reconstructionist center. Moreover, the bolsheviks sensed a shift in revolutionary potential or revolutionary dynamics in 1920 and made efforts to adjust to this shift.

This is not to say that the many obscurities and ambiguities of bolshevism as it appeared in 1919 were completely cleared up in 1920. On the contrary, while the nature both of bolshevism and the Communist International became far clearer by the time of the Second Congress of the Comintern, certain obscurities remained, obscurities which one might say were never clearly resolved, and which remained part of the communist tradition.

For the ardently pro-bolshevik extreme left in western Europe, late 1919 and early 1920 was a time of sobering reevaluations of bolshevism, especially on such questions as the nature of Russian soviets, the bolsheviks' attitude to party discipline, participation in parliament, and work in nonrevolutionary trade unions. The anarchic "sovietist" view of the revolution had to be rejected in the face of incontrovertible evidence. The centrists of the USPD and SFIO had to face incontrovertible evidence as well of the bolshevik's deep hostility to them. Yet, puzzlingly and contradictorily, the centrists became aware that the Russians at the same time *were* interested in negotiating with them on the question of their parties' joining the Moscow international.

The USPD opens negotiations: A letter from Moscow

The USPD's initial efforts to establish direct contact with the bolsheviks had very limited success. At first, this may have been due to the Allied blockade, but communications between the USPD and the Comintern remained unsatisfactory long after Russia obtained easier access to the West, and the reasons for these irregular and often confused contacts are difficult to untangle. There is no reason to doubt that Radek, who reached Moscow by January 28, gave his comrades a full account of his contacts with the USPD and delivered to them the letter with which he had been entrusted.[1] However, throughout the months of February, March, and early April of 1920, the USPD leadership received no answer from Moscow. And without word from Moscow further action became difficult, especially since the left so objected to Crispien's conduct in Switzerland; it now insisted that the party refrain from taking any further measures that might seem designed to put pressure on the Russians.[2]

Even if the Russians had promptly responded to the USPD letter, it is doubtful that in this particular eight- to ten-week period the USPD would have felt free to devote much of its time and energy to the problem of international affiliations. For from mid-January to early April the USPD's attention, like that of most Germans, socialist and nonsocialist, was fixed on the dramatic struggle for political domination within Germany.

On January 13, 1920, against a background of railroad and coal mining strikes, crowds of workers gathered in front of the Reichstag to protest a bill limiting the political functions of the *Räte*—a bill that, if passed, would probably have meant the absolute end of any hopes that the *Räte* in Germany might take up the role the soviets had in Russia. When some of the demonstrators, without any restraining influence from their leaders, tried to storm the Reichstag building, the police opened machine-gun fire, killing forty-two and wounding 105. Immediately afterward, the government declared a state of siege for the whole north of Germany and awarded Noske extraordinary powers. The USPD suffered from a series of repressive acts, such as arrests of leaders (including Ernst Däumig) and summary executions, as Noske again "unleashed" the *Freikorps*—which he was having greater difficulty keeping under control, and whose members now often voiced open contempt for him and for the Republic.

The demonstrations of January 13 may be seen as the opening stage of a complex period of urgent crisis which culminated in the so-called Kapp-Lüttwitz Putsch in mid-March, when reactionary forces around General Baron Walter von Lüttwitz attempted to seize power. These forces were at first able to gain control of Berlin, but by March 17 the Putsch was strangled by a massive general strike, at the time the greatest ever seen in Germany or in the world. The power of the German working class was reaffirmed; the strike made clear that no regime that totally lacked working-class support could survive.

No regime could rule against the workers, but this did not mean that the workers could rule by themselves. Several days after the fall of the Kapp regime, Karl Legien, the leader of the trade unions, asked the USPD if it would enter a new government under his leadership and based on the program of thoroughgoing social and economic reform demanded by the unions at the time of the general strike. The USPD had been enthusiastic in backing the strike, and now a significant part of the party leadership wanted to give Legien a chance. But the party's left was absolutely opposed, saying that participation in government with men like Legien had not worked in late 1918 and would not work now. Thus, rather than risk throwing the USPD once again into internal turmoil, the party's leadership finally declined Legien's offer. Ironically, the KPD, when consulted about its own attitude to a USPD-coalition government, affirmed that it would not try to overthrow it but would rather offer "loyal opposition." Earlier the KPD leaders had refused to participate in the general strike—but then had changed their minds when it became clear that the strike had gained the overwhelming support of Germany's workers. In the end, the USPD came out looking not only more competent than the KPD but also more radical and uncompromising.

The only action the USPD took before April on the question of the international was without any immediate consequence and was taken during the period of relative calm in late February, between the stormy periods of January and March. On the twenty-seventh of February, an enlarged meeting of the *Zentrale* met and decided, other methods having failed, to send a delegation directly to Moscow. The *Zentrale* was informed by a bolshevik representative in Germany that in order to secure a visa to enter Russia the USPD would have to make application to the Western European Secretariat (WES) of the Communist International. But, oddly, the USPD was unable to find either the address or the names of the members of the Secretariat. Efforts to obtain visas through direct application to Russia were as fruitless as the former attempts to get an answer to the letter sent in December.[3]

It was not entirely correct to say that the Comintern had failed to respond to the USPD's letter, because in fact it *had* replied—tentatively by mid-January and more fully in early February. But, for reasons that remain obscure, these answers were very long in reaching the offices of the USPD. The first reply to Crispien's letter was, in any case, not of much significance. The Western European Secretariat[4] composed a letter, dated January 15, which, while observing with favor that the pressure of the masses was causing the USPD to turn left, deferred final judgment on the matters brought up in Crispien's letter to the ECCI. The USPD probably received or at least saw this letter in January,[5] but perhaps felt that its biting, critical tone and the uncertain status of the WES made its publication inadvisable.

The Comintern's next reply, dated February 5, was more official and far more substantial.[6] It came directly from the offices of the ECCI and was composed by Zinoviev from an earlier draft by Lenin.[7] Both probably worked in conjunction with Radek, who had returned from Germany about a week before. The reply elaborately examined the points brought up in Crispien's letter and

clarified the Comintern's attitude to the USPD. However, this letter—which was the document from which Grumbach read excerpts
at Strasbourg—did not reach the USPD leadership until April 9,
and then under rather peculiar circumstances.

On April 9 the bolshevik leader Michael Borodin visited the
offices of the USPD and presented the letter. The USPD leaders
present naturally asked why it had been so long in coming and why
its arrival date was so much later than the date on its heading. Borodin explained that on his way back to Moscow from a trip in western Europe and America he had "found" a letter in Berlin (presumably in the offices of the WES) which seemed to be a reply of
the ECCI to the Leipzig congress. For some reason it had not been
passed on to the USPD.

It is possible that Paul Levi, the head of the KPD and a member
of the WES, stalled delivery of this letter because he feared that its
hostile tone would poison his own contacts with the USPD. As will
be discussed in a later section of this chapter, Levi hoped to lure a
large part of the USPD membership into the KPD; the broadsides
of the ECCI's letter were hardly consistent with Levi's own assurances to certain members of the USPD left that the entire USPD
would be accepted into the Comintern and even be given a seat on
the ECCI.[8] Conceivably, Borodin and Levi quarreled over the matter, since the former wanted nothing to do with USPD centrists.[9]

The letter that Borodin brought was addressed not only to the
USPD but, first of all, to the workers of Germany, next to the KPD,
and last—and presumably least—to the USPD. Yet the main body
of the letter dealt with the USPD and the questions brought up in
its own December letter. In harsh and unequivocal language, the
"sins" of the USPD leadership in holding back the revolutionary
drive of the masses were recounted; much of the responsibility for
the unfavorable turn of events in Germany since 1918 was placed
on the shoulders of the present leaders of the USPD. The compromise decision of the Leipzig congress was described as merely one
more proof of the way the USPD leadership strove to suppress the
revolutionary push from below and stifle the clamor of the rank and
file for immediate affiliation to the Communist International.

Predictably, the ECCI rejected out of hand the idea of an international conference to deal with the question of rebuilding the international. Any parties that were dissatisfied with the Second International or the attempts of the Bern organization to reestablish it, and that were now contemplating joining the Comintern, should come alone to Moscow and negotiate directly with the Comintern leadership. Haughtily, the letter remarked, "This hopeless attempt to found a fourth, bastard international . . . is of course doomed to failure." [10]

Yet the ECCI's letter was not exclusively hostile or negative. It obviously was concerned, for reasons more fully explored in a later section of this chapter, not to discourage all of the party leadership, and it seemed intent on so clouding issues that the USPD hierarchy could still harbor hopes for an eventual understanding. The letter asserted, for example, that the Communist International did not expect all revolutions to follow exactly the Russian Revolution; the "specific peculiarities" in revolutionary development in each country would be respected. Further, it asserted that the program of the Comintern was not fixed; it would be perfectly possible to "amend and extend" the program of the new international as it enlarged its membership.[11] And, in spite of the general attacks on "right-wing leaders," no specific USPD leaders were unequivocally ruled out by name.

In effect, then, the ECCI had administered a slap across the face followed by what surprisingly resembled an offer of a handshake. This was one of the first examples of a peculiarly Russian mannerism—the "hot-cold" or "Scotch bath" treatment. It was a mannerism that profoundly disoriented many western socialists, who were used to more straightforward exchanges. In the next year of contact with the bolsheviks, it was to become painfully familiar.

After he and other members of the party had looked through the letter, Arthur Crispien asked Borodin if a written answer was expected. Borodin suggested an immediate written reply so that he could take it back to Russia. But Crispien did not think that a proper answer could be composed so quickly. The USPD leadership would have to discuss the letter at greater length. To begin with, the suggestion that the USPD rid itself of its right wing and work to unite with the KPD was especially upsetting; in this as in other matters the Comintern betrayed a lack of understanding of conditions in Germany. For instance, did the Comintern leadership know about the present chaotic conditions within the KPD? Borodin avoided these questions but was especially interested to know the USPD's position on some of the points made in the letter, even though Crispien felt that an official, written reply was not possible on such short notice. For example, did the resolution voted at Leipzig mean that the USPD would be willing to negotiate directly with Moscow, or would it attempt to approach Moscow in the company of other parties? Crispien answered that it would be quite possible to negotiate alone with Moscow; the Leipzig resolution did not exclude such a possibility. And further, if Moscow wanted to negotiate directly with the USPD—as it had in fact made clear in its letter—then the German party would be entirely ready to do so. (One may detect a very different Crispien from the one who had spoken to Frossard in Switzerland.)

Borodin also wished to know what parties the USPD had already contacted and what agreements had been concluded. Crispien replied that no binding agreements had been made, but that the French and Swiss socialists had spoken favorably about the idea of a reconstructionist gathering. Finally, Borodin asked precisely what the USPD meant when it referred to "revolutionary elements" in certain parties not yet affiliated with the Comintern. Crispien answered that the USPD expected that such matters could be defined in negotiations at a preliminary meeting; but, in spite of all efforts on the part of the USPD, nothing at all had been heard from Moscow until that day. Now perhaps negotiations could proceed.

Borodin's visit opened a new stage in USPD-Comintern relations. Meanwhile, the other most important party with "revolutionary elements," the SFIO, had begun its own initiatives in the reconstructionist movement.

The SFIO approaches Moscow

During the last days of the Strasbourg Congress the final stages of the extensive postwar labor unrest in France had begun. In late February 1920, the victimization of a worker for the Paris-

Lyons-Mediterranean railway provoked a local strike, in the course of which several union members who tried to induce soldiers to disobey orders were arrested. Protests over this blossomed into a full-fledged general strike, beginning in early May. To many overoptimistic anarchosyndicalists, who had visions of Russia in 1917, this seemed the long awaited moment when the bourgeois state would tumble. However, the decided superiority of the forces available to the bourgeoisie was made quite clear: both employers and state responded forcefully. Against this onslaught the general strike collapsed. Extensive repression followed, during which the government seized the CGT headquarters and declared it dissolved (although this was never followed through). Employers refused to rehire the strikers. The consequences for organized labor were disastrous. From over 2 million members in February 1920, the CGT membership dropped to 600,000 after the strike.[12]

Although the SFIO had no direct part in the strike, this syndicalist failure in the spring of 1920 was interpreted as a complement to the electoral failure of November. Both reflected the inadequacies of France's labor organizations and served to strengthen the appeals of bolshevism, which by 1920 stood victorious over all its enemies. But although the strike aided the cause of the Committee for the Comintern by increasing the allures of membership in the new international, in the short term it greatly damaged it. For, even though they played no part in the strike, the leaders of the Committee were arrested shortly afterwards for plotting "against the security of the state" and remained in jail for the rest of the year, leaving the extreme left in the SFIO virtually leaderless.

The SFIO followed the lead of the USPD by selecting a delegation to go directly to Moscow, but it did not give up the idea of allying with other western socialist parties before approaching the bolsheviks. The departure of the delegation to Moscow was set for early May, while by early March the CAP of the SFIO had sent delegates to every important western socialist party to discuss the problem of reconstructing the international and to explain in detail the SFIO's position as laid down at Strasbourg.[13] The SFIO felt it particularly important to get the support of some of the parties already in the Comintern, and it was able to interest three of them, the American Socialist party, the Norwegian Workers' party, and the Left Socialists of Denmark.[14] But these were relatively unimportant parties; the key party of those already in the Comintern was the PSI.

In early March, Daniel Renoult, one of the leading figures of the Reconstructionist Committee, traveled to Italy to try to dissuade Serrati and the rest of the *Direzione* from their earlier refusal to participate in a reconstructionist conference. His entreaties were coldly received. The leaders of the PSI repeated that they "did not believe themselves authorized" to participate in such a conference. Moreover, they warned him that the SFIO should be careful not to send its delegation to Russia with the intention of "judging" the Bolshevik Revolution, as had many of the speakers at Strasbourg. Renoult assured the Italians that the SFIO delegation would go to Russia only as admirers of the new regime.[15]

In spite of this rebuff, Renoult returned to France believing that a reconstructionist conference would meet even without the Italians, no matter how important their participation had seemed in earlier reconstructionist plans. Even without their aid, he reasoned, the SFIO delegation to Moscow would easily be able to placate the Russians.[16] Frossard displayed similar optimism. He concluded toward the end of April that arrangements for a conference were well under way and that the reconstruction idea had developed into a "powerful movement." He also voiced great optimism that the SFIO delegation to Moscow would be able to clear up whatever "misunderstandings" had emerged between the SFIO and the Comintern.[17]

Renoult and Frossard were obviously whistling in the dark, for the only other important party—and not very important at that—which seemed to concur completely with the SFIO was the British Independent Labour party (ILP). Longuet, who had been delegated by the CAP to confer with the ILP, discovered that the latter had already written to the Swiss socialists, assenting to the idea to hold a meeting in Switzerland.[18] But the SFIO, the ILP, the Swiss Socialist party, and an indeterminate number of tiny parties and groups could hardly be called a "powerful movement."

The most important party of all was of course the USPD. Paul

Mistral was sent to Germany in March, but he found the USPD *Zentrale,* which had not yet received the ECCI's reply to its letter of December, unwilling to take any further initiative until it heard from Moscow. Clearly the left of the party had put its foot down, and the centrists feared any further efforts that would provoke new dissension within the party, especially since national elections were not far away.[19]

Thus by the time the various SFIO missions had returned to France, it was clear that no conference of any significance could be arranged until definite word was received from Moscow. The French were not willing to admit that the letter read by Grumbach at Strasbourg, notifying the USPD of the ECCI's categorical opposition to a reconstructionist conference, was really the last word on the matter. Thus the proposed French delegation to Moscow took on particular importance.

When the CAP had tentatively named the delegates to Moscow in early March, its Reconstructionist members had asked the Loriot left to form with them a common delegation to Moscow, based on proportional representation of the vote at Strasbourg. But again, as before Strasbourg, Loriot and his companions disdainfully rejected such overtures.[20] Writing in *Bulletin Communiste* (the Moscow-supported journal of the Committee for the Comintern) under the pseudonym "Flory" (since he was now in prison), Loriot asserted that the Reconstructionists were in a state of panic, because of the heavy attacks on them by the bolsheviks and because of the continued growth of the left wing within the SFIO. He saw little hope for a successful course to the negotiations in Moscow and believed that the pasts of SFIO centrists were too filled with equivocation and faithlessness to their duty as socialists to be favorably received by the leaders of the Comintern. Their last hope, he noted, of appearing in Moscow in a *"posture convenable"* was to attach themselves to the USPD delegation and together try to fend off the fury of the bolsheviks.[21]

The center *was* concerned with the growth of the left wing and the hostile attitude of the Comintern, but its actions in the spring of 1920 betrayed little panic. Quite the contrary, the center seemed to feel that the best attitude was one of "wait and see," and thus a final designation of the delegates to Moscow was put off and left uncertain, much as it was for the USPD. Jean Longuet and Marcel Cachin were the first delegates decided upon by the CAP in early March. But partly because of difficulties in arranging transportation and obtaining passports, the months of March and April passed and the delegation remained in France.[22] Finally, Frossard was selected to replace Longuet. It is not clear whether Longuet was replaced merely because he was unable to obtain a passport, as reported at the time. It is likely that the CAP, taking into account the harsh attacks on Longuet by the leaders of the Third International, decided that negotiations might go more smoothly if someone else were sent in his place.

That the Committee for the Comintern had refused to join the delegation to Moscow further complicated the situation because Renaudel and his wing could not then accompany the delegation without "unbalancing" it. The Italian socialists had already warned Renoult that the SFIO must not go to Russia planning to "judge" the Revolution; yet a center-right delegation would certainly tend to give an impression of SFIO hostility or at least suspicion of the Revolution, especially after the speeches the right-wing and center delegates had delivered at Strasbourg. Thus Cachin and Frossard refused to allow Renaudel to accompany them because they felt that such an "unbalanced" delegation would be ill-received by Moscow and would inevitably make negotiation more difficult.[23]

By the last week of April, all preparations for the voyage to Russia seemed in order, and on April 23 a written, formal mandate was given the delegates by the Secretariat of the party, signed by Frossard—composed before he knew that he himself would be one of the delegates. The delegation planned to leave for Russia shortly after the traditional May 1 celebrations.[24] But the abortive general strike of early May caused a further postponement. Cachin and Frossard finally left Paris on the evening of the last day of May, with the bitter working-class defeat of that month in the background—a defeat that could only serve to weaken the prestige of the French delegates vis-à-vis the bolsheviks. Even before the May defeats, Frossard had expressed his party's willingness to indulge in *"sacrifices d'amour propre"* in dealing with the Comintern;[25] now the defensiveness of the French delegation was intensified.

The written mandate given the delegates on April 23 was merely an elaboration of the Reconstructionist resolution presented at the Strasbourg congress. Since at Strasbourg the Reconstructionists had asserted that no "essential differences" divided the Comintern and the SFIO, they had to explain why the party had resisted joining the Comintern immediately. The mandate gave very definite instructions that the delegates should make these reasons clear. To begin with, the Third International did not yet represent all revolutionary parties. Probably the best way to assure a "real" international, one that adequately represented all European countries, would be to arrange a conference of the Comintern and these parties; then whatever differences existed could be ironed out, resulting in a new organization composed of both the former Comintern parties and those revolutionary parties now outside its ranks.

Before such a regrouping would have any chance of success, the mandate affirmed, the SFIO must receive definite "assurances" (*apaisements*) concerning Moscow's attitude toward certain peculiarities of French socialism. The USPD, the mandate noted, had expressed a similar concern. One of the peculiarities of the French situation was the relation of the party to the *syndicats* and cooperatives. In the past these labor organizations had insisted that the SFIO not meddle in their affairs; now the SFIO could not consider changing this relationship, and especially not in the direction of *noyautage* or "boring from within," which was the bolshevik notion of gaining political control over labor unions and other working-class organizations. The relationship between the party and the *syndicats* must be one of "full agreement" (the old formula of Jaurès) without control of one over the other. The mandate weakly observed that Lenin himself had said that each member party of the Communist International should be left "a certain liberty of movement," and for France this liberty would entail independence of the *syndicats* from the political party.

On the question of exclusions the mandate set down forthrightly and unequivocally the party's position. As was evident at Strasbourg, this was a point on which there was the widest consensus: the Comintern should not hand down excommunications against individual members of the SFIO. The mandate thus flatly stated that "the party intends to deal sovereignly with its own internal discipline," and it added that the demands for exclusions that had reached France from Moscow had "greatly disturbed" the members of the SFIO.[26]

The final specific point of "assurance" concerned the various "anarchist groupings" in France and the attitude of the Comintern toward them. It was important to determine Moscow's exact stance toward the several small *"so-called French communist parties"*[27] existing in France at the time. The mandate made no secret of its ridicule for these small groups, which it termed "actually of very little importance,"[28] serving only to divide the working class.

Finally, the mandate urged the delegates to approach the leaders of the Comintern "in the most fraternal manner," remarking that every effort should be made to come to an agreement, and again employing Frossard's phrase that *"sacrifices d'amour propre"* might be necessary. Equally, in order to dispel the "misconceptions" caused by the blockade, the delegates were to gather during their stay as much information as possible about the social, economic, and political conditions of Russia.[29]

Cracks in the Maximalist majority

As the leaders of the USPD and SFIO were making preparations in early 1920 to negotiate with Moscow, the PSI itself entered into a period of "negotiations" in the sense that each faction of the PSI began to discover that the doctrines of the Comintern were different in significant ways from what had first been believed and that Moscow would not give its unqualified support to any faction of the party. Thus just as the centrist leaders of the French and German parties feared for their unity in approaching Moscow, so also did a more secure knowledge of bolshevism by the Italians tend to threaten the unity of the PSI. However, the internal breakup of the Italian party was primarily due to the spring wave of revolutionary unrest in Italy, a wave that paralleled the general strike in France and the Kapp Putsch in Germany and subjected the ruling Maximalist Electionist majority to internal pressures with which it was not equipped to deal.

The months immediately following the Bologna congress marked the high point of success and prestige for Serrati and his followers. Not only did Serrati enjoy overwhelming popularity in the party, but the few messages that arrived from Moscow seemed to confirm his political and ideological leadership of the PSI. For example, a letter from Lenin "To Comrade Serrati and the Italian Communists," dated October 28, 1919, congratulated the Maximalists for their decision to participate in the November elections. The letter even expressed hope that the example of the PSI would favorably influence the KPD, which had abstained from the German immediate postwar elections.[30] It further warned the party to exercise great care before taking revolutionary action and specifically advised that before a proletarian dictatorship could be established it would be necessary to have the support not only of "all of the industrial proletariat" but equally that of the rural proletariat and even the small landowners—support the party certainly did not have by late 1919 or early 1920. Thus Moscow seemed to be recommending a postponement of revolutionary action for some time, contrary to what both Bordiga and the *Ordine Nuovo* group had been urging. An earlier letter of the ECCI had also seemed to support Serrati over Bordiga by urging the "utmost unity . . . for all groups and organizations which are genuinely fighting for soviets."[31] (There was some equivocation here since it was doubtful that Turati was "fighting for soviets." Moreover, the unity the ECCI had in mind was not between the reformist right and revolutionaries but between those revolutionaries who favored participation in parliament and those who opposed it—groups that had split in England and Germany. Still, it was possible to interpret this call for "utmost unity" in terms of general support for the unity of the PSI, and certainly this was the way Serrati interpreted it.)

Thus Serrati seemed to have Moscow's support for his positions on participation in parliament, preparation for revolution, and party unity. Yet this apparent support did not prevent the growing alienation of a large part of the party's left from his leadership. Gramsci was particularly upset by Serrati's continued failure to give strong impetus to the creation of workers' councils in Italy, and he was deeply disappointed in the letters from Moscow which seemed to sanction the present habits of the party leadership.[32] By early 1920 Gramsci had also become concerned about the PSI's lack of interest in winning over the peasantry to socialism. Gramsci believed, and in this matter, at least, he found support in Lenin's letter, that winning over the peasantry was essential to the victory of socialism in Italy. Yet the PSI had done virtually nothing to establish contact with the peasants when they began to occupy land at the end of the war. Serrati in fact was hostile to the idea of such contacts: since the peasantry, especially in the *Mezzogiorno*, was led by "veterans and *popolari*," the whole affair was "a demagogic and petty bourgeois movement."[33] Serrati's hostility to the peasantry's desire for land was to become a central point of contention with Moscow later in the year. Already by early 1920 he explicitly affirmed that one of the factors that made revolution in the West and in Russia fundamentally different was that the peasantry in the West would not support proletarian revolution as the Russian peasantry had.[34]

Gramsci himself freely admitted that socialists could not regard redivision of lands pure and simple as an adequate solution to the plight of the peasantry. He had in mind some form of peasant cooperatives, directed by peasant councils, which would make it possible to raise the productive level of the countryside above what was possible with individual peasants farming small plots. Still, unlike Serrati, he firmly believed that socialist revolution could succeed only with the mass support of the peasants; thus he urged the party to strive to convince the peasants that the industrial proletariat was the only class truly interested in radically increasing productive levels in the countryside and in equalizing urban and rural standards of living.[35]

Serrati's attitudes to the creation of soviets in Italy not only alienated Gramsci but began to make him suspected by the Comintern agent in Italy, Carlo Niccolini (Nikolai Markovich Lyubarsky).[36] Information about Niccolini is vague, but he seems to have been a Russian by birth who had lived in Italy as an exile for some time before 1917. During the Russian Revolution he returned to his homeland, and in early 1919 he was selected by Zinoviev to be a representative of the Communist International in Italy. Returning to Italy sometime in the fall of 1919, Niccolini became a close collaborator of Serrati, and together they launched a new magazine, *Communismo, revista della terza internazionale*, supported by bolshevik funds. Niccolini was able to provide some much needed clarity for the PSI on a wide range of issues, beginning with the question of soviets. In fact this question quickly became a point of contention between Serrati and Niccolini, since Niccolini considered wholly wrong and even preposterous the Maximalists' compromise plan, adopted at a meeting in May; the compromise was to abandon the plans to set up soviets throughout Italy and to experiment instead with soviets in one locality.[37] (This was a "compromise" between the right wing's desire to forget about the whole question of soviets and the left wing's desire to establish them immediately.) These difficulties encouraged Niccolini to move away from Serrati and to move cautiously toward the *Ordine Nuovo* group and toward the Abstentionists[38]—toward the two groups, in other words, which would be the founding pillars of the Italian Communist party.

Serrati's difficulties with Niccolini were paralleled by the difficulties he and his followers were having with another Comintern agent, Vladimir Degot'. Degot', who also had arrived in Italy in the fall of 1919, urged the leaders of the PSI to follow Lenin's advice (in his previously mentioned letter) to change the name of their party to "communist" as had the bolsheviks and the Spartacists. He further urged the Maximalists to expel the party's reformist wing—a subject Niccolini did not press.[39] But the Maximalist leaders stubbornly resisted these entreaties, arguing that since the name "socialist" had not been besmirched in Italy as it had in most other countries, there was no real need to abandon it. Similarly, since the PSI's right wing had avoided the patriotic excesses of other right-wing socialists, there was no reason to expel it.[40] In these matters, as in the question of the soviets and in the PSI's attitude toward the peasantry, rumblings could be sensed within the party, rumblings that would develop into a storm by late 1920.

Undoubtedly what most served to turn much of the extreme left of the party against Serrati was his attitude and that of the *Direzione* to the wave of unrest that rolled over Italy in the spring of 1920 and that culminated in a general strike and an attempted revolutionary insurrection. Early in 1920 peasants in the south began to occupy and work the land of large estates. Peasants in the north followed suit, and soon the unrest spread to the cities. In Naples the factory of Milani and Silvestri was occupied by strikers, and when the police tried to force the workers out, a local general strike was called. From Naples the unrest spread to Turin, where the situation took on far more serious dimensions.

After the continual working-class unrest of 1919, the employers at the Turin-Fiat complex prepared for a showdown. In particular they were intent on destroying the *consigli di fabbrica*, which had begun to grow up in their plants. On March 23 the management of the Fiat works fired certain leaders of the *consigli*, and in response a strike was called. The employers closed down the factories and locked out the workers. The workers then occupied the factories. From this start a general strike spread to all of Piedmont, including by mid-April about one-half million workers, both in cities and in the countryside. The Turin working-class leaders, with visions of their city as "Italy's Petrograd," pressed for general insurrection.[41]

Just as the bourgeoisie and the democratic state in France were able to put decisive military force into the field, so in Italy the police and troops ultimately forced the Turin strikers out of their factories. Significantly, throughout the crisis the *Direzione* did not try to spread the movement to the rest of Italy. In fact the PSI *Consiglio Nazionale* (composed of *Direzione*, provincial leaders, and parliamentary deputies) met in Milan in April at the very height of the strike, but ignored the Turin events (even though the meeting had at first been planned for Turin but was unable to meet there because of the military blockade); instead it engaged in another exhausting and ultimately fruitless discussion of soviets in Italy—while the only existing soviets in Italy were under siege in the factories of Turin.

After the strike ended in failure, Gramsci accused the party leadership of deliberately isolating Piedmont from the rest of Italy

by refusing to spread the unrest. Serrati, in reply, argued that the
Piedmont leaders were to blame in taking revolutionary initiative
without seeking coordination with or approval of the national leadership.[42] In any case, Serrati and much of the Maximalist leadership,
although they continued to talk of a revolutionary situation in general terms, did not believe that the moment for revolution had yet
come to Italy—and of course in this they had Lenin's recent written
support.

It is difficult to believe that the Turin leaders themselves believed in the possibility of spreading the revolution outside of Piedmont at this time. Within the *Ordine Nuovo* group there were
strong differences of opinion about the meaning of the Turin
events; this crisis marked an important stage in the breakup not
only of the PSI Maximalist majority but even of the *Ordine Nuovo*
group[43]—a development that increased the attractions of Bordiga's
steadily growing and well-organized Abstentionist faction for certain of the young Turin intellectuals.

By the late spring nearly all the factions of the PSI had received
indications both of favor and of reproach from the bolsheviks. And
while the greater clarity concerning Comintern doctrines reduced
confusion in one sense, nevertheless neither Serrati, Bordiga, nor
Gramsci knew exactly where he stood with the Comintern leaders.
This was not quite the "Scotch bath" treatment meted out to the
USPD and SFIO, and it is possible that the bolsheviks did not consciously encourage these ambiguities. Nevertheless the interfac-
tional situation in the PSI was not unlike that in the SFIO and
USPD, and it put the ECCI in a favorable position to extract from
the PSI whatever concessions it desired, by playing upon the rivalry
of the various factions.

Adjustments in Comintern policy:
The extreme left

As noted in chapter two the parties and groups that first
became members of the Comintern came largely from the extreme
left of the prewar Marxian socialist parties and were joined by certain anarchist organizations. By early 1920 these initial members be-

gan to present special, unforeseen problems for the leaders of the new international, problems that required important adjustments in policy. In order to understand the nature of these shifts, it is necessary to analyze some of the less obvious implications of Lenin's theories in relation to developments within the communist ultra-left in Germany, France, and Italy.

Lenin has often been denounced as a "splitter," a perennial schismatic for whom party unity had no particular value. Actually, the willingness of Lenin and the bolsheviks to provoke splits was based upon a proposition of syllogistic reasonableness: a revolutionary had the obligation to break away from a party and establish a new one when he believed that the old party was making revolution impossible. The implication—central to Lenin's thought—was of course that no revolution could succeed without the leadership of a truly revolutionary party and that a revolutionary situation might easily be lost through the betrayal of social-democratic pseudorevolutionaries.

The notion of splitting away to form a new party assumed that a revolutionary found himself in a minority. If he was a member of the controlling majority, then his duty was to rid the party of any elements within it that were making revolution impossible, although at the same time *among revolutionaries* disciplined unity was absolutely essential. Such reasoning was the basis of Lenin's foundation of the separate Bolshevik party, breaking away from the older Russian Social Democratic Workers' party. It was also the rationale for founding a new international and for the appeal from the First Congress of the Communist International to all revolutionaries to break away from their social patriotic parties and form pure, revolutionary ones.

However, such a proposition is deceptively simple and entails a number of significant complications. For example, according to what standards does one determine that a particular organization is making revolution impossible? And how does one select the proper moment to split: should one act as soon as it becomes clear that a particular party lacks revolutionary will? Or would it not be better to remain inside a party in order to expose its leadership and *eventually* win it over to a revolutionary program—and then expel the nonrevolutionary elements? And in the latter case, what should a revolutionary do when, having remained in a party with the expectation of winning it over, he suddenly finds that the situation in his country has become revolutionary? Should he then at all costs strive to form a pure revolutionary party in order to exploit the revolutionary situation, or would this be an impractical measure because of the time and care necessary to build a revolutionary party?

These questions would be posed time and again in 1920, but the pronouncements of the First Congress and the declarations of the ECCI in 1919 were of little aid in dealing with them. The advice from Moscow was simply to "establish a revolutionary party free of social-democratic corruption." This did not make clear which factions of the old parties were to be considered irrevocably lost to the revolution and thus inadmissable in a revolutionary party, nor whether a split should be undertaken immediately or only according to particular tactical considerations. But although the question was confused by the PSI's presence in the Comintern, the implications were strong that the split should be immediate and that the new party should consist exclusively of the extreme left of the current parties, without any remnants of the centrist and right-wing members. For example, in September, 1919 the ECCI applauded the initiative already taken by Raymond Péricat to form a separate, pure party of the extreme left in France.[44]

In this advice was a latent danger: by sanctioning a party split whenever one faction of a party decided that another was ruining the prospect of revolution—especially given the self-confident and even self-righteous mentality of many revolutionaries—the Comintern seemed to be opening the door to unending and uncontrolled schisms within its member parties. Of course Lenin had stressed the importance of "utmost unity" among revolutionaries. But suppose that one small faction of a party declared that all others were not revolutionary; or that one revolutionary faction decided that certain other factions, even if revolutionary, were making revolution impossible because of their lack of discipline or because of their faulty analysis of the present situation. Obviously Lenin's guideline on when to split poses as many difficult questions as it is designed to answer, and it tends to put great weight on the discrimination of individual revolutionaries. Alfred G. Meyer, who has written one of the best studies of Leninism, has remarked on this persistent tendency of Lenin's theories to offer mere verbal or deceptively simple solutions to particularly difficult questions "so that in every concrete situation decisions still have to be made."[45]

The vicissitudes of the pre-Comintern left in Germany, France, and Italy strongly underlined these complications and dangers. The KPD, for example, after its split with the USPD, further split into two parties; and even within these two there raged dissensions and the threat of further splits. Lenin approved of the establishment of the KPD out of the USPD, since he believed that the latter was an obstacle to revolution in Germany. But the further split of the KPD deeply troubled him; he feared that the KPD would destroy itself through selfrighteous factionalism. Thus by late 1919 he began to stress particularly the need for "utmost unity" among revolutionaries rather than the duty to split.

The Bremen-Left-Spartacist coalition of the young KPD had been hesitantly agreed to by the Luxemburgist wing of the Spartacists. Throughout 1919 the party remained isolated from the mass of the German working class because of its wild, terroristic reputation. After the disasters of early 1919, Paul Levi, the friend and collaborator of Luxemburg who took over the leadership of the party after her death, set out to remedy this situation. Levi reasoned that the only way the KPD could escape its isolation was to get rid of its more undisciplined members on the left and then seek to attract the left of the USPD—making up, in other words, for the lost opportunities of December, 1918 and for the bad advice given by Karl Radek. To Levi's way of thinking these two moves were logically connected, since the USPD left would have nothing to do with the KPD as long as it retained its "putschist" and terroristic wing. Thus at the KPD's second national congress in October, 1919 at Heidelberg, Levi maneuvered a forced departure of the party's anarchic left wing, which some months later formed the KAPD (*Kommunistische Arbeiter Partei Deutschlands*). At the same time he established regular contacts with the leaders of the USPD left to discuss the possibility of an eventual merger—and two of the latter, Kurt Geyer and Walter Stoecker, in the summer of 1919 spoke publicly in favor of such a merger.[46] (It will be recalled that Levi probably attempted to block what he felt was the unfortunate influence of the Comintern by withholding the ECCI's letter of February 5, which he felt would endanger his contacts with these leaders.)

In effect, then, Levi was acting contrary to the advice of the First Comintern Congress to seek out the anarchic left as a revolutionary ally. Yet at the same time he was acting in conformity with Lenin's proposition that a split was justified if a wing of the party was making revolution impossible. Moreover, insofar as Levi was seeking to attract the USPD left he was following the explicit recommendation of the ECCI's letter of February 5, although his *personal* evaluation of *how* the USPD left was to be attracted was not shared by the ECCI, which disapproved of his actions at Heidelberg and which hoped to retain the KPD's left wing *and* attract the USPD left.

Although Levi provoked the split at Heidelberg, he was not a schismatic like Bordiga or Péricat. He split the KPD not in order to make it purer or more elitist but rather to open the possibility of a large or "mass" communist party in Germany. Levi did not believe that a small, pure communist party could be effective in the western European context. He felt that the experiences of the KPD in 1919 were conclusive proof that such a party would remain isolated and impotent, while the success of the USPD indicated the advantages of a large and legal mass party.[47]

Whether a western communist party should be a democratic mass party or an authoritarian elite party is one of the more elusive notions of Lenin's thought. The question is a particularly important one because many western socialists—such as Frossard, Stoecker, Gramsci, and Levi himself—hoped somehow to combine what they saw as the bolsheviks' elitist revolutionary know-how with the mass democratic traditions of the West. The difficulty is partly due to the lack of exact definition for the words "mass" and "elite." Does a mass party contain 100,000, 500,000, or 1,000,000? Does an elite party include only those professional revolutionaries able to handle the abstractions of the dialectic, or does it also include factory working proletarians who are untutored but profoundly revolutionary? Similarly, do conditions in the West necessitate a more democratic party, while those in the East a more elitist party? One can find in

Lenin's writings the most diverse answers to these questions, but his prevailing tendency before 1920 was to favor an authoritarian, elitist party—which was the point on which he first differed with the mensheviks, who favored a more open and democratic party.

Lenin clearly recognized that an elite party, in order to be effective, had to develop firm and intimate contacts with the masses. In this respect the soviets provided a perfect complement to an elite party. However, in countries like France and Italy which had no mass soviet institutions—and even in Germany, where by early 1920 the *Räte* were rapidly fading in importance—the problem remained of how communists were to have access to the masses. There were of course other nonparty mass organizations, such as trade unions and cooperatives, but the *tendency* for communists in these countries—although the question is hardly clear-cut—was to aspire to mass membership in the communist parties *themselves* rather than to strive for control by a revolutionary elite over nonparty mass institutions.

Certainly Levi thought in such terms. He freely agreed that the task of a revolutionary party was to give firm and clear leadership to the masses, but he still favored, as had his teacher in these matters, Rosa Luxemburg, far greater democracy within the party than did the bolsheviks. Moreover, he believed that in the West a revolutionary party could be less homogeneous than the Bolshevik party; he even seemed willing to accept members of the USPD center and right wing into the reformed German Communist party. In many ways, then, his concept of a revolutionary party resembled that of Serrati more than that of the bolsheviks.

In 1919 these matters were not openly aired, and Lenin did not directly oppose Levi's views—as he did not clearly oppose those of Serrati. At times he seemed even to agree with them, but always with a certain qualification or equivocation. He seemed to stand between those in the Comintern who clearly and openly opposed the idea of a relatively heterogeneous mass party (such as Rakosi and Borodin), and those who were more favorable to the idea (such as Zinoviev, Kamenev, and Radek). The question would become much more explicit when Levi broke with the Comintern in early 1921.[48]

Levi's belief that an elite party on the bolshevik model was not appropriate for the West and his sense that it might have been better for the *Spartakusbund* to have remained in the USPD found further confirmation in the development of the extreme left in France. Loriot and most of his followers ignored, resisted, or doubted the authenticity of the injunctions of the ECCI that the extreme left of the SFIO should split off to form a separate party with the revolutionary elements of French anarchosyndicalism. Throughout 1919 and especially 1920 Loriot's wing benefitted from the groundswell of new members in a way similar to the left of the USPD. The only group that did follow the injunction to split and form a separate party was the small band around Péricat, largely of an anarchist orientation. Their "French Communist party" was even less successful than the KPD, in spite of the ECCI's description of it as the "kernel" of the new French Communist party.[49] It remained totally isolated, an insignificant clique. (It was this group, no doubt, that was the object of Frossard's ridicule in the mandate to Moscow.)[50]

Loriot and the other "political" members of the Committee for the Comintern apparently shared Levi's reticence to work with the anarchist left. Shortly after the Strasbourg congress the Committee purged some of its less disciplined, anarchist, and antiparliamentarian members.[51] Moreover, Loriot had earlier resisted the demands of these and other members of the Committee to split from the SFIO by arguing that the pro-Comintern left was too small and weak to form a separate party; it would be more effective inside the SFIO, where it had a better possibility of spreading pro-Comintern propaganda among the rank and file. After Strasbourg he reversed his argument and insisted that a split would be a mistake because the Committee was strong enough that it could expect to take over the SFIO in the near future.[52]

Perhaps the KPD's experiences caused the bolsheviks to be sympathetic with Loriot's hesitation to form a new party immediately. Interestingly, in a message to the Strasbourg congress the ECCI no longer explicitly urged the creation of a communist party as such; instead it ambiguously called for the formation of a "unified organization"[53]—something Loriot and the extreme left had already established with the Committee for the Comintern. After Strasbourg the ECCI did not persist in its earlier, explicit demands for a split. In fact, as will be explained more fully in the following section, by the early summer of 1920 the bolsheviks retracted their earlier appeals to form a pure communist party immediately and instead openly approved of the policy of working within the SFIO to win a majority of it.

The notion of establishing a pure communist party from the left of the PSI strongly appealed to Amadeo Bordiga. After the First Congress of the Communist International he had confidently asserted that only his elitist, abstentionist position was in perfect harmony with that of the Comintern. It is difficult to believe that Bordiga himself gave full credence to these assertions, especially in the matter of participation in parliament, unless he grossly mistranslated or misinterpreted some of the Comintern documents available to him by the summer of 1919.[54] In any case the ECCI's letter of September 22 and Lenin's of the following month seemed to support the Maximalists and to reject conclusively many of Bordiga's particular views.

However, Bordiga was not convinced by the reasoning of these letters. On November 10, 1919 and January 11, 1920 he sent off letters of his own to Moscow. In them he insisted that his views were completely and orthodoxly Marxist, and he rejected as totally unfounded Moscow's description of all parliamentary abstentionism as anarchist or syndicalist. Bordiga noted that his faction was distinct from and even refused to collaborate with those latter groups. He described the Italian Abstentionists as basically similar to the KPD, which also had boycotted parliamentary elections. Bordiga further asserted that Moscow was mistaken to give its support to the Maximalists, since they were in fact little different from the ruling centrist faction of the USPD.

Bordiga was especially concerned to stress how little the Russians seemed to appreciate the much greater difficulties of fighting parliamentary and bourgeois ideals in Italy than in Russia. In Italy parliamentary and bourgeois traditions were deeply rooted, while in Russia they were not; the Russian masses had very little experience with bourgeois representative institutions and little attachment to parliament—as their failure to object to the bolsheviks' dispersal of the Constituent Assembly clearly demonstrated. A similar dispersal of Italy's parliament would be far more difficult and would not be accepted by the Italian masses. Thus Lenin's examples, drawn from Russia's past, to confirm the need for parliamentary activity were simply not relevant to Italy.[55] Bordiga's comparison of his faction to the KPD had a certain ultimate purpose; he announced in his January 11 letter that he and his followers planned to break away from the PSI to form the Italian Communist party by about July 1920,[56] because the many reformists in the PSI made revolutionary action impossible. Yet he wanted Moscow's support for this step and specifically asked for it in his letter.

Bordiga's letters did not reach Moscow. They were confiscated by the Italian authorities and deposited in the archives of the Italian police.[57] While he received no reply from Moscow he did get a kind of response from the Comintern's agent, Niccolini. The first indication of the latter's favorable attitude to Bordiga's ideas was in an article in *Communismo*, in December 1919.[58] The article dealt with the establishment of soviets in Italy, and a large part of it was devoted to warning against the dangers of "workers' control," using examples from Russia to show how factory councils could easily lose sight of the interests of society as a whole in favor of their own narrow interests. Rather than this "syndicalist" notion of soviets, Niccolini maintained that it was necessary to establish "Marxian" soviets that would emphasize centralized control for the good of the whole society—points very similar to those earlier made by Bordiga. Niccolini seemed further to favor Bordiga by emphasizing that the seizure of political power was the first essential step in making revolution, *after* which soviets could be created and given the power to direct the transition to socialism. (A strange interpretation for a bolshevik, it seems, since in Russia the soviets existed before the bolshevik seizure of power.)

Although he thus criticized the Turin group's notion that the *consigli di fabbrica* could begin to establish socialism in the factories even before the actual seizure of political power, Niccolini soon afterward warmly supported the Piedmont factory council movement—probably because it was the only significant soviet movement in Italy and because it seemed a center of revolutionary action. Moreover, Niccolini did not back Bordiga on all points, since he explicitly opposed the intentions of the Abstentionists to break away from the PSI by July.[59]

Niccolini, in other words, upheld in early 1920 the same policy that the Comintern had maintained since early 1919: that the PSI should remain united. Yet beyond this simple assertion Niccolini failed to provide any doctrinal principle that would justify this unity or explain to Bordiga why he should stay in the Italian party while Loriot and the USPD left had been urged to break away.

The failure of the German revolution to advance to a stage of proletarian dictatorship in late 1918 and early 1919 was obviously a bitter disappointment to the bolsheviks, especially after their un-bounded enthusiasm at the outbreak of revolution in Germany. This failure inevitably forced them into a rethinking of their situa-tion and into a reformulation of their previous doctrinal positions. One particularly significant aspect of this reformulation was their tendency to abandon the earlier assumption that revolution in the West would be more "civilized" in aspect, less harsh and bloody than in Russia, and that once started it would solve the problems of the transformation from capitalism to socialism with much greater ease than was possible in Russia—that, in short, western revolution-aries would show the Russians "how it is done."

As it happened, the Spartacists, the leading revolutionaries of the advanced West, did not move rapidly and easily into power, and a highly brutal and bloody repression followed their half-hearted attempt to do so in January 1919. Certain conclusions were to be drawn from these developments. To the bolsheviks it seemed clear that decisive factors in the failure of the German communists had been their lack of preparation and organization and their inability to give adequate leadership to the masses. In these respects the bol-sheviks were superior to the German communists. According to the strictest Marxism this did not make sense, because the German revo-lutionaries should have been superior in preparation to their back-ward Russian counterparts. But for Lenin and Trotsky this paradox became a "trick of history," or a "dialectical contradiction."

Beginning in the spring of 1919 both Lenin and Trotsky began to hypothesize that the German revolution of 1918 was in fact not the counterpart of the Russian in 1917 but rather of the Russian in 1905.[60] Like the Russian upheaval fourteen years before, the German revolution underlined the unpreparedness of the revolutionary elite and the still widespread illusions of the masses. In other words the Russian leaders began to feel that they, because of the lessons learned in 1905 and the party struggles in the years following, to say nothing of 1917 itself, had revolutionary experience and training superior to that of revolutionaries in the West, and this more than compensated for Russian backwardness.

A similar tendency could be perceived in the bolshevik response to the failure of revolution in Hungary. As previously described, Lenin had at first entertained the possibility that the Hungarian communists, by allying with the social democrats, would give the Russians a better example of the kind of proletarian dictatorship possible in countries farther west than Russia. But the collapse of the Hungarian regime caused Lenin to reassert strongly his earlier belief that social democrats would always betray the revolution.

In October 1919, after the collapse of the Hungarian soviet regime, Lenin composed an article insisting that in spite of Russia's backwardness in relationship to the capitalist West, "the basic forces and structures" were the same in Russia and in the West.[61] By the time Lenin was writing *Left-Wing Communism, an Infantile Disorder*, in April 1920, he asserted that not only were the basic aspects of revolution in the West and in Russia the same, but so were many "secondary aspects."[62] At the Second Congress of the Communist International (July 1920) Zinoviev proclaimed that there were no important differences between revolutionary dynamics in the two areas.[63]

These were not in fact entirely new tendencies, since even before the war Lenin had played with the notion that developments in Russia would have special value for western revolutionaries.[64] But by 1920 these tendencies became far stronger. The bolsheviks asserted not only that the Russian model of revolution had direct and detailed relevance for western revolutionaries but in addition that the model of the Bolshevik party had precise relevance for western revolutionary parties. Moreover, they not only abandoned the earlier assumption that revolution in the West would be more "civilized," they openly declared that the *Russian* model was more "civilized" and that revolution had been "easier" in Russia than it would be in the West.[65]

This last assertion, while at first appearing extravagant, had a solid foundation. The revolutionary failures in the West during 1919 strongly impressed upon the bolshevik leaders one difference between Russia and the West which the more clearsighted socialists in the West had long stressed: the repressive forces open to the bourgeois democratic state under advanced capitalism were far more effective than they had been under the tsar or under the Provisional Government. For many western socialists, especially those in whom the will to revolution was weak, this difference underlined the great dangers of illegal activities and the possibility of massive and bloody repression of the working class. For the bolsheviks, in whom the will to revolution was much stronger, it meant that the final showdown between the proletariat and the old order would be extremely violent—more so than it had been in Russia—although of course in the end victory would come to the proletariat. Moreover, the bolsheviks strongly emphasized that the established leaders of western socialist parties aided the bourgeois democratic state in putting down revolution. Thus for the Russian leaders an essential task was to cast aside such leaders and build truly revolutionary parties.

Beyond these assertions that the bolsheviks were superior in revolutionary training and that the Russian model of revolution was more civilized lay some important implications. Did the bolsheviks' superior training mean that western revolutionaries were to acquiesce in the Russians' judgments, even in matters intimately related to developments within western countries? Were westerners to accept as natural and appropriate the overwhelming dominance of the Russians in the new international? In reading *Left-Wing Communism* one certainly gains the impression, which will be discussed below, that Lenin had come to accept as perfectly natural the unqualified superiority of his evaluations and of his theories over those of western revolutionaries. By the early summer of 1920 Lenin had even begun to assume, perhaps without fully realizing it, that the Russian Revolution and the Bolshevik party were not only infallible models for others to study but even that *only* the Bolshevik party was capable of properly interpreting these models for other revolutionaries. Somehow, the Bolshevik party, and ultimately Lenin himself, was becoming the keeper of revolutionary secrets that were closed to the view of other men.[66]

If revolution in the West was to be even more violent than in Russia, did the sacrifice not exceed the gain? Was revolution really worth it? The violence and bloodshed of the Bolshevik Revolution had repelled many from the notion of a proletarian dictatorship, and most western socialists were willing to entertain the possibility of such a dictatorship only if it were less violent and terroristic than it had been in Russia. If the bolsheviks themselves asserted that communist revolution in the West would be even more barbarous than in Russia, it is hardly surprising that many westerners were not attracted to communist revolution. It was previously observed that Lenin's wartime theories concerning the manipulative and deceptive powers of the bourgeois-democratic state implied a lasting impotence on the part of proletarian revolutionaries in the West; in a paradoxical way, the theories worked out in late 1919 and early 1920 concerning the necessary violence for making revolution gave new reasons for believing that communist revolution would never come to western Europe.

The failure of revolution in the West and the bolsheviks' own success were not the only factors that impelled them to assume the attitudes described above. It was widely recognized that the Comintern *needed* much greater discipline and clearer direction than it had had in 1919. And, given the undisciplined tendencies of many of those who first joined the Comintern, one might agree that even unquestioned authority—the kind of authority the bolsheviks began to exercise in 1920—might serve useful and necessary purposes. Certainly the bolsheviks themselves felt a particular need to exercise greater control over the anarchic left that had been invited to join the Comintern in 1919.

Lenin's *Left-Wing Communism, An Infantile Disorder*, composed in the spring of 1920, was the most fully elaborated statement of this new caution vis-à-vis the anarchic left. As the title implies, a central purpose of this work was to criticize the immaturity or "infantilism" of many left-wing revolutionaries. What Lenin called immature was in particular the ultraleft's sterile sense of uncompromising purity, its distaste for party discipline and centralized authority, its inability to make tactical retreats in the interest of the revolution, and its unwillingness to participate in such "bourgeois" institutions as parliament and the reformist trade unions.

In many ways the issue of whether revolutionaries should participate in parliamentary elections had become a central issue, one of symbolic significance extending beyond the specific problems of parliamentary activity itself. Lenin seems to have felt at first that the issue was of secondary importance. Thus the pronouncements of the First Congress, while condemning bourgeois parliaments, were vague about the question of whether revolutionaries should engage in parliamentary campaigns. But as the issue came to assume central importance in many parties, Lenin and the ECCI, in their letters of the autumn of 1919, urged participation, while emphasizing that the issue was not important enough for revolutionaries to split over.[67] (Shortly before, Lenin had, oddly, advised Sylvia Pankhurst, the English abstentionist, that it might be necessary— and, implicitly, acceptable to the Comintern—for the English communists to split and form *two* communist parties, one electionist and one abstentionist.[68] But after the German communists split into two such parties, Lenin moved sharply away from this position and emphasized the need for unity among revolutionaries. It was in this context that he praised the unity of the PSI.)

Clearly, by the spring of 1920 a more complete and solid theoretical justification for participation in parliament was needed to put an end to the growing confusion and contention on the issue. In the West the antiparliamentary revolutionaries, such as Bordiga and the Dutch Tribunists, had formulated a fairly clear principle to justify *abstention* from parliament: in a revolutionary situation —and Europe was, they believed, in such a situation—parliamentary activity was a waste of time; revolutionaries should concentrate their activities on the building of revolutionary institutions preliminary to a seizure of power. But Lenin's own attitude to the question was less simple and far more elusive, even though at times it seemed to resemble that of the antiparliamentary left. On the most general level Lenin's views seemed very similar to those of traditional orthodox Marxism: a revolutionary should combine both parliamentary and nonparliamentary activity, using the parliamentary platform to expose parliament as a tool of the bourgeoisie. On the other hand, Lenin *did* recognize that there were occasions when a boycott of parliament was justified; but he seemed unable or unwilling to articulate a clear and explicit general principle of when such occasions had developed. Between 1905 and 1917 his statements fluctuated confusingly,[69] and in *Left-Wing Communism* he merely stated, "I cannot attempt here to formulate the conditions under which a boycott is useful, since the object of this pamphlet is far more modest, namely, to study Russian experience in connection with certain topical questions of international communist tactics."[70] Elsewhere he had observed, "sometimes, in an individual case, in an individual country, abstention from parliament is correct, as it was for example, when the bolsheviks abstained from the 1905 Duma elections."[71] In discussing the bolsheviks' boycott of 1905, Lenin in *Left-Wing Communism* did not offer a general principle so much as tactical observations: ". . . we succeeded in *preventing* a reactionary government from *convening* a reactionary parliament in a situation in which extraparliamentary mass action (strikes in particular) was developing at great speed, when not a single section of the proletariat and the peasantry could support the reactionary government in any way, and when the revolutionary proletariat was gaining influence over the backward masses through the strike struggle and through the agrarian movement."[72] If one can glean a general principle from this passage—and it may well be that the effort is futile—it would seem to be that a boycott is appropriate only when the revolutionary situation is *so* intense that parliamentary participation would only slow the development of revolution in other areas. Thus one might hypothesize that Lenin actually agreed with the general principle that parliamentary activity in an intense revolutionary situation was a waste of time but did not believe that the situation in western Europe in 1920 was nearly so intensely revolutionary as it had been in Russia in 1905. He says as much in the sentence following the above passage: "It is quite obvious that *this* experience is not applicable to present-day European conditions."

The entire matter is further obscured by the fact that Lenin and the Bolsheviks approved of participation in the elections to the Constituent Assembly in 1917—certainly an intense revolutionary situation. It seems safe to conclude that on the question of parliamentary participation Lenin's position was elusive, highly subtle, and ultimately not reducible to a general proposition that others could understand and use as a guide to action. Thus Lenin's position here was typical: he was always ready to contradict theory if the revolutionary potentialities of a given situation seemed to justify it.

Such being the case, it was difficult for Lenin to argue on a purely theoretical level against the antiparliamentarians in the West. Thus the arguments of *Left-Wing Communism* are at times exasperating in the extreme. Lenin time after time ignores the most difficult issues brought up by the antiparliamentarians and obscures his own lack of clear and substantial positions through high powered barrages of irrelevant, condescending, and even insulting verbiage. For example, although Lenin granted Bordiga's point that parliamentary illusions were more profoundly rooted among the masses in Italy and the West than in Russia, he would not accept Bordiga's conclusion that especially in Italy this justified abstentionism. Quite the contrary, Lenin insisted that precisely because parliamentary prejudices were so strong among the western masses it was necessary to participate in parliament; only by doing so could parliament be effectively undermined. But this ignored Bordiga's most telling point: the Marximalist Electionists, while they formally followed a policy of "revolutionary" participation in parliament, in fact had geared the party's main energies to obtaining parliamentary seats rather than spreading revolutionary propaganda to prepare for the violent seizure of power.

If Lenin had granted Bordiga's main contention—that it was necessary to establish a "pure" revolutionary party in Italy *immediately* by breaking away from the main body of the PSI—these ambiguities might not have existed, for such a party would not have allowed reformist parliamentary deputies in its ranks, nor would it

have allowed parliamentary activity to assume the kind of hegemony which it had assumed in the PSI. Yet again Lenin skirted the
issue; while condemning Serrati's tolerance of Turati, Lenin still
left the impression that the bolsheviks wanted a mass rather than
an elite party in Italy. In what amounted to a slap in the face for
Bordiga, Lenin observed: "You think, my dear boycottists and antiparliamentarians, that you are 'terribly revolutionary,' but in reality *you are frightened* by the comparatively small difficulties of
the struggle against bourgeois influence within the working-class
movement."[73]

Adjustments in Comintern Policy: The Centrists

The arguments of *Left-Wing Communism* implied, although they did not say explicitly, that the revolutionary wave of
1917–1919 had crested and that now it was necessary to focus on the
long-range organizational work necessary to prepare for the next
wave of revolution. Throughout this pamphlet Lenin emphasized
the very great difficulties of building a revolutionary party, and repeatedly he marveled at how fortunate the bolsheviks were to have
had fifteen years of internal party struggle to prepare themselves
for 1917. Underlying his arguments, then, was the assumption that
western communists had before them a long period of organizational efforts rather than revolutionary action. The Third Congress
of the Comintern was to pursue this line of reasoning, in its most
evolved and explicit form, in 1921, when it was unmistakeably
clear that revolution would have to be postponed to an unforesee-
ably distant future. But in 1920 Lenin and his followers stood un-
certainly between the revolutionary optimism of 1919 and the pessimism of 1921. It is in this context that one must seek to understand
the new and extremely ambiguous attitudes of the bolsheviks to the
centrists in western Europe.

The past chapters have had a number of occasions to remark
that while Lenin's polemical style tended to give the impression of
a man of extraordinarily narrow dogmatism, he maintained a ca-
pacity to respond to the opportunities of given situations with a

remarkably undogmatic flexibility. He seemed able to sustain an attitude of radical doubt about all propositions, including his own, and to respond creatively to a situation that did not correspond to what theory had predicted. Yet at the same time he was the perfect opposite of the Hamlet-like intellectual who suffers soul-wrenching uncertainty from such radical doubting. It seemed almost psychologically impossible for Lenin to express openly and clearly that he was puzzled or perplexed by a certain situation, except of course when he completely lacked information about it. Once informed he always had an answer, a set of "theses" drawn up in the most self-assured and unequivocal terms. This combination of radical doubt and extreme self-confidence lent to Lenin's thought an oddly elusive quality. It is often impossible to say with finality what his position was on a given subject at a given time, even when he seems to have spoken in the most unequivocal fashion.

These generalizations are especially apt in relation to Lenin's theories about and expectations of revolution in the West, which, as we have seen, tended to fluctuate in the most remarkable fashion, from the great pessimism at the time of Brest-Litovsk to the enthusiasm of late 1918 and early 1919. In 1920, in spite of the pessimistic implications of *Left-Wing Communism*, Lenin continued to maintain an attitude of expectant tentativeness; while trying to give direction to the arduous work of building revolutionary parties, he could not yet give up hope entirely for immediate revolution; he continued to examine eagerly any new possibility, no matter how unorthodox in aspect, of ending the isolation of the Soviet Republic.

The Kapp Putsch seemed to offer just such a possibility. After the failures in the first half of 1919, the bolsheviks had at times appeared to abandon hopes for immediate revolution in the West and instead to concentrate on Asia, with the hope of undermining western European imperialism. But the Putsch, followed by the massive general strike in Germany, dramatically reawakened the bolsheviks' hopes for Germany. The party press was full of the most varied and even contradictory speculations about the possible meaning of these events. Nearly all commentators tried, often in the most far-fetched manner, to extract some proof of the proximity of proletarian revolution in Germany.[74] And since the Russian model had now taken on such importance, the attempted take-over by Kapp and the German military seemed especially promising: in Russia in 1917 General Kornilov's abortive coup had been a decisive step in the victory of the bolsheviks.

Lenin's own ideas fluctuated similarly. Even after Kapp was deposed and events in Germany began to settle down he still seemed to harbor hopes that revolution would come to Germany. And, aside from developments inside Germany itself, he had another reason to hope that Russia might yet break out of its isolation: after the Poles had invaded the Ukraine earlier in the year in an attempt to regain their "historic" boundaries, the Red Army had pushed them back and was now driving steadily for Warsaw. If the bayonets of the Red Army could "probe" Germany from the Polish border, Germany's workers would be inspired to rise up to greet their Russian comrades. And in spite of the strong current of antibolshevism in Germany, even many nonproletarian Germans might welcome Russia on its borders; a Russian alliance—and even perhaps a communist takeover—would be a way to break out of the isolation imposed on Germany at Versailles. The Kapp generals had hoped to end Germany's isolation with a Russian alliance, and the idea of "national bolshevism"—an alliance between the extreme right and extreme left to fight the Entente—was in circulation in Germany at this time.

In his ardent desire to make contact with the German proletariat, Lenin seems to have lost some of his usual realism. Trotsky, Radek, Dzerzhinsky, and Markhlevsky—the last three of whom were Poles and thus were familiar with Polish conditions—each insisted to Lenin that the Polish masses could not be expected to rise up in favor of the Red Army. On the contrary, they said that Polish nationalism was so strong that Polish workers preferred to be ruled by their own bourgeoisie rather than by an international working-class regime. Such would be all the more true if the international regime was to be installed with the aid of Russian bayonets. But Lenin angrily refused to listen to these objections and chose to believe the Pole Lapinsky, who alone stressed the strength of communism in Poland.[75] Lenin equally bristled when Levi and Meyer, the leaders of the KPD, were unwilling to confirm his optimistic predictions of revolution in Germany after a bolshevik take-over in Poland.[76]

Lenin's lingering hopes for revolution in Germany ran contrary to his earlier conclusion that the KPD was an insufficient vehicle for revolution and that a merger with the USPD left was essential. The efforts to unite with the USPD that Levi had already begun were long-range; and they explicitly precluded the possibility of revolutionary action until the new mass Communist party in Germany was on its feet. Lenin himself, by repeatedly emphasizing in *Left-Wing Communism* the very great difficulty of establishing an effective revolutionary party, implicitly agreed with Levi. Yet the Polish invasion seemed to open new possibilities which Lenin was not willing to neglect. Thus he continued to discuss the possibility of revolution in Germany while approving of the negotiations with the USPD and the arduous work of establishing a mass Communist party in Germany.

Lenin's uncertainties were mirrored in the different drafts he composed for the "Basic Tasks of the Communist International," which were to be presented to its Second Congress. In an early draft, dated July 4, he stated that the main task of communism was *not* to accelerate revolution but to work for the preparation of the proletariat.[77] This was consistent in emphasis with the letter he had sent Serrati in late 1919 and even more with *Left-Wing Communism*, which he had finished sometime in June. But the final draft of the Basic Tasks, no doubt composed under the influence of the victories in Poland, spoke far more hopefully of the possibility of revolution in the immediate future. While recognizing that the preparation of the proletariat was highly inadequate in many countries, Lenin rejected the conclusion that revolutionary action should be avoided:

It does not follow that the proletarian revolution is impossible in the immediate future. It is quite possible, for the entire economic and political situation is unusually rich in inflammable material and in reasons for its suddenly catching fire. . . . It follows that for the communist parties the immediate task is to accelerate the revolution, taking care not to provoke it artificially before adequate preparations have been made. The preparation of the proletariat for revolution must be promoted by action.[78]

These were ambiguous and even enigmatic words. They flatly contradicted Levi's contention that revolutionary action and organizational activities were incompatible, at least in the West where such action inevitably called down upon itself the enormous repressive powers of the state. Lenin did not deign to offer a reasoned rebuttal of this contention; and his ambiguous theses at the Second Congress would prepare the way, as will be later described, for another disastrous revolutionary *Putsch* in Germany.

The earlier notion of splitting the USPD by denouncing the actions of its leaders to the masses was the tactic of a revolutionary situation, a tactic which presumed rapid changes of allegiance by the masses, as had occurred in Russia in 1917. The new tactic of negotiating directly with the leaders of the USPD was of a longer and more laborious perspective. It was also one that recognized that the earlier propagandistic tactic had been ineffective. So far the left of the USPD, instead of entertaining the idea of leaving the party to join the KPD, had become reconciled to working with the right of the USPD and seemed to think that the saner elements of the KPD should now join the USPD.

Within the councils of the Bolshevik party the strongest partisan of direct negotiations with the USPD leadership apparently was Karl Radek, who found strong support from Zinoviev and Kamenev.[79] Radek's stay in Germany had convinced him that revolution there in the immediate future was impossible, and like Levi he believed that the task at hand was to avoid further clashes with the government and to rebuild the KPD.[80] His meeting with the USPD *Zentrale* before leaving for Russia seems to have convinced him that direct negotiations between the USPD and the Comintern would bear fruit. But as the above quotation testifies, Lenin was not yet willing to accept Radek's advice in its entirety.

If the absence of an effective revolutionary party and the lack of a revolutionary situation in Germany spoke for negotiations with the USPD, a similar reasoning could apply to negotiating with the SFIO; and Radek also favored inviting the leadership of the French party to Moscow. If the reasons to believe that revolution would not break out immediately in Germany were substantial, they were overwhelming in the case of France. France's victory in the war, the numerical and organizational weakness of her proletariat, the conservatism of her peasantry, the power and confidence of her ruling classes—all weighed heavily against revolution. With the November victory of the *Bloc national* and the collapse of the spring general strike, reaction was triumphant in France. The bolsheviks were well aware of this, especially since France had become the principal supporter of the antibolshevik forces in Russia and was now giving military aid to Poland.

The leaders of the Comintern were also aware of the inadequate leadership of the extreme left in France; Lenin even made derogatory remarks about it when talking with Cachin and Frossard in Moscow in June.[81] Moreover, nearly all of the revolutionary leaders of any prominence were thrown into jail after the spring general strike and remained there until early 1921. Thus by June the extreme left in France lacked even the second-rate leadership it had had before.

This lack of both revolutionary conditions and revolutionary leaders encouraged the bolsheviks to adopt a highly unorthodox strategy in dealing with the SFIO, one which was probably not worked out until after the arrival of the SFIO delegates in Russia, when the possibility of manipulating them was perceived. What the strategy entailed was to invite the *center* of the SFIO to affiliate itself formally with the Comintern and to consent to a *centrist* leadership of the new French Communist party. This policy went beyond advocating that a communist faction attempt to win over a mass party by boring from within; it entailed actually incorporating centrists—those very types who were still being vehemently denounced as infallible traitors to the revolution—into positions of responsibility within the structure of a communist party. This was a variation of what the bolsheviks had at first approved in Hungary in 1919, but now it was not a question of the bolsheviks being presented with decisions already made while a revolution was in progress. This time the bolsheviks themselves openly sought out the centrists as allies of the communist left in France.

What were the goals of this surprising alliance with centrism? From the standpoint of Lenin's hopes for revolution in Germany a compelling reason for working with the French centrists was conceivably the expectation that they could create a communist party which, if not really capable of revolutionary initiative within France, would at least become an impediment to counterrevolutionary action by France's reactionary government. Perhaps even the presence of a large communist party in France that would threaten to take action—organizing munitions strikes, sabotage in war industries, protest demonstrations, agitation in the army—against French intervention would so intimidate the French government that it would hesitate to take action abroad. It is clear that French intervention abroad was extremely unpopular with the working class—and also with other sections of the population in France—and to organize action against it would not require great revolutionary audacity.[82]

Obviously the area of possible intervention that counted most heavily in bolshevik calculations was Germany. France could easily cripple a German revolutionary regime by moving into the areas of heavy industry in western Germany. If revolution were to succeed in Germany, something had to be done to oppose this threat from across the Rhine. France offered a similar threat to revolution in Italy, since Italy's northern industrial regions were also within fairly easy striking distance of French armies.

If revolution failed to come to Germany—as it clearly had after the defeat of the Red Army outside Warsaw in August 1920—then the centrists of the SFIO could still have uses, and the bolsheviks continued to cultivate them in late 1920 and in 1921. As noted in the previous section, 1919 and 1920 was a time of doctrinal reformulation for the bolsheviks, and in the late summer and autumn of 1920 they had begun to work out a theoretical resolution of the dilemma they had posed for themselves in 1917. At the time of the Revolution they had asserted that a proletarian socialist regime in Russia could not possibly survive alone. Yet by late 1920 it was obvious that Soviet Russia would in fact remain isolated for some time. The new theoretical position emphasized that the soviet regime could survive for an extended period by exploiting the divisions and contradictions of the capitalist world. This would be facilitated by the presence of a strong "mass" communist party in each of the western capitalist nations.[83] A large communist party in France was particularly important because of France's role as the bulwark of reaction in Europe.

These goals made it important to avoid a major schism in the French party—to avoid, in other words, the kind of schism that the ECCI had encouraged in 1919. A pure, elitist party in France promised to be as isolated and impotent as the KPD and thus of no value to the Soviet Republic.

As might be expected, the idea of accepting centrists as full-fledged members of the Comintern encountered a mixed reception by both its leadership and other members. The dissatisfaction of the latter was made abundantly clear at the Comintern's Second Congress, as will be seen. Within the councils of the Bolshevik party the idea was not received with equal enthusiasm either. The leaders who forwarded this "centrist strategy" most enthusiastically were Zinoviev, Kamenev, and Radek.[84] Of these three Zinoviev made negotiations with the French his particular concern and used his special talents to wrench from them far greater concessions than they had been prepared to grant when leaving Paris. As will be explained more fully in the following chapters, Zinoviev gave a rather frank account at both the Second and Third Congresses of the Communist International of the "separate agreement" made with the French, and he justified it by emphasizing that the left wing of the SFIO was still too weak; by dealing with the centrists, the ECCI gave the SFIO's left wing "time to organize and regroup."[85] Within the Bolshevik party he had often argued for greater understanding of the mensheviks—the Russian "centrists"—and had strongly urged allying with them immediately after the bolshevik seizure of power.[86] Interestingly, Zinoviev's own sympathies for the centrists went hand in hand with what Lenin had so strongly warned against: cowardice and betrayal at the crucial moment of revolution. But Lenin seemed willing to forgive Zinoviev his falterings in 1917, perhaps because of his many oratorical and polemical talents.[87]

Zinoviev had also earned for himself the reputation of having a special talent for duplicity and subtle maneuvering: during the war he had been a kind of "hatchet man" for Lenin in the intrigues of the antiwar minorities. Obviously the intricacies of incorporating a centrist party into the Comintern while officially declaring war on centrism required some such talent, and Zinoviev went to work with genuine expertise. It is significant in this respect that Angelica Balabanoff, a Zimmerwaldian left-wing socialist, who was earlier active in the PSI and had worked with Zinoviev in the high councils of the Comintern throughout 1919 and early 1920, described him as a "master of intrigue and calumny" and stated that "after Mussolini . . . Zinoviev is the most despicable individual I have ever met."[88] At the end of 1920 after their experiences at the hands of Zinoviev, the SFIO delegates would have cause for similar reflections.

Lenin's own attitude to the idea of a special role for centrism in France is obscure, but he seems to have evolved slowly toward Zinoviev's position as he came to accept the desirability of large or mass communist parties in the West. That he was moving away from the idea of a pure communist party in France formed by immediately splitting away from the SFIO was reflected in a conversation he had in June 1920 with Alfred Rosmer, a representative of the Committee for the Comintern. Rosmer informed him that after the Strasbourg congress many in the Committee who had previously been anxious to break away from the SFIO decided to stay in, since they believed that they would soon win a majority and take over the entire party. Lenin, who had just reproachfully asked Rosmer why the Committee had waited so long to set up a new party, replied, "If that is the case, I have written nonsense [*une bêtise*] in my theses; ask for a copy of them from the Secretary of the Communist International, and send me the corrections you propose."[89] The thesis in question was undoubtedly number sixteen of Lenin's Basic Tasks, which in its final form, presumably with Rosmer's corrections incorporated, recommended that communists now in a minority of a centrist party remain in it in order more effectively to criticize its leadership and to retain contact with the masses. "Whenever the left wing of a centrist party has become strong enough, and the development of the communist movement requires it, it may leave the party and form a communist party."[90] The emphasis, in other words, was now much more on carefully planning the appropriate time for a split, in order that communists take as much of a mass following as possible with them.

But of course to recommend that communists stay inside a centrist party was not quite the same as actually using the centrists themselves to attract the masses. But that the latter concept was not far from Lenin's mind can be discerned in the following passage from *Left-Wing Communism*:

> The petty-bourgeois democrats [i.e., the centrists] . . . inevitably vacillate between the bourgeoisie and the proletariat, between burgeois democracy and the soviet system, between reform and revolution. . . . The proper tactic for communists to adopt is to *utilize* these vacillations, not ignore them; and utilizing them calls for concessions to those elements which are turning toward the proletariat.[91]

Opposition to the special strategy for France found its most highly placed representative in the person of Leon Trotsky. Trotsky at the time of the Second Congress was probably too preoccupied with the Polish war to devote full attention to the problems of the Communist International, but it is clear from his speeches and articles of the period that he still felt nothing but contempt for the French center socialists.[92] During the war Trotsky had developed close friendships with the leaders of the revolutionary anarchosyndicalists, and he apparently persisted in 1920 in believing that they should form the nucleus of any communist party in France.

But in spite of his distaste for the "centrist strategy," Trotsky acquiesced in it, and he seems to have decided to let Zinoviev have a free hand in the matter. Significantly, in a note added to his *Terrorism and Communism*, dated June 17, 1920, he stated, "the moment of formal split with the open *and disguised* Kautskyans, or the moment of their expulsion from the ranks of the working class party, is of course to be determined by considerations of usefulness from the point of view of circumstances." He could not help adding: "but all policy of real communists must turn in that direction."[93] In other words, it would be all right to make momentary tactical arrangements with the centrists, but they must be purged in due time.

The goals of the Comintern leadership are more difficult to determine in relation to the PSI than for the SFIO and USPD, probably because the bolsheviks themselves were more perplexed concerning the proper strategy for dealing with the Italians and because they were frustrated in their attempts to manipulate the factions within the Italian party. Ironically, while discovering that the French centrists, who wanted to join the Comintern, could be humbled and manipulated, Zinoviev found that Serrati, who was already a member in good standing of the Comintern, stubbornly resisted bolshevik recommendations and himself began to talk very much like a centrist.

Yet if Serrati was a "hidden" centrist, he enjoyed a very significant popularity among the Italian masses. Thus any attempt to dislodge him from the leadership of the Italian party would have to be made with caution. Clearly the bolsheviks did begin to look for alternate leadership in Bordiga and in the *Ordine Nuovo* group. But none of the latter came to Moscow in 1920, and Bordiga seemed to be afflicted with the "infantile disorder" of left-wing communism, which the bolsheviks at this time were particularly concerned to combat. Moreover, neither Bordiga nor the Turin group had a significant mass following. Thus any communist party led by them could well remain impotent and isolated.

The Comintern leaders found themselves pushed into an uncomfortable position. They wanted a "mass" Italian Communist party, purged only of the present PSI's small reformist wing. But only Serrati could provide such a party, and he refused to purge the right wing. A party led by Bordiga and purged of Serrati would mean a narrow, pure party, just when the bolsheviks were beginning to feel the necessity of larger mass parties in the West.

The most obscure aspect of the bolsheviks' policy toward the PSI was their attitude to revolutionary dynamics in Italy. Certainly revolutionary conditions seemed more auspicious in Italy than they did in France. Moreover, Italy did not lack, as did France, a choice of competent and charismatic revolutionary leaders; if anything there were too many such figures, or at least so it must have seemed in early 1920. Yet Lenin's advice to the PSI had been mostly words of caution, and in early 1920 he showed constant awareness of Italy's vulnerability to blockade, her lack of raw materials, her lack of a broadly revolutionary peasantry. Strangely, however, in late 1920 when revolutionary conditions in Italy were obviously at their lowest ebb since the war, the bolsheviks reversed the thrust of their earlier advice and began to assert that Italy was closer to revolution than any other country in the West.

Little solid documentation is available that will help resolve this seeming paradox. It is conceivable that the bolsheviks hoped to keep the prospect of revolution open in Italy in case the Polish and German gambits paid off. However, this would not account for the Comintern leaders' continued assertion, even after the defeat of the Red Army outside Warsaw, that the situation in Italy was immediately revolutionary. Perhaps a certain amount of rhetorical inertia played a role here, and perhaps, as will be discussed in the final chapter, there were still, even as late as the winter of 1920–1921, those in the leadership of the Comintern who hoped for a last-minute revolutionary outbreak in the West.

What seems more likely, especially in light of what has been said about the tendency of Lenin and the bolsheviks to stress one theme for propaganda purposes while keeping their own realistic and un-dogmatic counsels, is that the fiat "make revolution" was a subtle way of humbling the Italians and imposing discipline on them. Certainly the largest part of the leaders of the PSI, while enthusiastically praising the bolsheviks and the Bolshevik Revolution, tended to ignore bolshevik advice except when it suited their own, independently attained notions. By constantly urging the Italians to make revolution—even while knowing that this was not possible—the bolsheviks underlined the fact that they had been successful while the Italians had been mere talkers; equally such an imprecation underlined the point that the Italians should show more respect for the authority of experience.

Chapter **V**

In the Land of Revolution

The delegations of the PSI and SFIO were in Russia for over a month before the convocation of the Second Congress in mid-July. During this time they traveled extensively and thus were able to become familiar with conditions in revolutionary Russia, to carry on extensive negotiations, and to develop personal acquaintances with most of the bolshevik leadership.

By the time the delegates had returned to their respective countries a most surprising transformation had occurred in the French delegation. Having made the trip as members of the Reconstruction Committee they came back as ardent partisans of immediate affiliation to the Comintern. To understand their about-face it is necessary to follow with some care the complex evolution of their negotiations with the bolsheviks. It is a remarkable story, one of an almost unbelievable repetition of "hot-cold" treatments and of humiliations and reconciliations that virtually dissolved the ability of the French to resist.

The Italian delegation, going to Russia not really as negotiators but as honored friends of the Soviet Republic and members of the Comintern in good standing, discovered that the PSI was in fact not so securely in the good graces of the Comintern as had at first seemed the case. In particular for Serrati the weeks in Russia were a disillusionment and even a trauma. Entering the land of revolution as a regaled hero, he departed as a harassed apostate.

The delegation of the USPD did not arrive until mid-July, during the opening days of the Second Congress. With the short time thus available to them the bolsheviks made every effort to split the USPD delegates, just as they had turned Serrati's companions against him. The task was not easy, and many heated quarrels be-

tween the Germans and Russians developed. But in the end the latter succeeded, and the four USPD delegates returned home, two
strongly in favor of affiliation and two strongly opposed.

The delegates of the SFIO

In the personal qualities of the two delegates of the SFIO
to Moscow and in their past positions in the party are to be found a
key to understanding the development of the negotiations in Russia, since their past "sins" and their weaknesses of character were
played upon skillfully by the bolsheviks after their arrival in Moscow. It is doubtful, indeed, that if Longuet had gone instead of
Frossard—as originally planned—or if Cachin had been replaced by
almost any other centrist leader, there would have been such a
"fruitful" turn to the negotiations or finally such a heavy majority
in favor of the Comintern in December, 1920. It is thus worth-
while to pause briefly to examine the characters and pasts of these
two men.

In an article in *Bulletin Communiste*, "Flory" (Loriot), while
asserting the impossibility of the reconstructionist goals, succintly
put his finger on important aspects of the two delegates' characters
by predicting that "neither the enthusiasm [*enthousiasmes*] of
Cachin nor the suppleness [*souplesse*] of Frossard will be able to resolve the difficulties they will encounter. . . ."[1] As the following account of the course of the negotiations should make clear, it was, on
the contrary, Cachin's emotional, enthusiastic nature and Frossard's
flexibility and negotiating skill that finally allowed them to "resolve" the difficulties they did encounter.

Marcel Cachin's *enthousiasmes* were well known in the SFIO.
Although he had been affiliated before the war with the Guesdist
wing of the party, he shared little of Guesde's stiff Marxist orthodoxy and humorless estrangement from bourgeois society. Cachin,
on the contrary, was a colorful but not too complex individual, the
bon enfant of the party, whose combination of joviality and selfless
devotion to the SFIO earned him much popularity among the party's leadership and local officials. Yet at the same time, and unlike
many other SFIO *parlementaires*, Cachin kept in close contact with

the working masses, not only in his Parisian constituency, the Goutte-d'Or, but in other parts of France as well, where he gained the reputation of a tireless speaker and campaigner, combining a powerful voice with a robust handsomeness and eloquent rhetoric. The applause and warm affection of the masses became a very important part of his life. As Frossard observed in a later book, "the bravos of the crowd touched his heart like a woman's caress."[2] To retain this popularity became Cachin's most pressing concern.[3]

It was thus hardly surprising that in August 1914, when the overwhelming majority of the French working class, like the overwhelming majority of France, burst into patriotic frenzy, Cachin was there to rally them. What was for other leaders of the SFIO, like Guesde, a relatively rational course of action, was for Cachin an overwhelming emotional experience: ". . . a whole dormant heritage of near mystical patriotism rose abruptly from the heart to the lips of this robust Breton."[4] Cachin was a "social patriot" of the first order, developing into one of the most stubborn of the "bitter-enders" of the *Union sacrée*.[5] Early in the war he became a representative of the French Ministry of Foreign Affairs in Italy, where he supplied funds to none other than Benito Mussolini.[6] At the time of the February Revolution in Russia, Cachin was sent along with Thomas, Moutet, and Lafont to try to convince the Russians to stay in the war; while there, Cachin, in his speeches to the Soviets, accused the bolsheviks of being spies for the *"boches."*[7] After the Treaty of Brest-Litovsk—which cruelly stung his patriotism—and under the pressure of a new German offensive, Cachin wrote in *L'Humanité* as follows: "We are not bolsheviks . . . and we do not want to sign, as they did, a new treaty of Brest-Litovsk. Since the assassination of Mirbach, the bolsheviks have managed such a close *rapprochement* with the German government that it has taken them openly into tutelage. . . . Everywhere revolutionaries watch with horror as the bolshevik police, in the service of Berlin, track down and shoot socialists. . . ."[8] At the end of the war, during the ceremonies dedicated to the French takeover of Alsace-Lorraine, Cachin, tears streaming down his cheeks as he witnessed the popular acclaim which greeted the French *"Piou-pious"* tramping down the street of

Strasbourg, blurted out to those around him, *"Le plebiscite, le voilà!"* [9]

The list of Cachin's "crimes" could be lengthened, but the essential point to emphasize is that in each instance his position was at the head of the prevailing popular passion: patriotic frenzy in 1914, fear that Russia would leave France to face Germany alone in 1917, joy at recovering the lost provinces in 1919. In the same way, Cachin's cautious move to the left after 1917 corresponded to a popular revulsion from the war and a growing revolutionary restiveness among the working masses. Cachin thus first maneuvered to a center position between the *Majoritaires* and the *Minoritaires*, then joined the Reconstruction Committee, and was finally to become an enthusiastic partisan of the Communist International. [10] In this amazing journey across the breadth of socialist opinion, little can be found to suggest a bolshevik or communist nucleus of belief. Indeed, quite the opposite would seem the case, in spite of Cachin's surprisingly lasting acceptance by the French Communist party. Probably the most accurate final description, in Leninist terms, of Cachin's position would not be "social patriotism"—since he soon enough abandoned that—but *khvostism* ("tailism"), the tendency to follow rather than lead the working class, which Lenin professed to see in his menshevik opponents. One might say, then, that Cachin was "true to the working class" at the expense of any semblance of doctrinal integrity as a socialist.

Yet, although practically all observers concur that Cachin was "... a man without character, who followed the current" [11] and who showed "neither fidelity to his friends nor consistency in his opinions," [12] it must be granted that he was still in a sense an "honest" representative of the working class, who always maintained close and warm contact with the rank and file. Cachin never sought to enrich himself or make his position as parliamentary deputy a stepping-stone to success and prestige in the bourgeois world as had been the case with, for example, Millerand and Briand. He lived modestly, even suffering real deprivation at times, and kept his reputation of selflessness and devotion to the working class.

Whatever Cachin's saving graces, in retrospect his selection by the leaders of the SFIO to negotiate with the Comintern seems strangely ill considered. Certainly the party leadership was not unaware of his particular failings, and certainly none could have believed that he had the firmness and composure characteristic of a skillful negotiator. Perhaps it was hoped that Cachin's charm might work to soothe the nasty disposition of those in Moscow, while Frossard could be relied upon to keep Cachin in line. Whatever the reasoning, his presence in the delegation to Moscow must be seen as a major error by the CAP, for his charm was to have little effect, while his weaknesses were to be exploited by the bolsheviks, and it was he who would pull Frossard along rather than Frossard holding him back.

L. -O. Frossard was in nearly every respect the antithesis of Cachin. Indeed, two more strikingly different men could hardly be imagined. Although only thirty-one years old (b. 1889) at the time of his voyage to Moscow, Frossard gave more the impression of middle age than did Cachin, who was in fact twenty years his senior (b. 1869).[13] Prematurely bald, bespectacled, rather frail and reserved in comparison to Cachin's hearty ebullience, Frossard did not enjoy the kind of ardent popularity that surrounded Cachin. In Frossard's memoirs, even when he defends Cachin, one can detect an undercurrent of resentment or jealousy of him.[14] Frossard admits that he opposed Cachin's appointment to the position of editor-in-chief of *L'Humanité*, but acquiesced finally under pressure from other members of the CAP.[15] Quite unlike Cachin, Frossard won his position in the party—taking over the post of General Secretary, amazingly, at the age of twenty-eight—through the exercise of a subtle and brilliant intellect and by demonstrating a real administrative talent. Although quite capable of effective oratory, Frossard's tendency was to appeal to his listeners' reason; he did not possess Cachin's emotional appeal and ability to move large crowds. It was in the written word that Frossard best displayed his talents, either in the smooth and subtle working of formal statements and resolutions, or—and much more impressively—in moving, colorful description, striking phrases, perceptive characterization, charming wit.

Frossard's past, while not as erratic as Cachin's, was still not that of a radical revolutionary. He was, in Lenin's terms, a "social paci-

fist." As a *Minoritaire* he had opposed the war and socialist participation in it for pacifist reasons, and he certainly had no sympathy
for Lenin's slogan "turn the imperialist war into a civil war." Frossard's position at Bern—where he joined with Loriot in support of
the Russian Revolution—may have won him some favorable attention from the bolsheviks, but he had of course not come around to
Loriot's point of view on any other matters, and had instead joined
hands with the Reconstructionists.

As Cachin's *"khvostism"* separated him fundamentally from being a "true" bolshevik or communist, so it can be said that Frossard's taste for tolerance and liberality put him in a camp very different from Lenin's. When Frossard first joined the SFIO at the age
of sixteen, he had done so partly out of admiration for the tolerance
within a party that had achieved unity while allowing different internal tendencies to remain. It is obvious, then, that Frossard could
have little real admiration for Lenin's trenchant dogmatism. Of
Loriot, in temperament probably Lenin's closest equivalent in
France, Frossard observed bitterly, "He knows nothing of the art of
nuances. . . . He has no desire either to entice or to convince—instead
he affirms, he slashes!" [16]

Frossard not only felt scant sympathy for the rigid orthodoxy
that emanated from Moscow, but experienced deeply the anguish
of seeing both sides of a question, even to the extent of tormenting
himself with doubts about the truths of socialism.[17] He seems to
have had an intellectual's distrust and even distaste for the working
masses, although he was himself the son of a poor artisan.[18] For him,
unlike Cachin, the attraction of socialism lay in its ideals of equality
and justice, its promise of a better future, and not in a natural affection for the seething masses in their current state.

Perhaps in Frossard's humble origin, which was not so common
among the leaders of French socialism as it was in the SPD, can be
found a key to understanding his own particular weakness: an intense and driving ambition, an ambition formed and tempered in
the factional maneuvers of his own party and the intrigues of the
Chamber of Deputies. Frossard's father, a hard-working saddler,
had sacrificed everything for his son's education and success, and his
son had not disappointed him. Certainly to land at the head of the

SFIO at the age of twenty-eight was no small accomplishment. But, shortly after Frossard attained his position, Loriot's wing threatened to replace the *Minoritaires*, just as the latter had replaced the *Majoritaires* at the end of the war. And thus Frossard, though more concerned than Cachin with socialist principles and personal consistency, was himself susceptible to "going with the current" by assuming a more left-wing stance in order to keep his position at the head of the party.

The CAP cannot be blamed as easily for poor judgment in selecting Frossard as in selecting Cachin, because the extent of Frossard's *souplesse* had not yet come into the open. In the following years he was to pass from the SFIO to lead the Communist party, then back to the SFIO, then to a cabinet position in a Laval ministry, then to serve in succession under Blum, Daladier, Reynaud, and finally Pétain, under whom he exchanged courtesies with the ultraconservative Maurras and Henriot.[19]

These were, then, the two men who set out for Russia to bargain with the bolsheviks. From the standpoint of the Reconstructionist majority of the CAP, probably no two men of their faction less likely to fulfill its wishes could have been found.

The delegates of the USPD

In the meantime the USPD had itself been making preparations to send a delegation to Russia. The leaders of the USPD were actually slower and more cautious than the French. Even after they had carefully examined the ECCI's letter of February 5, they were hesitant to make it public or to encourage intraparty debate on it. In later accounting for this hesitation, the party leaders explained that because of the chaotic conditions in Germany in April and then the pressing demands of preparing for the June elections, there simply was not time to publish the letter. These hollow excuses convinced no one, least of all the bolsheviks, who saw in them another example of how the leaders of the USPD deceived the masses and how they were more concerned with parliamentary electioneering than in preparing for revolution. It *is* clear that the party leadership avoided publishing the letter because it feared the disruptive effects the letter would have on USPD unity. And party unity seemed particularly vital in the post-Kapp period and the May electoral campaign.

The first mention of the letter in the USPD's *Die Freiheit* was not until mid-June, a full two months after Borodin's visit. Even then it was only in direct response to an attack by the KPD's *Die Rote Fahne*.[20] In the weeks following, the text of the letter was published in *Die Freiheit*, accompanied by a detailed editorial rebuttal and a long defense of the party's leadership, which recounted at length all the initiatives concerning the international it had taken since Leipzig.[21]

The USPD leadership also repeatedly postponed making definite arrangements to send a delegation to Moscow. It will be recalled that the ECCI's letter had urged sending such a delegation; since then the USPD had received several other indications of Moscow's desire to negotiate directly with it.

On April 30, G. Shlyapnikov, a member of the ECCI and president of the Russian Metal Workers' Union, visited Berlin and, while there, stopped by the offices of the USPD.[22] Like Borodin, he urged sending a USPD delegation directly to Moscow as soon as possible; but unlike Borodin, he consented to answer the USPD's leaders' questions. In a second meeting, on the seventh of May, he assured them that there would be no question of forcing exclusions upon the USPD if it joined the Comintern, not even a requirement to fuse with the KPD.[23]

On the thirty-first of May, a telegram sent from Moscow by Karl Radek on the twenty-seventh reached the offices of the USPD. This telegram expressed regret that the USPD had not yet answered the ECCI's letter of February 5 and that the letter had not even been published by the USPD. The USPD was specifically requested to send a delegation to Moscow to clarify things.[24] In answer to this the USPD *Zentrale* sent back a telegram noting that the letter of February 5 had not been received until April 9, when there was little time to devote to it because of the approaching elections. In any case, the letter had been published on May 20, though in a limited number of copies because of Germany's "chronic paper shortage." Furthermore, the USPD all along had intended to send a delegation to Moscow and would do so as soon as possible.[25]

But by mid-June, when the SFIO and PSI delegations had already arrived in Russia, the ECCI still had nothing but the promise of the USPD to send a delegation. It thus apparently decided to exert pressure on the USPD *Zentrale*: on June 21 an official ECCI appeal was sent to the local USPD units authorizing them to send individual delegations to Moscow.[26] Given the highly decentralized and heterogeneous nature of the USPD and the suspicion of the left of the party that the *Zentrale* was not carrying out the wishes of the rank and file, it was likely that this appeal would find a sympathetic response.

However, the USPD's leadership had already met on the eleventh and the nineteenth of June to designate four delegates to Moscow, who were to leave in time for the Second Congress of the Communist International, which had now been set for the first week of July. The four delegates apparently were chosen with an eye to a balanced representation of the main trends of the party. The left, unlike its counterpart in the SFIO, agreed to accompany the delegates representing the right and center of the party—though none of the four was closely associated with the extremely antibolshevik wing of the party—and all four agreed to represent the party according to a common mandate.

Unlike the two SFIO delegates, who left after the dismal failures of the strike movement in the spring and who were thus in a poor negotiating position, the USPD delegation set out for Moscow after its impressive victories in the June elections, and thus felt itself in a strong negotiating position. Furthermore, while the French delegates could not speak for the growing left of their party, Walter Stoecker and Ernst Däumig represented the USPD's own powerful left.

The mandate the USPD delegates were given[27] took a much more aggressive position than did the mandate of the SFIO delegates, although the mandates otherwise had much in common. The German mandate was especially concerned to rebut the attacks on the USPD made in the ECCI's letter of February 5. Beginning by calling the letter "totally false," the mandate rejected the accusation that the party's leadership or its right wing was sabotaging the push from the masses for revolution and for immediate affiliation with the Comintern. The personal attacks on some of the leaders of the USPD were described as either ill-willed slander or evidence of a basic ignorance of conditions in Germany. The Russians were lectured on their "un-Marxian viewpoint" in arguing that a small group of men could block the drive of the masses for revolution. The mandate also included an elaborate defense of the USPD's decision to enter the Council of People's Representatives in November, 1918 and its actions while allied with the SPD. In sum, the mandate charged the bolsheviks with inadequate knowledge of western conditions and a too facile willingness to apply Russian methods—which were repeatedly termed "un-Marxian"—to the entirely different needs of western socialism.

Wilhelm Dittmann stood the farthest to the right of the four delegates, although at one time he had been a friend of Rosa Luxemburg.[28] It will be remembered that he had served with Haase and Barth on the Council of People's Representatives, and he seems generally to have been associated with Haase during and immediately after the war. As a young man he had been a carpenter, but he soon began to work his way up the hierarchy of the SPD, showing special talents in newspaper work. He had spent five years in Frankfurt as local party secretary before coming to Berlin to work in the party headquarters. Before the creation of the USPD, he had been the secretary of Haase's parliamentary antiwar faction, and once Haase's group had broken off formally from the SPD, Dittmann played a prominent role in the USPD. At Leipzig, he made an effort to distinguish his position from that of the right wing, and thus he spoke not for Hilferding's resolution but for Ledebour's and also for the final compromise resolution. Dittmann obviously did not believe that a bolshevik type of revolution would be appropriate for Germany; yet he was not a "formal democrat": in November, 1918 he favored making fundamental reforms while the revolution was still in motion and before the calling of a constituent assembly. He left for Moscow with little enthusiasm for affiliation to the Comintern unless the bolsheviks could, through negotiations, be convinced that they must moderate their language and their demands on prospective members. Once in Moscow, Dittmann became the most pugnacious negotiator of the four USPD delegates.[29]

Arthur Crispien had entered the SPD as a painter, and had, like Dittmann, made his way up the party hierarchy largely through newspaper work. At the outbreak of war he had attacked the SPD leadership for its support of the war, and because of his stand he lost his job with the *Schwäbische Tagwacht,* which he had been the editor of since 1912.[30] During the war he had joined the Spartacists, but broke with them, as he later explained, before the formation of the KPD because he did not agree with their defense of the use of terror.[31] At Leipzig he spoke for the compromise resolution, although he later misinformed Frossard concerning its import. Like Dittmann, Crispien had little esteem for the bolsheviks, who had personally attacked him on a number of occasions. Zinoviev had named him as one of those who could not possibly be accepted into the Communist International,[32] and in *Left-Wing Communism* Lenin described him as a "snivelling, philistine democrat," who was "incapable of thinking and reasoning like a revolutionary."[33]

Ernst Däumig, with whom we are already familiar from his speeches in the *Räte* congresses and at Leipzig, had a much more unorthodox background than either Dittmann or Crispien. He had spent his younger years in the army, partly in the Foreign Legion, after which he had written a book on his experiences entitled *Modern Mercenaries* and had become a journalist for the social-democratic newspaper *Vorwärts.* After the November Revolution, he had tried to organize a "Red Guard" to oppose the *Freikorps,* but was unable to interest the German revolutionary soldiers, who felt that their present organizations were adequate.[34] After the Leipzig Congress, when it had become increasingly clear that his notion of the primacy of the *Räte* would not be accepted by Germany's workers, he moved towards an acceptance of the role of the political party as the necessary organizer of revolution. In fact, although he had earlier ridiculed those who made a "fetish" of bolshevism, by the time he left for Moscow he seems to have moved toward a bolshevik position; and under pressure from the bolsheviks he would abandon even more of his earlier beliefs.[35]

Walter Stoecker, who is also familiar from his speeches at Leipzig and before, was of the four perhaps the most imbued with the spirit of "*la révolution ou la mort*," the feeling that revolution *must* come to the West in the immediate future. Like many others who felt this way, he was young (twenty-nine years old in April) and had spent tragic years during the war. When the revolution broke out in Germany, he was still ill, from malaria picked up in Macedonia, but he nevertheless enthusiastically entered the fray. He became a leader of the *Räte* in Cologne, like Däumig entertaining high hopes that they would supplant organized parties in the revolution. Shortly after the outbreak of revolution he joined the USPD and became an editor of the USPD newspaper *Volkstribüne*.[36] Although before the war he had been a left-wing activist in the SPD youth movement, he, like so many other future communists—Gramsci, Togliatti, Loriot, Cachin—was momentarily swept up in the patriotism of late 1914.[37] But after the war he became an ardent admirer of the bolsheviks and felt in a rather vague way that to join the Comintern without delay would somehow speed revolution in Germany.[38] He also shared with many young, ardent admirers of the Bolshevik Revolution an uncritical and careless optimism about the relationships of bolshevism to western socialism. It will be recalled that in late 1919 he had confidently affirmed that "pure bolshevik" methods would not be imposed on new members of the Communist International. Even by July, 1920 he still believed that the USPD could join the Comintern without splitting and that men like Hilferding could remain in the party. Like Däumig and much of the left of the USPD, and even the KPD, he was suspicious of a highly centralized party organization and seemed to feel on this point too that the bolshevik model was not relevant for the West.

The delegates of the PSI

The Italians who left for Russia did not go with the goal of negotiating with the Comintern. The Italian delegation was not even, strictly speaking, a political delegation; rather it was a group consisting of thirteen representatives of the PSI, labor unions, co-operatives, and various other organizations whose official task was to study the bolshevik regime and to negotiate certain trade agreements. It left with the full approval of the Nitti government.[39] The members of the PSI that went along did not yet know that the Second Congress of the Comintern would be held in mid-July, and the members who were not leaders of the party returned in late July without attending the congress.

G. M. Serrati has played a leading role in the preceding pages as the leader of the wartime intransigent faction and afterwards of the Maximalist Electionists. In his youth he had wandered over most of Europe and America, trying every kind of job from cabin boy to journalist, and becoming a socialist activist at a very early age.[40] He was, as his actions during the war demonstrated, a man of great devotion to the cause of socialism and of unusual firmness and independence of conviction, even to the point of stubbornness. Thus, in important ways he was cut from a different cloth than were Cachin and Frossard, especially in terms of his ideological integrity and his disdain for parliamentary and intraparty maneuvering. Yet at the same time, as Serrati himself was later to admit,[41] he too was concerned about the threat to his leadership from the extreme left, a threat which would become more serious if the Turatian right were expelled from the party as the bolsheviks demanded. Significantly, Bordiga's faction at the Milan *Consiglio Nazionale* in April won nearly eight times the support it had won at the congress of Bologna.[42] Bordiga and the *Ordine Nuovo* group did not yet present such a threat to Serrati as did Loriot and his followers to Cachin and Frossard, but still Serrati feared that Moscow would support them over him, and thus he went to Russia harboring certain suspicions and anxieties.

Nicola Bombacci was one of the more notorious revolutionary firebrands of the left wing of the Maximalist faction. His provocative manner, revolutionary posturing, and flaming beard made him for many the symbol of the Italian "bolshevik." Yet in fact he was something of a comic figure, and his emotional and unintellectual approach to socialism was very different from that of Lenin or Trotsky. Perhaps because he had a scant theoretical foundation for his beliefs he seemed most willing of all the Italians to accept the unquestioned authority of the bolsheviks. The plan for the building of soviets in Italy which he worked out for the *Direzione* was little more than a shallow, rote-imitation of what he understood, often mistakenly, to exist in Russia; it largely ignored the peculiarities of Italian development and relegated the *consigli di fabbrica* to a purely economic and implicitly nonrevolutionary role—little more, in fact, than an adjunct to the trade unions. Very plausibly Bombacci's admiration for the bolsheviks was connected to his own ambitions, for he no doubt came to appreciate that any future leader of communism in Italy would have to be distinguished by greater respect for bolshevik leadership than had been the case with Serrati and Bordiga. In any case, his ideological integrity was far less firm than that of the latter two; with Mussolini's rise to power, Bombacci was to abandon socialism in favor of fascism.

Antonio Graziadei, a professor of political economy from a wealthy and conservative family, was the pedagogue of the PSI. His speeches and articles were interlaced with learned quotations from Marx and Engels, a practice that generally characterized the Turatian wing of the party. Until the end of the war Graziadei had been associated more with the right wing of the party than with its left. Like other right-wing members of the party, he had made deprecatory remarks about the Bolshevik Revolution, and he had frequently underlined the difficulties of making revolution in Italy.[43] However, by late 1919 and early 1920 Graziadei began to drift leftward, for reasons that remain obscure; perhaps he also feared for his future in the party. It will be recalled that during his trip in France in early 1920 he encouraged the French centrists in their hope that they could gain certain concessions from the bolsheviks in joining the Comintern. In Moscow he would serve as a contact and buffer between the bolsheviks and the SFIO delegation.

Amadeo Bordiga is by now too familiar to require further introduction. Typically, he departed for the Second Congress with a very specific and clear-cut plan in mind. (He was not a member of the larger delegation which departed in June, but came instead in July specifically as a representative of the Abstentionist faction to the Second Congress.) He was the only delegate, aside from the bolsheviks and the Indian, Roy, to present a set of theses for discussion at the congress. Bordiga had not been won over by the reasoning of Lenin and the ECCI concerning parliamentary participation, nor was he convinced by Niccolini that the PSI should remain substantially united. He sought out the support of the Second Congress for his conception of an elite abstentionist revolutionary party.

A young Italian revolutionary who talked to Bordiga just before the latter's departure asked him if he were excited at the prospect of seeing the land of the revolution at first hand. Bordiga replied that the revolution itself did not particularly interest him; what was important was that he gain the support of the congress for his theses and that they be recognized as rigorously and orthodoxly Marxian.[44] This remark was typical of the man, and it underlined his profound differences from the many delegates who went to Russia as if they were on a pilgrimage to the Mecca of Revolution.

En route to Petrograd

The large Italian delegation left Italy on May 25, traveling through Switzerland to Berlin, Copenhagen, Malmö, Stockholm, Helsingfors, Reval, and finally reaching Petrograd on June 6. During their five-day stopover in Berlin, the Italians had a chance to observe at firsthand the workings of the USPD, KPD, and KAPD, and presumably to talk with the leaders of each. From the standpoint of Serrati's later difficulties with the bolsheviks it is interesting to note that already, as he wrote back to Italy, he recognized that the USPD was the party in Germany that had the overwhelming mass of the revolutionary proletariat behind it. He further added that the KPD was still a small and unimportant group, lacking in leaders, unity, and organization. The KAPD, he concluded, was a band of impossible sectarians.[45]

The voyage through Scandinavia was psychologically a poor preparation for the later weeks in devastated and backward Russia. All of the Italian delegates were deeply impressed with the clean, efficient, and prosperous aspect of the Scandinavian countries. Vincenzo Vacirca, who represented, like Serrati, the PSI *Direzione*, touchingly jotted down in his diary, "we all feel the deep humiliation of being . . . Italians."[46] Apparently Graziadei was so taken with Copenhagen that he wanted to stay there while the rest of the delegation proceeded on to Russia, and only with much difficulty was Serrati able to dissuade him from this odd whimsy.[47]

At any rate the Italians entered Russia with relatively little of the sense of cultural superiority that characterized many other western socialists, especially the French and Germans. This may have been part of the reason why the Italians received such a consistently warm welcome throughout Russia. But equally, as has been observed, the bolsheviks felt a special affection for the PSI as the only major western party that had remained true to the principles of internationalism during the war, and that had, more than any other western party, struggled for the defense of the Soviet Republic. Once inside Russia the Italians were feted and regaled; they were, as Graziadei put it, the *enfants gâtés* of the delegates to Russia.[48] On the train ride from Reval to Petrograd on June 6 the Italians' car was greeted, even in small villages, with bands and banners. At Iamberg, the first soviet village of their voyage, they encountered large poster pictures of Lenin, a phonograph recording of the speeches of Lenin and Trotsky, and fervent singing of the *Internationale*.[49]

At Petrograd they were met by Zinoviev and Angelica Balabanoff (a Russian revolutionary who had been active in the PSI before the war), with hugs, kisses, tears, hurrahs, and military music. Soldiers lined their way for some distance along the streets as they traveled by automobile from the station to their hotel.[50] In the following week the Italian delegation was given an extensive tour of the city, including a visit to Kronstadt, the Putilov steel works, the headquarters of the Bolshevik party, a mass meeting in the Uritsky Palace, and an evening with Maxim Gorky. Gorky, an ardent Italophile, was able to obtain some bottles of chianti, left over from tsarist times. While Balabanoff, the clucking, prudish auntie of the revolution, was scandalized at these luxuries in the midst of mass suffering, Zarin, with a boyish, ironic grin, whispered to Vacirca, "how wonderful it would be if Italians arrived every day!" Later Balabanoff wrote, "I have seen many huge gatherings and mass demonstrations in Russia, with beautiful banners, parades of the youth and military forces, manifestations of joy and mourning, but none so spontaneous and unanimous as those attending the arrival of the Italian delegation in Petrograd. There were demonstrations every evening until we left for Moscow."[51]

The Italians had prepared themselves for the worst, as far as the material conditions in Russia were concerned.[52] Even so they were shocked. Emilio Colombino, the representative of the FIOM (the Italian metalworkers' union), described the famed Putilov steel works as a "ghost factory."[53] The other major factories were in the same condition. The whole city had a brutalized, deserted look: empty shops, filthy streets, barges sunk in the Neva, miserably dressed people, and disgusting food. The bolshevik leaders openly recognized that they could do nothing about the rampant black market in the city, since the government was not able to provide the population with the goods it obtained only through the black market.[54] Colombino, himself obviously distressed by what he saw, later pleaded, in a book concerning his travels, for a "socialist consciousness" to understand these various distresses, which were the results of war and blockade rather than the rule of the bolsheviks.[55]

While the Italians rarely engaged in invidious comparisons between Russia and Italy, they were obviously surprised and often bewildered by the character of the Russians they encountered, both on the street (especially later in Moscow) and among the leaders of the Bolshevik party. They were particularly struck by the indolence, apathy, and superstition of the Russian population. Vacirca recounted seeing a man do fifteen genuflections and 454 signs of the cross.[56] The only answer Colombino could get from most of those he met on the street was "*nichevo*" (a noncommittal "nothing").[57] All of the Italians were surprised to see that Lenin, whose picture was everywhere, was revered as a demigod by the population at large, even by those who were apolitical or hostile to bolshevism.[58] Among the bolshevik leaders themselves the Italians noted a curious lack of a sense of time and an absence of personal preoccupations; any such concern on the part of the Italians was good-naturedly ridiculed by the Russians. Vacirca, with obvious delight, recounted how Bordiga, the ultrarevolutionary, had lamented to Bukharin that he had lost his new leather traveling bag at the station. The Russian leader looked the young engineer up and down and derisively uttered "petty-bourgeois!"[59]

Yet there was also much that favorably impressed the Italians. The homes of the rich were now turned over to war orphans and retired workers. Surprisingly, the theater and ballet had survived, and first-rate performances continued, attended by enthusiastic working-class audiences. The Italians were astonished to encounter an excellent version of *Rigoletto*.[60] And in spite of the apathy of the general population, there was no denying the ardent enthusiasm of a large part of the working class for the bolshevik regime, especially in Petrograd and Moscow.

On a special train that had once belonged to the Tsar, the Italians left Petrograd for Moscow on June 14. The purely festive part of their Russian voyage was now ending, for on the train south Zinoviev began to press the inquiries he had made just after the Italians' arrival; in particular, why had the PSI not yet excluded the Turatian right wing? But before looking into this new stage of the Italian delegates' stay, it is important to follow the progress of the delegation of the SFIO, which had arrived in Petrograd the day before and which was traveling toward Moscow on the very same day, although under very different conditions.

On the evening of May 31, that is, six days after the departure of the Italian delegation, Cachin and Frossard were able to leave Paris, traveling by way of Cologne to Berlin, where on the second of June they were met by the correspondent of *L'Humanité*, O. Cohen. Because the mandate the two delegates carried with them said nothing about a stopover in Berlin, it can be assumed that their two-day stay there was unofficial. Perhaps Loriot's charge that Cachin and Frossard were still hoping for some sort of last minute "attachment" to the USPD to help fend off the bolsheviks had some foundation. Frossard's memoirs,[61] the only source that mentions the contents of the discussions carried on with the USPD during these two days, make no mention of any attempt to arrange a common front with the USPD. In principle, the USPD delegation was supposed to leave at the same time as Cachin and Frossard,[62] and it might be guessed that if Frossard did bring up the question of a common mandate or common tactical plan, the leaders of the USPD demurred because of the demands of the electoral campaign (the elections were less than a week away) or because the left was not interested.[63] (Cachin and Frossard met with Däumig in the offices of the party *Zentrale*, and presumably he informed them of the left's hostile attitude to such common tactical plans.) Most of the conversations Frossard does mention were uniquely concerned with Germany's internal affairs. Hilferding, whom Cachin and Frossard met in the offices of *Die Freiheit*, seemed little preoccupied with the USPD's international affiliations and far more concerned with Germany's future, about which he was very pessimistic, expecting a new *Putsch* at any time.[64]

The only figure with whom Cachin and Frossard spoke who did not seem to be completely absorbed in Germany's internal affairs was Georg Ledebour. Cachin was especially anxious to meet this old veteran of revolutionary struggles, and the two delegates thus made a special trip to Seidlitz, a suburb of Berlin, to see him.[65] Frossard has left substantially different accounts of their conversation. In his earlier writings,[66] while still at the head of the French Communist party, he reported that Ledebour had insisted that only "misunderstandings" separated the Russians and the USPD; for its part, the USPD wanted "passionately" to join the Comintern. Ledebour asked the French delegates to pass on his best regards to Lenin and Trotsky. But in his later writings after he had broken with the Party[67] Frossard's account corresponds more closely to what would be expected, given Ledebour's position at Leipzig, and is thus probably the more accurate one.

According to the later version, Ledebour insisted that bolshevik methods could not possibly be applied to Germany, and that the USPD could not accept the imposition of methods that were applicable only to Russia. To this Cachin replied with great conviction, "You can count on me, Ledebour. I'll tell Lenin all that, I promise."[68] However, ten days later, Cachin confided to Frossard: "It seems impossible to me that we won't join the Comintern. Those Germans don't understand anything. . . ."[69]

Cachin and Frossard also had occasion in Berlin to meet their first important representative of the Comintern, Shlyapnikov. As will be remembered, Shlyapnikov had been in contact with the USPD leadership. He was now staying in Berlin as a representative of the Russian trade unions at the congress of German metal workers, presumably doing some preliminary work for the Red International of Labor Unions.[70] By accident, on the same day that Cachin and Frossard went to visit him, Shlyapnikov had made plans to meet with Alfred Rosmer, who was traveling illegally to Russia as the official representative of the Committee for the Comintern. (He had tried to arrange a "cover" by traveling with the Italian delegation. But the Italians, hesitating to put the legality of their own delegation in jeopardy, refused to take him.)[71]

Rosmer, an anarchosyndicalist, devoted internationalist, and lifelong friend of Trotsky, was one of the few that had opposed the war in France from the beginning. An enigmatic and romantic figure—the name "Rosmer" he had borrowed from Ibsen's *Rosmersholm*—he would remain in Russia for the next several years as the permanent representative on the ECCI of the Committee for the Comintern and then of the French Communist party. Victor Serge, a revolutionary of a similar background who knew Rosmer well in Moscow, aptly characterized him: "beneath his half smile, Rosmer incarnated the qualities of vigilance, discretion, silence, and dedication."[72]

Shlyapnikov apparently planned a reunion between Rosmer and the SFIO delegates, but Rosmer demurred: he had profound contempt for both Cachin and Frossard, whom he considered typical of what was worst about the SFIO. For Rosmer, Cachin was a "man without character," who had "condemned the October Insurrection, and at heart, hated the bolsheviks."[73] He was now going to Moscow not out of any real attraction to bolshevism but in order to save his position in the SFIO. As for Frossard, Rosmer considered him a "mediocre imitation of Briand"[74] (the one-time revolutionary socialist who had made a career as a bourgeois parliamentarian).

Cachin and Frossard left Berlin on June 4, passing through Stettin and Helsinki on their way to Reval. In the course of their five-day journey they talked and thought much about what they could expect in Russia. Again relying only on Frossard's memoirs, it seems that Cachin experienced the most severe ups and downs in his feelings. At one point, Cachin blurted out to his traveling companion, "our heads and the Russians' heads, you know, are just not made of the same stuff!"[75] Yet, as they approached Russia, Cachin voiced greater and greater hopes for smooth and fruitful negotiations with the bolsheviks.[76]

On the ninth Cachin and Frossard reached Reval, where they were received by the Soviet diplomatic legation. Here they were informed that the Second Congress of the Communist International had been officially scheduled for late July,[77] and here they waited for the next mail train for Petrograd, which did not leave until the thirteenth. During their stay the SFIO delegates had the feeling that the Soviet legation's coldness in receiving them reflected their status as representatives of a suspect party, "a party of dangerous confusionists."[78] They soon had more striking confirmation of their suspicion.

Upon arriving at the Baltic Station in Petrograd, the two delegates found no one waiting for them and no one who could give them any indication of what to do or where to go. Frossard was quick to interpret this as a crude snub; he asked Cachin, who had recently been talking so optimistically, what he made of it. Frossard could see that Cachin was suspicious, but said nothing and shrugged his shoulders while "tugging nervously at his mustache."[79]

They spent the day and night of the thirteenth in the Baltic Station in quite a bewildered state. Finally, the next afternoon their car was attached to a train heading for Moscow, and they began a very slow trip south lasting twenty-two hours.[80] On the way they learned from a "talkative Bulgarian" in the next compartment about the Italian delegation's gala reception in Petrograd. The Italians, moreover, had a special train which was about to leave that evening (the fourteenth). Frossard's suspicions were now confirmed, and he felt certain that negotiations were not going to be easy.[81]

Moscow

On the train trip south, and no doubt even before, Zinoviev sought to make contacts with those Italians who desired to expel the right wing of the party. He enlisted Balabanoff to sound out the most radical members of the delegation, who were few in number, since a significant number of them represented the more conservative unions and cooperatives. When Serrati was approached he firmly opposed these efforts; in spite of Zinoviev's most insistent entreaties, the Italian leader refused to consider a split in his party.[82]

Before the Italians' arrival in Russia the bolsheviks were probably not fully aware of the extent of Serrati's opposition to the idea of a split in the PSI. Since he himself had often attacked Turati and other right-wing socialists in the strongest terms, perhaps the Comintern leaders felt that he would simply require a little prodding to consent to a purging of the PSI. Serrati's stubborn resistance to these proddings was obviously a disappointment to them and caused them to suspect that he was now defending Turati not so much out of principle but because he had come to fear the growth of the left wing in his party. Serrati's stubbornness also put the bolsheviks in a particularly awkward position; they had previously so glorified him as one of the very few reliable revolutionary leaders in the West that he enjoyed a tremendous popularity not only among the delegates to the Second Congress, who were now arriving, but also among the Russian masses.

These initial encounters convinced the bolsheviks of the need to launch an all-out attack on the Turatian wing, a measure they had so far resisted taking, and certainly one Niccolini had not pushed in late 1919 and early 1920. The bolshevik Central Committee entrusted Chiarini-Heller, who had been in Italy earlier in the year, with the job of collecting incriminating evidence on Italian reformism in order to prepare an unequivocal denunciation of it at the Second Congress.[83]

In Moscow the Italians were again festively greeted, with military honors and speeches by leading bolsheviks. In the following days they were taken to see the principal sights of the city, and they met with various delegations of Russian workers and foreign socialists. In the evenings they had long talks with Kamenev, Chicherin, Bukharin, Rakovsky and other prominent figures about the nature of the Soviet regime and the many difficulties it faced.[84] Zinoviev continued to work on the delegates and was able gradually to con-

vince Bombacci and Graziadei to dissociate themselves from Serrati's stubborn opposition to excluding the right wing. In other
words, members of both the right and left wings of Serrati's Maximalists now moved away from him under pressure from the bolsheviks.

After extensive tours of Moscow and the surrounding areas, the
Italians on June 26 finally were taken inside the Kremlin walls to
meet Lenin. The interview with him was long and covered a wide
variety of subjects. Repeatedly the problem of Turati came up.
Lenin insisted that the PSI was wrong to permit the treacherous
right wing to remain in the party, and he declared himself stupe-
fied to read that Serrati, in an article in *Communismo*, referred
to Prampolini (a prominent right-wing figure) as "dear" ("*caro*").
Serrati's attempt to defend himself by emphasizing the deep regard
between left and right in the PSI obviously impressed Lenin very
unfavorably.[85]

If the other bolsheviks had impressed the Italians as strangely
"Russian," Lenin did so even more. With his lively, slightly Asiatic
eyes, his ironic, scrutinizing looks, his alternation of good-natured
bons mots and oddly smiling polemics, he gave a most disarming
and confusing impression.[86] When Lenin urged Serrati to expel
Turati and then, afterward, offer to cooperate with the reformists
for specific reforms, Serrati insisted that Russian and Italian manners and traditions were profoundly different; such a procedure,
while perhaps possible in Russia, was inconceivable in the Italian
national context.[87] In discussing the use of violence in the dictatorship of the proletariat, Vacirca insisted that it was necessary for a
revolutionary party to have a majority of the proletariat behind it
before attempting a violent seizure of power and the establishment
of a dictatorship. Lenin termed this a "democratic prejudice" and
insisted that it was necessary to exercise dictatorial methods over
the more "backward" parts of the proletariat as well as over the rest
of the population; what was far more important than a formal majority was to have control of the army.[88] (This was an interestingly
different emphasis from the one Lenin had made in his letter to
Serrati after the Bologna congress—when he talked about the need

for mass support and the danger of a premature revolution—but no one seems to have pointed out the discrepancy.) Vacirca retorted that for one part of the proletariat to assert that the other part was more backward—and especially to thus justify acts of violence by a minority of the proletariat—would mean to turn the proletariat against itself. Lenin only shrugged, as if to say that there was no other way.[89]

A few days afterward the Italians joined a large number of other foreign visitors, including Cachin and Frossard, for a leisurely journey down the Volga. But between this time and the time of their arrival, the French delegates had been through some rather peculiar experiences.

After their painfully slow journey from Petrograd, Cachin and Frossard arrived in Moscow on June 15. They found the train station ornately decorated—red flags, decorated pine branches, emblems everywhere—but all for the benefit of the Italian delegation, which had arrived some time before. "For us," Frossard bitterly observed, "naturally, no one. All right: we got the message." [90] Again the two delegates were given no indication of where to go or what to do. Fortunately, this time their Bulgarian acquaintance helped them, though not without considerable confusion, to find a hotel.

Since they had not been able to contact any Comintern officials, Cachin and Frossard wandered about Moscow on their own, encountering, to their dismay, closed shops, empty and dirty display windows, filthy streets, and a black market tolerated everywhere.[91] After a full day of being ignored Frossard began to grow angry and was ready to go back home.[92] His frame of mind was not improved by the supper offered them at their hotel; the food of revolution and blockade was more than his French palate could bear. After a few bites he returned to his room to consume a can of sardines brought along for such an emergency. Cachin was also upset, but he kept repeating that there must be some kind of mistake, that this failure to encounter any Comintern officials was due only to the great disorder in Russia at the time.[93]

Although Frossard mentions nothing about it in his memoirs, in frustration he apparently sent back to France a telegram stating that he and Cachin had been able to finish their business in Russia much sooner than they had planned and thus would be back in Paris by July 1.[94] It seems entirely possible that Frossard's telegram was intercepted by the Comintern leaders, and that they then decided that their game had lasted long enough. It is equally possible that Frossard intended that they would get wind of it, and that he sent it less out of disgust or discouragement than in the hope of forcing the bolsheviks to knuckle down to business.

This explanation seems plausible because on the evening of the fifteenth, the day Frossard presumably sent off the telegram, the quarantine of the French delegation ended. At about 10:00 P.M. Jacques Sadoul, his wife, and Taratouta (Kemerer)—the latter a Russian whom both Cachin and Frossard had known earlier in France, when he worked with the Committee for Comintern—suddenly appeared at the hotel, welcoming the two Frenchmen with open arms and assuring them that their neglect had been a terrible mistake, since their arrival was earlier than expected. They added, "Lenin is terribly sorry."[95]

Frossard was little impressed by this sudden and effusive welcome. He still felt that the entire interlude had been staged in order to make him and Cachin feel vividly the difference between "real communists" and "vulgar social democrats." But, as he dryly put it, "since they still want something from us, they are careful not to let their little joke last too long."[96]

Now all doors opened to the French delegates, and they enjoyed a very short period of easy and friendly relations. This transition from the cold of being totally ignored to the effusive warmth manifested by Sadoul and Taratouta, who now escorted them around Moscow and arranged for their transfer into the more comfortable hotel where other delegates were staying, was a first sampling in Russia of the "cold-hot" treatment they were to experience in the coming weeks. Frossard described this initial transition as one from "purgatory to paradise" and described the hurried efforts of Sadoul to "inform" them on doctrinal matters as a desire to "put us in a state of grace before we were called to appear before the most redoubtable of tribunals—the Executive Committee of the Communist International."[97]

Frossard's remaining suspicions about the warm welcome they had finally received were certainly justified, for the Comintern leaders were about to turn on the cold again. The next day, June 16, before the ECCI was ready to meet them, the two delegates were taken to a meeting of the Executive Council of the All-Russian Council of Soviets, which had assembled in order to welcome the delegates to the Second Congress of the Communist International. The meeting took place in the Moscow Theater and was attended by 3,000 to 4,000 very enthusiastic and attentive Muscovites. During the meeting Cachin was pushed to the stage and asked to address the crowd. This was his element, and, caught up in the enthusiasm of his audience, he addressed them "with great pathos and rhetorical skill."[98] He begged forgiveness for the crimes of the French bourgeoisie and for the inadequacies of the French working class, which was still too weak to help the Russians by making revolution in France.

As soon as Cachin had finished, Kamenev and then Bukharin stepped to the stage to deliver blistering attacks on the SFIO, on Cachin's speech, and on Cachin personally. Kamenev said that it was not necessary to ask forgiveness for such comrades as Loriot and Monatte, who were at the time in jail for their struggle on behalf of communism in France; pardon need only be asked for those leaders of the working class who were misleading it—and who had indirectly caused the death and starvation of hundreds of thousands of Russian workers, women, and children by their cowardly, nonrevolutionary work. Bukharin called the attention of his audience to Cachin's last visit to Russia, in 1917, as part of a French delegation when he had tried to rouse the Russian workers against the "*boches*" and had branded the bolsheviks as "German spies."

These speeches were a severe jolt to Cachin. The audience repeatedly interrupted Bukharin and Kamenev with approving applause and shouts.[99] Cachin, for whom the bravos of the crowd were like a woman's caress, and who had argued against Frossard's suspicions that an agreement with the bolsheviks would not be reached easily, finally could take it no longer and burst into tears.[100] (The incident caused Rosmer to remark to a Russian friend, "Oh, he cries easily; in 1918 he cried at Strasbourg, in front of Poincaré, celebrating the return of Alsace to France.")[101]

The next day Cachin and Frossard met informally with the semiofficial "French Group" in Moscow, composed of Henri Guilbeaux, Inessa Armand, Pierre Pascal, a few French prisoners of war, and a number of others. The meeting was presided over, significantly, not by any of the French, but by a Russian, Zalkind, who, it was explained, was married to a Frenchwoman. Cachin and Frossard were not particularly happy about meeting this group, partly because Sadoul, in whom they seemed to have found a real friend, was "in difficulty" with it. As they feared, the meeting turned into an unpleasant scene, much as had the meeting the day before in the Moscow Theater. Guilbeaux delivered a violent attack on them and on nearly every other prominent figure in the SFIO.[102] Cachin became extremely irritated and defensive, and shouted, "I am just as good an internationalist as you, but I am also a good Frenchman!"[103] The meeting came to a close as Cachin and Frossard, red with anger, left abruptly, vowing that the "French Group" would never see *them* again.[104]

Cachin and Frossard before "the most redoubtable of tribunals"

On the nineteenth of June, after a few short preliminary encounters with Comintern officials, the French delegation met with the ECCI to discuss the question of the SFIO's relationship to the Comintern. Normally the ECCI met in the building of the old German embassy, but on the nineteenth it met in the Kremlin so that Lenin could easily attend. On arriving at the meeting, Cachin and Frossard noted a much larger attendance than the day before in the embassy, when they had been allowed to sit in on a session. Frossard concluded that the numerous spectators had been "lured by these choice morsels: two victims prepared for sacrifice—and handed over defenseless to the claws of Lenin."[105]

Cachin addressed the ECCI first, reading from a prepared speech and obviously trying to counter some of the accusations which he knew from experience were forthcoming. This time he did not beg forgiveness for the failings of the French but rather stressed the "constant and energetic protests" that the French had made against intervention in Russia. He elaborated in detail all that the SFIO had done—meetings, demonstrations, the whole November electoral campaign—and summed up by insisting that "all that could have been done in this respect has been done." He especially emphasized the power of the bourgeoisie in France: "On the 16th of November the bloc of capitalist parties defeated French socialism in the political arena just as it has more recently defeated French syndicalism. . . . Now our bourgeoisie is all-powerful."[106]

After Cachin, Frossard read a rehash of the party mandate he had earlier composed, although this time he deleted the derogatory reference to the ultra-left in France. No doubt he had concluded that such remarks were not likely to please the bolsheviks, who had made several favorable references to the anarchic left. Frossard also formally requested to be admitted, along with the USPD delegation, to the sessions of the Second Congress.

The members of the ECCI followed with a series of probing questions dealing with such matters as the exclusion of the right wing of the SFIO, *noyautage* in the *syndicats*, the relationship of the communist left and the center in the SFIO, and the reconstructionist movement. A stenographic record of the answers Cachin and Frossard gave to these questions unfortunately is not available. Frossard merely remarked in his later report to the party leadership that "we answered with whatever facts we could"—except in the case of the questions of Bukharin (which dealt with the SFIO's "treasonous attitude" during the war and with some incidents from Cachin's past). The delegates refused to answer these out of consideration "for the dignity of our party. . . ."[107]

But these initial exchanges, as Frossard later wrote, were only the *"hors d'oeuvres"* everyone in the audience was anxiously awaiting the *"plat de résistance"*—Lenin's interrogation of the French delegates. They were not disappointed. Lenin trenchantly informed Cachin and Frossard that their viewpoints were not those of the Communist International. There was no "fundamental agreement" between the SFIO and the Comintern; there were "profound differ-

ences." The SFIO did not understand the dictatorship of the proletariat or the role of a communist party in it. Lenin insisted, as he
would a week later when meeting with the Italians, that the most
advanced section of the working class, formed into a disciplined
party, must become the state itself, imposing a firm dictatorship not
only on the bourgeoisie but also on the less advanced ranks of the
proletariat. He concluded, "The reformists in Russia either bend
to our will, or leave, or we prevent them from bothering us!"[108]

Lenin made it clear that he rejected Frossard's formula of "full
agreement" between party and *syndicats* in France. The proper
course for the French should be the same as for the Russians in 1917.
Communist cells should be built within the CGT in order to expose and discredit its leaders and to bring the rank and file around
to the communist leadership.

Yet in spite of this gruff tone, Lenin did not seem intent on
chasing Cachin and Frossard back to France. He thanked them for
coming to Moscow and complimented them on the honesty of their
speeches. He then launched into a tirade against the USPD, which
had continued to postpone its departure and whose leaders had recently explained that the Communist International's pronouncements were not published in the USPD press because of the chronic
"paper shortage" in Germany.

Lenin assured the SFIO delegation that he did not expect the
French to foment revolution in the immediate future; but revolution must at least be prepared by the party; and this was not being
done. Most certainly there was no evidence of it in the party press.
Even the Committee for the Comintern was only "sometimes" properly engaged in this revolutionary preparation. If one objected
that the bolsheviks themselves had not made such preparations
before 1917 in Russia, then it should be recognized, he insisted,
that conditions had changed. And one should learn from the Russians' mistakes.

Lenin also seemed conciliatory when dealing with the question
of exclusions. He affirmed that they were not important, at least not
"in a personal sense." What was essential was to purge the party of
the *ideas* represented by certain members of the party and to make
the guiding principles of the party clear and straightforward. Fi-

nally, Lenin suggested that what he personally had to say on these questions was not the last word. The Second Congress, when it convened, would prepare a "detailed reply" to the points brought up by the SFIO delegation. The SFIO could then make its decision about joining the Comintern. (This reply was handed to the French about a month later, during the deliberations of the Second Congress. As will be seen, it nearly provoked a complete breakdown in negotiations.)

Although Lenin's conciliatory tone was unmistakable, Frossard was still inclined to return immediately to France. Cachin, however, wanted to stay, and thus things remained up in the air for a few days, during which time the two delegates were shown around Moscow, in the company of the Italian delegation, passing an affable and leisurely Sunday (the twentieth) at the home of Steklov, the editor of *Izvestia*.[109]

At approximately this time, the two were given stronger and more explicit assurance of the bolsheviks' desire to prolong negotiations. Kamenev visited them with the news that Lenin wanted them to stay for the Second Congress. He added reassuringly, "Lenin wants an agreement with you."[110] Then a veritable parade of Comintern representatives—Radek, Sadoul, Deslinières, Bukharin, and members of the Italian delegation—passed through Cachin's and Frossard's hotel room with the same message. Sadoul stressed the importance of staying longer in Russia to reach a better understanding of bolshevik ways, and affirmed, "Lenin has confidence in you." Bukharin, who had earlier attacked Cachin so strongly, now apologized for his outbursts. He virtually implored them to stay, talking with them into the early hours of the morning. He stressed how important it was that the Second Congress become a truly international affair and assured them that the Comintern would not require the SFIO to split or expect it to start a revolution immediately. He explored with them the possibility of a future "proletarian blockade" in response to a bourgeois blockade of Russia, and he stressed the intimate interrelationship of any future German and French revolutions.[111]

Frossard at first resisted these entreaties. But after a while he had to admit "it is clear that they want the affiliation of the French party, that they attach the most extreme importance to it, that they consider it of capital importance for the future of the International." [112] And in the light of repeated assurances of Lenin's desire to come to an agreement with them, Bukharin's apologies, and the actual concessions mentioned (no exclusions, no split in the party, no immediate revolution), Cachin and Frossard could easily conclude that the bolsheviks somehow *had* come around to a more reasonable attitude than at first had seemed the case. So, on Sunday, June 27, they made the decision to stay and sent off a telegram to France for permission to do so. The SFIO's *Conseil national*, which had assembled just before their telegram arrived, granted them the permission.

These first weeks in Soviet Russia had a powerful emotional impact on Cachin and Frossard. In spite of the crude and humiliating manner in which they were first received, both seemed deeply impressed with the Russian people's immense struggle against all odds to preserve its revolution. Cachin was predictably more swept up in the emotions of this drama, but Frossard did not exclude himself when he wrote that

the Russian Revolution overcomes us with a new atmosphere, it accustoms and forces us—almost against our will—to feel, understand, think [in new ways]. . . . It encloses us, tightens around us, conquers us, penetrates us, uproots us. . . . Outside of it nothing counts, nothing is worth the trouble. The necessities of the Revolution are the supreme law. [113]

After their return to France, Cachin and Frossard sought to give the impression that they had "seen the light" in Russia, had renounced their pasts, and had decided to work for a different and purer socialism. This was certainly an exaggerated picture, especially in Frossard's case. Yet it would be difficult to believe that his emotions as a socialist were not engaged at all during his stay in Russia, even if his material position, his future as a leader of socialism in France, was protected by coming around to a new point of view.

The shift in the attitude of the bolsheviks in dealing with Cachin and Frossard can best be explained in terms of a calculated "hot-cold" treatment, rather than by any genuine change of mind about the French party. On their arrival and in the first meeting with the Executive Council of the Soviet Congress and the ECCI, the SFIO delegates had been made to feel sharply the humiliation of being "dangerous confusionists"; now the bolsheviks set out to demonstrate to them how sweet existence could be when one entered the land of bolshevik favor. This rapid switch from cold to hot not only confused the delegates about the real attitude of the bolsheviks but also made them—especially Cachin—anxious to avoid further humiliation by showing a "positive attitude," a readiness to make concessions.

On June 29 Cachin read before the ECCI the answers he and Frossard had composed to the questions asked them on the nineteenth.[114] Even aside from its emphatic avoidance of references to personalities, this answer was not a point by point consideration of the ECCI questions. It was rather a general statement of Cachin's and Frossard's evolution in favor of communism. Compared to Cachin's speech on the nineteenth it took a more conciliatory and self-deprecating position, conceding more than before to the bolshevik point of view and going distinctly beyond the general statement of SFIO principles voted in the April 1919 party program.

Cachin began by asserting that the SFIO could no longer be called a reformist party, since the majority of the party had explicitly rejected reformism two years before and now recognized the need for the dictatorship of the proletariat. (This was stretching things a bit, since the new party program had been adopted in April 1919, closer to one year before, not two. The new program referred to the dictatorship of the proletariat only as the "probable" form of the revolution. The Strasbourg congress had made a slightly stronger statement.)[115] Further, Cachin accepted as necessary that a revolutionary initiative by a professional elite need not wait until the majority of the population was behind it, since the proletarian mass under capitalism was "poisoned" by bourgeois control both of the state and of all means of communication within it. Thus he recognized that the play of parliamentary votes under capitalism could have no real significance. Finally, Cachin accepted the point that such an elite would initially have to resort to force and terror to attain and implement its power. (Cachin here flatly contradicted the April party program, which stressed that "all means"—parliament included—were acceptable to forward the revolution, but that revolution could come only when the objective conditions were ripe and the proletariat educated to its task of political power.)

Instead of stressing, as he had on June 19, the SFIO's many actions in support of the Russian Revolution, Cachin admitted "the insufficiencies and weaknesses of our past action" and recognized that the Russians had a perfect right to criticize the SFIO's lack of vigor in helping beleaguered Soviet Russia. He promised that hereafter his party would go beyond words to the "acts of bravery" so conspicuously lacking before. He vowed that he would return to France to prepare the French proletariat, on the political *and* syndicalist level, to imitate the methods that had allowed the bolsheviks to seize and to retain political power. Further, he would join hands with the Committee for the Comintern to assure that the SFIO would join the Communist International "as a whole."

The bolsheviks were obviously pleased with this declaration, especially with its penitent tone, its promises to change, to adopt bolshevik ways, and to work for the affliation of the SFIO with the Comintern. On the part of the two delegates the declaration was offered as a major concession, one which can be understood only in light of the conversations they had had in the past few days with Sadoul, Taratouta, Bukharin, and others. The French felt that they were being offered most of the *apaisements sérieux*, or real concessions, mentioned in their mandate; in order to clinch the negotiations they themselves offered important concessions as well. It is interesting that shortly afterwards *Izvestia* reported, "Comrades Cachin and Frossard, the official representatives of the French Socialist party, are on their way between complete social-patriotism and the camp of the proletarian revolution; the future will tell how far they progress." [116]

Voyage down the Volga

The day after their final declaration to the ECCI Cachin and Frossard joined a large company of bolshevik dignitaries and other foreign delegates, including the Italians, for a long and festive voyage down the Volga, with stops at Nizhni Novgorod, Kazan, Samara, Saratov, and the factories of Tula. This voyage gave the French a greater sense of "belonging" and permitted them to fulfill in a more complete way the second part of their mandate: to investigate the social and economic condition in Russia.

The Volga itinerary was a standard "prepared" tour for foreign visitors to Russia and was undoubtedly designed to mask some of the most unpleasant or damning aspects of bolshevik rule.[117] Still, both the Italian and the French delegates saw much that did not redound to the glory of the bolsheviks. Colombino was touched by the tired, hungry, and resigned faces he saw in the factories and countryside. At Tula, one of the most concentrated industrial areas of Russia, the foreign delegates of the Volga tour were very coldly received. According to Colombino, most workers in this area were menshevik, and they were still deeply resentful of the massive arrests carried out by the bolshevik regime after a recent strike.[118]

The Italians apparently obtained much hostile information from menshevik sources, but the French refused to meet with the mensheviks or any other opponents of the regime,[119] obviously for fear of ruining the progress of their negotiations. Still, Frossard wrote that "we . . . did not close our eyes or our ears"; and the French managed to hear a good deal about the vast emerging bureaucracy of the Bolshevik party, the inefficiency and cruelty of the Soviet regime, the opposition of the peasantry to the requisitions imposed on them, and the generally stifling despotism everywhere.[120]

The right wing of the Italian delegation did not hesitate to seek out conversations with the mensheviks and socialist-revolutionaries. Apparently Serrati met with them also. Significantly, those members of the Italian delegation who had already reached an agreement with the bolsheviks about excluding the right wing did not even go with the rest of the delegates on the Volga tour. Bombacci and Graziadei stayed in Moscow and continued the conversations they earlier had held with Zinoviev. By the time of the Second Congress they were well prepared for the attack the bolsheviks had worked out for Serrati.[121]

The late arrival of the USPD delegation

The USPD delegates reached Petrograd about a month and a half after the French and Italians, on July 18, just in time for the festive opening day of the Second Congress on the nineteenth. Thus the bolsheviks did not have a chance to manipulate and pressure the USPD delegation, as they had done so effectively with Cachin and Frossard. Immediately upon their arrival, the Germans turned over to the ECCI their party's strongly worded reply to the Comintern's letter of February 5 and then joined the other delegates and members of the Petrograd Soviet in the Tauride Palace for the speeches of the first day. After sharing in the festive gaiety of the first day in Petrograd they accompanied the other delegates in the special train to Moscow, where the congress was to continue its deliberations.[122] However, once in Moscow, difficulties began for the USPD delegates, too. On July 21 the four delegates met privately to map out the tactical positions to be taken in the forthcoming negotiations. But at the very start Stoecker, with Däumig's support, refused to participate. He wanted nothing to do with negotiations, he said, since he had always favored immediate and unconditional affiliation to the Comintern. Thus he would leave the negotiations up to Crispien and Dittmann.[123] This attitude surprised and irritated the latter two, who reminded their colleagues that the delegation had been selected to represent the party as a whole and should thus work together. They pointed out that Däumig and Stoecker had signed their party's answer to the Comintern's letter of February 5 and that this answer clearly indicated numerous differences of opinion with the bolsheviks which would have to be ironed out in negotiation. But the two left-wing delegates still refused to participate. Crispien and Dittmann were therefore obliged to take upon themselves most of the negotiating.

It appears that Stoecker and Däumig had already initiated a series of separate, semisecret talks with various Comintern representatives, talks that were probably a cause for their sudden reluctance to assume an active part in negotiations. Moreover, the four delegates had travelled from Stettin to Petrograd in the company of

Paul Levi, with whom they all had what Dittmann termed "congenial" conversations. Possibly Levi had already prepared the way for the semisecret talks that began when the delegates arrived in Russia.[124]

On the afternoon of the same day, July 21, the Germans arranged a meeting with Cachin and Frossard in order to exchange views and discuss the possibility of assuming complementary tactical positions, since they had failed to do so in Berlin. But the French, who now seemed reticent to talk with them, revealed that they had completed negotiations and had decided to join the Third International. Therefore they were not interested in making any common tactical argreements.[125]

This was surprising news, but in one sense it encouraged Crispien and Dittmann, for it was plain to them that the SFIO delegates, who now seemed in the good graces of the Russian leaders, were anything but doctrinaire bolsheviks. Cachin, especially, did not talk like a "revolutionary firebrand" (revolutionäre Himmelsstürmer),[126] and when Frossard described the course of their negotiations (at this time apparently successful), there seemed no reason why the USPD could not come to a similar agreement with the Comintern. In fact, the conditions that the French had described as essential to their joining the new international—autonomy for their party in its internal affairs, no forced exclusions, no change in the party name—were largely the same that the USPD delegates sought. Yet, on reflection, Crispien and Dittmann could not help observing that "those French comrades took things more lightly than we." [127]

Däumig and Stoecker were particularly encouraged by the information given them by the French and now felt justified in their earlier contention that Moscow would not be overly dogmatic. The two right-wing delegates could not deny that the French had been accepted and that the bolsheviks had compromised on a number of issues. At least so it seemed. The USPD delegates had of course no way of knowing that the French were basking in a deceptive and short-lived period of favor, soon to end.

Further comforting to the Germans were the conversations they had with Serrati and Graziadei, who were very friendly to them and who seemed to share most of their political positions. Indeed, Serrati defended the USPD later against the attacks of the bolsheviks.[128] The PSI's honored position among the foreign delegations seemed strong evidence that the USPD could also be accepted.

The German delegates thus went to their first meeting with the ECCI, in the evening of the same day, with genuine optimism. This optimism was rudely crushed. Wijnkoop, the representative of the Dutch "Tribunists" (who had earlier protested when the ECCI agreed to receive Cachin and Frossard), was vehement in his denunciation of the USPD delegates; all four of them, he loudly announced, were corrupt agents of the bourgeoisie and should be immediately ejected from the room. Henri Guilbeaux took a similarly dark view of the USPD, which he considered a diffuse party of reformists and pacifists, hardly acceptable to a revolutionary organization like the Communist International.

This unexpected reception stunned Däumig. Flushed with anger he stamped to the speakers' stand and vigorously defended his party, in spite of his earlier assertion that Dittmann and Crispien must carry on the burden of negotiation. Wijnkoop hooted insults back at him. Finally Zinoviev intervened to express his opinion that only the right wing of the USPD need be attacked; the party still had the support of millions of revolutionary workers, and these workers must be won over to communism.[129] Paul Levi added his support to Zinoviev's words, and both he and Zinoviev heaped ridicule on Wijnkoop. A majority of the ECCI supported Levi and Zinoviev, voting to invite the USPD delegation to attend both its sessions and the sessions of the Second Congress.[130]

Crispien's formal declaration to the ECCI in many ways resembled that earlier given by Cachin. He described the development of the USPD since its inception and defended its revolutionary record. Since he and his fellow delegates had already handed over their party's answer to the ECCI's letter of February 5, he ended his declaration by suggesting that the latter formulate questions that could serve as the basis of discussion and negotiation.[131]

The ECCI had actually already formulated such a set of questions,[132] certain of which merely reiterated material already contained in the February 5 letter (such as the refusal by the RdV to accept Russian grain). Certain others were clearly designed to increase tension among the four delegates. The first question by Radek, for example, asked whether the entire delegation agreed with the USPD's answer to the ECCI's letter. Levi asked exactly what were the "conditions and concessions" mentioned by Crispien in Switzerland when he met with the French and Swiss; also, did all the delegates agree with Crispien? Certain other questions were designed to attack the "errors" that even the left of the USPD had fallen prey to: what was the meaning of the distinction Stoecker had earlier made between "force" and "terror"? Why did he refuse to proclaim openly the inevitability of civil war in revolution? Finally, the delegates were asked to explain their position on the question of party centralization and exclusions (particularly of Kautsky and Hilferding).

At first the ECCI intended that the delegates answer the questions immediately, but then it was decided, ostensibly because of the late hour—but also, probably, to allow relations within the delegation to fester for a while—that they could be answered at a later session of the ECCI.[133] As it finally turned out, the delegates were asked to read their answers to the full Comintern congress on July 29.

After the meeting with the ECCI, around midnight, Crispien and Dittmann were called in for a personal interview with Lenin. Why only these two were summoned was not explained, but again one can surmise that the purpose was to get Däumig and Stoecker alone for an informal discussion of the questions asked them. The interview with Lenin was abrasive. Dittmann expressed astonishment at the Russian leader's "ignorance" concerning the provisions of the Versailles treaty and at his "wild notions" (*phantastische Vorstellungen*) about the number of troops in the occupied zone[134] —all of which was further evidence for Dittmann of the Russians' isolation from events in the West. Dittmann testily remarked that if the USPD had done in Germany the kinds of things that the bolsheviks had done in Russia, Lenin would certainly have condemned the leaders of the USPD as the "greatest imaginable of opportunists." Even now, much of the bolshevik criticism of the USPD reminded one of the dreary and petty-minded creations of a clique of literati.[135] Dittmann later affirmed that he said these things "with a smile," but he could tell the Russian leader was stung. He surmised that this midnight encounter convinced Lenin, if he had had any doubts before, that it would be necessary to purge the two right-wing delegates before the USPD could be permitted in the Comintern.[136]

The next day, July 22, the four delegates again met in private to consider the questions asked them by the ECCI. They reached agreement on a number of points but not on Radek's first question. Stoecker insisted that, no matter what may have seemed the case previously, he and Däumig were not in agreement with their party's reply. Crispien angrily insisted that in Berlin Stoecker had gone over the reply "pencil in hand," point by point, making adjustments and comments; surely now he could not say that he did not bear full responsibility for it. But that was precisely what both Stoecker and Däumig *did* say.[137]

With this impasse, the effort to work out a commonly acceptable reply to the ECCI's questions was temporarily dropped. The opening sessions of the congress in Moscow were beginning, and these sessions provided the USPD delegates with new hopes for an eventual accomodation with the Comintern.

The Second Congress of the Communist International

Although preparations for the Second Congress of the Communist International had been hurried and inadequate compared to the meetings of the prewar Socialist International, the Second Congress was a considerably more impressive affair than the First Congress had been. Statutes carefully laying down the organizational structure of the Comintern and lengthy theses on a wide range of subjects were drawn up for the approval of the some 200 delegates from thirty-four different countries, most of whom had legitimate mandates from significant parties or groups. The Second Congress thus made possible a full exchange of views among world revolutionaries and put a final, official stamp of precision on such previously confused issues as the proper organization of a communist party, the role of the soviets, the nature of proletarian dictatorship, the relationship of communists to parliament and trade unions and the role of communist parties in the struggle for liberation in the colonies.

As at the First Congress the bolsheviks exercised complete hegemony over the proceedings. Nearly all of the documents drawn up for the approval of the congress were composed by the bolsheviks, and leading bolsheviks presented the main speeches at the sessions of the congress. As at the First Congress most of the delegates with full voting powers were handpicked by the bolsheviks. The new statutes made *de jure* the extensive *de facto* powers of the ECCI, the Presidium of which had a bolshevik majority. Less tangibly the Russians exercised an enormous psychological superiority over the other delegates; as leaders of the first victorious social revolution in history, Lenin, Trotsky, and Zinoviev had immeasurably greater prestige than any other delegate.

Still, there was not at this congress the robotlike approval of all bolshevik proposals and the monotonous unanimity that would characterize later meetings of the Comintern. The delegates to the Second Congress were a very heterogeneous conglomeration of anarchists, syndicalists, ultra-left Marxists, centrists, as well as unquestioning admirers of the bolsheviks. Many of the delegates did not hesitate to criticize the bolsheviks, and at times the exchanges on the congress floor were harsh and acrimonious.

As all observers testify, the general mood of the congress, in spite of the many defeats of revolution outside Russia, was optimistic and even euphoric. No doubt a good part of this was due to the natural good spirits of revolutionaries meeting for the first real international gathering organized by a victorious revolutionary regime. But the excitement of the congress was intensified by the advance of the Red Army into Poland. On a wall of the congress was a great map with markers, changed each day, showing the approach of the Soviet forces toward Warsaw.

Much of the real work of the congress went on in the committees set up to discuss and revise the text of the theses drawn up by the bolshevik leaders. One of the most important of these committees was the one charged with considering a draft, drawn up by Lenin, of the conditions for admission into the new international. In the meetings of this committee the bolsheviks continued their game of bluff and parry with the SFIO delegates, their efforts to divide the USPD delegation, and their pressure on Serrati to yield on the question of his party's right wing.

The opening days of the Second Congress

The ceremonial first day of the Second Congress, on July 19 in Petrograd, was obviously intended to buoy up the Petrograd population as much as to inaugurate the proceedings themselves. Music, flowers, banners, children's demonstrations, and overwhelming masses of marching workers came out to greet the foreign delegates. The bolsheviks' genius for pageantry, already well developed, was put to impressive use. In the evening fireworks punctuated an improvised satiric review with hundreds of actors, in which the social patriots were held up for searing ridicule. The tribulations of world socialism were finally ended by the arrival of Lenin.[1] To the ironic amusement of bystanders, Cachin joined in the applause of the crowd while the patriotic socialists were being vilified.[2]

Most of the speeches of the first session of the congress, held in conjunction with the Petrograd Soviet, were grandiloquent "greetings" to the workers of Petrograd, to the Red Army and Navy, and to the workers of the world, read by leading western members of the congress' Presidium—Serrati, Rosmer, and Levi. Lenin's speech, in Russian for the benefit of his Petrograd audience,[3] received over ten minutes of applause, and only Zinoviev's urgings finally quieted the audience.[4] The speech sought to make clear the new emphases of the Second Congress and to complement the arguments in Lenin's "Basic Tasks of the Communist International" and his *Left-Wing Communism, an Infantile Disorder*, copies of which had been handed out to every delegate at the congress. He thus spoke with greater circumspection than he had at the First Congress concerning the prospects of an immediate or inevitable capitalist collapse in the West, using John Maynard Keynes as his text; and he paternally chided the ultra-left for its "childish" errors.

Zinoviev also spoke on the same day; both he and Lenin obviously made a conscious effort not to attack the ultra-left as much as the center. Lenin warned, "opportunism is our main enemy."[5] Zinoviev expressed sympathy for what he termed the "honest revolutionary elements of syndicalism, anarchism, industrialism, and the Shop Stewards"[6] represented in the hall; but he was scornful of the "old bourgeois parties" that were now approaching the Comintern. He vowed that no "fundamental compromise" would be permitted in their case, although the Comintern was interested in establishing a "communist union" (*kommunistische Bund*) with the "honest revolutionary workers" within the old bourgeois parties.[7]

Yet these speeches were only one side of the coin, for in the following sessions, which were transferred to Moscow, Zinoviev, Radek, and Levi spoke quite favorably of negotiating with the leaders of the USPD and SFIO. They continued to heap ridicule on Wijnkoop, the ultra-left Dutch communist, who vociferously opposed these negotiations.[8] Radek conceded that he himself had doubts about the centrist delegates, but he asserted that the Comintern should not approach them with the inquisitional attitude of "what have the accused to say in their defense?" but should listen to them open-mindedly and give them a fair chance to explain their positions.

The sessions in Moscow, beginning July 23, were more business-like than the first day in Petrograd had been. Now each national group was assigned a table to work on; this put Cachin and Frossard side by side with Rosmer, Guilbeaux, and several other ultra-left figures. The USPD delegates and the KPD delegation were seated at the same table. James Murphy, a delegate from England, could not help noticing Frossard's discomfort in this situation: "He certainly looked out of place in this camp of revolutionaries, very uncomfortable and worried."[9] All the other delegations were dwarfed by the enormous Russian delegation, seventy-two in all, five with deliberative and sixty-five with consultative voice.

Since one of the most significant areas of misunderstanding among revolutionaries in the West about the bolshevik regime concerned the relationship of the Bolshevik party to the soviets, it was appropriate that the first set of theses taken up for discussion by the congress were those composed by Zinoviev "On the Role of the Communist Party in the Proletarian Revolution." These theses carefully explained the bolshevik conception of the "leading" role of the party (as the representative of the rational elite of the working class) and "democratic centralism" (in which lower echelons of the party elect upper echelons but then must accept unquestioning obedience). They further emphasized the need to establish communist cells in all important institutions of society and the impossibility of gaining majorities in favor of communism, even in the working class, until *after* the revolution.

In his speech defending his theses Zinoviev attacked the various revolutionary tendencies, such as those of the I.W.W. and the English Shop Stewards, which denied the necessity of a party and assumed instead that trade unions or soviets could lead the revolu-

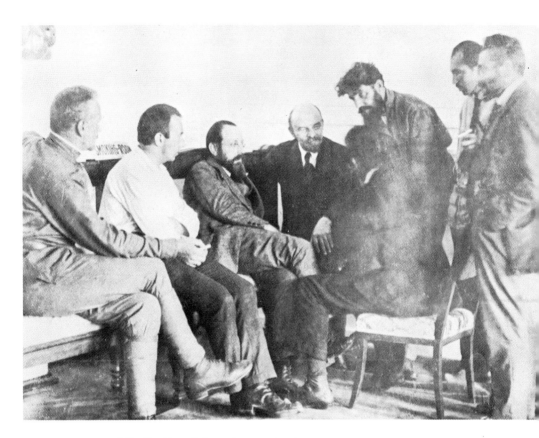

The Italian delegation to the Second Congress of the
Comintern in conversation with Lenin. Serrati is seated on
Lenin's right, Bombacci is standing on his left.

Crispien and Dittmann at the time of the congress of Leipzig.

Lenin addressing the Petrograd masses on the opening day
of the Second Congress of the Comintern.

Lenin marching with foreign delegates, at one of the ceremonial parades of the Second Congress. Beside Lenin is Paul Levi. On the extreme right is Lenin's wife, Krupskaya.

tion. He singled out the Dutchman Pannekoek, whom he criticized for making a "fetish" of the masses, and he especially ridiculed the idea that the general strike—a "negative measure"—would be sufficient to bring down a capitalist regime. It was necessary to be "positive" and to *seize* political power through armed insurrection.

As they made clear in the debates that followed Zinoviev's speech, the representatives of the Shop Stewards and the I.W.W. were not convinced.[10] Interestingly, however, neither Däumig nor Stoecker, both of whom had earlier argued in favor of a leading role of the *Räte*, had anything to say in opposition to Zinoviev's theses. The left USPD delegates, like the anarcho-syndicalist Rosmer and, later in the year, Gramsci, were among those who were gradually moving away from the democratic traditions of western socialism and syndicalism toward the elitist bolshevik concept of the revolutionary party.

Cachin and Frossard opt publicly for the Comintern

These opening days of the congress came at a time of growing uncertainty and confusion for Cachin and Frossard, feelings which were not diminished by Lenin's and Zinoviev's speeches at Petrograd. The French delegates had returned from their Volga journey thinking that after the ups and downs of their first weeks in Russia they had finally established firm foundations for fruitful negotiations with the Comintern and all that remained was to clear up a few details. The Russians, however, had not yet finished their "hot-cold" treatment. Once back in Moscow Frossard found that those who previously had been so cordial and conciliatory were suddenly cool and distant. Kemerer informed them that the Comintern really did not give much importance to their joining, and they were made to understand that Rosmer would serve adequately as the only representative of the Comintern for France.[11] Frossard began to sense that a "network of intrigues"[12] was spreading around them and that new, unacceptable conditions were being prepared. He and Cachin were falsely told that the SFIO *Conseil national* had just voted, by a very small majority, in favor of joining the Comintern. (This was an utterly transparent attempt to play on the centrist delegates' fear of the growing left wing in the SFIO; the *Conseil national* was composed of parliamentary deputies and party bureaucrats, largely members of the right wing of the party, who would not in any case have made such a decision before Cachin's and Frossard's return.) At the same time the two delegates' conciliatory declarations before the ECCI, in a summarized and exaggerated form, had been sent back to France without their knowledge.[13]

Thus Frossard was suspicious when Cachin proposed to him that they send a telegram back to the SFIO announcing they now favored joining the Communist International. He was not sure what the bolsheviks were brewing up, and this telegram (obviously proposed to Cachin by a bolshevik representative) seemed an imprudent public commitment. Yet Cachin insisted. He finally informed Frossard that if necessary he would send it under his name alone.[14]

It was clear that Cachin had become a confidant or at least a willing agent of the bolsheviks. Frossard now had to decide if he would go along or offer further resistance. The two delegates plunged into a long and extremely frank discussion of the probable effects of joining the new international: what could be expected from the bolsheviks and what might happen in France if the SFIO delegation returned without the backing of the Comintern. There was no question in their minds that the SFIO was unavoidably bound to split because of its wartime experiences and because of the continuing pressure from Moscow. But *where* the party would split—on its left or on its right—still appeared an open question. No doubt if they came back to France empty handed the split would occur on the left, leaving them, as leaders of the center, face to face with the old right-wing leaders of the SFIO. But if they could win the blessing of Moscow they could presumably return to France and lead the campaign for affiliation. This would permit them to pull the center of the old party into the new Communist party and to outmaneuver the left. Thus Frossard concluded, "we were resigned to split from our reformist right."[15]

With lists of party and parliamentary leaders in front of them,

Cachin and Frossard checked off one by one those who might be convinced to enter the new Communist party and those who would resist or be forced out. They concluded that they would lose half of the *parlementaires*, but they felt confident that centrists like Longuet, Faure, Pressemane, Mistral, Le Troquer, and Verfeuil would stay.[16] (Only the last two, in fact, did stay.) Frossard still lamented that "a crushing responsibility weighs on us—what if we are making a mistake?"[17] Yet he concluded that "there is no other course than to place ourselves at the head of a movement that is clearly irresistible. We will lose some parliamentary deputies—would it be better to lose the masses?"[18] He tried to cool his resentment over the Russians' aggressive and insulting behavior by reasoning that it was a result of their harsh experiences in civil war and revolution. Time would soften these "Homeric" manners. Yet Frossard, the cultivated Frenchman, could not help reflecting that "the sense of *mesure*, in words as in actions, is after all one of the means by which an advanced civilization expresses and affirms itself."[19]

It is easy to see in Frossard's calculations the play of narrow self-interest, the wheeling and dealing of the traditional SFIO politician. Yet, given the basic premise that the SFIO would unavoidably split, his decision was entirely rational in a broader sense. That is, a center-left coalition would assure a less damaging split than would a center-right coalition. It happened, at this juncture, that Cachin's and Frossard's self-interest coincided with what seemed the most rational measure to assure the greatest possible working-class unity in France.

Frossard finally consented to make his commitment more public and to send the telegram to France. In his diary he wrote that he had abandoned his last hesitation when he was shown an article in *L'Humanité* in which Renaudel gleefully announced the French delegation's "sudden return" from Russia. The right-wing leader sighed with relief that the "nightmare" of negotiating with the Comintern was over. Frossard pretended to be indignant over this article, but if in fact he had sent the telegram on June 16 (announcing that he and Cachin would be back in Berlin by July 1), then one cannot give much credence to his indignation.[20] He no doubt felt the need to *appear* indignant in order to stay in the good graces of the Comintern leaders.

Cachin and Frossard expected that this telegram would, like their earlier declaration before the ECCI, preserve good relationships with the bolsheviks. Yet the ambiguous speeches by Lenin, Zinoviev, and Radek in the first days of the congress were disturbing. On July 18 the official delegation to the Second Congress of the Committee for the Comintern arrived in Petrograd. The members of this delegation were obviously surprised and upset with the progress the centrist delegates had made in negotiation and no doubt complained to the Comintern leadership. Moreover, they seemed to be filling the Russians' ears with stories of the immediate approach of revolution in France—the opposite of what Cachin and Frossard had been saying.

The centrist delegates had become so apprehensive by July 24 that they arranged a special meeting with Zinoviev and Kamenev. They strongly reiterated that there was no revolutionary situation in France and that exclusions within the SFIO could not be permitted. They remarked that the bolsheviks were now being very badly informed by men who had utterly utopian perceptions of conditions in France. Zinoviev and Kamenev acted surprised at the French delegates' anxieties and assured them that the ECCI had no intention whatsoever of presenting them with a list of SFIO members to be excluded. Moreover, they clearly understood that revolution in France could not be expected in the near future. All that the ECCI asked was that the French adopt a new policy and forsake old ways. Thus reassured, Cachin and Frossard returned to their rooms.[21]

The SFIO and USPD delegates before the Committee on Conditions

Delegates of both the SFIO and USPD were invited to attend the meetings of the committee which was to draw up the conditions for joining the Comintern. The committee's first meeting, on July 25, seems to have been devoted to presentations by the USPD and SFIO delegates; it was graced by the presence of Trotsky, who had so far had little to do with the activities of the Second Congress. Perhaps Trotsky wished to check on the progress Zinoviev was making in negotiating with the centrist parties.

The conversation the day before with Zinoviev and Kamenev apparently had had a remarkable impact on the French delegates, although Trotsky's presence may also have played a role, for they made far-reaching concessions to the bolshevik point of view. Cachin announced to the committee that he and Frossard had been doing a great deal of thinking and reading during their stay in Russia. Now they saw more clearly the necessity of a radical break with their party's past. They recognized the justice of the criticisms made of the SFIO, and they professed general agreement, with a few minor qualifications, on all the theses drawn up by the bolsheviks. One of the most important of these qualifications concerned the problem of revolutionary and defeatist agitation in the army. Cachin, the former ardent patriot, rather feebly explained that such agitation would be difficult in France because most of the French army was in the Rhineland and thus inaccessible to French socialists. However, he recognized that the SFIO had not done enough in this respect, and he promised to spread antimilitary propaganda, if not directly inside the army at least in parliament, in the party press, and among young people who would later be going into the army. Cachin skirted the problem of illegal agitation, which the bolsheviks had so insisted upon in their theses.[22]

Cachin replied point by point to the question asked the SFIO in an article by Trotsky in *Izvestia*.[23] To the first question, dealing with the problem of national defense, he affirmed that he and Frossard now understood the necessity of putting class interests above national interests; they would vote against military credits "at this time," since France had become "so military and hateful."[24] Trotsky interrupted to express dissatisfaction with Cachin's answer. As far as he was concerned the French socialists' position on national defense was entirely unacceptable and was filled with equivocation and vagueness. The French, if they wanted to become members of the Comintern, must openly and clearly recognize that patriotism and nationalism are deceptions used by the bourgeoisie to divert the working class from revolution and class war. Trotsky termed

Longuet a "stubborn patriot" whose verbal distinctions between *patrie* and *nation* (the very ones made earlier by Jaurès) masked a bourgeois attitude and could not be accepted by the Communist International. Cachin, obviously intimidated by this lecture from the leader of the Red Army, meekly replied, "I agree."[25] Frossard held his tongue, although he would write two days later in his diary "we cannot give in concerning Longuet's exclusion, since we are convinced that our honor is at stake."[26]

Cachin was able to formulate more acceptable answers to Trotsky's second and third questions (regarding strict control over parliamentary deputies and agitation to liberate France's colonies); but he again hedged on the fourth, which asked his attitude toward party control over the *syndicats*. He emphasized the utter opposition of nearly all syndicalists, of both the right and the left, to political interference in their affairs. Frossard interrupted to observe that if men like Monatte and Rosmer (mentioned favorably in Trotsky's questions) accepted the theses of the Second Congress, then there would be no trouble in cooperating with them.[27]

Cachin promised that since he and Frossard had come to a "basic agreement" with the Comintern, they would return to France, resign all their party positions, and work for the direct affiliation of the SFIO to the new international. As for the ideas of the reconstructionists, he observed, "we do not have any intention to 'reconstruct.' The concept and the word are absurd."[28] He concluded by saying that he did not expect the leaders of the Comintern to believe him immediately. So far he and Frossard had only made promises, but once back in France they would translate those promises into deeds.

The French delegates thus assumed a very humble, even abject attitude at this meeting, and they were gently treated. In fact, as previously suggested, it may well have been their submissiveness that convinced the bolsheviks that these centrists might be useful. But the USPD delegation was more combative and was far more severely attacked. Zinoviev and Radek subjected the USPD delegates to a long recital of the many failings of their party—their "catalogue of sins" (*Sündenregister*), as Dittmann later put it—including the expulsion of the Soviet representative Joffe in late 1918, the refusal of Russian grain (both of these while the USPD shared power with the SPD), and the party's inadequately revolutionary response to the Kapp Putsch.[29] The USPD delegates replied in kind. Dittmann even dared to attack the bolsheviks' revolutionary accomplishments and repeated his earlier description of Lenin as "the greatest opportunist of them all." He asked why the bolsheviks, who had made so many compromises with their principles, could not be more sympathetic to the compromises the USPD had been forced to make. Crispien vigorously defended his party's actions during the Kapp Putsch, and he ironically compared the USPD's actions to the absurd and incompetent figure cut by the KPD during the crisis—to which Zinoviev surprisingly replied: "the KPD is a small party from which no political action can be expected and which has every reason to be excused."[30]

Dittmann was visibly irritated by the declaration Cachin had made; the French seemed to be making much larger concessions than they had indicated would be necessary just four days previously. Their attitude undermined the position of the USPD delegation in that the latter could no longer point to the "reasonable" conditions given the French and demand only as much for the USPD. Peevishly acknowledging the extent of the French concessions, he observed that "Germans" would not be so quick to make promises that might not be upheld; "when a German makes a promise, he keeps it."[31] Frenchmen apparently did not.

All of the USPD delegates were concerned about the attacks that had been made on individual members of their party, and all resisted the idea of obligatory exclusions. Although the left of the delegation normally remained quiet, on this point Däumig too spoke up. Crispien stressed the complete isolation of Kautsky, the principal target of the bolsheviks' ire, and insisted that it was wrong to equate Hilferding with Kautsky as the Comintern leaders tended to do. But again it was Dittmann who was most aggressive—"sehr oft maliziös," as he was later to admit.[32] He insisted that it would serve to useful purpose to exclude Kautsky, since he had no influence in the party and his books were not even read by its members. The "literary squabble" (Literatengezank) between Trotsky and Kautsky had become tiresome and was a waste of time.[33]

Frossard chuckled inwardly at this—Trotsky a *"littérateur"*! In his diary he described the scene that followed: "Trotsky, his arrogance stung, sprang up from his seat in outrage. Tightening his lips in an ugly, contemptuous sneer and speaking in a hiss," he indignantly declared that the proof of Kautsky's influence in the USPD was in Dittmann's own words, which were infused with the spirit of Kautsky.[34] Moreover, among comrades one did not make invidious distinctions between nationalities, especially since the "Germans" had in fact repeatedly broken their promises, starting on August 4, 1914 and most recently by the rejection of fraternal ties with Soviet Russia by the USPD representatives of the "revolutionary" German government, that is, by Kautsky, Haase, and *Dittmann*. Dittmann was not intimidated. He shouted back, "liar!"[35]

This angry scene was severely distressing for Däumig and Stoecker, both of whom sought to disassociate themselves from their fellow delegates. To demonstrate that he did not share Dittmann's boastful nationalism, Däumig angrily whispered to Shablin, the Bulgarian representative on the committee, *"Ils sont boches!"*[36] But Crispien and Dittmann remained unflustered at the ire of the bolsheviks. They quickly perceived the purpose of the "hot-cold" treatment, and they resolved to ride out the storms caused by it. Later, back in Germany recounting the course of the negotiations in Moscow, Dittmann remarked that he and Crispien were "old, experienced Thebans"[37] who were not awed by the Russians and who were used to maneuvering and subterfuges. He commented that he had straightforwardly approached Zinoviev, who was usually "friendliness itself," with the taunt, "do you play the flute and then Trotsky and Lenin come in with the thunderbolts?"[38]

But the two right-wing delegates increasingly sensed that the bolsheviks were not sincerely interested in working out an agreement with them. The Comintern leaders concentrated their attention on the left-wing delegates, using every device to force them into a more submissive attitude. But by the time of the meeting of the Committee on Conditions these efforts had had only limited success. Däumig still stubbornly insisted, against all that Zinoviev and Trotsky had said, that he would not accept a list of USPD members to be excluded and that a split in the USPD would do nothing to forward revolution in Germany.[39]

New pressures from the bolsheviks

Cachin and Frossard had a private and more cordial meeting with Trotsky on July 26, the day after their meeting with the Committee on Conditions. They were surprised to find him extremely well informed on developments in France. Cachin, having bowed to Trotsky's strictures on the previous day, tried now to convince him that the French worker was "naturally warlike" and patriotic, citing as further evidence the Commune of 1871. But Trotsky insisted that the French workers had cooperated with the *Union sacrée* only because of the failure of their leaders to oppose it. He did not hide his opinion that Jaurès, now sacrosanct in the SFIO, had been a bad influence in this matter, although he politely avoided dwelling on Cachin's own patriotic past. He assured the two delegates that he did not overestimate the importance of the anarchosyndicalist minority around Rosmer and Monatte. Still, he stressed that only in such circles in France could one find real contact with the workers. Men like Rosmer and Monatte made a sharp contrast to Longuet, who was petty-bourgeois reformist and not a revolutionary socialist.[40]

Frossard, who harbored a profound distaste for Trotsky's "haughty superiority," did not try to argue with him, but he was little impressed with his arguments. He later wrote that he and Cachin accepted Trotsky's demand for a complete rejecion of national defense under capitalism, "less out of acquiescence to his questionable arguments" than because the threat of a proletarian uprising might prevent another war.[41]

Shortly after their conversation with Trotsky the French attended the day's meeting of the congress, and while listening to the speeches they were handed a stinging "Answer of the ECCI to the French Socialist Party,"[42] which presumably was the document earlier promised them by Lenin. It was drawn up in the "language of a legal indictment" (*ton d'un réquisitoire*), as Frossard put it, and it stunned both of them. They considered it absolutely unacceptable, and as a consequence they left the congress hall in a huff, Frossard first and Cachin soon after. Back in his hotel room Frossard seethingly set to work on his own "answer to the Answer," promising not to mince his words.[43]

In the course of the same day, July 26, the USPD also encountered new difficulties. In the meeting of the Committee on Conditions which they, but not the SFIO delegates, attended, several new and more stringent conditions were proposed. Lenin sat in on the meeting and during its deliberations proposed, as he had in fact already done in his theses on "The Basic Tasks of the Communist International," that all parties wishing to join the Comintern must agree to allocate two-thirds of the seats of their central committee to men who had declared themselves in favor of joining the Comintern *before* the Second Congress. For the SFIO and USPD this would mean that the minority factions of Strasbourg and Leipzig would be given a decisive majority on the directing bodies of their respective parties. This was a particularly significant step in light of the power to be awarded to the central committee—and was in fact the very thing Cachin and Frossard hoped to avoid by coming to an agreement with the bolsheviks. In addition to Lenin's new proposals a more detailed list of "notorious reformists" to be excluded was presented; this time it explicitly named Hilferding, Longuet, and Turati.[44]

These new conditions met with solid resistance from all four USPD delegates and even from the KPD delegate, Meyer. Both Däumig and Stoecker insisted, as they had on the previous day, that such a list would do nothing to forward the will to make revolution in Germany, as it was supposed to do. Nevertheless, the committee adopted the new proposals by a vote of five to three, with two abstentions.[45]

Crispien and Dittmann went directly to the hotel room of the SFIO delegates and informed them of what had transpired in the committee. Having just received the "Answer of the ECCI" the Frenchmen were all the more indignant. Zinoviev had repeatedly assured them that no such list would be drawn up. Frossard informed the Germans that "absolutely under no conditions could the exclusion of Longuet be accepted." Dittmann urged him to go to the ECCI with them to insist that the new conditions could not be allowed to stand. But Frossard told them, "no, I'm through, I've had enough," and they departed without him.[46]

The actual depth of Frossard's disillusionment is uncertain, since he himself has left differing accounts,[47] but there is no question that he bitterly regretted having made so many concessions to the Russians. He equally regretted not having resisted the enthusiasm of Cachin, who, typically, soon yielded to the entreaties of the emissaries of the ECCI that he return to the congress.[48] But, in spite of the numerous representatives of the ECCI who came to see him, Frossard remained adamant.

That the ECCI continued to be interested in winning over Frossard, instead of contenting itself with splitting the SFIO delegation, is worth emphasizing. For it is abundantly clear that the bolsheviks were not content to have only Cachin; they wanted the support of both centrist delegates, and they were willing to work very hard to win it.

Jacques Sadoul, who had esablished particularly friendly relations with Cachin and Frossard, was given the job of "softening up" the latter. On Tuesday, July 27, he was at Frossard's side constantly. But in spite of Sadoul's repeated insistence that Frossard was making too much of the "Answer" and that the new conditions of affiliation need not be taken so seriously, Frossard remained firm in his opposition. Still, he jotted down in his diary that after much discussion Sadoul confided in him, "we'll come to an understanding, I'm sure; the International needs you as much as you need it."[49]

Serrati versus the bolsheviks

The stormy encounters on July 25 and 26 were paralleled by the deteriorating relationships between the Italian delegation and the Russian leaders. Their first meetings with Serrati had disappointed the bolsheviks, but they could not easily accept the inevitability of complete break with him; they seemed to hope that they could still pressure him to follow the lead of the French and German delegates and accept more completely the bolshevik point

of view. However, Serrati did not respond at all to their pressure—
or rather he responded negatively, since throughout the congress
proceedings he repeatedly criticized the bolsheviks' theses. These
criticisms were highly embarrassing to the Russian leaders, since
Serrati was, along with Rosmer, Levi, Zinoviev, and Lenin, a member of the Presidium of the congress. It was relatively unimportant
that centrists like Dittmann or factionalist intellectuals like Wijnkoop and Guilbeaux criticize the bolsheviks; but when Serrati, the
truly popular and previously much praised leader of the largest
western party in the Communist International, found fault with
them on a wide range of important issues, it was a grave and even
intolerable situation.

In Lenin's previously mentioned theses on "The Basic Tasks
of the Communist International," the Turin *Ordine Nuovo* group
was singled out for special approval in thesis seventeen because of
the report the Turin section had prepared for the PSI's *Consiglio
Nazionale* in April 1920. This report, titled "For a Renewal of the
Italian Socialist Party," contained a strong criticism of both Serrati's and the Maximalists' leadership of the PSI, describing them
as indecisive, verbal revolutionaries who lacked contact with the
masses and who still thought exclusively in terms of parliamentary politics. The report favored the expulsion of the Turatian
wing and the formation of a homogeneous, disciplined party which
would take advantage of the revolutionary epoch Italy was then
passing through and which would prepare for a violent seizure of
political power in the near future.[50]

It is unclear who were the actual authors of this document; its
later attribution to Gramsci alone is almost certainly inaccurate.[51]
Without knowing much of the Turin intellectuals, Lenin approved
completely of their report and deplored their lack of representation
among the Italian delegates. Serrati was naturally upset, since the
Turin report so sharply criticized his leadership, but so too was
Bordiga, who had come to Russia with the hope of obtaining the
support of the Second Congress for his own revolutionary conceptions. In fact the entire Italian delegation opposed thesis seventeen.
Serrati and Graziadei recalled the insubordination of the Turin
intellectuals during the spring strike; Bombacci stressed their syn-

dicalist tendencies; and Bordiga pointed out that the views expressed in *L'Ordine Nuovo* were in conflict with the Second Congress' theses concerning soviets and unions. (He might also have
observed that the Turin report was not typical of the views of the
ordinovisti and was far closer to his own point of view.) Faced with
this united opposition, Lenin retreated a bit, admitting that he
"lacked documentation"; but he still insisted that the report itself,
whatever the other ideas normally expressed by its authors, was a
correct analysis of the situation in Italy which advocated the proper
reforms within the PSI.[52]

In order to get around this impasse, Graziadei met with Zinoviev and worked out a reworded form of thesis seventeen, such that
the criticism of the Maximalists was slightly less direct. But the reworded text still recognized the correctness of the Turin report. It
was thus no more acceptable to Serrati than was the original text.
He later complained in the congress hall that "perhaps a lawyer
could see some difference [in the two texts] but we are not a congress of lawyers but of communists. This thesis means a disavowal
of the leadership of the Italian party and of *Avanti!* That should be
clearly stated."[53] But Bombacci and Polano signed Graziadei's reworded version—although, significantly, Bordiga did not—and all
of the theses on "the Basic Tasks of the Communist International"
were passed by the congress, with only two votes opposed and one
abstention.[54]

Relations between Serrati and the bolsheviks were worsened
further when the latter refused the Italian leader's urgings that
D'Aragona (a leader of the CGL and of the right wing of the PSI)
be allowed to represent the CGL in the committee dealing with the
theses on the trade-union movement and factory councils. As a result D'Arragona, Vacirca, and Colombino angrily left Moscow, and
Serrati boycotted *all* of the meetings of the committees set up to
consider the bolsheviks' theses.[55] Yet, while refusing to participate
in the preliminary committee discussions, Serrati continued to use
the platform of the Presidium to criticize in full congress session
what he repeatedly termed the "confusion" and "opportunism" of
those theses.

He made critical remarks on nearly every set of theses before the congress. Of particular interest was his objection to the assertion in the "Theses on the Agrarian Question" that it was possible to win over or neutralize the small and middle peasant to the cause of communism through the promise of land redistribution. He insisted that even to try to do so tended to confuse issues and to dilute the revolutionary awareness of the propertyless agricultural proletariat. Such would be the case especially in Italy, where the agricultural proletariat had been engaged for years in a bloody class war with the property-owning peasantry. Moreover, in western countries the peasants were far more politically sophisticated than in Russia, and communists had not the slightest chance of weaning them away from other parties, since bourgeois politicians could make more credible campaign promises for the redistribution of land.[56]

Serrati's differences of opinion with Gramsci over the peasant question have been described previously. It is interesting to note that Serrati's hostility to the peasants' striving for land was quite similar to that of Lenin before 1905. At that time Lenin categorically refused to support the peasants' aspiration toward the division of the gentry's land; he said that the proletariat had no interest in supporting a new class of capitalist farmers. Like Serrati, he had stressed the necessity of organizing the agrarian proletariat in the same manner as the industrial proletariat—as an independent class, led by a revolutionary party, battling for the socialization of land. But after 1905 Lenin moved away from these policies and came to view more sympathetically the revolutionary potential in the peasantry's "bourgeois" striving for land. He reasoned that proletarian revolutionaries should exploit, as a temporary, tactical device, the unrest of the peasantry. Otherwise the peasants could become the most imposing bulwark of the old order. Once the proletariat had seized political power, it would be in a better position to bring the land-holding peasantry under its control and to abolish private property in land.[57]

Serrati's criticisms of the "Theses on the National and Colonial Question" were of a nature similar to his criticism of the bolsheviks' agrarian policy. The theses recommended that communists in colonial areas cooperate with their "national-revolutionary" bourgeoisie in the struggle for national liberation, so long as this bourgeoisie allowed the communists to organize the peasantry and exploited masses along revolutionary lines. Serrati, who had spent long months in jail for his opposition to nationalist passion in Italy, simply could not accept this "opportunistic" policy. He insisted that communists could not collaborate, even "provisionally," as the theses stated, with the nationalist bourgeoisie without "undermining the class consciousness of the proletariat." Communists must fight consistently and unequivocally for an internationalist program, and they must strongly condemn nationalism to the masses.[58]

Serrati's remarks repeatedly evoked indignant rebuttal from the other members of the Presidium and from the congress floor. Zinoviev termed them "uncomradely," and Bombacci was quick to dissociate himself from Serrati before the congress. Trotsky compared Serrati's criticisms to those of Kautsky, a comparison he had earlier made in his confrontation with Dittmann. But it was obviously not so much the content of Serrati's criticisms that angered the bolsheviks as the way in which he criticized, particularly since he boycotted all the preliminary committee discussions. In fact Bordiga shared Serrati's objections to the theses on the colonial and on the peasant questions, but he said nothing on the congress floor. Similarly, Graziadei voted with Serrati against the colonial theses, but he did so discreetly, without bringing up the issue in full congress.[59] Bordiga agreed with Serrati's objection to thesis sixteen of the Basic Tasks (which recommended that the British communists stay within the Labour party), but he said nothing of his reservation,[60] while Serrati again loudly deplored the opportunism of the bolsheviks.[61] In short, the bolsheviks had good reason to suspect that resentment, rather than purely doctrinal differences, was behind Serrati's constant objections. This suspicion inevitably pushed them closer to a complete break with him, much as they wished to avoid it.

The compromise with Cachin and Frossard

The stubborn resistance of Frossard and of the entire USPD delegation to the new conditions presented them on July 26 apparently convinced the bolsheviks that they had overplayed their hand. According to Frossard, his angry departure from the congress caused "great alarm,"[62] and soon afterwards the bolsheviks began to moderate their demands. On the evening of July 27, Frossard finally consented to a new meeting with Zinoviev. The French delegate came ready to do some aggressive and straightforward bargaining. He reported in his diary that Zinoviev was now in a more conciliatory frame of mind and "did not much resist."[63] Frossard brought with him a prepared memorandum and announced, "I am not fooled by certain of your actions; we had better make things clear."[64] The memorandum listed twelve specific points which, even taking into consideration the "habitual polemical violence" of the bolsheviks, demanded rectification.[65] On the point of Longuet's exclusion, Zinoviev again backed down; he affirmed that it was not Longuet personally whom the ECCI wanted to attack but rather the tendency he had come to represent. "If Longuet agrees to accept the platform of the Communist International," Zinoviev assured Frossard, "we will be happy to accept him among us."[66] On the question of "packing" two-thirds of the central committee, Zinoviev explained that this should henceforth be considered merely a "wish of the Russian delegation," not an official condition of admission.[67]

On other points, such as changing the name of the SFIO to the French Communist party, Zinoviev insisted more strongly, but in none of these did Frossard feel that essential questions were at stake.[68] He left Zinoviev without making any firm commitments, and plunged into another of his Hamlet-like periods of uncertainty. The next day, July 28, was one of anguished indecision for him. Sadoul remained at his side, urging him to reconsider. In a moment of ostensible frankness, Sadoul confided that doctrinal matters were not at the heart of Frossard's difficulties with the Russians; rather, the bolsheviks feared putting confidence in him because of the "dangers of his well-known craftiness" (*habilité dangereuse*),[69] learned in the school of French parliamentary socialism. (This view was probably urged on the Russians by Rosmer, one of the bolsheviks' principal informants on French matters, who later commented that the bolsheviks "did not and could not know . . . the extent of the skill at maneuvering of these two men formed in the practices

Delegates to the Second Congress of the Comintern. The tall figure is
Paul Levi. Immediately behind him, to his right, is Frossard, and par-
tially obscured by Levi's left shoulder is Cachin. Zinoviev, Sadoul, and
Radek (with glasses and pipe) are to Levi's right in the front row. To
his left is Bukharin (with cap, facing forward).

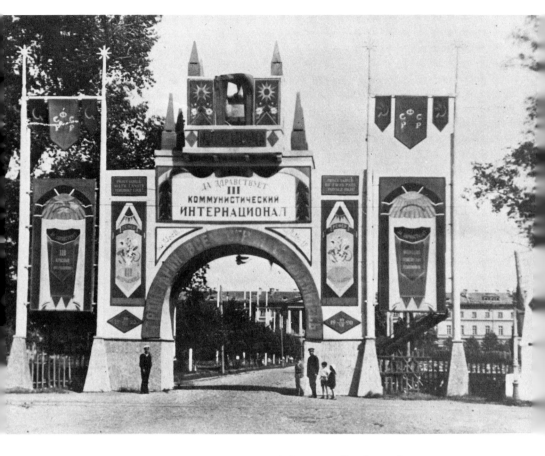

Entrance to the hall of the Second Congress. On the arch
is inscribed "proletarians of the world unite!" Above that,
"Long live the Third International!"

A meeting of a committee of the Second Congress. Lenin
is in the middle and at the end is the typically scowling
countenance of Paul Levi.

Zinoviev (moving head) at the train station with Cachin and Frossard as they depart for France, converted to the cause of communism.

of parliamentary democracy. They had more tricks in their bag than even the suspicious Russians could imagine.")[70]

Frossard now especially regretted his earlier loss of "prudent reserve" and his failure to stand up to Cachin. But in weighing his many ideas and feelings, he was forced to conclude that he had more to lose by breaking with the Comintern and returning home empty handed than by making every effort to come to a new agreement. He later reflected,

> If I feel for certain [bolsheviks] . . . an insurmountable repulsion, if I rebel against their duplicity, if I detest the haughty superiority of Trotsky, the venomous treachery of Zinoviev, the air of false bon-hommie of Kamenev, more and more am I attracted by the Revolution. We had a choice between despair and resignation. The unity of the party, the unity achieved by Jaurès, could not survive the war. We could do nothing to prevent its being torn apart. Our goal was to preserve the maximum unity possible. . . . We will stay with the working class, at the side of the first successful revolution in the world.[71]

On the evening of July 28, Frossard again went to meet Zinoviev, and they reached a new agreement. Although Frossard left no account of this meeting, it is clear that Zinoviev yielded to the French delegates' objections on a number of points, because the declaration he consented to have Cachin read to the congress the next day was considerably more reticent than the declarations the SFIO delegates had made earlier. In it Cachin repeatedly stressed that he and Frossard had come only on a "mission of information" and thus could not speak for their party as a whole. Instead of stressing their essential agreement with the theses of the Second Congress, as he had done on the twenty-fifth, he merely observed that they had "talked over" many points with the representatives of the Comintern and had "taken notice" of the "most important, central ideas."[72]

Cachin and Frossard had also prepared another short declaration, which they did not read to the congress but only handed over to its Presidium; it was even more negative and reticent than the declaration Cachin did read. This second declaration was a kind of reply and mild rebuttal to the open letter of the ECCI which they had agreed to take back with them to France. The letter was directed "To All Members of the French Socialist Party, to All Class Conscious Proletarians" and was no doubt a modified form of the "Answer" of the ECCI which had previously so angered Frossard. It still contained many stinging criticisms of the French socialists, and in the declaration they handed to the Presidium, Cachin and Frossard, while promising to give the letter full publicity, added "as far as we are concerned, we cannot avoid stating our reservations concerning the form and content of several of the judgments which it contains."[73]

Immediately after their declaration to the congress, the two French delegates returned to their rooms to make preparations to return to France. Even in view of their long absence, their hurry to depart is difficult to understand, especially because while packing they received word from the USPD delegates that their declaration had been very coldly received and that sharp attacks against them were being delivered on the congress floor.[74] In the face of such attacks, Cachin and Frossard should have remained until it was clearer what the final pronouncements of the Second Congress would be. They would later regret their hurried departure.

Zinoviev obviously knew that Cachin's declaration would make an unfavorable impression on the congress. Thus he devoted the beginning of his speech on the twenty-ninth, titled "What the Communist International is and what it ought to be," to a defense of the SFIO delegates. A general theme of the speech was that the Comintern must be strictly disciplined and uncompromising toward the opportunistic elements that were now being attracted to it. Yet he defended Cachin by insisting that there was no question of his "personal honesty" and that "everyone can err and then later regret his errors."[75] (Coming from Zinoviev, who regretted his own errors at the time of the October Revolution—when he had broken ranks and denounced the bolshevik plans to take power—this statement was quite understandable.) But these remarks did not forestall the attacks that were being prepared.

Their bags packed, Cachin and Frossard went on the afternoon of the twenty-ninth for a final meeting with Lenin. This time the

Russian leader showed them more cordiality than he had in their first encounter in June. He spent much of the meeting describing for them the recent successes of the Red Army in Poland and made repeated references to the importance of the SFIO's doing more to stop the flow of munitions from France to the Polish regime. He apparently said nothing about immediate revolutionary action in France.[76]

Earlier that afternoon Zinoviev had sent a note to the SFIO delegates, observing flippantly, "they're very unhappy about you!" (*on est très mécontent de vous!*"), in reference to the attacks on Cachin's declaration which were being delivered from the floor. But Zinoviev expressed regret for the attacks and presumably assured the French that there was no cause to be alarmed.[77] By 8:00 P.M., thus reassured, Cachin and Frossard were on their way back home.

The attack of the extreme left

The attacks referred to in Zinoviev's notes were more serious than he implied. After Cachin had read his declaration, a series of speakers, largely of the extreme left wing of the congress, launched into bitter denunciations of the SFIO delegates and the policy of negotiating with the leaders of centrist parties. While these attacks seem to have embarrassed Zinoviev, they gave him at the same time an excuse to renege on some of the vague promises he had made to both the SFIO and USPD delegates and to reintroduce the stringent conditions that had been temporarily retracted.

The first speaker after Cachin was Raymond Lefebvre, a youthful revolutionary firebrand of the Committee for the Comintern. He had arrived shortly before, after a journey of great hardship, in the company of Vergeat (an anarchist) and Lepetit (a revolutionary syndicalist).[78] Lefebvre, like Rosmer, was an official representative of the Committee and was hence awarded full voting powers at the congress. In Moscow, even more than he had in France, he displayed an attachment to a showy and crudely orthodox Leninism, one long on revolutionary enthusiasm and short on genuine understanding of the principles involved. In this spirit he devoted a good part of his speech to a description of conditions in France, asserting that revolution would soon break out there.

Surprisingly, Lefebvre was relatively easy on Cachin and Frossard—surprisingly, because he stood to lose from Moscow's acceptance of them. With the explicit backing of the ECCI, the two centrists could now return to France and expect to reassert their sagging leadership over threats to it from Lefebvre's friends. But, nevertheless, he limited himself to expressing concern that Cachin and Frossard would have difficulty in escaping their long pasts as opportunists and would become only "platonic communists."[79]

Lefebvre was followed by Henri Guilbeaux, who had been the delegate from France to the First Congress and who had already clashed with Cachin and Frossard. Guilbeaux openly accused the Comintern leaders of developing a "new tactic" in dealing with the center, a tactic that went contrary to the theses of the First Congress. He emphasized the inconsistency of the ECCI's unequivocal criticism of the PSI's right wing, while it labored at the same time to find an agreement with the SFIO and USPD. He could see little difference between Cachin and Turati, and at least Turati had opposed the war. Guilbeaux went on to expose the machinations of what he termed "a certain right wing" in the leadership of the Comintern—obviously referring to Zinoviev, Radek, and Kamenev—which expected much of the USPD and SFIO. This right wing hoped to use the "old leaders" of the centrist parties to attract the masses still in those parties to the Comintern. But Guilbeaux predicted that this new scheme would not work. Men like Cachin and Frossard, once back in the "polluted air" of the French parliament, would quickly slip back into their old, corrupt habits.[80]

Guilbeaux's speech was followed by an even more unrestrained attack on the "new tactic" from a young man named Goldenburg, the representative of the French "Group of Revolutionary Socialist Students." He also urged fidelity to the intransigent policies of the Comintern in 1919. Unlike the other speakers so far, he ignored the distinction between Cachin's personal honesty and his political actions, and he openly voiced his doubts concerning the honesty—personal or political—of the SFIO delegates. He asked how any socialist who could announce his willingness to vote for credits to support Kolchak and Denikin, as Cachin had done, could suddenly become a sincere communist. For Goldenburg the reason that Cachin and Frossard wanted to join the Comintern was clear: they feared losing control of their party if they did not.[81]

After Goldenburg the attacks continued.[82] From his chair in the Presidium Serrati was obviously gratified by them. Early in the next day's session he himself remarked on the hypocrisy of the attacks on Turati from the very men who were ready to admit Cachin, the worst kind of social-patriot who had "in the course of the war filled [certain] pockets with French money and who had travelled all over Europe in order to corrupt the working class."[83] It was a comparison that greatly pleased Serrati, and he would return to it time and again in the following months.

The split in the USPD delegation

Although Zinoviev had made great efforts to make Cachin and Frossard acceptable to the Second Congress, by the concluding days of the congress he and the rest of the bolsheviks had decided irrevocably that it would not be possible or desirable to make such compromises with the right of the USPD delegation. Thus pressure was stepped up to split the delegation. Crispien and Dittmann, after their return to Germany, complained that Däumig and Stoecker received "daily beatings" from the bolsheviks and responded like submissive curs.[84] That this treatment was having the desired effect is obvious from a conversation Frossard had with Däumig on July 29. The latter confided to Frossard that an open break with Crispien and Dittmann would be the "only way to avoid exposing myself to the humiliation that I have felt most deeply since I arrived in Moscow."[85] That same day Däumig and Stoecker agreed to their first public statement recognizing differences of opinion with Dittmann and Crispien.[86]

On the twenty-ninth the USPD delegates addressed the full congress, for the same reason the SFIO delegates had: to answer questions the ECCI had asked, on the twenty-first. They had not been able to formulate a common statement and hence addressed the congress separately. The two right-wing delegates remained as combative as they had been on July 25, and they refused to recognize any merit in the attacks of the ECCI on their party. Crispien, who spoke first, rejected the accusation that the leaders of the USPD had betrayed the masses and had come to Moscow because of pressure from the rank and file. If such were the case, then why had the same USPD leaders been repeatedly elected? After all, the USPD, unlike the Bolshevik party, was a democratic organization whose policy and leadership were closely controlled by its congresses. These crude accusations might be believed "in some countries," but not in Germany. The German worker had a socialist education and required that facts be put before him; he was not responsive to such simple-minded demagoguery.[87] Crispien objected pugnaciously to the Russian hegemony in the new international, noting that virtually every party but the bolsheviks had been heavily criticized at the Second Congress. Yet, when the USPD had presented a few needed criticisms of the Comintern leadership, the bolsheviks had become outraged. Crispien quipped, "why suddenly such maidenly sensitivity?"; the USPD had received a "peppery letter" (that of February 5) from the ECCI and had merely replied in kind —without sniveling.[88]

In their declarations, Däumig and Stoecker also defended their party and emphasized that it had been the USPD, not the KPD, that had won over the majority of the revolutionary workers in Germany since the war. This demonstrated the fundamental error the KPD had made when it decided to break away from the USPD in December, 1918. Now, since there was very little difference remaining between the two parties, the KPD and USPD should be able to work together. The reason many members of the USPD had until recently resisted joining the Comintern was that its first member party in Germany, the KPD, had presented a bad example of the kind of action the new international seemed to be encouraging, since anarchistic and irresponsible elements had controlled the actions of the KPD on the local level in most areas of Germany, and the KPD *Zentrale*, which was more responsible and reasonable, had been able to exercise relatively little influence. Thus workers in Germany for the most part had formed a very low opinion of the

KPD as a whole and had avoided it. The USPD had done likewise. Even now, Däumig observed, in view of the speeches that had just been delivered (by the extreme left), one could easily conclude that the Comintern was and would continue to be nothing more than a band of fire-breathing sectarians (*"Propagandagesellschaft"*), although he was certain that the Russian comrades did not want it to remain so.[89]

Both Däumig and Stoecker made it clear that their desire to work with the KPD did not mean that they would look favorably upon a split in their own party. They were quite willing to get rid of Kautsky—and had indeed been in favor of that before coming to Moscow—but they were not ready to see a whole wing of their party secede or be excluded.

Stoecker forthrightly stated that he did not accept all of the theses presented at the congress. In particular he could not swallow the bolshevik notion of terror. It would no doubt be necessary, he recognized, to resort to revolutionary terror when reactionary terror threatened the existence of a proletarian regime; but this would be the exception. There was no reason to adopt terrorism openly as a part of the party program and as a normal way of holding political power; and certainly none of the non-Russian parties already in the Comintern had such provisions in their party programs. Stoecker emphasized that "Russian methods cannot be adapted mechanically to western European lands."[90] Germany was a vastly different country from Russia: it was highly industrialized and did not have millions of revolutionary peasants. In fact, the German peasant was generally reactionary and was one of the greatest obstacles to the progress of the revolution. Germany's more highly evolved economy and society provided a totally different class structure, including significant numbers of "intellectual proletarians" (*"geistiger Arbeiter"*): clerks, technicians, and engineers, whose presence would require very different forms of revolutionary development and dictatorship from what had been required in Russia.[91] In short, Stoecker made it clear that, while he remained attached to the idea of world revolution, he could not submit to what he considered the dogmatic interpretations the bolsheviks were attempting to impose upon all the Comintern membership.

The "daily beatings" had clearly not been as effective as planned. A few more lashes were necessary. Zinoviev addressed the congress after the USPD delegates had finished. He now categorically stated that the Comintern could never accept men like Crispien and Dittmann, let alone Hilferding. The USPD would have to be thoroughly purged and would have to change its character entirely before being accepted into the Comintern. Towards Däumig Zinoviev adopted the tone of a disappointed and impatient schoolmaster; he demanded, "Is this all you have to tell us, comrade?"[92] To say, as Däumig did, that the USPD was developing in the right direction by becoming more responsive to the revolutionary pressure from below, was hardly satisfactory: it was not the masses that should lead a revolutionary party, but just the opposite. Däumig's signature on the Kautskyite answer to the ECCI's letter of February 5 was symbolic of the weakness of the USPD left; it had allowed itself to be influenced by the right wing and had not developed a correct, independent revolutionary position. All this must change.

In a similarly intransigent tone, Zinoviev sought to reassure the left of the congress about the SFIO delegates. He acknowledged that Cachin's last speech had been a "retreat" from earlier declarations of the SFIO delegation, and he strongly implied that he did not seriously expect Cachin and Frossard to become communists.[93] He read to the congress the document he had given the French delegates to take back with them to France—that is, the "answer"— which bitterly attacked Longuet and the past actions of the SFIO. He further assured the congress that he did not propose that the French centrists be accepted immediately. All he asked was that the ECCI be given full authority by the congress to determine whether at some future time it would be possible to accept some of the former centrists. His principal intent in dealing with Cachin and Frossard was to use them as a vehicle to obtain direct and widespread access to France's working class. They had promised to publish in all the SFIO press the document they had been given; and what better way to expose the centrists in France than by a document critical of centrism, published by centrists themselves![94] Zinoviev strongly implied that once Cachin and Frossard had been

sufficiently "used," they could be cast aside. He also implicitly admitted that the Comintern had failed in its previous attempts to
establish a communist party in France and secure meaningful contacts with the French working class. A new direction was therefore
indicated. In any event, he stressed, all he was asking for was the
authority to act flexibly. There would be no danger to the ideals of
the Comintern, for the conditions of admission would be severe
enough to assure that only genuine communists would finally be
accepted.

Since Däumig and Stoecker had already openly stated their differences with their companions, the force of Zinoviev's attack was
a surprise and even a shock to them. But the Russian leader had
them where he wanted them—giving ground and still deeply committed to joining the Comintern. Thus he knew he could continue
his pressure to elicit ever greater concessions. In the following days
the two delegates met frequently in private and presumably stormy
sessions with representatives of the ECCI.[95] No stenographic account of these meetings is available, but their effectiveness became
clear in the last meeting of the ECCI with the entire USPD delegation, over a week later, on August 9.

The four were asked by the ECCI if the theses of the Second
Congress were clear to them, and if so, what was their attitude to
the positions taken by the Comintern. Dittmann replied that while
he could see a "fundamental" agreement on the "main questions,"
on certain specific points, such as the need for an illegal organization and the use of terror, the USPD differed with the Comintern.
Moreover, the USPD could not accept the new conditions added in
the last days of the congress; to do so would mean a major split in
the party.[96]

Däumig's reply constituted what Dittmann was later to call,
somewhat implausibly, an "about face" ("grosse Wendung"). He
announced that after "long and thorough thought," he was convinced that the USPD must join the Comintern, with all that membership would entail. Conditions in Europe required tightly organized revolutionary parties, and therefore he now accepted all
the theses of the Second Congress and the Twenty-one Conditions.
On all these points he was seconded by Stoecker.[97]

Crispien, when his turn came, launched into another long recitation and defense of his party's history—he and Dittmann were absolutely untiring in this—and criticized the Comintern by recounting in detail the relations between the USPD and the ECCI since the Leipzig congress. Finally, he stressed that the mandate he and his fellow delegates had brought to Moscow was clearly contrary to the theses and Twenty-one Conditions of the Second Congress.[98]

It would seem that by now all these men would have grown extremely weary of the same old arguments. But after the four delegates had spoken, Crispien, Dittmann, Zinoviev, and Radek fell into another interminable squabble about the same questions that had originally been brought up by the ECCI's letter of February 5. On this squalid note, the negotiations between the USPD and ECCI ended, and the four delegates finally prepared to return to Germany.

Bordiga at the Second Congress

After his disappointing exchanges with the bolsheviks in late 1919 and early 1920 and after being awarded only consultative rather than full voting voice at the Second Congress, Bordiga must have been gratified to observe the ever intensifying conflict between Serrati and the bolsheviks. The possibility of forming a bolshevik-sponsored communist party in Italy free of the dominance of the Maximalists now seemed much greater.

In the discussion on the congress floor of the conditions for admission, Bordiga proposed a new one, later accepted by the congress, which was obviously designed to further his plans to establish a pure communist party. This condition was that anyone who rejected the theses of the Second Congress (as Serrati was obviously doing) should be expelled from any party wishing to be a member of the Communist International. Bordiga also requested that Lenin's "two-thirds" condition be reintroduced and remarked that he personally would prefer that 100 percent of the leading organs of all communist parties be composed of long-standing communists.[99]

Although Bordiga was not happy over the favorable mention of the *Ordine Nuovo* group in thesis seventeen of the Basic Tasks, the Turin report was actually much closer to his own views than were those of Gramsci, and the report was probably worked out by some of his own followers in the Turin section of the PSI. Thus to a certain extent he could feel satisfaction that thesis sixteen was accepted by the congress. However, he met solid resistance from the congress on the one subject that seemed most important of all to him, the abstention from parliament.

Bordiga had come to Moscow with a set of theses defending parliamentary abstentionism. The arguments contained in them were the same ones he had tirelessly defended in Italy. The committee charged with deliberating on the question of parliamentarism favored the theses prepared by Bukharin, and in fact Bordiga's received only two votes in the committee.[100] Bordiga succeeded at least in getting a grudging recognition from the bolsheviks that there were two kinds of antiparliamentarism—Marxian and anarchist—and that his was of the former variety (something Lenin had not recognized in *Left-Wing Communism*). Moreover, in his speech to the congress Bordiga effectively made the point that the kind of "revolutionary parliamentarism" advocated by the bolsheviks—that is, using parliament to spread revolutionary propaganda—was possible only when a party had been purged of all its nonrevolutionary elements,[101] which the PSI had obviously failed to do and which Serrati refused to do.

Bordiga was still not convinced by the arguments in Bukharin's theses, any more than he had been by the earlier letters of the ECCI or by Lenin's *Left-Wing Communism*. But he declared himself ready to accept "communist discipline" by trying to implement the theses accepted by the congress, and he agreed that the question of parliamentary participation was not important enough to justify splits among genuine revolutionaries.[102] Yet he still insisted that "revolutionary parliamentarism," while it may have been effective in Russia where national traditions were so different and where parliamentary illusions were less deeply ingrained, would not work in Italy.

Bordiga was normally careful to avoid any association with Serrati's criticisms of the theses of the Second Congress, even when he was in agreement with those criticisms; but he did not hide the fact that he shared Serrati's objections to the negotiations with Cachin and Frossard. Even more, Bordiga believed that both the left and right of the USPD were opportunist and unworthy of membership in the Comintern. (Serrati did not speak up on the question of the USPD, but he seems to have favored the entry of both the left and right wings; Hilferding was after all not much different from Turati.)[103] In fact, the entire Italian delegation, with the probable exception of Graziadei, was upset over Zinoviev's dealings with Cachin and Frossard, and they all supported the additional condition of admission proposed by Serrati which would have prohibited all Free Masons from entering the Comintern.[104] Since the PSI had outlawed the Free Masons in 1914, this was not a stringent condition for the Italians. Serrati proposed the condition because he knew that Cachin and many other leaders of the SFIO were Free Masons. Interestingly, although the congress seemed perfectly willing to include this condition in the list already being made up, it did not appear in the final Twenty-one Conditions. Very plausibly Zinoviev stalled its acceptance in the committee because he knew it would embarrass his agreements with the French.

On the next to final day of the congress, August 6, the KPD representative Meyer reported on the progress of the Committee on Conditions. He noted that a subcommittee had suggested altering somewhat the conditions approved on July 30, and he announced the following changes and additions: (1) Hilferding's name was again added to the list of "notorious reformists," including Turati and Longuet, who must be excluded; (2) two-thirds of the central committee must be composed of men who had favored joining the Third International before the Second Congress; (3) a special congress must be called in each country within four months of the Second Congress in order to decide whether the party would join the Comintern and accept its conditions of admission; and (4) those members who wanted to join the Comintern but who did not agree with all its principles must be excluded. A few other adjustments in wording had been made: the ECCI was given the right to make exceptions in the case of both the "two-thirds" condition and the condition requiring exclusion of those not agreeing "fundamentally" (a word added by Zinoviev to Bordiga's condition) with the theses of the Second Congress.

Now the full form of the famous Twenty-one Conditions was immediately put to a vote. The congress passed it, with only two votes opposed. Debate on the question was then quickly closed.[105]

August 7, the last day of the Second Congress, was devoted to ceremonial speeches in joint session with the Moscow Soviet, the Executive Committee of the All-Russian Soviet, and the All-Russian council of Trade Unions. The huge audience, assembled in Moscow's Bolshoi Theater, enthusiastically applauded the glowing predictions about the war in Poland, and they joined in the singing of the *Internationale*. Appropriately, Trotsky, the leader of the Red Army, delivered the main speech, the theme of which was how Russian socialism or bolshevism had assumed leadership over world socialism: "if the world proletariat has suffered defeat and has had to retreat while we have been successful, it is because it has not yet wholly entered upon the road indicated by the Communist International."[106] He concluded with an ardent appeal: "We say to the workers of the world: 'in the Moscow forge, on the Moscow anvil, we have hammered out a sharp sword. Take it in your hands and strike international capitalism to the ground.' "[107]

Chapter VII

The Campaign
for Communism

The delegates from the USPD, SFIO, and PSI returned to their countries to launch ardent campaigns for or against acceptance of the Twenty-one Conditions. The period between the end of the Second Congress and the national congresses of the three parties, in October, December, and January, respectively, was one of factional reshuffling and intense polemic, a time which would in many ways define the nature of communism and socialism in each country for the next generation. The Twenty-one Conditions and the theses of the Second Congress made reasonably clear—to those who studied them, although not many did—the ideological and organizational foundations of the new communist parties that were to be established in each country. Yet uncertainties and equivocations still remained, and were in fact consciously encouraged by the bolsheviks, particularly in the case of the French and Italian parties.

Thus behind the enthusiasm of the campaign for communism were undercurrents of suspicion, jealousy, and duplicity—an appropriate beginning, perhaps, in light of the subsequent history of communism in western Europe. The plans to split the USPD worked smoothly, although the following amalgamation of the KPD and USPD left promised to be more difficult, and the effort to reincorporate the KAPD into the new united party contributed to a major crisis in German communism in early 1921. Zinoviev continued to manipulate the French centrists in a successful manner, but the bolsheviks encountered tremendous obstacles in getting their way in Italy, where the alignment of factions went contrary to what was desired in Moscow.

Cachin and Frossard return to Paris

Cachin and Frossard returned to Paris on August 12, three days after the USPD's last meeting with the ECCI.[1] They found the SFIO—right, left, and center—in an uproar of concern and disbelief over the telegram the two men had sent affirming their belief that affiliation with the Comintern was "necessary."

The most stunned were the members of the Committee for the Comintern. Before the departure of Cachin and Frossard, Loriot had confidently predicted that they would have no success in Moscow. Thus even the news that the SFIO delegation had been admitted to the sessions of the Second Congress was received by the Committee with surprise. "Varine" (Boris Souvarine, like "Flory," in jail) wrote in *Bulletin Communiste* that "our comrades of the Executive Committee in Moscow *have certainly overestimated the representative value of the two centrist delegates,* and their admission to the Congress, even with simple consultative voice, can only be explained by the [self-condemning] declaration which they made. . . ."[2] (The declaration is that of June 29; it was published in the Committee's *Bulletin Communiste* on August 5.) However, Varine was convinced that the Comintern would pose conditions that Cachin and Frossard and their supporters back in France would find completely unacceptable. Even now the declaration that Cachin and Frossard had made went beyond what the right wing of the Reconstruction Committee would accept. Varine had no doubt that "the proof will soon be loud and clear that only the followers of the Committee for the Comintern represent true communist ideology and action."[3]

But the proof that came was that the committee did not have a monopoly on communism; whether they liked it or not, Loriot and his followers were forced to acknowledge that Cachin and Frossard *had* come to an agreement with the Comintern leadership. This was a bitter pill to swallow, and at first Souvarine insisted that the two delegates submit to the leadership of the Committee and map out their campaign for affiliation under its direction.[4] But he soon had to face the unpleasant truth that the extreme left of the SFIO had been neatly outmaneuvered. The members of the Committee could not even openly protest, since Cachin and Frossard had the direct blessing of Zinoviev and the ECCI. Thus Loriot and Souvarine were constrained to accept the leadership of the two former centrists in the campaign.

The center and right wing of the party were scarcely less surprised and concerned. Cachin's and Frossard's telegram, published by *L'Humanité* on July 21, and their declaration to the Second Congress (published only in *Bulletin Communiste*, since its authenticity was doubted by the other papers) deeply disturbed many of them and started widespread speculation.

Thus the small group of SFIO leaders waiting at the station in the morning of August 12 was understandably anxious and tense as the train from Cologne carrying Cachin and Frossard pulled into the station. The delegates emerged from their compartments obviously exhausted from the long journey, but Cachin, in spite of his fatigue, was bubbling over with enthusiasm. "We come back utterly amazed at what we have seen" he told his waiting friends.[5] Frossard said little while Cachin excitedly described their "most fraternal welcome" by the bolsheviks in Petrograd and Moscow. The two delegates were asked almost immediately about rumors spread by the bourgeois press that Cachin had been booed by a crowd of workers in Moscow. Frossard flatly denied the truth of such rumors, calling them "vulgar lies." He affirmed that both his and Cachin's speeches had been enthusiastically received by the Moscow crowds.[6]

To worried inquiries concerning the stringency of the theses and conditions of affiliation laid down by the Second Congress, Cachin responded reassuringly that the Comintern's theses "are just like those formulated by Guesde"[7] and thus nothing to disturb the SFIO. But when some of those waiting at the station began to reproach the two delegates for their overly sudden announcement in favor of the Comintern—which had put their friends back home in an awkward position—fatigue got the better of Cachin, who blurted out, *"foutez-moi la paix!"* ("damn it, leave me alone!").[8]

After a night's rest the two delegates arrived the next day to address a crowd of 10,000 packed into the Cirque de Paris. They told their cheering listeners that they now were wholeheartedly in favor of joining the Communist International. They described in glowing terms the revolution in Russia and their conversion to communism while there.[9]

These speeches at the Cirque de Paris were the overture to a long and energetic campaign in favor of affiliation that Cachin and Frossard undertook soon after. They composed brochures, addressed rallies, and wrote innumerable articles for *L'Humanité* and *Le Populaire*.[10] From August 12 until the end of September, they offered a daily front page report on "What We Saw in Russia" for *L'Humanité*, describing life in Russia, its schools, factories, farms. They drummed up enthusiasm for the revolution as part of their campaign for affiliation with the Comintern, equating support of the Soviet regime with affiliation to the new international. Their articles and speeches were by no means a whitewash of conditions in Russia; the failures of the new regime were described as well as its successes. But the articles emphasized that most of the failures were due to the many years of war and blockade, and to the generally low level of the Russian economy before the war.

The articles in *L'Humanité* seem to have been written mostly by Frossard. The same images, phrases, and literary devices show up in his later writings in a more polished form. One might guess that Frossard was especially concerned to appear objective and balanced in order to counteract his party's natural skepticism of Cachin's "enthusiasms." If Cachin's reason had been clouded in Moscow, few could think the same of his companion. From the first days back in France Frossard declared confidently that he knew the party trusted him and Cachin enough to be certain that they would tell the whole truth about their experiences in Russia.[11]

It scarcely need be commented that the two delegates did not in fact present the whole truth. The only detailed published account of their negotiations was in a pamphlet put on sale in early September, "The Socialist Party and the International: Report on the negotiations carried out in Moscow." The text of this pamphlet provided the basis of a long special meeting in late August between the two delegates and the CAP, but unfortunately no stenographic account of this meeting was ever published. The main body of the pamphlet, all of which seems to have been composed by Frossard, consisted of a factual and fairly complete account of the course of negotiations in Moscow, leaving out, however, some fairly significant points. No mention was made of the initial incidents that had marked their arrival in Russia and their first day in Moscow. Instead of noting Cachin's and Frossard's frequent differences of opinion the report stressed their "perfect agreement" at all times. Similarly, there was no mention of Cachin's hostile reception at the Executive Committee of the Soviets or of Lenin's speech at their meeting with the ECCI. The breakdown of negotiations regarding the "Answer of the ECCI" was glossed over; it was merely noted that the Answer had been written in a way that threatened to compromise a fruitful development of negotiations.[12] Obviously, the impression that the report attempted to give was that the Communist International had demanded things of the French representatives which they had refused to accept, and that their firm opposition and skill at negotiation had forced the Comintern leadership to moderate its demands.

Appended to the report was the document that Zinoviev, in the name of the ECCI, had given Cachin and Frossard upon their departure, titled "To all Members of the French Socialist Party, to all Class-Conscious Proletarians," which ended with the nine "essential" conditions Zinoviev had finally agreed upon for the affiliation of the French party. All the wartime sins of the *Majoritaires* were dredged up in this document. Albert Thomas and Pierre Renaudel were denounced for their "treachery to the working class" and were equated with Noske and Scheidemann in Germany. The attack on the *Minoritaires* was scarcely less vehement: they were condemned for not breaking cleanly with the *Majoritaires* and for not making crystal clear to the working class that the war was a war of imperialism on all sides. The leaders of the minority had consistently followed a policy of spinelessness and equivocation and were in fact worse than the leaders of the USPD, who had at least broken away from the SPD social-patriots. Now the French centrists, the former equivocating *Minoritaires,* were hoping to worm their way into the Third International and water down its revolutionary determination as they had that of the Second International. But it would not work, because the ECCI was perfectly aware of their plans.

Although the report compared Longuet to the archenemy Kautsky, the attack on him was modulated, no doubt because of Frossard's adamant stand concerning Longuet's exclusion. Longuet "as a person" was not important; but it was essential to cast aside the policies his name had come to represent. On the other hand, no concessions were offered on the question of *noyautage* in the unions. The necessity of "declaring war" on "Jouhaux and Co." (the reformist leaders of the CGT) was pressed strongly, and the traditional formula of "full agreement" between party and union was ridiculed as impossibly unclear and equivocal.

The nine conditions of admission to the Communist International that were appended partly repeated the points already made in the text, but they were laid down in direct and simplified form, purportedly in order to outline the "essential" conditions. They demanded militant revolutionary propaganda by the French party press; a campaign against French imperialism, directed toward liberating all French colonies; a clear rejection of "social-pacifism" and the expulsion of the reformists still in the Party; *noyautage* in the unions; strict subordination of the *parlementaires*; change of the name of the party to "Communist party"; arrangements for illegal as well as legal work; and acceptance of all decisions of the Comintern unconditionally.[13]

This document and the conditions it contained were of course a shock to the right and center of the party, but before examining their response to it, it is useful to turn to the USPD delegation's arrival in Germany, which took place shortly after Cachin and Frossard reached Paris.

The return of the USPD delegates

The USPD delegates' return to Berlin was under conditions quite different from those of the French. Whereas the latter, both centrist reconstructionists before they left, returned to Paris to proclaim their united enthusiasm for the Comintern, the former, divided into pro-Comintern and reconstructionist factions before they left, returned to Germany bitterly split—one side campaigning for the Comintern, the other attacking it, with each side doing its best to discredit and besmirch the other. Crispien and Dittmann, unlike the opponents of affiliation in France, had easy access to the major party newspapers, especially *Die Freiheit*, which they used to fight affiliation to the Comintern. Däumig and Stoecker had greater difficulty in getting their point of view published, because the right wing of the party controlled most of the party press. A final difference was that the four German delegates carried back the full text of the Twenty-one Conditions, which were far more stringent than the nine conditions the French had brought back. As a result of these different circumstances, lines were quickly drawn within the USPD—which was not at all the case in France—and the dénouement came with little delay.

Shortly after its return on August 24, the USPD delegation met with the party *Zentrale*, which decided to call a *Reichskonferenz* for September 1–3 in Berlin so that the delegates could give an account of the negotiations in Moscow. This *Reichskonferenz* provided a public and lengthy airing of all the twists and turns of the developments in Moscow, an airing where no holds were barred: each side of the delegation wished to embarrass and "expose" the other as much as possible. (It is interesting to speculate on what might have been the result if similar conditions had obtained in France—Frossard denouncing Cachin's weak resistance to bolshevik pressure, the initial bolshevik hostility to negotiations, Zinoviev's duplicity; and Cachin accusing Frossard of ruining the possibility of easy negotiations by his suspiciousness and lack of cooperation.) Indeed, the speeches of the *Reichskonferenz* were a study in Germanic thoroughness; no detail was neglected, concerning either the long course of the negotiations at Moscow or the many arguments for and against joining the Communist International. For the most part, the speeches, articles, and brochures that proliferated in the next six weeks, before the full party congress at Halle, merely repeated themes laid down at the *Reichskonferenz*.

That the USPD was irrevocably split was immediately evident at the *Reichskonferenz*. The polemic in the party press for and against the Comintern had been raging throughout the last week of August, and now the exchanges between the opposing factions became bitter and at times ugly. Both sides openly recognized the necessity of a split.[14] Ledebour refused even to employ the customary term "comrade" (*Genosse*) when referring to the pro-Comintern representatives; instead he referred to "those people" (*Leute*).[15] With obvious *Schadenfreude*, he asserted that Däumig had hid himself in fear during the January Uprising.[16] Dittmann vowed that never again would he accept any position of leadership in the party along with Däumig or Stoecker.[17] Däumig and Stoecker, for their part, made no secret of their profound contempt for Crispien and Dittmann.[18]

Judging from the stenographic account of the *Reichskonferenz*, it seems that the anti-Comintern speakers got the best of the exchanges and received the general support of the Conference. If the vote on affiliation had been up to the *Reichskonferenz*, the USPD probably would have rejected the Comintern, although it should be remembered that this body was largely composed of party bureaucrats. Their strong showing at this meeting seemed to give the right-wingers a renewed sense of security,[19] for during the *Reichskonferenz* and in the subsequent period before the preliminary elections for the party congress, Crispien, Dittmann, and other anti-Comintern figures took the offensive against Däumig and Stoecker. The right of the delegation emphasized how the other two delegates had earnestly promised to oppose Hilferding's exclusion, but then backed away under the "daily beatings" administered by the bolsheviks. Crispien and Dittmann constantly emphasized that the conditions of affiliation would never have been so stringent if Däumig and Stoecker had not been so fainthearted in their opposition to them.[20]

Däumig and Stoecker made no particular effort to rebut or even reply to the charges of misconduct at Moscow. Instead they asserted that Dittmann and Crispien were themselves to blame for the stringency of the conditions: if they had not been so hostile to the bolsheviks from the very beginning, and especially if Dittmann had not insulted Lenin and provoked the row with Trotsky, the Russians would have been more conciliatory.[21]

Däumig and Stoecker made much of Cachin's and Frossard's decision to join the Comintern. That the two Frenchmen, who had previously been reconstructionists, had now been accepted by the ECCI seemed ample proof that the bolsheviks could be broad-minded with those who were willing to meet them halfway. Cachin's and Frossard's campaign in favor of the Comintern was also held up for unfavorable comparison to Crispien's and Dittmann's sharp criticism of the new international and the conditions in revolutionary Russia. One pro-Comintern delegate to the *Reichskonferenz* asserted that the French delegates' account of conditions in Russia was more reliable, since Cachin and Frossard had spent a longer time in Russia than the German delegation, and more objective, since the French told both the good and the bad about Russia, while Crispien and Dittmann dealt only with the bad.[22]

Cachin's and Frossard's names came up again in the debate over the Twenty-one Conditions. Dittmann recalled his meeting with the French delegates in Moscow (after the new conditions recommended by Lenin had been adopted by the committee on conditions) and stressed that Frossard had explicitly said that he would never accept the Twenty-one Conditions. Dittmann further observed that he himself had written down the full text of the conditions for Frossard, and thus it was impossible that the latter did not know them. Yet Cachin and Frossard were now maintaining in their campaign for affiliation to the Comintern that the SFIO had only nine conditions to fulfill. Dittmann strongly implied that some kind of shady dealings were going on in France.[23] And in fact the impression persisted in Germany that somehow the French *were* receiving special treatment, which was of course greatly resented, since the Twenty-one Conditions were officially announced to hold for all.[24] Their resentment was soon seconded by the Italian delegates.

The return of the Italian delegation

The nonpolitical members of the Italian delegation returned to Italy in early July, before the opening of the Second Congress. D'Arragona, Vacirca, and Colombino had left in disgust, it will be recalled, in the midst of the congress proceedings. Of those who remained for the Second Congress, Graziadei returned first, reaching Italy on August 21. Serrati, Bordiga, Bombacci, and Polano did not return until mid-September, more than a month after the return of the French delegates and after the *Reichskonferenz* had met.

The first returnees published nothing about their impressions until early 1921. However, word got around that they had been very unfavorably impressed by conditions in Russia and by the nature of bolshevik rule.[25] When approached, Graziadei insisted that he could not properly discuss his impressions of Russia until the rest of the delegation returned. He limited himself to a very general discussion of the theses of the Second Congress and of the conditions of admission, seventeen of which he brought back.[26]

In early September the party's curiosity was temporarily diverted from the question of the International by a massive general strike and occupations of factories, in full course when Serrati arrived in Italy. His return, however, quickly revived the discussions concerning the PSI and the Comintern. He brought back with him the full text of the Twenty-one Conditions and a letter from the ECCI, dated August 21 and addressed "To the central committee and all members of the Italian Socialist party." This letter was the opening salvo of the long polemical battle that Serrati and the Comintern would wage throughout the autumn and early winter.

In tone and intent the ECCI's letter was broadly similar to that which Cachin and Frossard finally agreed to take back with them to France. Immediately after the closing of the Second Congress the Italian delegation had been invited to a meeting of the ECCI, at which a rough draft of this letter was read to them. Serrati criticized the draft on a number of points and further opposed the idea of a letter to the Italian proletariat directly from the ECCI which criticized the leadership of the PSI. Zinoviev and Bukharin, who had drawn up the rough draft, agreed to a few small changes, but they insisted upon the right of the ECCI to send such a letter, and on this point they found support from the other members of the delegation.

Shortly afterward Serrati temporarily left Moscow for a tour of the Ukraine, and when he returned he was given a revised draft of the letter to take back with him to Italy.[27]

The letter began by noting that the ECCI felt itself obliged to discuss the "involuntary and voluntary errors" of the PSI.[28] Predictably, the principal error that the ECCI wished to point out was the failure of the Italian party to rid itself of its reformist wing. But, in elaborating the reasons for expelling Turati and his followers, Zinoviev and Bukharin introduced what was for them a new theme: Italy was now on the verge of proletarian revolution; it was closer to revolution than any other country in western Europe, and since it was so close it was necessary to impose upon the PSI more stringent conditions than was the case for other parties. In fact, one of the principal crimes of the party's reformist wing had been to mask the imminence of revolution and to frighten the proletariat with stories of an inevitable blockade and intervention by the Entente if the working class assumed power in Italy.

In attempting to demonstrate that Italy was ripe for revolution the letter introduced some highly dubious arguments. It made vague and contradictory strictures against "premature putsches" and against allowing the bourgeoisie any more time for its counter-revolutionary preparations. The letter's assertions that the Italian proletariat was "astonishingly unanimous" in its desire for revolution, that the majority of the peasantry also favored revolution, and that the army would rally to the revolution at the "decisive moment" were themselves astonishingly divorced from the reality of Italy in the autumn of 1920. In their confident predictions that the "Entente *will not be able*" to intervene in Italy, Zinoviev and Bukharin revealed their own doubts by immediately adding that, even if blockade and intervention were likely, it did not mean that revolution in Italy could not come until revolution had begun somewhere else in western Europe—had not Russia survived blockade and intervention?

Although the letter avoided explicit mention of the speculations within the Bolshevik party that revolution in the West would be even more painful and "uncivilized" than it had been in Russia, it repeatedly emphasized that the Italian proletariat must be ready for great sacrifices and suffering. It furthermore conceded that "if revolution does not come quickly in other countries it is possible that the Italian proletariat will have to travel the same hard path as the Russian proletariat since the great October Revolution of 1917."[29] Strangely missing in these speculations was any mention of the point repeatedly emphasized by many members of the PSI: intervention and blockade would be almost immediately effective in Italy; the "breathing space" that Russia's great distances and relatively sparse population permitted the bolsheviks would not be permitted Italian revolutionaries because of Italy's accessible industrial centers, her dependence on imports, and her relatively dense, urbanized population. It was thus inconceivable that an isolated Italian soviet republic could travel the "same hard path" as the Russian Soviet Republic had, especially for years on end. (In an article in November, Lenin would openly recognize these important differences between Russia and Italy, and would grant that without revolution in central Europe a proletarian regime in Italy would be rapidly crushed. Yet the only conclusion he drew was that communists should not use the fear of intervention and blockade to *weaken* the revolutionary determination of the Italian proletariat; rather, these possibilities should be brought into the open in orden to *harden* that determination. It was, to say the least, a subtle and difficult distinction.)[30]

The letter asserted that the only important thing missing before revolution could succeed in Italy was a truly revolutionary party, and the description of the "involuntary and voluntary errors" of the PSI amounted to an accusation that it was, in spite of its status as one of the leading parties of the Comintern, little different from the other centrist or reformist parties of western Europe. The PSI did not lead the masses but only responded halfheartedly to the revolutionary push from below. Its leaders valued formal unity above doctrinal clarity, discipline, and revolutionary determination. It tolerated a reformist parliamentary faction in its ranks, one that confused the masses and turned the left of the party toward abstentionism. And the fiery rhetoric of the party *Direzione* was not complemented by *real* revolutionary will, since the party leaders had failed to make concrete preparations for a violent seizure of power.

Significantly, Serrati did not publish this letter upon his return, as he was supposed to do, but merely handed it over to the *Direzione*, which decided to discuss it at a later date. Hence it was kept from the rank and file for over a month. When it finally was published, Serrati appended a long series of ironic and biting footnotes, terming the entire letter a "puerile" document.[31] Moreover, he was able to obtain the *Direzione's* unanimous agreement that the letter showed the bolsheviks' inadequate understanding of conditions in Italy.[32]

Serrati's first articles after his return were devoted to a defense of his conduct in Moscow and an attack on the theses of the Second Congress for their "excessive opportunism, inconsistencies, and lack of clarity." He laid out more fully the basis for his opposition to the theses on the unions, colonies, and peasants, and once again he bitterly objected that while Cachin was being accepted, men like Turati, Modigliani, and D'Arragona were being hounded out of the party. He consistently ignored the ECCI's assertion that particularly stringent conditions were necessary for Italy because of the proximity of revolution there, and he asserted that all he wanted for the PSI was the independence being given the SFIO.[33]

On September 28 the *Direzione* met to hear the report of the Italian delegates and to discuss the question of the International in general. This meeting, which lasted four days, resembled the USPD's *Reichskonferenz* in that each of the delegates presented long and formal speeches, and were divided in their attitude to the Twenty-one Conditions. Graziadei, Bombacci, and Polano argued in favor of the Conditions and in particular in favor of expelling the right wing, while Serrati insisted that greater leeway should be allowed the Italian party in handling its own affairs. In the final vote a resolution favoring the expulsion of the right received seven votes. A resolution favoring Serrati's position received five votes.[34]

Since he no longer enjoyed a majority in the *Direzione*, Serrati offered his resignation as editor of *Avanti!* (the *de facto* position of leadership in the party). However, even though a majority of the party's ruling body disagreed with Serrati's attitude to the Twenty-one Conditions, they refused to accept his resignation. Even a month later, in the context of worsening relations between Serrati and the Comintern, the *Direzione* in large part accepted his objections to the ECCI's letter of August 21. In short, Serrati continued to exercise a strong influence in the PSI, even though his Maximalist faction was splitting up. Even the left Maximalists were rarely willing to accept Bordiga's thesis that Serrati was just as much an obstacle to revolution as was Turati. Nor were they always willing to accept bolshevik criticism of the PSI's past actions.

Significantly, the left Maximalists stressed not so much Moscow's contention that the Turatian wing was an obstacle to revolution as the purely practical consideration that, given the inevitability of a split in the PSI, it would be better to lose the small right wing than the vigorous and growing left wing. Graziadei argued the same way: if a split was not really desirable, it was in any case unavoidable, and thus its proportions should be reduced as much as possible.[35] This line of reasoning was much closer to Frossard than to Bordiga, and it made clear that the defection of many of Serrati's followers was of a practical rather than a doctrinal nature.

In retrospect it seems strange that Serrati himself could not acquiesce in the simple logic of this position. Why did he so stubbornly oppose the idea of purging the right wing? His opposition seems doubly puzzling since he continued to affirm his basic agreement with Moscow and since he had himself often delivered slashing attacks on Turati and the reformist wing.[36] It has already been suggested that Serrati was concerned about the growing strength of the extreme left of his party and that he hoped to keep the right wing in the party as a kind of counterbalance to Bordiga and the *ordinovisti*. He considered the Neapolitan to be an impossible sectarian, who in his revolutionary "purity" isolated himself from all possibility of realistic action. He believed the young Turin revolutionaries to be too intellectual and too immersed in the special problems of industrial Piedmont to be effective leaders of the party as a whole. Moreover, the earlier association of many of the Turin intellectuals with the cause of intervention in the war seemed to him clear evidence of their unreliability.

Serrati feared that Bordiga, the *ordinovisti*, and the bolsheviks would destroy the network of working-class institutions which his and Turati's generation had so laboriously built up. As Serrati repeatedly emphasized, he himself wished to preserve the traditions of Italian socialism, not to destroy them. At the Leghorn congress he would sum up his feelings in simple terms: "it is easy to destroy and difficult to build" ("*è facile abbattere, è difficile ricostruire*").[37]

But less tangible, more temperamental factors probably explain Serrati's resistance to the bolsheviks. He was a stubborn, proud, and independent man. While admiring the Russians, he simply could not stomach their overbearing, cocksure, and condescending manners. Thus when he emphasized that Russia was a backward country unprepared for socialism and that the bolsheviks were ignorant of conditions in the West, he was in effect arguing for the dignity and independence of western socialism.[38] Ironically, similar criticisms of Russia's backwardness and her cultural barbarity had earlier been expressed by Turati, for which he had been criticized by Serrati. After his trip to Moscow Serrati could not help feeling that Turati had been right.

Serrati's new hostility to the bolsheviks meant a complete break with Niccolini, the Comintern agent in Italy, and thus an end to their collaboration in *Communismo*. It meant also that Niccolini quickly strengthened his earlier contacts with Bordiga and the *Ordine Nuovo* group. Serrati and Niccolini engaged in acrimonious and tedious polemics from the pages of *Avanti!* and *L'Ordine Nuovo*,[39] and the Turin editors began to publish a series of harsh criticisms of Serrati's past leadership of the PSI. Serrati replied in kind: in an ironic and biting letter to *L'Ordine Nuovo* he admitted that he had made mistakes, but he ardently defended his actions through the terrible years of the war. He observed that the young editors of *L'Ordine Nuovo* were very wise after the fact; yet in the past two years the Turin section of the PSI had always unanimously approved the work of *Avanti!* He ended his letter,

Well then, comrades Pastore, Gramsci, Galetto, Togliatti, Zino Zini, and co. of the new order, tell us—while we in our humble condition of men in the land of Pulcinella turn to admire you from your splendid height in the land of the sun—tell us: where were you and what were you thinking when the war broke out?[40]

Factory occupations and municipal elections

The renewed discussion in the PSI, inspired by the ECCI's letter, concerning how best to prepare for revolution in Italy was not taking place in a vacuum. In early September an enormous wave of strikes and factory occupations spread over Italy. Just as these difficulties were resolved Italy went to the polls for administrative elections. These two developments had important yet contradictory influences on the internal conflicts in the PSI.

The occupation of factories in Italy, like the French general strike in the spring and the German general strike following the Kapp Putsch, seemed to some uncareful observers the long awaited time when western revolutionaries would follow the lead of the bolsheviks. Yet the factory occupation had not been intended by its initiators to be a revolutionary measure; rather, it was a new way of putting pressure on management to sit down and negotiate. Matters accelerated beyond all expectations: between the first and fourth of September virtually all metal workers in Italy, some 400,-000 in all, occupied their factories.[41]

On the fourth and fifth of September there was a meeting of the "estates general" of the proletariat, headed by the directing council of the CGL and *Direzione* of the PSI. After a full examination of the question, they came to the conclusion that if the situation did not resolve itself otherwise, either by concessions from the employers or violent intervention by the state, the organizations of the proletariat would make the collective control over factories and the socialization of the means of production the goal of the conflict. This was in effect to threaten revolution, but to cool-headed observers it was obvious that these were merely further bluffs designed to frighten the employers. Significantly, no preparations for a seizure of power were being made.

Giolitti, the cagey prewar politician, was for one final time back in power, and he was not taken in. In spite of strong urgings from the leaders of Italian industry and from conservatives to intervene with force, he made up his mind to handle this crisis just as he had handled the general strike of 1904. That is, while making certain that he had control over such vital power centers as the army, the *carabinieri*, and the *guardie regie* (the recently created "royal guards"), he merely waited out the workers: he would allow them to see for themselves the utter impossibility at this time of a socialization of production in Italy with the meager forces available to the proletariat.

The neutrality of the government, which had not obtained in the spring Turin strike, allowed the factory occupation to gather momentum. In the south there was an intensification of the occupation of feudal lands by landless peasants which had been going on sporadically since the end of the war. On the sixth the PSI issued a manifesto to the peasants and soldiers in Italy urging them to sympathize with the striking metal workers, since "perhaps the day of liberty and justice is near." [42] Factory occupations began to spread to other industries, workers tried to begin production on their own, and the bourgeois press was full of stories concerning the arming of the working class. [43]

But Giolitti's calculations were sound. On the tenth and eleventh the PSI *Direzione* again met with the directing committee of the CGL in Milan. These leaders had to come to grips with the flagrant disparity between their revolutionary rhetoric and their actual preparation for a seizure of political power; their discussions made clear a complete incapacity to launch a military attack on the power centers of the Italian state. It was a most striking confirmation of the point repeatedly stressed at the Second Congress of the Comintern: a general strike was merely a "negative" measure that could never lead to proletarian revolution without the "positive" measure of a violent seizure of power.

On the evening of the tenth the leaders of the CGL absolved themselves of responsibility for violent revolutionary action and informed the leadership of the PSI that if it wished to make a revolution it would also have to assume the leadership of the CGL. The party leaders, including Gennari and Terracini (but not Serrati who was still in Russia), then took the issue to the national council of the CGL, hoping for a vote of confidence from the rank-and-file leaders of Italy's unions. A vote was taken, and 591,245 votes went to D'Aragona's nonrevolutionary resolution and 409,569 to Bucco's resolution advocating revolutionary measures.[44] Insofar as the proletarian masses were capable of speaking through their traditional organizations, they had rejected revolutionary action. In the following weeks Giolitti met with representatives of the unions and management, and a resolution of the conflict was worked out.[45] It was again easy to see in these developments a confirmation of bolshevik contentions that the right-wing bureaucrats of the unions and party would always back away from a revolutionary situation and that the masses needed firm direction from a truly revolutionary party.

Although a formal victory for the unions, the agreements worked out under Giolitti were felt within the party and within the unions to be a failure for the Italian proletariat. This was true even though a referendum in the unions strongly approved the agreements. However, the sense of defeat was certainly not so strong as it had been in France and Germany after the spring strikes. Moreover, the factory occupations were quickly followed by a working-class victory similar to that of the parliamentary elections of November 1919.

The communal and local elections of October 31 and November 7 gave the socialists a victory in 2,162 communes (out of a total of 8,069; they had formerly held 300) and in 26 provinces (out of 69).[46] Inevitably these victories added to the sense of *situation acquise*, of hard earned gains, which were so important to the Turatian and Serratian wings of the PSI. By the end of 1920 the PSI had almost 220,000 members,[47] 156 parliamentary deputies, and controlled about one-third of the nation's communes and about one-third of its provincial councils; there were approximately 8,000 socialist-oriented cooperatives and about 2,000,000 members in the CGL.[48] If the PSI were split into warring communist and socialist parties, these gains would be put into great danger.

The communal elections in Bologna constituted the most striking socialist victory in all of Italy. Although the bourgeois parties had formed an electoral bloc against the socialists, the PSI still won 20,000 votes to 8,700 for the bourgeois parties.[49] But this victory had an ominous sequel. In the following weeks the fascists took over the streets, terrorizing the population and finally achieving a kind of *de facto* control of the city in spite of the socialists' legal control of it. Throughout the autumn of 1920 the level of fascist violence in other cities also steadily rose. It became clear that Giolitti's policy of giving the workers enough rope had an unexpected side effect: it sharply accelerated the sense of disillusionment among large sectors of the bourgeoisie with the parliamentary-democratic state. The socialist victory in the provincial and communal elections merely served to increase the fears of many of those who had already been badly frightened by the factory occupations. The continued revolutionary rhetoric of the PSI and the urgings from Moscow added further fuel to the fire. Thus the fascists took on new appeal for much of the Italian bourgeoisie.

The Twenty-one Conditions in France

The center and right wing of the SFIO had been shocked sufficiently by the nine conditions brought back by Cachin and Frossard. But when news began arriving that there were in fact eighteen or nineteen, then twenty-one, and even twenty-two—conditions falling like hailstones—their shock dissolved into confusion and finally turned into outrage.

The first indication that Cachin's and Frossard's nine conditions were not a full text came on August 26, when *Bulletin Communiste* published eighteen conditions.[50] A few days later, news of the publication of the Twenty-one Conditions in *Die Freiheit* reached France,[51] and this newest version of the conditions was published in *Le Populaire*.[52] Confronted with this new development, Varine, having now accepted the partnership of Cachin and Frossard, explained confidently that the eighteen conditions published in *Bulletin Communiste* were merely an elaboration, with no new elements added, of the nine conditions brought back by Cachin and Frossard.[53] But no amount of clever interpretation could convert the Twenty-one Conditions into an elaboration of the nine conditions, as members of the party's right and center were quick to point out.[54] To begin with, condition seven of the Twenty-one Conditions, dealing with the necessity of breaking with the "reformists" and "opportunists," specifically named Longuet as one of those that the Comintern could not allow within its ranks. The eighteen conditions published in *Bulletin Communiste* named only Turati and Modigliani, and Frossard's nine conditions mentioned no names at all. Moreover, the last four of the Twenty-one Conditions were clearly new and unrelated to the earlier versions: number eighteen obliged member parties to print all important documents of the ECCI; number nineteen demanded an extraordinary congress within four months to vote on the question of affiliation; number twenty —and this was the real nettle—made it obligatory that two-thirds of the executive committees of new member parties be composed of those who had openly declared themselves in favor of affiliation with the Communist International before the Second Congress (although exceptions were allowed, with the permission of the ECCI, to this condition and to condition number seven); and number twenty-one, which also was received with particular shock, demanded that all those who "in principle" refused the conditions and theses of the Communist International were to be automatically excluded.[55]

Cachin and Frossard continued to insist that the conditions they had brought back were the only conditions for France, and they did their best to minimize the force even of those relatively mild conditions, since nine conditions were still too many for many in the SFIO. Replying to a question about the stringency of Moscow's conditions, Frossard explained that "it is not really proper to speak of 'conditions.' The Communist International simply gave us a memorandum which contains a critical examination of the present state of affairs and ends by presenting certain points concerning which we are asked to give a clear answer."[56] Again Frossard emphasized that he and Cachin had resisted the efforts of the Comintern to make stronger demands.

But Cachin and Frossard were fighting a losing battle. More and more evidence appeared that the Twenty-one Conditions were the final and definitive text and that they applied to all countries. Crispien sent word to France assuring the members of the SFIO that the Twenty-one Conditions had been voted by the Second Congress and were meant to be applied everywhere.[57] Soon after, Däumig and Stoecker sent a more formal letter giving the same information.[58] While Frossard's friends continued to insist that there were, in spite of what the Germans said, special conditions for France,[59] Frossard himself began to falter: ". . . unless a new order arrives, I recognize nine and only nine conditions."[60]

A new order did arrive on the first of October, in the form of an "Open Letter of Lenin to the workers of France and Germany,"[61] which confirmed that the Twenty-one Conditions applied to all countries. A few days later further confirmation arrived with the publication of a letter of Lenin to Serrati, who was complaining so loudly about the special treatment given the French. Lenin stressed that the Twenty-one Conditions were a *sine qua non* for all parties," pointedly including the French Party. Serrati added, in a note quickly sent to the French, "that is very clear and distinct."[62]

The Twenty-one Conditions were thus established with Cartesian certainty. Cachin and Frossard were beginning to pay the price for having so hastily departed from Moscow. They had been outmaneuvered not only while in Russia but even now that they were back in their own country. Frossard later bitterly remarked, "We never stopped being outmaneuvered."[63] By now he and Cachin had committed themselves so deeply to affiliation that if they backed out they risked being totally discredited. Moreover, since the Red Army had been pushed back at Warsaw and was now in retreat, it was even more difficult for them to withdraw their support. The cornerstone of their campaign had been that joining hands with the Communist International would be the best way of protecting the Russian Revolution. They could not withdraw their support for the Comintern without risking the appearance of turning their backs on the bolshevik regime when it was down. "It was too late to get out"[64] Frossard later observed; "they [the bolsheviks] knew we were already too committed."[65]

Thus Frossard resolved not to give up his support for the Comintern. He maintained his outward display of enthusiasm for it and continued his vigorous campaign in favor of affiliation. But he had grave inner doubts about the Twenty-one Conditions; he doubted that within them he could find room for his kind of socialism.[66]

He prepared for the congress of Tours "with uncertain steps, filled with anxiety."[67]

Cachin's and Frossard's plans to pull over the Reconstructionists seemed fairly well launched in the first weeks after their arrival. They had a formal meeting with the Reconstruction Committee on September 6,[68] and two weeks later a large number of the leading figures of the Committee resigned[69]—among them Daniel Renoult, Paul Louis, and Amédée Dunois—and declared their intention to work for direct affiliation. But a number of other Reconstructionists resisted the idea of joining the Comintern under the Twenty-one Conditions, among whom were Jean Longuet, Paul Faure, and Léon Blum.

By early October attitudes and alliances began to crystallize, although the exact forms that would result were not yet entirely clear. Cachin and Frossard still did not give up hope of winning over the rest of the SFIO center in spite of the Twenty-one Conditions, and they worked diligently in that direction. In the meantime, the USPD congress of Halle had been called to meet on October 12, and the eyes of all factions in the SFIO turned anxiously to Germany. It seemed clear that the decisions made at Halle would have an effect on the forthcoming SFIO congress, just as the Leipzig congress had powerfully influenced the outcome of the congress at Strasbourg. The Longuet wing of the center was especially concerned with events in the USPD—the pages of *Le Populaire* were filled with the USPD debates about the Comintern—and Longuet finally decided to accompany Renoult (a leading representative of the *ralliés* of the Reconstruction Committee) to Germany to attend the USPD congress.

The new factions of the PSI

The worsening relations between Serrati and the bolsheviks, his break with Niccolini, and his quarrels with the *ordinovisti* were welcome developments for Bordiga. For while Maximalists such as Terracini and Graziadei were trying to broaden the pro-Comintern alliance as much as possible, Bordiga was working in the opposite direction. Even after the Second Congress he did not abandon his hope of building a small, elitist communist party which would separate from the main body of the PSI and be free of the influence of the Maximalists. He did not accept the idea, which the leaders of the Committee for the Comintern in France finally accepted, of diluting revolutionary purity and working with the "centrists" (which he considered the Maximalists to be). He persisted in his earlier ideas of "separation" rather than simply purging the party of its reformist right. Bordiga was thus acting contrary to the desires of the bolsheviks, who hoped to get an even heavier majority of the PSI than of the SFIO and USPD, in order to establish a "mass" rather than an elite party in Italy.

It was impossible to obtain a majority of the PSI without Serrati's support, although this may not have been completely clear in Moscow. At the same time the position he had assumed made it next to impossible for the ECCI to accept him. Bordiga made the most of the bolsheviks' dilemma. He did what he could to intensify the alienation between Serrati and the left of the PSI, and he worked assiduously to assure that the new Communist faction that was being established in Italy after the Second Congress would remain firmly under his leadership. In open defiance of the instructions from Moscow he sought to limit the number of Maximalists, such as Bombacci, Gennari, and Graziadei, who would enter the new faction, since they might easily swamp his own Abstentionist followers. *Il Soviet* was openly critical of the left-center alliance in France and of Zinoviev's opportunism in agreeing to it: one of its writers, Ludovico Tarsia, even suggested that Zinoviev was again showing the weakness toward opportunists that he had earlier shown at the time of the Revolution, and Tarsia appealed to the "intransigence of Lenin."[70]

Bordiga also strove to assert his dominance over the *ordinovisti*, a task he considered especially important because of the favorable mention of the Turin group in Lenin's theses. This was not difficult, since by the fall of 1920 the doctrinal differences and personal antipathies among the Turinese intellectuals had nearly dissolved whatever organizational unity they once had. Even at its height their organization was limited to Piedmont, whereas Bordiga had been able to establish a broadly national organization. The impact of Lenin's favorable mention of the Turin report was diminished because the report was not a typical document of the *ordinovisti*; it was actually more Bordigan than Gramscian. In abandoning many of his earlier positions in favor of the resolutions of the Second Congress, Gramsci, like many other young leftists in the PSI, moved toward Bordiga's position on a number of questions, particularly on the need for a disciplined revolutionary party.[71]

In the first half of October representatives of the Abstentionists, the *ordinovisti*, the socialist youth group, and the left Maximalists met in Milan to work out a manifesto of the new Communist faction.[72] A little over a month later, on November 28, Bordiga's leadership of the new faction was ratified at a conference at Imola, called to prepare the resolutions for the forthcoming full party congress. Although all of the factions mentioned above were represented at Imola, the resolutions of the conference had been drawn up beforehand by Bordiga, and he insisted that no alteration of them could be allowed. The resolutions called for acceptance of the Twenty-one Conditions and of the theses of the Second Congress, without reservations. After some difficulty, Bordiga finally had his way and no alteration was made.

Ironically, the Imola conference, which was to establish a united alliance of determined and genuine revolutionaries in Italy, was the scene of backstage maneuverings, petty jealousies, and squalid bickering, an omen of things to come in the Italian Communist party. Only the intervention of the Comintern representative prevented the collapse of the whole effort. The main problem was that the Abstentionists, and particularly Bordiga, insisted that only a few carefully chosen former Maximalists be allowed in the Communist faction. Bordiga was hostile to the presence of such men as Bombacci, Gennari, and Repossi—to say nothing of Graziadei (who only sat in on the conference without voting powers and who later helped to set up a separate faction). The non-Abstentionist representatives at Imola demanded categorically that the Abstentionist faction be dissolved as a prerequisite to the formation of the Communist faction, and the Comintern representative put pressure on the Abstentionists to respect this demand. However, while some of his followers acceded to this pressure, Bordiga announced a few days after the conference that the Abstentionist faction would not be dissolved until the establishment of the Italian Communist party.[73]

A week before the Imola conference, Serrati and his followers had met in Florence. Assuming the new name "Unitary Socialist-Communists," the former Maximalists formally accepted the positions that Serrati had laid down in his articles and speeches since his return: the Twenty-one Conditions were acceptable only if the Italian party were given full freedom to apply them according to its own lights; the vital unity of the party would be destroyed at this time by exclusions, which would not be understood by the masses; the Italian socialist right wing should be considered the equivalent of the *center* in such parties as the SFIO; the Unitarians only asked that the Italians be given as much freedom to deal with their centrists as the French were being given—something Moscow should easily accept since the Italian centrists, unlike the French, had not supported the war.[74]

Turati's faction, meeting in late November at Reggio Emilia, reiterated many of the criticisms of bolshevism and the Bolshevik Revolution that it had formulated since 1918. But its members significantly avoided describing themselves as reformists, and in order to complement Serrati's description of them as centrists, they assumed the name "Concentrationists." They even affirmed their readiness to accept the Twenty-one Conditions "with application ... according to the special needs of each country," and like the Unitarians they affirmed their desire to remain in the Comintern.[75]

Aside from these three main factions, two smaller factions were established in late November. Both of these were led by men who hoped to save the party's unity and who shared Serrati's concern to preserve Italian socialism's established institutions and traditions. Graziadei and Marabini headed the "Committee for Communist Unity," which favored both an unconditional acceptance of the Twenty-one Conditions and a unification of the Communist and Unitarian factions. Of all the factions, then, this "Committee" attempted to follow most faithfully the desires of the ECCI. But, significantly, Graziadei's faction elicited less support than Turati's, Bordiga's, or Serrati's. The old party secretary, Lazzari, headed an even smaller faction of "Intransigent Revolutionaries," with a following of many older party members. The Intransigents urged fidelity to the "glorious history of the party" and opposed their Marxian economic determinism to the "voluntarism and opportunism" of the extreme left. Just as Graziadei's group hoped to bring the Communists and Unitarians together, so Lazzari's group sought to act as mediator between the Unitarians and Concentrationists, although after the schism of the PSI a certain number of the Intransigents, including Lazzari himself, rallied to the new Communist party.[76]

Serrati and centrism

By early December 1920 the PSI had divided itself into right, center, and left. Formally, at least, these divisions suggested the Leninist categories of reformist-right, equivocating-center, and revolutionary left that existed in the other mass socialist parties in western Europe. In other words, the new divisions of the PSI gave a certain external plausibility to Bordiga's long-standing contention that the PSI was in fact little different from such parties as the SFIO and USPD. The ECCI's letter of August 21 seemed to accept Bordiga's contention, although only indirectly and ambiguously. But if Bordiga was correct about the PSI, then logically he was correct about the leading figure of the PSI; and by late autumn he more openly and confidently described Serrati as a centrist, very similar to the leaders of the USPD and SFIO.

At the Second Congress Lenin and Zinoviev had accused Serrati of talking like a centrist. Niccolini took up this theme in his articles after breaking with Serrati, and it would be more and more frequently employed in the autumn of 1920. Certainly a good case could be made that in this period Serrati reasoned very much like the centrists in the USPD and SFIO. His strong attachment to party unity, to preserving the established traditions of Italian socialism, was not very different from Léon Blum's attachment to what he would call the *vieille maison* (old house) of French socialism. As the right wing of the USPD had done, Serrati now often lectured the bolsheviks on their "un-Marxian" assertions that a few reformist leaders could prevent revolution and on their "miraculist" belief that revolutionary organization and determination by a small elite was more important than mature objective conditions."[77] As Dittmann had, he frequently made supercilious references to the low cultural and educational level in Russia, and also as the German leader had done, he emphasized that the bolsheviks were an "insignificant minority ruling over an enormous passive majority."[78] He resentfully criticized the bolsheviks' authoritarian control over the institutions of the Comintern, and he berated them for their bad manners and ignorant intransigence in exercising their authority.[79] In short, Serrati—at least as he appeared in the autumn of 1920—ostensibly had more in common with the European socialist center than he did with the bolsheviks or with the pro-bolshevik extreme left in western Europe.

Yet in spite of all this Serrati seemed to believe that he could remain in the Comintern, and unlike many other centrists he seemed genuinely to *desire* membership in it. Perhaps this paradoxical desire was the reason he continued to express his "general agreement" with the theses of the Second Congress while combating them (although this too was a common attitude of the centrists in western Europe), and the reason he even agreed to Turati's expulsion—though at a time and in a manner appropriate to Italian conditions, not at a command from the Russians.[80] Contradictorily, while emphasizing the need for mature objective conditions, Serrati agreed with Moscow's assertion that Italy was ripe for revolution[81]—something that even most of the members of the Communist faction no longer believed. In fact in his report to the ECCI in June Serrati not only asserted that revolution was imminent in Italy, he also agreed with the idea that revolution in Italy would be *more* painful than it had been in Russia.[82] In the autumn of 1920 he made no consistent effort to discard these positions; yet he refused at the same time to recognize the justice of the criticism that the party had failed to prepare for revolution, and he did no more than before to prepare for a seizure of power.

At the Second Congress and in the months following, Lenin had been more circumspect than Zinoviev in equating Serrati to the centrists. Lenin felt a genuine affection for Serrati, especially since he was the only important western socialist leader, aside from Paul Levi, who had opposed the war from a revolutionary perspective and who had rallied immediately to the Communist International. It was then difficult for Lenin to accept that the leader of the Comintern's most numerous party was a "hidden" centrist, in reality little different from Kautsky. (Lenin often retained warm personal feelings for men whom he had first admired and then later differed with: Martov was another example, and soon Levi would enter their ranks.)

Lenin tried to work out a solution to these dilemmas in an article he wrote on November 12, "On the Struggle in the Italian Socialist party."[83] In agreement with the ECCI's letter of August 21, he asserted that Italy was going through a revolutionary period fundamentally similar to that which Russia had experienced in 1917 and, further, that this situation demanded especially stringent measures for the PSI, in particular getting rid of reformists and "waverers."[84] He recalled the difficulties of Zinoviev and others on the eve of the bolshevik seizure of power, and how later, after the decisive struggles had been won, they returned to the party and were allowed to play important roles. Thus Lenin's "solution" for the troubles of the PSI was that Serrati should resign his party positions and allow more resolute leaders to take over, with the assumption that once the decisive battles had passed, he would return and serve the party in the building of socialism. (Lenin probably did not know that Serrati had already offered his resignation in early November or that his offer had been rejected by the *Direzione*.) Lenin emphasized that a withdrawal of men like Serrati, Baratono and Bacci—who were "probably . . . excellent communists"[85]—would not weaken the party but strengthen it, and would in fact make revolution possible.

Lenin's letter was published in *Avanti!* on December 10, and the next day's issue contained a long and often sarcastic reply by Serrati,[86] reiterating the positions he had formulated since his return and showing no interest in Lenin's solution. Indeed, instead of retiring from the scene, Serrati strove, with considerable success, to strengthen his position within the PSI. Far more than Longuet or Dittmann, Serrati won a broad following in the autumn of 1920.

His articles were widely read and discussed, and his speeches were enthusiastically applauded, even when he criticized the bolsheviks. His stubborn independence obviously hit a deeply responsive chord among a large segment of the party militants. The extent of the favorable response that Serrati's resistance to bolshevik control found among the former Maximalists suggests that, even if he himself had campaigned in favor of the Twenty-one Conditions, he would not have been able to pull all of his former followers with him into the Comintern. Large numbers of Italian socialists were no doubt repelled by the prospect of a new party in which Bordiga would assume a leading role.

If Serrati had reached some compromise agreement with the bolsheviks in the fall of 1920, Bordiga and the *ordinovisti* would in all likelihood still have established a separate party, creating a situation similar to that between the KAPD and KPD.[87] One must keep in mind the intense distrust of Serrati by Bordiga and the extreme left before blaming the bolsheviks for causing the split of Italian socialism. As has been stressed frequently, the bolsheviks wanted the "maximum unity possible" in the Italian party, although they insisted upon the absolute necessity of purging the right wing. But neither Serrati nor Bordiga was willing to give them that kind of unity.

Chapter VIII

The Split in Western Socialism

The split of the three main western socialist parties into communist and socialist or social-democratic branches was consummated at the congresses of Halle, Tours, and Leghorn. These congresses came as a climax to the opening of direct contacts with the bolsheviks in early 1920; they marked a decisive stage in the growth of influence of the bolsheviks in the internal affairs of western parties. The debates at the congress also constituted a final and elaborate recapitulation of the differences between western and Russian socialism.

In each congress a central point of discussion was the possibility of revolution in western Europe. Paradoxically, even after the decisive defeats of the western proletariat in 1920, the ECCI continued until the spring of 1921 to talk as if revolution in the West, or at least in Germany and Italy, was still rapidly approaching. The right-wing speakers at each of the congresses argued strongly and convincingly that such talk was nonsense, but they could not engage the left in a genuine debate on the question. The continuing incitements to revolutionary action from Moscow would contribute to the disastrous March Uprising in Germany.

The ECCI's advocacy of policies that even many probolsheviks in the West considered ill suited to the conditions in western Europe resulted in the first major "purge" of a western communist party: Paul Levi dramatically broke with the ECCI and the pro-Comintern wing of his party. In conjunction with the March Uprising, Levi's break marked a decisive end to the *biennio rosso*.

The Halle Congress

After the *Reichskonferenz* the anti-Comintern leadership of the USPD seemed anxious to get things over as quickly as possible. It succeeded in arranging that the party congress be called within six weeks instead of the originally planned eight weeks (in the second week of October rather than the beginning of November).[1] The antiaffiliation forces seemed to believe that their best chance to win a majority lay in calling a congress as quickly as possible, a likely interpretation in view of the bitter complaints of the proaffiliation wing about the rush.[2]

Within this fairly short period the polemics, accusations, and counteraccusations hurled about at the *Reichskonferenz* were taken to the country as a whole. The intraparty struggle became even more acrimonious, personal, and shrill. The party's right made much of the unorthodox pasts of Däumig and Stoecker, who had now become so ardently bolshevik—"Moscow's court chaplains,"[3] as one right-wing leader complained.

The pro-Comintern partisans returned blow for blow. Däumig asserted that behind all the rhetoric of the USPD *Bonzen* about the "Un-Marxian" Twenty-one Conditions was the simple fear of losing their party offices if the USPD merged with the KPD and was subject to ECCI discipline.[4] This charge especially outraged the anti-Comintern forces,[5] although they could hardly deny that a very heavy majority of the party bureaucracy *did* in fact reject the Comintern.

Slightly more than a week before the congress at Halle, the preliminary elections to determine the mandates of the delegates to the congress gave a comfortable majority (220 to 158) to Däumig's and Stoecker's wing,[6] quickly destroying whatever hopes Crispien's and Dittmann's wing may have had about being able to win a majority by calling the congress quickly.[7] However, the turnout at the preliminary elections was surprisingly light, considering the great importance of the issue at hand. Many areas showed an attendance of only 25 to 40 percent,[8] and while these votes were in a majority for the Comintern, such low attendance hardly demonstrated a mighty upsurge of popular enthusiasm for the cause of world revolution. This lack of broad popular support for the idea of revolutionary action was completely inconsonant with the assertions of many of the speakers at Halle that revolution in Germany was still possible and even imminent. Symptomatic of the bitterness of the intraparty struggle, local splits began to occur in advance of the party congress. The left either forced out the right when it had the majority or departed to form a new organization when it found itself in the minority.[9]

The selection of the city of Halle for the congress was to the advantage of the pro-Comintern forces, since the local USPD organization was heavily pro-Comintern.[10] Thus the congress hall was decorated in a way that made it appear to be already a meeting of a communist party: Soviet emblems were everywhere, bolshevik slogans decorated the wall, and on each table were placed brochures and pamphlets from the press of the Communist International.[11] The opposing delegates formed two very distinct groups on the right and left of the hall, leaving a wide aisle down the middle, and refused even to exchange courtesies with one another.[12] The resolutions presented by each wing were clearly and simply stated, with no suggestion of equivocation: one side accepted the Twenty-one Conditions, the other rejected them.[13]

Since their return Crispien and Dittmann had tended to maintain the offensive against Däumig and Stoecker. This was true not only in the accounts of the course of the negotiations in Moscow, but also in their more general discussion of the nature of the Russian Revolution, the doctrinal foundations of bolshevism, and the personal leadership of the Comintern. Dittmann continued to "expose" the lamentable material and political conditions of revolutionary Russia.[14] He drew a picture of a profoundly backward, Asiatic Russia where 75 percent of the population could not even read, and where the bolsheviks had come to power not for socialist reasons but merely through opportunistic appeals to the material interests of the ignorant workers, soldiers, and peasants, none of whom had the slightest notion of the meaning of communism. (Karl Radek asserted that Dittmann's articles did more harm than three years of the bourgeois press campaign against Soviet Russia.)[15] Ledebour added that because of what the bolsheviks had done, a real socialist revolution in Russia would be more difficult in the future. Both agreed that not the working class but a bureaucratic party machine ruled in Russia.

In short, the observations of the right-wing delegates while in Russia reinforced the right's long-standing assertion that bolshevism had no relevance for socialists in the West, where conditions were totally different, where the peasantry was a distinctly reactionary force, and where the working class was sufficiently well educated and organized that it would not submit to the kind of despotism the brutalized Russian lower classes had come to accept. Yet, the right wing complained, the bolsheviks stubbornly insisted that German revolutionaries establish a rigid and exaggeratedly centralized hierarchy over the German working class, a hierarchy that would give the Russians final voice on all important decisions affecting Germany. The Twenty-one Conditions, they warned, would merely kill the vitality of the German workers and frustrate their revolutionary instincts.

The prospect of Russian control of German socialism was doubly unacceptable because the bolsheviks were unable to keep themselves adequately informed about conditions in the West. Yet in spite of their limited knowledge, they had already proved themselves stubbornly intolerant of all arguments opposing their point of view, even when those arguments came from men who were in a position to know intimately the conditions involved.[16] Dittmann cited Lenin's condescending pronouncements on the measures to be adopted by German revolutionaries and then observed that Lenin was ignorant of the simplest matters of fact concerning developments within Germany.[17]

Däumig's and Stoecker's defense of the Comintern and its leaders rested on the simple assertion that the Russians need *not* be followed as strictly as the right wing said and that particular pronouncements of the bolsheviks need not be taken literally.[18] They were quite defensive at first about the Twenty-one Conditions, admitting openly and frankly that they did not like them.[19] They kept repeating that the Conditions would not have been so severe if Crispien and Dittmann had been more cooperative in Moscow.

Däumig and Stoecker did not dispute their fellow delegates'

ideas that conditions in Russia were very different from those in Germany.[20] Their arguments, now as before leaving for Russia, avoided specifics. Their speeches were thus especially repetitive and superficial; at Halle Däumig was repeatedly heckled with the irritated cry of "platitudes!" (*Selbstverständlichkeiten!*).[21] They asserted that the only way revolution could be accomplished in Germany was to decide in favor of the Communist International. It was not possible to "sit on the fence"[22] and quibble over details. It was not possible to say that one supported the Russian Revolution against its bourgeois enemies and yet at the same time reject the Comintern and criticize particular aspects of the Revolution. They frankly admitted disliking the "eastern orientation" of the new international, the large numbers of anarchists and other non-Marxists within its ranks, and the rude manners of the Russians.[23] But they had realized, once in Moscow and surrounded by the Revolution, that their own views needed a "powerful revision"[24] and that the future of the revolution in Germany and in the world depended on the creation of a united, powerful revolutionary international, an international that would combine the revolutionary *élan* of the East with the democratic mass parties of the West.[25]

As at the *Reichskonferenz*, the Halle congress disintegrated into utter chaos on several occasions. But there was a difference in that now it was the pro-Comintern speakers who received most of the applause. Those who attacked the idea of affiliation encountered jeers, repeated interruptions and objections, and constant heckling. The old party regulars explained this change by pointing to the influx of new, unschooled masses that were swamping the structures of the party.[26] Indeed, in Germany, France, and Italy, the struggle over affiliation to the Communist International had strong overtones of a conflict of generations. Dittmann, at the *Reichskonferenz*, had blurted out, "You young brat" (*Säugling*) to one of the pro-Comintern speakers, and Dahlem told the delegates that he had heard someone near him muttering "silly, naive kid!" (*dummer, grüner Junge*).[27] Similar outbursts would occur at Tours and Leghorn.

Zinoviev was granted a passport to come to the Halle congress. His speech there,[28] which lasted four hours, was delivered with great rhetorical skill and fire, and the pro-Comintern side of the hall received it with frenzied enthusiasm. He repeated and elaborated the standard fare of bolshevik propaganda, but he played down the Twenty-one Conditions and openly promised that the Conditions would be applied with the "greatest tolerance" once the real enemies of the Comintern had departed.[29] He implied that even changes in the Conditions were still possible. This caused a storm of indignation on the right wing, which complained, "Why wasn't this offer made before?" "Retraction!" (*Rückzug*) and "cover-up!" (*Verkleidung*).[30] Most of the antiaffiliation delegates refused to believe in the sincerity of Zinoviev's words, passing them off as another Russian trick.[31]

A recurring theme of the pro-Comintern speakers was that the revolutionary leaders of the German proletariat had to gird their loins for the approaching revolution in Germany. Zinoviev did not push this idea with such recklessness and questionable reasoning as he and other bolsheviks were then doing in application to Italy; yet, as will be discussed in the final section of this chapter, it was perfectly consistent with the theory of the "revolutionary offensive" forwarded by the ECCI in late 1920. Certainly among many of the left-wing USPD speakers a lingering hope for revolution in the near future was apparent, and most seemed to believe that unification with the KPD under Comintern leadership would somehow powerfully enhance the chances for successful revolution in Germany. These were not propitious signs for Levi's hopes to reorganize the party while avoiding clashes with the government.

At last the ballots were cast. To no one's surprise, Däumig and Stoecker's resolution received 236 "yes" votes and 156 "no" votes.[32] With this Crispien announced that anyone who had voted for the proaffiliation resolution had automatically excluded himself from the party. The right-wing delegates then slowly filed out, showered with insults, shouting back "Long live the USPD! Long live world revolution![33]

Negotiations at Halle

In his speech at Halle Zinoviev made an obvious attempt to appear as conciliatory as possible toward those who had not yet made up their mind concerning affiliation to the Comintern. He did this to reassure not only the left of the USPD but also the French and Italian delegates who were present at the congress. In fact, before his speech Zinoviev had met in his hotel room with Longuet. The French centrist explained to Zinoviev which of the Twenty-one Conditions he found unacceptable; Zinoviev assured him that these should present no insurmountable obstacles to joining the new international.[34]

Daniel Renoult, representing the left of the French Reconstructionists, also travelled to Halle to confer with Zinoviev. He came specifically to obtain Zinoviev's approval to the draft resolution in favor of affiliation to the Comintern which Cachin, Frossard, and the members of the Committee for the Comintern had agreed upon. This resolution, which will be discussed more fully in the following section, was composed in a way that allowed Longuet and the right of the Reconstruction Committee to be admitted if they agreed to follow the decisions of the majority of the SFIO and the directives of the ECCI.

That Zinoviev freely consented to this draft and made every effort to assure Renoult that the Longuet faction, and the SFIO's unity, could be saved is strong evidence that in spite of the manner in which Zinoviev had manipulated Cachin and Frossard on the conditions of admission, the bolshevik leader still intended to uphold the overall agreements he had made with the SFIO delegates in Moscow. Once he had returned to Russia Zinoviev continued in the meetings of the ECCI to defend his agreements with the French centrists.[35] Yet Zinoviev's friendliness to Longuet and Renoult made the relationship between the ECCI and the Italians more difficult. Il Soviet complained publicly about Zinoviev's conduct at Halle,[36] and the resolution Serrati's faction drew up at Florence in late November in certain ways strongly resembled—no doubt intentionally—the draft Renoult had brought to Halle for Zinoviev's approval.

Renoult returned to France convinced that his party could join the Comintern and still maintain a substantial unity.[37] However, Zinoviev's assurances did not seem to sway Longuet. He suspected that Zinoviev's new concessions were just a maneuver,[38] and he made clear in his speech at Halle that his real sympathies lay with Crispien and Dittmann, not with the proaffiliation faction. When the right wing retired from the congress hall, Longuet went with it.[39]

Delegates from many countries visited Zinoviev's hotel room in Halle, including Bombacci and Niccolini, but significantly not Serrati. On October 22 Zinoviev composed a strongly worded letter to Serrati observing how the right-wing speakers at Halle had cited him as an authority in their attacks on the theses of the Second Congress. The letter ended with a warning to Serrati that he had to choose between coming over completely to the side of the Comintern or joining hands with the centrists and reformists; there was no other alternative.[40]

Zinoviev was thus much less conciliatory with Serrati than he had been with either the USPD right or the SFIO center. Even so he apparently had not yet given up hope that Serrati would finally give in, for a few days later he wrote another letter, more courteous and friendly in tone and probably not intended for publication, assuring the Italian leader that once the reformists had been expelled from the PSI, the genuine revolutionaries in the party would be given wide rein by the ECCI. Yet he also kept up the pressure on Serrati by informing the Italian Communist faction that now it alone represented the Comintern in Italy and thereafter if Serrati wished to work with the Comintern he would have to enter the Communist faction and accept its present leadership.[41]

Serrati also continued to hope that an eventual agreement could be worked out with the bolsheviks, that they would finally make some of the concessions and rectifications he demanded. These last letters of Zinoviev prompted Serrati to make more of an effort himself to reach a reconciliation with the bolsheviks. On November 17 and again on December 7 he wrote to Zinoviev asking for a meeting in Reval, Estonia, in order to explain the position of the Unitary Communist faction. He emphasized that no one in the PSI wanted to leave the Comintern and that a schism in the party would only aid the reactionaries in Italy, who were ready to profit from the inexperience of the "leftist insurrectionists" of the Communist faction.[42]

Zinoviev's reply arrived on December 25. He said that he would be "most happy" to meet with Serrati, urging him to fix a date. (If the reconciliation at Reval was to be according to Lenin's "solution," one can imagine an interesting scene with Zinoviev, the former "waverer," proposing that Serrati do as he had done in 1917 and resign all his positions. . . .) However, in the meantime, relations between Serrati's and Bordiga's factions had continued to deteriorate. By the time Zinoviev's reply arrived the national congress was so near that it was obviously impossible to travel to Reval in time to return for the congress. Thus the trip was abandoned and with it the last faint hope for a reconciliation between Serrati and the bolsheviks.[43]

The factions of the SFIO

After Halle three basic groups took definite form in France in preparation for the party congress at Tours, then planned for the end of December. The Reconstruction Committee was shattered into three parts: those who had been won over by Cachin's and Frossard's campaign and by Zinoviev's pledge at Halle (e.g., Renoult, Dunois, Louis); those who affirmed their desire to enter the Comintern but who still had reservations about the Twenty-one Conditions and remained suspicious of Zinoviev's assurances (Longuet, Paul Faure); and those who rejected the Comintern outright (Léon Blum, Mayéras, Adrien Pressemane). The first group, following the lead of Cachin and Frossard, worked together with the Committee for the Comintern behind the resolution approved by Zinoviev at Halle. The resolution they agreed upon, which came to be known as the resolution of "affiliation without reservations," was a long and carefully composed document.[44] While affirming its basic acceptance of most of the Twenty-one Conditions, the resolution skirted direct criticism of Longuet's center, called special attention to those of the Twenty-one Conditions (especially condition six) that recognized that each national member party would "in general" be the best judge of its own internal situation, and stated that the exceptions allowed in condition twenty (on the question of the exclusion of centrists and those who voted against the Twenty-one Conditions) should apply in the case of the SFIO. Further, the question of *noyautage* was lost in a tangle of words which in effect rejected the bolshevik point of view. Finally, even the name "Communist party" was avoided; the party would call itself, "Socialist party, French Section of the Communist International," and it promised to explain later in a meeting with the ECCI the reasons for this name. In effect, then, what this resolution proposed was "affiliation without reservations"—but with reservations. Yet it won the acceptance of Zinoviev and the ECCI.

Longuet and his followers composed a resolution[45] that came to be known as "affiliation with reservations," the reservations representing a more complete form of the objections to the Twenty-one Conditions that Zinoviev had invited Longuet to spell out at Halle.[46] But if Zinoviev had found nothing particularly objectionable in Longuet's reservations at Halle, surely now something had been added that Longuet had not mentioned before. Indeed, it is hard to believe that those who composed this resolution had any sincere intention of its being accepted by the ECCI. To begin with, the notion of the dictatorship of the proletariat was so defined as to criticize the bolshevik regime implicitly: the dictatorship should be short-lived, "impersonal"—in order that it not "degenerate into tyranny"—and directed not by the party alone, but also by the *syndicats* and cooperatives. Thus Longuet and his followers rejected the primary role of the party and denied any role at all to workers' councils or soviets. The resolution declared that while parliamentary deputies should reject ministerial alliances with bourgeois parties, they should at the same time carry on a "constructive" opposition in parliament. The kind of discipline under the ECCI laid down by the theses of the Second Congress was simply not acceptable; the Reconstructionists seemed to be proposing a return to the old practices of the Second International, where the central bodies had had the power only to proclaim general directives. Equally reminiscent of the Second International was the categorical rejection of all illegal, clandestine activity, which, the resolution observed, was "neither possible nor desirable," especially in the case of a democratic republic such as France.

The third group resulting from the fracture of the Reconstruction Committee took an unequivocally hostile position toward the Comintern. In this forthright hostility it was only natural that Blum and those other ex-Reconstructionists who rallied to the resolution he composed should make common cause with the Renaudel right wing, which all along had voiced stubborn opposition to the Communist International. However, this natural coming together was at first resisted, and when an amalgamation finally did occur, it was on the terms of Blum and his friends. The resolution he composed for the congress of Tours followed the lines of the party program voted in early 1919 (which also bore the imprint of Blum's hand)[47] and was thus more a centrist than a reformist document.[48] Similarly, the *Comité de la résistance*, formed to coordinate the work against affiliation, was founded by Blum and his group and was only subsequently joined by Renaudel's group.[49]

It was at this time that Léon Blum began to demonstrate most remarkably the qualities that were later to help him assume leadership of the SFIO. He already had a certain advantage over figures like Longuet and Paul Faure in that he had not become so clearly associated with any particular faction in the party; he had been known largely for his conciliatory work in the difficult months directly after the war. Even more than his lack of *parti pris*, Blum's rise to preeminence in the party in late 1920 can be explained by his penetrating analyses of the problems that beset the SFIO and of the nature of the communist threat to its unity. In his thoroughness, clarity, and lack of emotionalism, Blum elevated the level of discussion and tended to attentuate some of the petty bickering of the party's many *literati*.[50]

Although the stand taken by the Longuet wing in its resolution made it unlikely that the ECCI would accept it, Cachin and Frossard still strongly insisted that the ECCI would not exclude Longuet if he and his followers bowed to the majority of the party in the future. Frossard was especially ardent in trying to soothe and win over Longuet, for whom he felt a genuine personal sympathy. But Longuet grew more and more scornful of Frossard's efforts. Thus, on November 16 he observed in *Le Populaire*,

... in his [Frossard's]subtle mode of speech Moscow's most shocking and outrageous statements disappear as if by magic; what originally appeared harsh smooths out, mysteriously, as if bewitched: why, it is only a question of first truths that we have all learned in the primary school of socialism.[51]

Longuet's irony was particularly biting on this day because news of a letter from Zinoviev had reached Paris.[52] The letter informed the French that now the question must be put clearly to Longuet: did he want to follow in the footsteps of Crispien, Dittmann, and Hilferding, or would he stop his nonsense and consent to follow the lead of the majority of the party? Zinoviev ended his letter with the following instructions:

You ought to put a knife at the throat of Longuet and his followers and then ask them to answer; only if they say they accept and that they want to carry out the theses and conditions of the Communist International will the final decision be taken.[53]

The crudity of this letter jolted Longuet, and in the article mentioned above, he asked mockingly, "What does Frossard have to say about Zinoviev's knife?" Longuet's friends and supporters were equally stung, and the SFIO press was filled with outraged comments.[54]

To any realistic observer this incident must have seemed the end to any hope that Longuet could be reconciled to membership in the Comintern, or that the Comintern had much interest in accepting Longuet. But Frossard and his faction stubbornly refused to lose hope, and they expressed extreme irritation when "Varine" in *Bulletin Communiste* voiced his own belief that Longuet must be thrown aside.[55] They informed Longuet that he need pay little attention to Souvarine, whose writings did not bind the party and who was a "narrow-minded bigot—who does not represent the majority of the party."[56]

The Congress of Tours

In the final days before the congress of Tours Longuet and his followers publicly announced that they still hoped to join the Comintern directly and save the unity of the SFIO.[57] These proclamations were no doubt stimulated by the results of the preliminary federal elections, which gave the Cachin-Frossard resolution a three-to-one majority. The strength of this majority was a shock to the Longuet wing, which had at first, like the Crispien-

Dittmann wing in Germany, been fairly confident that the Twenty-one Conditions would be rejected by a majority of the SFIO. Even now Longuet insisted that the vote was not truly representative of opinion within the SFIO, but rather was based on a false fear, and one that the partisans of affiliation played up fully in France as they did in Germany, that a vote against the Comintern would aid reaction.[58]

In spite of the results of the federal elections, there was considerably more suspense, as the delegates assembled in the Salle du Manège at Tours on Christmas Day, than there had been at Halle. This was not because any of the delegates came to Tours uncertain of what course to follow and expecting to make up their minds on the merits of the arguments of one side or the other; most of them, as had been the case at Halle, carried mandatory votes and in any case had already formed unshakeable personal opinions through the months of debate on the question of the international. The debates were thus only a repetition and summary of all the passionate exchanges that had occurred before, reiterated and registered one final time. The suspense of the congress lay in the fact that, in spite of Zinoviev's "knife" letter and the outrage it had caused, Longuet still affirmed his desire to enter the Comintern with the rest of the party. Thus the Cachin-Frossard faction continued almost feverishly to proclaim that Longuet would be accepted by the ECCI if he would bow to the decision of the majority of the congress.

The Salle du Manège in Tours—small, run-down, and crowded with uncomfortable iron folding chairs—was hardly an appropriate setting for this historic congress. The local federation had done what it could to overcome the dingy surroundings: red banners were hung on the walls surrounding three large portraits of Jean Jaurès, and behind the speakers' stand were tacked up posters proclaiming in large letters, "The emancipation of the workers will be the task of the workers themselves," and, "Workers of the world unite!"[59] (Unlike the decorators at Halle, it would seem, the men in charge of decorations at Tours opposed the split of their party.)

It was decided on the first day, over the protests of the right and center, to hear reports from the provincial delegates before going on to the general discussion of the question of the international.

Thus for the next day and a half delegates from the provincial federations delivered brief reports on the state of affairs in their federations. As planned, this turned out to be an impressive showing of strength for the left of the congress.

The provincial delegates' reports underlined some interesting developments within the SFIO since the last party congress at Strasbourg.[60] Nearly all of the delegates remarked on the precipitous growth in their federations, something which had begun in mid-1919 and which by this time amounted in most cases to a swamping, if not total inundation, of the established prewar party structures. In all, the party membership had swollen to 180,000 (relatively small compared to the USPD's 800,000, but still about two-and-a-half times the size of the prewar SFIO). Yet this influx had several puzzling aspects. A very substantial percentage of the growth seemed due to new rural and peasant members.[61] Perhaps even more surprising, the rural districts were for the most part overwhelmingly in favor of the pro-Comintern resolution, while Longuet's resolution won favor in a large proportion of the working-class districts—in general those areas where the SFIO had established itself in the prewar period. It appeared that if the working-class districts alone had voted, the Twenty-one Conditions might have been rejected.

Time and again the pro-Comintern provincial speakers seemed more concerned to voice their resentment against the *parlementaires* and Parisian bigwigs, who ignored the problems of the provinces, than to praise the bolsheviks or explain why they thought joining the Comintern was necessary. It seemed as if these delegates saw their votes for the Comintern both as a way of punishing the old leaders of the party for their support of the war and of protesting against the Parisian supremacy over the other federations.

Mixed in with these resentments were undertones of a conflict of generations. Older members like Marcel Sembat complained that young enthusiasts "joined the party but knew nothing of socialism."[62] During the war such *Majoritaires* as Sembat, Renaudel, and Thomas had been known as *"les vieillards"* (the old men), while such younger *Minoritaires* as Frossard, Longuet, and Faure were called *"les jeunes"* (the young ones).[63] With the influx of new members after the war, even the relatively young *Minoritaires* felt that the party had been swamped by men ignorant of socialism. Frossard wrote:

Only hatred of the war attracted them to us. They arrived in the party filled to the brim with the dreadful bitterness of tragic years. The war had cruelly marked them, and the odor of death still floated over their martyred flesh.[64]

To Frossard these men seemed to be looking for a new kind of party, for a leader to give them marching orders, and they were enticed by the easy slogan of communism.

The general discussion at Tours in many ways resembled that at Halle. The question of when and if revolution would come naturally was an important part of the debates. The USPD left had repeatedly voiced its belief that socialist revolution would come to Germany in the near future. But few French socialists, either on the right or the left, genuinely believed that the twice-defeated French proletariat could challenge its all-powerful bourgeoisie until after an extended period of reorganization and recruitment. Those members of the Committee for the Comintern who had earlier emphasized that revolution was rapidly approaching in France were not much in evidence at Tours. Lefebvre had perished in an accident at sea during his return from the Second Congress, and most of the other leading figures of the Committee were still in jail. Cachin and Frossard normally spoke for the left, and they of course did not believe in the imminence of revolution in France.

In Germany and Italy, where in retrospect it seems that reaction was assuming more ugly and threatening forms than in France, the USPD and PSI seemed relatively unawed by it. In France the right wing and center fairly quaked before the power of the bourgeoisie: Marcel Sembat confessed to the congress that he was "frightened—horribly frightened" of the "new Commune" that the ruling classes in France desired, and even planned, to provoke.[65] As for the peasant support that the provincial delegates had so emphasized, Sembat pointed out that the peasants with socialist sympathies were a pitiful minority; the overwhelming majority of France's peasants now possessed land and had even grown rich from the war; these men firmly backed the bourgeois parties. Even those who now were toying with socialist notions could not be considered reliable allies. "Tomorrow you will find them against you in the elections—and their guns facing you in the streets!"[66] Paul Faure underlined with great cogency the lack of objective conditions in France for a revolution. In lugubrious detail he described the preparations, in the form of military units ready to use machine guns and poison gas, the bourgeoisie was making against any new working class outbreak.[67]

The pro-Comintern speakers' arguments resembled those of Däumig or Stoecker in that they avoided direct or detailed rebuttal of the criticisms made by the center and right and emphasized the need to show solidarity with Soviet Russia. The left's response to the dire predictions of reactionary violence in France was not to deny that the bourgeoisie was arming itself; rather, it complained that for socialists to dwell on such matters merely served to discourage and demoralize the proletariat.[68] (It was in any case obvious from the light turnout at the elections to the congress that demoralization of the rank and file was a problem in France as in Germany.)[69]

The left's discomfort with the Twenty-one Conditions was still obvious at Tours. In his speech Frossard did not hide his distaste for some of the Conditions, but explained soothingly that "no one will find in them his exact thought, but everyone can find in them what is essential to his thought."[70] What was most important was to join the Comintern in order to protect the Russian Revolution. At the same time Comintern membership would assure a new determination, a new purity of motive, and a new will to power that would prepare the party to face the unprecedented conditions thrown up by the war. Yet Frossard himself hardly sought to give the impression of a determined Leninist revolutionary. Later in the same speech he commented, "the most difficult thing, someone once said, is not to do your duty, but to know what it is. For my part, I have never more experienced the truth of that [saying] than in these last three months."[71]

The tension between the Committee for the Comintern and the followers of Cachin and Frossard had not abated by the time of Tours. The delegates to the congress remarked on it frequently, especially those who had come over to the pro-Comintern side under the influence of Cachin's and Frossard's campaign. They were also apprehensive: with whom would they be dealing in the future, Frossard or Souvarine? A few openly predicted that if Souvarine would gain the upper hand, then even Cachin and Frossard would not last long.[72]

The most substantial argument in opposition to affiliation was delivered by Léon Blum.[73] This speech was the culmination of his elaborate and penetrating criticism of the doctrinal foundations of bolshevism, which had begun in mid-October in *L'Humanité*.[74] Where Sembat, Faure and others had concentrated on the practical impossibility of revolution in France and the inapplicability of the Twenty-one Conditions, Blum focused on more purely doctrinal issues. He meticulously scrutinized the theses and statutes voted at the Second Congress and attempted to make clear the relationship of bolshevism to orthodox Marxism. He was particularly intent on demolishing Cachin's and Frossard's contention that bolshevism was little more than prewar Guesdism. He insisted that Lenin's theories were something almost totally new and certainly alien to Marxism in almost all essential respects. Bolshevism had developed in the peculiar setting of tsarist Russia and could thus have little or no application to western Europe.

Like the USPD right wing, Blum put special stress on the undemocratic tendencies of bolshevism, tendencies which, he asserted, ran contrary to a central concern of Marx and Engels and of all western Marxist parties since Marx's time. The bolsheviks' absolute disregard for majority opinion, the monolithic control they gave to the central committee over freedom of expression within the party, the organization of power from the top down instead of from the bottom up—all this would smother the life of a western socialist party. In the same way, the secret committees, the elaborate illegal framework, the general clandestinity the bolsheviks wanted to impose on the SFIO simply did not correspond to the needs of a legally recognized party in a democratic republic. Blum stressed that he by no means felt it necessary to give unqualified allegiance to bourgeois legality—at the proper time it could and should be cast aside—but asserted that what the bolsheviks envisaged would inevitably result in repression; a party that openly flouted the law could not take advantage of the organizational opportunities permitted by the law.

Yet these opportunities were essential to the proper preparation for the revolution. Further, what the bolsheviks intended would mean that a secret committee, unknown even to the party membership in France, appointed and controlled by Moscow, would be able to direct the party's actions and make its most important decisions. "Who will determine the most important acts for the life of our party?" Blum asked the congress, his weak and high voice scarcely penetrating through the tumult of protests, "—men whom you don't even know!"[75]

Blum strongly attacked the bolshevik conception of revolution and the socialist transformation of society. For a genuine Marxist, he insisted, the true "revolution" consisted of the transformation of private property into communal property, not the storming of the barricades, not the purely military aspect of seizing political power. This true revolution was possible only when the proletariat composed the immense majority of the population and when its education and awareness of its historical role was adequate to permit it to rule the new society. A professional elite, trained in the tactics of seizing power, could not possibly replace a united, educated working class composing a majority of the population. It was a perversion of orthodox Marxism to say that this elite should seize power in opposition to the majority of the nation, or even the majority of the working class, in order to supervise a *future* social transformation. To reason that the working class could never attain full socialist consciousness while under the sway of the bourgeois state was not Marxism but Blanquism, and such an attempt to organize and direct the "inorganic masses" would be certain to backfire:

We think that any movement concerned with the seizure of power that relies on a kind of instinctive passion, a herd-like violence of broad, inorganic masses, is based on very fragile material and will be exposed to very dangerous set-backs. . . . Those who marched with you the night before will be perhaps the first the next day to stand you against the wall![76]

Much more than any other speaker at Tours, Blum stung and angered the partisans of affiliation. He had to strain repeatedly to oppose his weak voice and flagging energies to the turbulence and heckling from the left in the congress hall. When, toward the end of his speech, he affirmed his belief in the necessity of national defense, even under capitalism, the hall exploded with protests. Delegates stood shouting, "*A bas la guerre*," hurled insults at Blum, and finally joined in a chorus of the *Internationale*.[77] Order had scarcely been reestablished when Blum, in his parting words to the congress, broached the problem of the future relations between those who would follow Moscow and those who would choose to stay with what Blum called the *"vieille maison."* Recognizing the inevitability of a split in the party, he asked,

Are we going to spend our time before the bourgeoisie calling each other traitors, renegades, fools, and criminals? Can't we, on each side, believe in the others' good faith? I ask: is there anyone here who doesn't think that I am a socialist?

From the back of the hall came the reply, "You're a confusionist!"[78] Another tumultuous interlude ensued before calm was again restored and Blum finally returned to his seat. Years later, Frossard would write, "Léon Blum, at Tours, was right and we were wrong."[79]

The debates raged on for several days after Blum's speech, but they were largely anticlimactic because of the events of the following morning (the twenty-eighth). Shortly after the initial speech of the morning session, a telegram arrived from the ECCI. It announced that while it was possible to accept the resolution with the "signatures of Loriot, Monatte, Souvarine, Cachin, Frossard, and others," the resolution signed by Longuet and Faure was "filled with a spirit of reformism and petty, quibbling diplomacy. . . . They [Longuet et al.] have been and remain determined agents of bourgeois influence in the proletariat. . . . The Communist International can have nothing to do with the authors of such resolutions."[80]

Immediately after the reading of the telegram, shouts of "Frossard! Frossard!" filled the congress. Vengefully they asked: could Frossard's verbal legerdemain conjure away this new apparition? But before Frossard could reply, a new communication arrived, this time from the veteran German revolutionary Clara Zetkin, who had planned to speak to the congress after Zinoviev had been re-fused entry into France. But she too was denied a passport, and so finally sent a letter to the congress. The letter was now read—a rous-ing appeal to the SFIO to forsake its old ways and enter the Comin-tern.[82] When Frossard was finally able to mount the tribune—after several more interruptions—and to try to deal with the "Zinoviev telegram" and other matters brought up in the course of the de-bates, he was again interrupted, this time by the spectacular appear-ance of Clara Zetkin herself, who had been able to sneak into the congress hall in spite of the police outside. Her appearance caused a sensation. She was wildly applauded by the left as she launched into another long appeal in favor of affiliation.

Frossard's explanations, when he was at last able to finish, were predictably feeble. The telegram of the ECCI had ended even his hope for a final *ralliement* of the Longuet wing. The following excerpt from the stenographic account of the congress gives some idea of the highly emotional last minutes:

LONGUET: Can we discuss the matter of our being agents of the bourgeoisie?

RENOULT: We consider . . . that it [the telegram] must be seen simply in terms of doctrinal polemic. . . .

LONGUET: The expression "agents of the bourgeoisie" is an impertinence! . . .

RENOULT: My dear Longuet. . . .

LONGUET: No! No! I am an agent of the bourgeoisie and I can't be dear to you.

RENOULT: I said to you, "my dear Longuet" (noise in the cen-ter of the congress). . . . You know we said to you in the course of our discussion this afternoon that we did not accept at all the interpretation that you have to this phrase of Zinoviev. . . .

LONGUET: It is not an interpretation; there are words.

FROSSARD: . . . I do not agree with Zinoviev. For me you are not an agent of the bourgeoisie.

LONGUET: Thanks![82]

When finally the vote was taken, the Frossard-Cachin motion received 3,208 votes to 1,022 for the Longuet-Faure resolution—more than a three-to-one majority, just as in the preliminary elections.[83] Blum and the *résistants* withdrew their resolution at the last moment and joined the Longuet wing when it withdrew from the congress.[84] Frossard mounted the tribune:

> The inevitable has come to pass. We can only say that we have done as much as could have been done to save as much unity as possible. . . . Together, with one heart, with one will, we will work for world revolution in this great socialist party which continues the tradition of those that went before it and which intends to remain faithful to its glorious past and to all revolutionary traditions.

To cries of *"Vive la révolution sociale!"* the meeting came to an end at 2:45 in the morning.[85]

The Congress of Leghorn

The PSI had at first planned to hold its national congress in mid-December in Florence. But, because of the power of the fascists there, Leghorn was chosen instead, and the congress date was put off until mid-January. A week of grey skies and drizzling rain preceded the opening of the congress. Nature thus complemented the mood of many of the delegates that filed into the spacious and comfortable Goldoni Theater, with its flower ornaments and large pictures of Andrea Costa, Karl Liebknecht, and Karl Marx.[86] A year and a quarter after the triumphant Bologna congress, Italian socialists were again assembling, but this time with spirits weighted down by the impending split of their party, the humiliating defeat of the September factory occupations, and the rising tide of fascist terror. Even the left wing of the congress could not enjoy the sense of triumph that the left wings of the SFIO and USPD felt, since in spite of the extraordinary influx of new members into the PSI the preliminary elections made it clear that Serrati and the Unitarian Communists still had a substantial majority of the party behind them. Approximately 110,000 votes had been cast for the Unitarians and only 65,000 for Bordiga's Communists.[87] (The PSI's total membership at this time was approximately 220,000, about 40,000 larger than the SFIO.)[88] Thus the left tended to be resentful and disruptive, though of course Bordiga himself was not disturbed to have such a limited following.

Serrati was repeatedly greeted with hate-filled taunts of "traitor!"[89] and the congress regularly dissolved into utter chaos. Bordiga repeatedly refused to respect the orders of the presiding officers that he remain quiet and allow the speaker to continue, and he was finally bodily carried out of the congress hall by two Unitarians, only to reenter immediately.[90] When Vacirca called Bombacci a "pen-knife revolutionary," the latter pulled out a revolver. Indescribable pandemonium followed.[91] There was no Léon Blum at Leghorn to raise the level of debate and to scrutinize the content of the bolsheviks' theses. More than at Halle or Tours, the Italian congress was a shouting match, a parade of slogans, and a circus, with little useful discussion or exchange of views.

As at Halle and Tours, the conflict of factions had overtones of a conflict of generations. Baratono, associated with Serrati's faction, was constantly interrupted by a young member of the Communist faction. In response a voice boomed out from the seats of the Unitarians: "he's just a kid. Give him his bottle and he'll be quiet!"[92] A few moments later Baratono himself referred to one of the Communist delegates as a "callow youth" (*pallido giovanetto*).[93] Later in the congress Serrati pleaded with the young Communists:

You expect us to give you our esteem . . . you who have joined the party only after the fraternal bloodbath. You shout at us that you are "most pure" (*purissimi*). We do give you our esteem. But, excuse me, can't you give a little to those who have been in the party for thirty years? . . . I urge you comrades, give a little esteem to the old-timers (*decrepiti*) because it is no sin to have grown old while holding high our red flag—never betraying it![94]

Zinoviev had hoped to come to Italy, intending to repeat his performance at Halle, but he was denied entry by the Italian government. At the last minute two special representatives of the Comintern arrived: Rakosi, a bolshevik of Hungarian origin, and Kabakchiev of the Bulgarian Communist party. Paul Levi also made his way to Italy, as did Dittmann and Rosenfeld of the USPD. Serrati engaged in long talks with all of them prior to the opening of the congress,[95] and both Levi and Kabakchiev made one final effort to bring Serrati around, with no success. Thus in his speech at the congress, composed after his talk with Serrati, the Bulgarian leader abandoned all moderation in his attacks on Serrati and the Unitarians.[96] (Kabakchiev was known within the Comintern to be in Zinoviev's entourage, and he had the reputation, as did Zinoviev, of being a harsh and unscrupulous polemicist. It thus seems unlikely that Zinoviev selected him with any sincere belief that he might reach a last-minute agreement with Serrati.) In an even more exaggerated and careless form, Kabakchiev reiterated the points the ECCI had first laid down in its letter of August 21 and had subsequently developed in a number of communications: the situation in Italy was revolutionary, and the urgent task of communists in Italy was to cast away all unreliable elements and prepare to seize power. But if in late August the thesis that Italy was on the verge of proletarian revolution could have been considered remotely plausible, by mid-January it had begun to appear ridiculous. Moreover, Kabakchiev's arrogant manners and wooden argumentation incensed the right and center of the congress.

Against Kabakchiev the speakers of the right and center emphasized the great obstacles to revolution in Italy and ridiculed the notion that the right wing of the party was responsible for the failure of revolution to develop. Vacirca, in his descriptions of the powerful resources open to the Italian government, sounded like Sembat at Tours.[97] He dwelled on the old issue of Italy's extreme vulnerability to blockade and on the foolishness of expecting that the proletariat of other countries, especially that of the Entente, would do anything effective against blockade or intervention if proletarian revolution came to Italy. He emphasized that proletarian revolution in Italy at the present time would be largely a northern affair and largely urban; it would thus quickly turn into civil war between north and south and between country and city—a war the Italian proletariat could not win. Vacirca was from Bologna, and he felt with particular sharpness the danger of careless revolutionary rhetoric and ill-planned action; he had seen what a very few well-armed and determined fascists could do.[98] (Vacirca had called Bombacci a "pen-knife revolutionary" because the latter had fled Bologna in the face of the fascists' attacks.)

Baratono carefully went over the development of the occupa-

tion of factories in order to disprove the contention that the reformists in the party were to blame for the occupations not turning into
a revolutionary seizure of power. He asserted that the right wing's
opposition to giving the situation a revolutionary turn was not due
to cowardice or treachery but simply to the belief that it would end
in bloody failure—a point of view many left wingers shared at that
time, in particular Gennari,[99] a leading representative of the *Direzione* while Serrati was in Russia. Baratono strongly emphasized his
belief that broad historical factors had to prepare a revolutionary
situation; when the situation was ripe for a seizure of power it could
not be undermined by a few individuals like Turati or D'Arragona.[100] He mocked the belief of many young Communists that
"revolution is no more than making a revolt tomorrow."[101]

A large part of Baratono's speech consisted of verbose and sentimental pleas for unity, which in many ways resembled the speeches
of the pro-Comintern centrists at Tours. He cited the concessions
Zinoviev had granted the French centrists and emphasized that, like
the French, all the Unitarians wanted was to be able to accept anyone, whatever his past, into the new party.[102] After the party had
been established, anyone who would not accept party discipline
would be expelled, but not mechanically, according to orders from
Moscow, and not in a way that would deeply split the party and de-
story the working-class institutions built up over the years.

The arguments presented against immediate revolution were
not refuted by the Communists. The left of the congress repeatedly
interrupted the right-wing and Unitarian speakers with shouts of
"we know, we know," or "that is what Nitti [the former prime min-
ister] says," or "defeatists, what are you trying to do?"[103] In fact
throughout the autumn and early winter campaign in favor of the
Twenty-one Conditions, only one serious attempt had been made
by the Communists to counter the arguments against immediate
revolution.[104] But the article that made this attempt was so shallow
and lacking in realism that it was subsequently attacked from all
sides—by Graziadei, Giungi Davide, and even Lenin himself.[105]

Serrati continued to complain bitterly about the special treatment given the French centrists; he was as tedious in this as were

the pro-Comintern speakers in their endless efforts to show that the French did not really have different conditions to fulfil.[106] He cited a letter he had received from members of the extreme left of the SFIO which expressed sympathy with his resentment over the ECCI's acceptance of Cachin and Frossard. They recognized that the PSI was being treated unjustly in relationship to the French party, but they urged Serrati to understand that Cachin's presence in the ranks of the pro-Comintern forces was necessary because of their weakness and because of the many rank-and-file adherents Cachin would attract to the new communist party in France.[107]

Oddly, Serrati was still unwilling to abandon his own earlier thesis that the situation was revolutionary in Italy. In spite of the stunning offensive of the fascists in the last few months he continued to affirm that the working class would take over because the Italian bourgeoisie was at the end of its resources and no longer capable of rule. In fact, contradictorily, he cited the fascists' victories as further evidence that the PSI should not split: a divided proletariat in Italy would not be able to stand up against the onslaught of Mussolini's followers (a doubly weak argument, since one could have more plausibly argued that Serrati's stubborn attachment to Turati was about to divide the Italian proletariat far more than if the right wing were excluded). Serrati even went so far as to assert that a united socialist party in Italy was *Russia's* only hope against the nations surrounding her; since the proletarian masses of France, England, and the United States followed "reactionary" labor organizations, Russia could no more expect real aid from them now than it could in July 1919.[108]

It was thus not only Kabakchiev who made a foolish impression or who put forth weak and implausible arguments at Leghorn. There was much vain and empty talk at this congress, although each faction seemed convinced that the others had a monopoly on it. An interesting interlude in this respect occurred when Abbo, a veteran party member, was heckled by the left with shouts of *"vana retorica!"* Stung by the remark, Abbo held up his calloused worker's hands to the congress and asked if they were the hands of a rhetorician:

Comrades, permit me to say that if in all our meetings there was less rhetoric, if there were fewer lawyers and members of the professions . . . [applause], and instead more authentic workers who know from experience the tearful sufferings of a toil-filled life, then we would not be experiencing this sad spectacle. [approval, noise] I believe that if the proletariat could be free of its tutelage and learn to defend its own cause, without so many subtleties, without so many words that end in "ism," which the poor workers—nine-tenths of whom cannot even read—do not understand . . . communism, socialism . . . [applause, noise].[109]

The final voting at Leghorn presented no surprises. Out of 172,-487 mandates the Unitarians won 98,028, the Communists 58,783, and the Concentrationists 14,695.[110] Serrati had won, but it was a pyrrhic victory, for his party was split down the middle. Bordiga was the real victor over Serrati and even over the leaders of the Comintern. After the results of the voting were read to the congress, Bordiga announced that his faction would meet in the San Marco Theater to establish the Italian Communist party. To the strains of the *Internazionale* the Communists filed out of the hall.[111]

In his final words to the congress Serrati blamed the bolsheviks for these sad developments. Their unwillingness to listen to the advice of those most qualified to judge conditions in the West was obvious not only in Italy, but also in Germany: in a meeting shortly before, Levi had complained bitterly to Serrati about the Russians' high-handed treatment of the KPD Central Committee. The ECCI had accepted the KAPD as a "sympathizing member" of the Comintern, against the strongest advice and then in spite of the complaints of the KPD leadership. But Serrati emphasized that, even with his great disappointment in the Moscow leaders, he was not defeated. He would take his case to the next congress of the Communist International.[112]

Paul Levi and the Comintern

Paul Levi's complaints to Serrati at Leghorn about the Russians' treatment of the KPD were the expression of long-simmering resentments on the part of the German leader, resentments he had harbored since the Second Congress and even before, but which he, unlike Serrati, did not openly express. A series of developments in late 1920 and early 1921 worked to bring these resentments into the open, causing him to lash out at the bolsheviks and to subject their control of the Comintern to searing scrutiny. Levi's break with the Comintern and the abortive March Uprising marked a distinct end to the *biennio rosso*. It sharply posed the question of whether it was possible for any independent western revolutionary to oppose the bolsheviks without seeming either a despised centrist or an "immature" anarchist. Levi made it clearer than ever before that the ideal of western communism as a synthesis of western and Russian traditions, as opposed to a narrow imitation of bolshevism, was untenable or at least unacceptable to the bolsheviks themselves.

In his memoirs Dittmann remarked that Levi seemed ill at ease in Russia and generally tense around the bolsheviks. On the trip back to Germany, when Levi accompanied the USPD delegates, he seemed to Dittmann deeply relieved to be leaving "Asiatic" Russia and returning to the West.[113] Dittmann may have exaggerated the extent of Levi's aversion to Russia and the Russians, but still there is little doubt that the KPD leader had long shared Rosa Luxemburg's distrust of the bolsheviks or that he was disturbed by their increasing readiness to assume an attitude of infallibility in relation to western revolutionaries.[114] It is even less doubtful that by 1920 he had come to share Rosa Luxemburg's extreme distaste for Radek and Zinoviev. Levi was not happy with the way the latter two had handled the USPD delegation at the Second Congress; and he was incensed to learn that they had tried to encourage his fellow KPD delegate, Ernst Meyer, to establish a faction in opposition to his leadership of the KPD.[115] Both Levi and Meyer threatened to leave the Second Congress when they learned of the bolsheviks' plans to grant the KAPD full voting rights at the congress.[116] Faced with this united opposition, the Russians backed down, but it seems that even Lenin, who was already disappointed in Levi's pessimism concerning the revolutionary effects on Germany of Russia's Polish victories, began to suspect the truth: that Levi harbored an "uncomradely reserve" in his relationship to the Russians and shared Rosa Luxemburg's hostility to the idea of the bolsheviks' leading role in world socialism after 1917.

Levi kept the USPD left informed of his dissatisfactions with bolsheviks,[117] and his attitude may well have convinced Däumig and Stoecker at the Second Congress that even if they did humble themselves before the Russians they would later be able to act with considerable independence in cooperation with him. And Zinoviev's efforts at Halle to give an impression of Russian tolerance and liberality served to encourage them in these beliefs. At the unity congress of the KPD and USPD left in December 1920, Levi openly voiced his discontent with the Twenty-one Conditions.[118] As he had intimated at the Second Congress, he felt that they imposed upon westerners the Russian practice of "mechanical" schisms and exclusions, which could have a disastrous impact in the West.

Levi had indeed left Russia in a deeply troubled state of mind. Among other worries he feared that the bolsheviks were not genuinely committed to building mass parties in the West, and he was apprehensive about the meaning of Lenin's theses which talked about "accelerating" the revolution through "action." He thus doubted that he would be able to carry on as leader of the KPD. But the failure of the Polish campaign and Lenin's subsequent assertion that revolution could not be expected in the West for a number of years encouraged Levi to believe that his own plans for the KPD could now be implemented with the cooperation of the Russian leaders.[119] But shortly after the unity congress, word reached Germany, as Levi informed Serrati at Leghorn, that the ECCI had accepted the KAPD into the Comintern as a "sympathizing party." Levi publicly criticized the ECCI for this action, which he termed "intolerable," and which had been taken without consulting any of the leadership of the KPD.[120] But more troubling to Levi than the unilateral manner in which this move had been taken were the reasons the bolshevik leaders gave for it: the injection of some of the revolutionary firebrands of the KAPD would help to overcome the "passivity" of the present KPD leadership. If this leadership had shown more aptitude in giving dynamic and aggressive leadership to the proletariat, in applying the theory of the "revolutionary offensive," then it would not have been necessary for the ECCI to persist on the question of the KAPD.[121] This was uncomfortably close to the arguments employed by the ECCI in dealing with Serrati and other "centrists."

The bolsheviks' attempt to force the KAPD on Levi was only part of his problems. In spite of the vote at Halle, which should have brought 500,000 to 600,000 new members to the KPD, only about 300,000 actually joined the party.[122] A significant part of the previously active, radicalized proletarians of 1919 and 1920 had become disillusioned and passive by early 1921.[123] They seemed uninterested either in Levi's ideas of reorganization and recruitment or in the ideas of the ECCI to engage in "action." Levi's efforts in January to improve the KPD's image by inviting Germany's labor organizations to join hands in submitting to the government a joint demand for a number of specific and limited reforms was met with a contemptuous rejection by Germany's labor leaders and by little or no response from the masses. This rebuff encouraged Levi's opponents in the party to step up their criticisms of him and of his "opportunism" and "passivism." In this they were, of course, aided and abetted by Radek and other members of the ECCI who were pushing the notion of the "revolutionary offensive."[124]

Levi never really had his heart in leading the KPD; he had taken over after the deaths of Luxemburg, Liebknecht, and Jogiches, more out of a sense of duty than out of the satisfactions of leadership.[125] He was never really a "popular" leader who could speak to the masses on their own terms. His forbidding exterior, mordant wit, and penchant for recondite literary allusions separated him from the rank and file. By early 1921 his growing irritations with the bolsheviks, the poor response his policies were finding in Germany, and the increasingly unrestrained criticism of these policies within the KPD seemed to undermine his will to continue. Then his experiences at the Leghorn congress and in Germany immediately after his return from Italy made him decide to relinquish the party leadership.

The actual course of events in the last part of January and their meaning have been obscured in the polemical tirades following Levi's expulsion from the KPD. The view generally accepted by scholars is the one Levi himself presented: the conduct of the Comintern emissaries to Leghorn caused the split in the PSI, and because of this Levi left the congress in disgust, which later resulted in his resignation from the KPD *Zentrale*.[126] But this view fails to take into account the development of the PSI in the autumn of 1920, and does not adequately recognize the extent to which Levi's will to continue was broken by the time he left for Italy. Quite simply, he was ready to be provided with an excuse to abandon the leadership of the KPD.

No doubt to Levi's eyes the array of factions at Leghorn was distressingly familiar. The Communist faction must have appeared to him like the anarchistic, antiparliamentarian KAPD: it was headed by Bordiga, the abstentionist ultra-leftist, and by Bombacci, the irresponsible revolutionary clown, with strong support from the "syndicalist" *ordinovisti*. The disruptive and abusive manners of the left of the congress recalled those of the KAPD or even those of the Left Opposition within the KPD. At the same time, the Comintern representatives, the Bulgarian Kabakchiev and the Hungarian Rakosi, were in Levi's eyes "Asiatics," who knew little of western conditions and were impossibly sectarian and insulting.

On the other hand, Serrati no doubt appeared to Levi to be a good western-style, "solid" revolutionary. Levi had known the Italian leader since the Zimmerwald meetings and had shared the Presidium of the Second Congress of the Communist International with him. Moreover, Levi could see that Serrati enjoyed the backing not only of the experienced members of the PSI but also of a heavy majority of the rank and file. For all these reasons Levi's sympathy went out to the Italian leader, and he was shocked to see him insulted and accused of treachery by the representatives of the ECCI.

Yet Levi did not openly side with the Unitarians at Leghorn. It is important to emphasize this because later, first in Germany and then at the Third Congress of the Communist International, Rakosi blamed Levi for not giving the Comintern's representatives enough support and for encouraging Serrati in his opposition to the ECCI's demands, implying that the Italian leader might have come around if he had found support from the leader of the party that was now the Comintern's largest outside of Russia.[127] Yet while it is clear that Levi did privately express sympathy for some of Serrati's views and did complain to the Italian leader about the bolsheviks' treatment of the German party, he did not voice these sentiments to the congress at large.

Quite the contrary, in his speech to the congress Levi supported the ECCI's demand for Turati's exclusion by emphasizing that "the unity of a party is not always a supreme good for the proletariat.... There are moments in the life of a party when it is no longer possible to remain united, when paths separate.... In Germany we had unity for a long time . . . and today we curse the murderers who emerged from the social democratic party." Levi drew explicit parallels between the situation in Germany and Italy, affirming that the Italian socialists were now on the path that the German socialists had already taken, "where the friends of yesterday become the enemies of tomorrow" (a statement that takes on unintended irony, in light of Levi's later break with the Comintern). The entire thrust of this speech favored the creation of a communist party free of reformists and was implicitly critical of Serrati.[128]

Thus if Levi genuinely believed, as he later told his friends in the KPD, that Kabakchiev and Rakosi had provoked an artificial split in the Italian party, he involved himself in a strong inconsistency when he gave a speech favoring a split. Of course Levi wanted a split that would retain Serrati in the new party and exclude only Turati. But it was Serrati who opposed such a split. How could Levi expect the leaders of the Comintern to accept Serrati when the Italian leader stubbornly refused to exclude Turati? Even more, how could Serrati be accepted when he would not accept the decisions of the Second Congress in anything but words, when he harshly and publicly criticized these decisions, and when he even criticized the nature of bolshevik rule in Russia? As Niccolini complained in a later article, Levi himself offered no solution concerning how to deal with Serrati and was not able to change the Italian leader's mind in his long conversation with him at Leghorn; but then Levi bitterly protested the measures the ECCI felt it was obliged to take because of Serrati's attitudes.[129]

If Levi felt that the demand for the exclusion of Turati was an example of the kind of "mechanical" exclusions to which he objected, then he should have said so openly, instead of appearing to accept the contention that reformists in the ranks of a revolutionary party undermine its ability to make revolution. If he felt that Serrati was correct and the ECCI wrong, then he should have said so, or at least he should have remained quiet; instead he explicitly declared that he did not agree with Serrati,[130] and, as will be seen, he later consented to a resolution of the KPD *Zentrale* which approved of the ECCI's policy in Italy. In any case, it seems strange that Levi, who had engineered the schism of the KPD a year and a half before, should now be so sensitive concerning "mechanical" schisms, since the split of the PSI was scarcely more mechanical than the earlier split of the KPD.

It is conceivable that Levi was ignorant enough of Italian conditions not to know that Serrati's differences with the bolsheviks were long-standing and deeply rooted, or that the left of the PSI was determined to split away from Serrati, even in opposition to the Comintern, which clearly preferred a broad party rather than Bordiga's narrow one. Or it may be that Levi, already deeply troubled by the bolsheviks' influence on western socialism, actually recognized a profound agreement with Serrati—even to the extent of sharing the latter's condemnation of bolshevik rule—but could not yet bring himself to an open declaration of this agreement. His abrupt and unexpected departure from the congress of Leghorn—he simply disappeared after his speech on its first day—would seem to speak for such a spiritual crisis. If this latter hypothesis has some validity, then Levi's return to Germany with the accusation that the Comintern's representatives had caused a disastrous split in the PSI can be seen as a kind of ill-tempered and ill-considered attempt to gain support for a major challenge to the authority of the ECCI and to the bolsheviks' preeminence in the Comintern.

But, just as Levi's speech at Leghorn undermined the position from which he could attack the ECCI representatives, so once back in Germany he showed no consistency or tactical shrewdness in fighting for his case. The resolution he put before the KPD *Zentrale* on the Italian question was only cautiously critical of the ECCI, and he withdrew it when sharply attacked by Radek. He then consented to a draft which cautiously approved of the action of the ECCI representatives at Leghorn but which blunted this endorsement by recommending further contacts with the Serratians in order to gain the honest revolutionary workers behind Serrati.[131]

With his own position thus profoundly weakened, Levi had to face Rakosi, who arrived in Berlin burning with resentment over Levi's and the French communists' failure to give more support in Italy (the latter failed even to make an appearance at Leghorn). If Levi had consistently and openly maintained that the ECCI had been mistaken at Leghorn, then Rakosi's appearance in Germany might have been a welcome opportunity, for the Hungarian assumed an almost absurdly exaggerated position. In defending his conduct toward Serrati's Unitarians he declared that "if regard for the clarity of the communist party makes such splits imperative, then they have to be carried out, if necessary ten times, whether in Italy, France, or Germany."[132] He pointedly remarked that after Halle the KPD had become "far too large" and that "it is not a mass party that is valuable to the Communist International, but a small, pure party."[133] This was clearly not the line being espoused by the ECCI in 1920, and it is highly doubtful that a majority of the KPD Central Committee agreed with Rakosi's views. But Levi had failed to articulate and organize consistent, principled opposition to them, and Levi's opponents saw Rakosi's attacks on Levi as a way of furthering their own campaign against him. Thus in the end a new resolution that demanded an "uncompromising struggle" against Serrati and gave unconditional support to the ECCI for its policies in Italy obtained 28 votes against 23. Shortly afterwards Levi resigned from the *Zentrale*, along with his cochairman Däumig; Clara Zetkin and a number of other leading figures in the party also resigned. They affirmed that it was no longer possible to continue as leaders of a party that supported policies with which they fundamentally disagreed and which they believed would be destructive to socialism in Germany. Levi's and Däumig's places were filled by Stoecker and Brandler, two men more acceptable to the Left Opposition.[134]

With the departure of Levi and many of the earlier associates of Rosa Luxemburg, and with the Left Opposition in control of the *Zentrale*, the stage was set for the so-called *März Aktion*, or

"March Uprising," which would be nearly as disastrous for the KPD as the January Uprising of 1919 had been, and which would see Levi's worst fears confirmed—that the KPD would once again become an undisciplined, irresponsible, "putschist" party and that the bolsheviks would encourage these tendencies.

The genesis of the March Uprising lies partly obscured and is unlikely to be cleared up until the archives of the Comintern are open to scholars. But again the truth that can be found is more complicated than either the view that the Uprising was provoked by the government in order to repress the communists (which became the official communist view) or the contention that Comintern agents were mainly responsible for it.[135] Certainly those members of the ECCI who pushed the so-called "theory of the revolutionary offensive" in Germany bear a large responsibility for the Uprising. Of these, Radek assumes a leading position, but even Lenin, although he no longer talked of "accelerating" the revolution and instead predicted that revolution in the West would be years in coming, did not see fit to reprimand the ECCI; indeed, as previously mentioned, he himself wrote the Italians as late as mid-November to say that their country was in the same stage of revolutionary development Russia had been in 1917.

But far more than Lenin, who was preoccupied with Russian domestic concerns, it was Zinoviev and Radek, speaking for the ECCI, who continued to talk as if revolution was imminent in both Italy and Germany in the autumn and winter of 1920–1921. Their position as revolutionary enthusiasts at this time seems inconsistent with the role they had played at the Second Congress in pushing negotiations with the centrist parties. Without access to the archives of the Comintern this apparent contradiction is difficult to resolve. However, the evidence that is available suggests that these two leaders pushed the theory of the offensive on the KPD in order to attack Levi, rather than out of a genuine belief in the proximity of revolution (similarly they spoke of revolution in Italy in order to attack Serrati), although Zinoviev may have hoped to counter his image— frequently evoked in the autumn of 1920—as a "waverer." The inconsistency also seems less flagrant if one keeps in mind that the bolsheviks' policy of "action" or "offensive" remained ambiguous:

did it really mean an attempt to seize power or merely a more aggressive policy on the part of communists?

Whatever the intentions of the leading members of the ECCI in early 1921, the selection of Bela Kun to go to Germany as a Comintern representative was hardly an indication of caution; for ever since his defeat in the Hungarian Revolution in 1919 he had been notorious for the ultra-extremism of his views and for the unscrupulousness of his methods in dealing with the struggling factions among the Hungarian exiles.[136] Kun's extremism found ready acceptance among members of the now controlling Left Opposition, although his exact role in encouraging their own plans for insurrectionary action is not known. He arrived in Germany at a time of crisis on many fronts. On March 8, the Entente decided to impose military and economic sanctions because of Germany's refusal to accept the reparations figures presented it. The Entente's demand for the disarming of the *Einwohnerwehren* ("Local Citizen's Guards") threatened to further envenom its relations with Germany, while the approaching plebiscite on Upper Silesia promised to do the same for Germany's relations with Poland. In spite of these many points of conflict, however, Kun found a passive working class in Germany; few workers showed an interest in "action" or even in a campaign for an alliance with Russia.

When government authorities announced that a police expedition would be sent into certain areas of central Germany (where there had been much labor unrest) to investigate the activities of "criminal elements," it seemed that the "provocation" hoped for by revolutionary firebrands in the KPD had finally been provided. Yet even the police expeditions were met with passivity by the workers. Moreover, this move of the authorities came before the KPD's own plans for insurrection were completely ready. But these inauspicious conditions did not deter Kun, who argued that a communist party could not passively wait for the workers to take the lead; its duty was to provide the example, to take independent "offensive" action to "force" the development of the revolution.

This was music to the ears of many of the leaders of the KPD left. But the forms that the communists' leadership finally took reproduced the worst putschist aspects of the KPD in early 1919, and was combined with utter confusion and ill-timing. This time even feigned attacks on working-class leaders were organized by the KPD in order to incite the workers. The final result was a bloody fiasco and an unmitigated disaster for the KPD: its membership dropped from about 350,000 to about 180,000.[137] An even deeper gulf was created between communist and non-communist workers in Germany, and the former lost almost entirely the influence they had exercised in the trade unions.

Levi, who had inexplicably left for a vacation after hearing of Kun's plans, was appalled when news reached him of the *März Aktion*. He at last decided that only a principled and open break with the policies represented by Radek, Kun, Rakosi, and the left of the KPD could possibly cure the party of its "sickness" and salvage it for the future.[138] If the party did not openly and explicitly recognize its errors and honestly seek to overcome them, then there was no hope of its eventually emerging from isolation and impotence. But Levi's efforts to have his criticisms accepted by the party leadership were futile; his resolutions were overwhelmingly voted down by the party's leaders. Thus blocked from working within the party, Levi felt that he had no option other than publishing his criticisms, even though he knew it would mean his exclusion from the party. Apparently the idea of waiting for the next meeting of the Comintern did not appeal to him; he had held his peace long enough.

Levi's public criticisms of the ECCI and the KPD *Zentrale* were in some ways even more searching than the criticisms of the anti-Comintern forces at Halle, Tours, and Leghorn, although his points of agreement with the anti-Comintern leaders were surprisingly numerous—particularly so in the case of Léon Blum. Levi's criticisms also underlined some of the contradictions and persisting ambiguities of the KPD's own position since its foundation in December 1918: especially, its vague associations with the humanistic-democratic Luxemburgist tradition as contrasted with its persistently shrill revolutionary rhetoric, which tended to appeal only to the most desperate and violent elements of Germany's working class.

Levi charged the KPD *Zentrale* with criminal irresponsibility and utter incompetence, and he demanded that its present members resign. He argued that disasters like the *März Aktion* were made possible by the Comintern's claim to unquestioned authority, a claim grossly inconsonant with the Russian leaders' inability to offer concrete guidance in given situations. And this insufficiency itself was related to the Russians' inadequate understanding of conditions in the West. In order to mask their incompetence the bolsheviks conducted witch-hunts in western parties for "menshevik" deviations, upon which they could lay the blame for whatever failings the party might suffer. And since the Bolshevik party's best minds and most talented leaders were preoccupied with pressing domestic problems, irresponsible incompetents like Kun and Rakosi were allowed to exercise the vast authority of the ECCI; their peculiar talents would have been better diverted to some place like Soviet Turkestan. In the West they destroyed all hopes of establishing mass communist parties that could work and grow in the context of bourgeois-democratic legality and that could aspire to leadership of all the working masses, not only a limited minority of them.[139]

Levi's criticisms created a sensation and earned him the exclusion and vilification he had expected. Not long afterwards, he arranged for the publication of Rosa Luxemburg's since famous critical reflections on the Bolshevik Revolution. He thus joined Serrati in attacking not only the bolsheviks' leadership of the Comintern but also the very nature of their rule in Russia. Ironically, at the Third Congress of the Communist International, the bolsheviks themselves recognized that Levi's criticisms of the "theory of the offensive" had been basically correct, and a few months later the Comintern initiated the United Front policy, which greatly resembled the policy Levi had advocated before he resigned from the *Zentrale*. Lenin even offered Levi the same kind of "solution" that he had offered Serrati; but Levi contemptuously rejected the offer.[140] In any case, the bolsheviks were not prepared to accept the full force of Levi's many criticisms. The men responsible for the *März Aktion* were not obliged to make an open declaration of their errors, the Uprising itself was described as a heroic act of revolutionary defiance rather than an ugly and stupid disaster, and the

ECCI hushed up all reference to the Kun mission. Moreover, the United Front policy did not really reverse the trends in western communist parties which so concerned Levi. The social divisions between communist and socialist workers persisted, and communist parties in the West long remained impotent representatives of a minority of the working class, totally under the direction of Russian leadership.

In the hands of a different personality, someone personally warmer, more open and straightforward, and tactically more clever, Levi's criticisms might conceivably have had important repercussions at the Third Congress. Levi possessed the intellectual tools to stand up for the values of western revolutionary socialism, but he lacked other necessary qualities.

Epilogue and Conclusion

The high hopes of the *biennio rosso* for revolution in the West were distinctly abandoned by the time of the Third Congress of the Communist International. Just as within Russia the NEP had been accompanied by a severe tightening of discipline within the Bolshevik party, so the United Front carried with it, after a period of delay following the Third Congress, an even stronger requirement of obedience from the communist parties of the West. Important elements within the KPD, PCF, and PCI resisted the United Front policy, though for different reasons; but all gradually bent to the will of Moscow, even though nearly a decade of extraordinarily complex factionalism passed before the member parties of the Comintern became as disciplined as the Bolshevik party itself. In the process nearly all of the original party leaders resigned or were purged.

The new French Communist party did not get a chance to act as the protector of revolution in Germany. After the schism at Tours most of the party's energies were spent in squabbles between the Cachin-Frossard faction and the followers of the Committee for the Comintern. In the first year of the PCF's existence, the ex-Reconstructionists kept control of its Executive Committee, although at the congress of Marseilles, a year after Tours, a new schism nearly occurred when the delegates to the congress refused to seat Boris Souvarine on the Executive Committee. This outraged the left and prompted it to threaten to leave the congress.[1]

The ex-Reconstructionists tried to run the party much as the SFIO had been run before and stoutly resisted the efforts of the ECCI to exert more control over them. They were particularly upset over the United Front policy because immediately after the split at Tours the new Communist party and the rump SFIO had fallen into using the very recriminations that Blum at Tours had urged them to avoid. Under the United Front policy the French communists were asked to arrange common action with the very men who had just been purged and who had been vilified by the leaders of the new party throughout early 1921. Ironically, the right wing of the French Communist party opposed the new "right-wing" United Front policy, while the left of the party defended it.[2]

In the course of these struggles the leaders of both wings of the party fell from grace, and the PCF suffered a steady loss of membership throughout the 1920s. Frossard, after several years of trying to buck ECCI control, left in 1923. Loriot simply withdrew from leadership positions, perhaps because of disillusionment, but claiming that he needed to tend his bookstore in order to provide for his old age[3]—a concern of a typical French *petit bourgeois* rather than a revolutionary, one is tempted to observe. Souvarine and Rosmer left the party with Trotsky's disgrace. Only Cachin survived, to become the venerable *"pépé"* ("Grampa") of the PCF.

In Italy as in France a great deal of the new Communist party's energies were devoted to factional rivalries rather than to revolutionary action. The bolsheviks cultivated these rivalries and, as they had done at the Second Congress, sought to elevate Gramsci and the *ordinovisti* over Bordiga and his faction. Bordiga was adamantly opposed to the United Front policies, especially insofar as they entailed cooperation with Serrati's PSI; his stubborn opposition to bolshevik leadership in this direction eventually cost him the leadership of the party.

Instead of growing more powerful the PCI destroyed itself from within, steadily losing membership and general influence. A similar process occurred within the PSI, which by the end of 1921 could count perhaps one-half the membership it had enjoyed immediately after Leghorn. By early 1923 its decline, like that of the PCI, had taken on disastrous proportions.[4] Serrati continued his efforts to reenter the Comintern, and after the PSI finally expelled Turati in 1922 the Comintern declared itself willing to accept the now much humbled revolutionary. Even so, Serrati was unable to pull a majority of his now depleted party with him into the Comintern; and, in any case, the victory of fascism in Italy lent a futile aura to all of these struggles. Serrati was arrested upon returning from Moscow, where he had gone to arrange his reconcilation with the bolsheviks.[5] Soon afterward he died suddenly of a heart attack.

Paul Levi eventually joined the rump USPD, which itself finally merged with the SPD. But his dramatic departure from the KPD was merely a prelude to the turbulent struggles within the party in the 1920s.[6] While those who took over from Levi were far more receptive to bolshevik leadership than he, they did not yet by any means respond to all bolshevik pronouncements in the robotlike manner characteristic of communist leaders in later years, when Stalin had assumed control over Russia and the Comintern, and when communist parties had come fully to accept their role as primarily that of protecting the Soviet Union through support of Russian foreign policy. The upheavals in Germany following upon the French occupation of the Ruhr valley in early 1923 resulted in a radicalization of Germany's workers and a sharp increase in the appeals of the KPD,[7] as well as a renewed hope on the part of the party leaders that Germany could be moved in a revolutionary direction. But again the KPD became mired in a struggle between the more cautious leadership and a left faction that accused the leaders of "passivity, opportunism, and revisionism"[8]—further complicated by the Trotsky-Triumvirate struggle in Russia—leading to another bungled communist uprising, the last before Hitler's coming to power.

From the standpoint of revolutionary socialism, the *biennio rosso* can be seen as a time of disastrously missed opportunities. The failure of proletarian revolution to transform and revitalize the shaken and war-weakened regimes in the West meant that these regimes festered into various varieties of reactionary and barbaric authoritarianism. Soviet Russia, without the helping hand of the industrialized West, was pushed to equally barbaric and costly solutions to her own problems.

Yet, the more that one investigates this period, the more it seems that the "missed opportunities" were illusory and that the arguments in favor of world revolution were based on extremely shaky foundations. Indeed, it is difficult to believe that even the proponents of these arguments were genuinely convinced by them. One may agree that the war underlined the "contradictions" of capitalism, but this did not necessarily mean that capitalism would collapse; even more, it did not mean that socialism would be able to replace capitalism. For as much as the war underlined the inadequacies of the existing capitalist regimes, it also made clear the "contradictions" of socialism itself, and in particular it exposed as chimerical the notion of world proletarian socialist revolution. No doubt the Bolshevik Revolution provided a "spark" of revolutionary optimism to many socialists in the West, but this aspect of the bolshevik accession to power was counterbalanced by the negative influence of bolshevik rule after 1917. The pervasive violence, the terror, the profound human suffering in Russia between 1917 and 1921, while clearly not the exclusive responsibility of the bolsheviks, greatly discredited the idea of socialist revolution. Thus the symbol of the bolshevik revolution was neither unequivocally detrimental nor beneficial to western socialism.

Similarly, the role of the bolsheviks as leaders of the Comintern had both negative and positive aspects. Many socialists in the West were anxious to blame the Russians for the many ills that plagued their parties immediately following the war, and a number of scholars in recent years have placed substantial responsibility on the shoulders of the bolsheviks for the split of western socialist parties, charging them with introducing an inappropriate eastern dogmatism and intolerance into the life of western parties.[9] Yet a careful study of bolshevik relations with western socialists reveals an ambiguous situation, one with so many elusive aspects that it lends itself to conclusions based on the political persuasion of the individual scholar rather than on a strongly persuasive array of documented proofs. It is this author's view that indigenous western conditions were the primary determinants of the misfortunes of western socialist parties during the *biennio rosso*.

The war brought out the profound divisions among prewar revolutionary and nonrevolutionary socialists; but, even more to the point, the war brought to the surface the deep differences between revolutionaries themselves. This was especially true in Germany, where split followed split between 1917 and 1921. The USPD and the KPD continued to suffer from intense and often paralysing internal differences. Quite aside from their inability to win over a majority of the population—or even a majority of the working class—Germany's revolutionary socialists were incapable of making revolution because they were incapable of working together. Some historians have argued that the logic of historical development by December 1918 indicated not a separation of the Spartacists alone from the USPD but rather the departure of the entire revolutionary left wing of the party; this wing had far more in common with the Spartacists than it did with the right and center of Kautsky and Haase. Thus the "necessary split" of the USPD failed to occur at the proper historical juncture, for reasons that might be called personal or accidental—again "missed opportunities." The schism at Halle, then, accomplished belatedly what had been necessary all along.[10] The problem with this line of reasoning, which of course has much in common with that of Paul Levi, is that even if the KPD had begun as a broader party, all evidence indicates that it would still have been torn by destructive factionalism and would hardly have been more able to effect successful revolution in Germany than it was as a smaller party.

Similar remarks hold true for the PSI. The revolutionary wing of the party, no matter how narrowly one defines it, was impossibly heterogeneous, each faction detesting the other. Even Bordiga's "pure" PCI was composed of a dizzyingly diverse variety of opposing ideological perspectives: Bordiga's elitist Marxian-Blanquism, the *ordinovisti*'s syndicalist-voluntarism, Tasca's pragmatism, and Graziadei's opportunism. There were uncritical admirers of the bolsheviks, like Bombacci; and others, like Graziadei, who retained a critical distance. There were those who wished to break entirely with the traditions of the PSI, like Gramsci and Bordiga; and those like Tasca and Gennari who hoped to preserve the traditions of Italian socialism. And even between Bordiga and Gramsci there were deeply felt differences concerning *how* the new party should break with the traditions of the past. Quite aside from the many other objective factors weighing against revolution in Italy, these profound divisions among revolutionaries themselves made a mockery of the hopes for revolution following World War I.

Of the three communist parties in question, the French was of course the most diverse internally, since it had large numbers of former centrists in its ranks and was led by a prominent former social patriot. But even among the left wingers of the French party the profound ideological and personal differences between men like Loriot, Rosmer, and Souvarine condemned the PCF to internal squabbling rather than revolutionary action. Significantly, by the time the French party was thoroughly "bolshevized" in the late 1920s, its following was perhaps one-quarter of what it had been immediately after Tours.

In attempting, then, to evaluate the influence of bolshevism on the unity of western socialism, it must be remembered that the bolsheviks had to work within a very definite set of given objective conditions. Try as they might, they could do little to remedy the KPD–KAPD split. Nor could they turn Bordiga from his stubborn determination to be rid of the Maximalists. Similarly, Comintern urgings that the left of the SFIO split away to form a new communist party in 1919 was ignored by Loriot and the Committee for the Comintern. In any number of given situations the bolsheviks had little or no power to enforce their will. Splits would have occurred without direct bolshevik interference, perhaps less "mechanically," perhaps at different times and with different factional alliances; but it hardly seems fair to shoulder the bolsheviks with primary responsibility for these schisms.

This is not quite the same as to assert that there would have been splits in western socialist parties if the Bolshevik Revolution had never occurred. The Revolution was an integral part of the world crisis of 1914–1920, and it is thus quite unrealistic to hypothesize what developments might have been elsewhere if revolution had not broken out in Russia. There is little question that the bolshevik model of the elitist "pure" party exercised attractions for certain western socialists, but the splits of western socialism had far deeper roots than an admiration for the bolshevik model. One should remember that the SPD–USPD split developed before the bolshevik victory in Russia; and the USPD–KPD–KAPD schisms also came to pass without substantial bolshevik interference. Similarly, the exclusion of Turati and his wing was often considered by the PSI leadership before the bolsheviks had any influence in the West; indeed, the party had already excluded a number of prominent right-wing socialists in 1912. Within the ranks of the SFIO's Committee for the Comintern there was a strong sentiment, independent of advice from Moscow, that men like Thomas and Renaudel would have to depart from the ranks of the socialists, just as Millerand and Briand had done before. Schisms and exclusions were hardly an innovation of the Russians.

It is reasonably clear, in fact, that by mid-1920 the bolsheviks were more concerned about unity than many western socialists; and that the Russians sought to *limit* the divisions of western revolutionary organizations, to bring the various quarreling factions together as much as possible, and especially to counter the mindless sectarianism of many extreme left-wing socialists in the West. No doubt part of the explanation for bolshevik efforts in this direction was that they wished to play the contending factions off against one another, allowing the bolsheviks to assume the powerful role of arbitrators. But to the accusation that the bolsheviks were full of duplicity and hungry for power in world socialism, it must be countered that they had no monopoly on these qualities. Frossard, Cachin, Bombacci, and Crispien frequently resorted to baldfaced lies in order to cover their tracks, and even Serrati, Levi, or Loriot were hardly models of straightforwardness. Bordiga, Souvarine, and the Left Opposition of the KPD hankered after leadership, and in striving for it they were scarcely less intolerant or unscrupulous than Zinoviev and Radek. In following the conflict between western socialists and bolsheviks, one encounters few unsullied heroes.

At the same time there were few unqualified villains. In many cases it is possible to see a less selfish purpose behind the actions of the men mentioned above. Frossard, while looking out for his own future, believed that he was preserving a maximum possible unity and injecting France's working-class movement with a new dynamism. Serrati, while striving to maintain his control of the PSI, was convinced that Bordiga and the *ordinovisti* would destroy the Italian socialist movement. The bolsheviks, while unquestionably savoring their new prestige in world socialism, also believed that western socialists needed more forceful and purposeful leadership.

The reactions of western socialists to bolshevism in the *biennio rosso*, the appeal communism held for them, varied widely, evolving as conditions shifted in Russia and the West and as the face of bolshevism itself altered. Yet there were certain interesting similarities in these reactions, similarities which cut across national lines and which can in very general ways be related to such factors as class background, previous experience in organized socialist parties, age, and psychological type. For the sake of convenience, the following labels can be applied to distinguish similar groups that emerged in each party: the "sycophants," the "syndicalists," the "opportunists," the "independents," and the "old Marxists."

The sycophants were those, such as Souvarine, Lefebvre, Bombacci, and apparently a number of second-level leaders, who were uncritical admirers of the bolsheviks; they seemed prepared to accept anything issued from Moscow as Gospel. This was not a large group, and the leading figures who shared these attitudes usually enjoyed relatively little personal prestige or following. The sycophants tended to be young, without previous experience in party work, without wide contacts in the working class, and of bourgeois origin. Typically, Souvarine was widely detested within the SFIO as a lisping and abrasive bigot who unfortunately had the ear of Moscow. Bombacci was passed off by many of his party comrades as a hotheaded revolutionary clown. And Lefebvre was condescendingly viewed as a callow, if somewhat appealing, revolutionary idealist who lacked any solid sense of the difficulties of making revolution.

A more common attitude among western socialists was one of basic admiration for the bolsheviks, coupled with a belief that revolution and revolutionary organizations in the West would be quite different—more democratic and more humane—than in Russia. This was the attitude of such men as Däumig, Gramsci, and Rosmer, and for much of the *biennio rosso* Lenin and the bolsheviks seemed themselves to accept this group's hopes for a "better" revolution in the West. These men were in one way or another associated with views that can be loosely termed "syndicalist": Däumig, in his hopes that the *Räte* would replace Germany's fractured socialist parties; Gramsci, in his theories concerning the role of the *consigli di fabbrica* in the struggle for socialism; and Rosmer, in his connections with the *syndicats* and the prewar anarchosyndicalist movement.

One might also say that these men were typical of an overall "Luxemburgist" emphasis in western revolutionary socialism in that they did not at first believe that a party machine should play a central role in making revolution. They looked to a spontaneous push from below, to a decisive role by class conscious proletarians who had acquired their socialist convictions through concrete experience in the factories. Typical were Gramsci's concern for raising the intellectual level of the working class before the advent of revolution and Däumig's belief in the importance of bringing to the revolution the widest possible spectrum of proletarians—including "intellectual" and manual workers.

Yet these figures, each in his own way and according to different modes of development, gradually became more elitist. They suffered repeated disappointments from the fickleness and short-sightedness of the masses and became increasingly disillusioned with the insufficiencies of democratically organized proletarian institutions, such as workers' councils, unions, and socialist parties. As the *biennio rosso* progressed they came to accept the necessity of an intellectual and moral elite, formed into a disciplined and centralized revolutionary party, at the head of the proletariat. Yet they moved cautiously and with many reservations toward Lenin's views; and what impelled them in his direction was not so much a heartfelt enthusiasm for the stringencies of bolshevik theory as it was a sense of personal failure, of the inadequacies of their own theories and the theories of other western revolutionaries in the arena of revolutionary practice. Whatever reservations they may have harbored about bolshevism, it remained for them the only successful revolutionary theory.

The syndicalists shared a number of traits with the sycophants. They also tended to be young, and they had had little or no contact with the prewar socialist movements. They were prone to the incautious enthusiasms of youth, and they strike one as *émotifs*, or at least as impressionable in comparison to those whose commitments to socialism dated to the prewar generation. Gramsci, Stoecker, and Loriot were at first carried away by the patriotic passions of the early stages of the war, but then, after the outbreak of revolution in Russia, they embraced with even more ardent passions the cause of world revolution.[11] In comparison to these young men in search of a *mystique*, the older generation of socialists, from Serrati to Dittmann to Blum, appear remarkably stable, even a little stolid.

It is easy to understand how young men or older men who had not devoted their energies to the arduous task of building working-class institutions in the prewar years could, on the one hand, put their hopes in nonparty organizations like the *Räte* or *consigli di fabbrica*, and, on the other hand, accept with relative ease the notion of a socialist party schism. In fact, for most of this younger generation the older organizations of the working class, as well as the older socialist leaders, came to represent obstacles to the success of revolution. In this respect, bolshevik propaganda merely intensified feelings that were already deeply rooted.

In the light of the limited information available it seems that the rank and file following of these two pro-Comintern groups shared certain characteristics with them.[12] This mass following seems generally to have been composed of a high proportion of men who had not joined socialist parties or other working-class organizations before the war and who were shocked into a revolutionary socialist consciousness by experiences at the front or in the new war industries. At the end of the war they flocked to the socialist parties and unions in unprecedented numbers. Prewar growth had tended to be steady or at least to change undramatically from year to year, and had generally proceeded at a rate that allowed the existing organizational structures to incorporate and indoctrinate in a regular fashion. But such regularity was obviously impossible in a party like the PSI, which grew from 30,000 at the end of the war to 220,-000 (a sevenfold increase) at the time of the Leghorn congress, or the USPD, which from early 1919 to late 1920 expanded from 300,-000 to 800,000 adding one-half million new members in less than two years.

Regular indoctrination and regimentation were also difficult because the new members were much less inclined to accept the old way of doing things. Far more than was the case for the prewar party members, these new recruits saw socialism or communism in terms of deeply felt revolt; they were little interested in the many "scientific" ramifications of Marxist theory. Thus the ideological differences between bolshevism and western socialism, which meant so much to men trained in the prewar parties, had little meaning to the new members. In the same way, the efforts of the older members to engage the new members in specific discussions of revolutionary potential were rejected with slogans or vague affirmations that revolution was inevitable. This remark holds even for Gramsci, who, while later becoming one of the most original and penetrating Marxian theoreticians of the twentieth century, greeted the Bolshevik Revolution as a liberation from the iron grip of scientific socialism, of Marxian determinism. To conclude that there was no hope for revolution in the near future seemed almost a psychological impossibility to men whose grievance against present society was so unqualified and "total." For them the arguments against revolution were merely façades behind which the older members hid their fear of change and their lack of revolutionary will.

Obviously, prewar socialist parties were also protest movements of Europe's exploited and disinherited masses, and malcontents of all sorts joined such parties. But the "total" rebels produced by the regular process of industrialization in the West between 1890 and 1914 were not nearly so numerous as those produced by the accelerated and "unnatural" industrialization of war time and by the experiences of trench warfare, demobilization, and the reversion to peace economies. Moreover, prewar socialist parties, particularly in Germany, had a core of "solid" working-class members whose complaints were balanced by a sense of accomplished position in terms of industrial skills and organization, who were in a sense integrated into capitalist society. It appears that this core was less attracted to communism and preferred to stay with the SPD or the right wing of the USPD, the right and center of the SFIO, and the Serratian wing of the PSI. Even in the case of the highly radicalized *revolutionäre Obleute* in Germany or the anarchosyndicalists in France, the communist policy of *noyautage*—which threatened to destroy the unity of the union—finally repelled many from joining the new communist parties. Even these fervent revolutionaries often harbored a paradoxical sense of *situation acquise*, which limited the intensity of their opposition to existing society.

There was thus a broad tendency for the pro-Comintern factions to find a significant proportion of their following among the perennially unemployed, the desperate and violent social strata cut off from production and divorced from recognized positions in society. This was the kind of member, in other words, that had tended to follow the KPD in 1919 in spite of the Luxemburgists' best efforts, or that was often associated with the anarchist organizations the Comintern tried to attract in 1919 and 1920. In the context of an intense revolutionary situation—as, for example, that of Russia in 1917—such violent and desperate men can be of use to a disciplined revolutionary party. But in the West they created problems with which western parties were not able to deal.

This analytical perspective suggests Lenin's division of the working masses into a "working-class aristocracy" and a "revolutionary proletariat," although Lenin himself did not push the logic of his position so far as to suggest that *all* of the workers in the West who had valued skills or who had deep roots in prewar socialist organizations had been bribed by capitalist society; nor did he affirm that *only* the desperate, lower levels of society could be expected to rally to revolution and to communism. But where Lenin hesitated, some of his lieutenants plunged in. Karl Radek, for example, in his writings of late 1920 and early 1921, asserted that the overwhelming majority of the SPD's prewar membership had remained faithful either to the old party or to the right wing of the USPD, while the overwhelming majority of those in the KPD by early 1921 were men who had had nothing to do with prewar socialism and who were awakened to revolutionary awareness by the shocks of war and revolution.[13] The rather unappealing implication of this line of argument was that the hundreds of thousands of "solid" workers who had filled the ranks of the SPD were lost to the cause of revolution; further, that only those uncorrupted by the relative security provided by industrial skills, unions, and other organizations would respond to revolutionary leadership. Radek sharply criticized Levi for his "centrist" hesitation to exploit to the full the revolutionary unrest among the unemployed and desperate lower levels of society.[14]

These remarks concerning the pro-Comintern forces in France,

Germany, and Italy are not really applicable to a third distinguishable group of pro-Comintern socialists: those who were motivated primarily by opportunism rather than by conviction. Most prominent in this group were Cachin and Frossard; in the SFIO their numbers were far greater than in the USPD and PSI. (In the PSI, Graziadei could be counted in the ranks of the opportunists, as could perhaps Lazzari.) Cachin, Frossard, and Graziadei had been associated with prewar socialism and were actually farther to the right politically than many of those who refused to accept the Twenty-one Conditions. But they were willing to swallow their pride and to follow bolshevik dictates, something other and more left-wing figures refused to do. In any case, most of the opportunists lasted only a few years, with the very important exception of Cachin, perhaps the most enduring communist of any European party.

In each of the three parties under discussion there was a fairly large group which, while defending the bolsheviks against the attacks of antisocialists, refused to accept the Twenty-one Conditions and insisted on the necessary independence of western socialists from Russian leadership. Virtually without exception these were men who had participated actively in the life of the prewar socialist parties and who had been associated with these parties' left wings. Longuet, Ledebour, and Baratono were typical representatives of this group, but one might easily place in it Serrati and, in a sense, even Levi. Certainly Ledebour, Serrati, and Pressemane, who all eventually opposed the Comintern, possessed more revolutionary conviction and courage than pro-Comintern figures like Frossard and Bombacci. Their primary difficulty with the Comintern related to their pride in and identification with western socialist traditions and organizations. They quite simply could not accept the self-abasement of a Cachin or a Stoecker, nor were they convinced by the subtle rationalizations of a Frossard or a Graziadei. Significantly, pressure by the bolsheviks, while bending men like Stoecker, Däumig, Cachin, or Graziadei, tended to work in the opposite direction when applied to Serrati, Longuet, or Levi.

Finally, there were those old Marxists who, while calling themselves revolutionary, were in no real sense tempted by the doctrines of the Comintern or impressed by the revolutionary accomplishments of the bolsheviks. As one might expect, they had all been active in the right and center factions of the prewar socialist parties, and most had attained positions of power and prestige in them. Ebert, Renaudel, and Modigliani are obvious representatives of this group, but such figures as Kautsky, Turati, and Blum fit into it also. Kautsky became a leading theoretical opponent of bolshevism but the positions of Turati and Blum were very close to his, and if their criticisms of bolshevism came across as less hostile than those of Kautsky, or Hilferding, or (in the end) Dittmann, it was largely due to tactical considerations and to differences in personal and national style. Turati really had little choice but to go along with his party's initial membership in the Comintern, and Blum sought to mitigate as much as possible the hostilities between pro- and anti-Comintern factions within the SFIO, in spite of his own profound opposition to the doctrines of the Comintern.

In sum, evidence does exist, though it is hardly of a conclusive nature, to support the conclusions that the postwar divisions of socialism occurred according to the prewar factions of the International, to social divisions within the working class, to generational divisions, and to divisions relating to previous experience in organized socialist parties and other working-class institutions. To view the schisms of western socialist parties in such terms further emphasizes the point made earlier: the bolsheviks cannot be made primarily responsible for them. Yet at the same time it should be reemphasized how Lenin's theory of the workers' aristocracy provided an oddly accurate theoretical explanation of the split of western socialism—oddly accurate because this theory, while part of an ardently revolutionary point of view, implied a lasting impotence of revolutionaries in the West. For the kinds of communist parties that were taking shape in France, Germany, and Italy in early 1921, by exercising their strongest appeal to the relatively small part of the population in western societies that harbored a "total" grievance with the status quo, further reinforced the impotence of western communist parties to make revolution. As long as the bourgeois state retained its vast repressive powers as well as its ability to manipulate and co-opt a decisive majority of the population, a small minority, no matter how determined, righteous, or clear sighted its leadership, could never hope to seize power. And ultimately communist parties themselves came to accept their impotence at home, turning instead to the protection of the Soviet Union as their only possible "revolutionary" role.

In the final analysis, not only did bolshevik theory imply a continuing postponement of revolution in the West, but most western revolutionaries suffered from a fundamental flaw in their perception of western reality: they expected that a majority of the working class (itself constituting a majority of the population) would become radicalized by its experiences and thus turn, sooner or later, to revolutionary leadership. Failing this turn of events, western revolutionaries had little to offer as an alternative to bolshevism, and their various efforts to find a middle ground between western socialism and bolshevism came to nothing. That relatively weak men like Serrati, Levi, and Frossard were the western leaders that emerged to defend western revolutionary socialism at a crucial point of development was symptomatic of deeper weaknesses. Faced with dynamic and clear-sighted leaders like Lenin and Trotsky, who stood at the head of the first socialist revolution in history and who suffered no uncertainties concerning the validity of their theories, western revolutionary socialists could not successfully resist.

Notes

Chapter I: Before the *Biennio Rosso*

1. Carl Schorske, *German Social Democracy, 1905–1917* (Cambridge, Mass., 1955), p. 13.

2. Gordon Wright, *France in Modern Times* (Chicago, 1960), p. 343.

3. Federico Chabod, *A History of Italian Fascism*, (London, 1963), p. 26.

4. J. P. Nettl, *Rosa Luxemburg* (London, 1966), 1:451.

5. Helmut König, *Lenin und der italienische Sozialismus, 1915–1921* (Tübingen, 1967), 10; from Franco Pedone, ed., *Il Partito socialista italiano nei suoi congressi*, 2 (Milan, 1963), 221.

6. J. Maynard, *Russia in Flux* (New York, 1948), 140; Merle Fainsod, *How Russia is Ruled* (Cambridge, Mass., 1954), p. 19.

7. Robert Wohl, *French Communism in the Making, 1914–1924* (Stanford, 1966), p. 95.

8. König, *Lenin*, p. 14.

9. Quoted in Edouard Dolléans, *Histoire du mouvement ouvrier, 1871–1920* (Paris, 1953), p. 221.

10. Joseph A. Berlau, *The German Social Democratic Party, 1914–1921* (New York, 1949), p. 73.

11. König, *Lenin*, p. 12.

12. Karl Landauer, *European Socialism* (Berkeley and Los Angeles, 1959), p. 537.

13. Wohl, *French Communism*, p. 66.

14. Vicenzo Vacirca, *Ciò che ho visto nella Russia Soviettista* (Milan, 1921), pp. 74–75.

15. Leon Trotsky, *A History of the Russian Revolution* (London, 1966), p. 318.

16. Olga Hess Gankin and H. H. Fischer, *The Bolsheviks and the World War: The Origins of the Third International* (Stanford, 1940), p. 158.

17. Alfred G. Meyer, *Leninism* (New York, 1963), p. 43.

18. Eugen Prager, *Geschichte der USP* (Berlin, 1922), pp. 124 ff.; A. J. Ryder, *The German Revolution of 1918* (Cambridge, 1967), p. 83.

19. Richard N. Hunt, *German Social Democracy, 1918–1933* (New Haven, 1964), p. 194.

20. Luigi Ambrosoli, *Nè aderire nè sabotare* (Milan, 1961), pp. 294–296.

21. Donald William Urquidi, "The Origins of the Italian Communist Party, 1918–1921" (Ph.D. diss., Columbia University, 1962), p. 13.

Chapter II: The Russian "Spark"

1. For a full discussion of this question see Peter Lösche, *Der Bolschewismus im Urteil der deutschen Sozialdemokratie, 1903–1920* (Berlin, 1967), pp. 166–167.

2. The form *"Räte"* is used throughout below because it is more precise and suggestive than the English term "councils" and because it renders the most convenient

equivalent of the Russian word for councils, that is, *"soviety,"* now anglicized and used currently as "soviets." It seemed better to avoid a similar anglicization of *Räte* ("rats").

3. Abraham Ascher, "Russian Marxism and the German Revolution, 1917–1920," *Archiv für Sozialgeschichte*, 6–8 (1966–1967), 403–404.

4. Eberhard Kolb, *Die Arbeiterräte in der deutschen Innenpolitik, 1918–1919* (Dusseldorf, 1962), p. 173.

5. Gerald D. Feldman, *Army, Industry, and Labor in Germany, 1914–1918* (Princeton, 1966), pp. 519 ff.

6. A. J. Ryder, *The German Revolution of 1918* (Cambridge, 1967), p. 158.

7. *Ibid.*, p. 181.

8. *Ibid.*, p. 182.

9. *Ibid.*, p. 183.

10. Eric Waldman, *The Spartacist Uprising of 1919* (Milwaukee, 1958), pp. 156–157.

11. Lösche, *Bolschewismus*, 193; Walter Tormin, *Zwischen Rätediktatur und Sozialer Demokratie* (Dusseldorf, 1954), p. 42.

12. Ernst Däumig, *Der Aufbau Deutschlands und das Rätesystem* (Berlin, 1919), p. 8.

13. *Ibid.*, p. 13.

14. *Ibid.*, pp. 28–29.

15. Waldman, *Spartacist Uprising*, p. 157.

16. J. P. Nettl, *Rosa Luxemburg* (New York, 1966), pp. 21–22, 471–472, 586–587.

17. Henrietta Roland-Holst, *Rosa Luxemburg, Ihr Leben und Werken* (Zurich, 1937), pp. 190–194. Cf. Waldman, *Spartacist Uprising*, 151–152, and Ryder, *German Revolution*, p. 198.

18. Richard Müller, *Der Bürgerkrieg in Deutschland* (Berlin, 1925), pp. 20 ff., from Ryder, *German Revolution*, p. 200.

19. *Ibid.*, pp. 200–201; Waldman, *Spartacist Uprising*, pp. 170 ff.

20. Richard N. Hunt, *German Social Democracy, 1918–1933* (New Haven, 1964), p. 112.

21. Tormin, *Rätediktatur*, p. 123.

22. Branko Lazitch. *Lénine et la Troisième Internationale* (Paris, 1951), p. 93.

23. G. D. H. Cole, *A History of Socialist Thought: Communism and Social Democracy, 1914–1931* (London, 1958), 4:297–298.

24. James W. Hulse, *The Forming of the Communist International* (Stanford, 1964), pp. 4–7.

25. Ascher, "Russian Marxism," p. 403.

26. Lazitch, *Lénine*, p. 96.

27. Jane Degras, ed., *The Communist International, 1919–1921: Documents* (New York, 1956), 1:17.

28. *Ibid.*, p. 4.

29. Cf. Rosa Luxemburg, *The Russian Revolution* (Ann Arbor, 1962), p. 79.

30. For a more complete discussion of Rosa Luxemburg's differences with Lenin see Richard Lowenthal, "The Bolshevization of the Spartakus League," in David Footman, ed., *International Communism* (Carbondale, Ill., 1960), pp. 26 ff. See also Nettl, *Rosa Luxemburg*, pp. 251, 294, 548–600, 787–841.

31. Hulse, *Forming*, p. 16.

32. Henri Guilbeaux, *Du Kremlin au Cherche-Midi* (Paris, 1933), pp. 206–207.

33. Secondary accounts of the First Congress can be found in Hulse, *Forming*, pp. 19–20, Lazitch, *Lénine*, pp. 111–113, and Branko Lazitch and Milorad Drachkovitch,

Lenin and the Comintern (Stanford, 1972), pp. 50–88. Firsthand accounts are in Angelica Balabanoff, *My Life as a Rebel* (New York, 1938), pp. 216 ff., and Arthur Ransom, *Russia in 1919* (New York, 1919), pp. 214 ff. See also *Der Erste Kongress der Kommunistischen Internationale, Protokoll der Verhandlungen in Moskau vom 2. bis 19. März, 1919* (Hamburg, 1921).

34. Lazitch, *Lénine*, pp. 111–113.

35. Hulse, *Forming*, p. 20.

36. F. Turati, "Socialismo e massimalismo," *Critica Sociale*, 1–15 Sept., 1920, p. 264.

37. Cf. Luigi Ambrosoli, *Nè aderire nè sabotare* (Milan, 1961), p. 261.

38. Donald William Urquidi, "The Origins of the Italian Communist Party, 1918–1921," Ph.D. diss. (Columbia University, 1962), p. 8.

39. Degras, *Communist International*, p. 20.

40. Cf. Pietro Nenni, *Storia di Quattro Anni, 1919–1922* (Rome, 1946), pp. 129–131.

41. John Cammett, *Antonio Gramsci and the Origins of Italian Communism* (Stanford, 1967), p. 66.

42. Ernst Däumig, *Der Aufbau Deutschlands und das Rätesystem* (Berlin, 1919), pp. 16–18.

43. See especially "Formiamo i soviet?" Sept. 21, 1919, p. 1, and "Per la costituzione dei consigli operai in Italia," Jan. 4, 1920, p. 2.

44. Direzione del Partito Socialista Italiano, *Resoconto Stenografico del XVI Congresso Nazionale del Partito Socialista Italiano, Bologna 5–6–7–8 Ottobre 1919* (Milan, 1920), p. 384.

45. *Ibid.*, p. 259.

46. "Vedara," *Avanti!*, Oct. 8, 1919, p. 1.

47. "I partiti della terza internazionale ed il metoda elezionista," *Il Soviet*, Oct. 5, 1919, p. 2.

48. *Bologna Resoconto*, pp. 75–78, 198.

49. *Manifest, Richtlinien, Beschlüsse des Ersten Kongresses. Aufrufe und offene Schreiben des Exeeutivkomitees bis zum Zweiten Kongress* (Hamburg, 1920), p. 151.

50. *Bologna Resoconto*, 98. It is debatable whether Graziadei should be grouped with the Maximalists at this time; but he was rapidly moving left and would be associated with them for most of 1920.

51. See *Manifest, Richtlinien*, pp. 150 ff. for relevant documents. Also, V. I. Lenin, *Sul Movimento operaio italiano* (Rome, 1962).

52. Cf. Helmut König, *Lenin und der italienische Sozialismus, 1915–1921*, (Tübingen, 1967) pp. 13, 15–18, 23 ff.

53. *Manifest, Richtlinien*, p. 151.

54. *Die Kommunistische Internationale*, no. 12 (July–Aug., 1920), p. 71.

55. The position of the Swedish left socialists was explained at some length at the USPD's Leipzig congress by the Swedish leader: *Unabhängige Sozialdemokratische Partei Deutschlands, Protokoll über die Verhandlungen des ausserordentlichen Parteitages vom 30 Nov. bis 6 Dez. in Leipzig* (Berlin, 1919), pp. 62–66. Also, "Überabstimmung über die Internationale bei den Schwedischen Linkssozialisten," *Die Freiheit*, Sept. 10, 1919, no. 438, p. 1.

56. Lenin, *Movimento italiano*, p. 112.

57. Cf. Willy Brandt and Richard Lowenthal, *Ernst Reuter* (Munich, 1957), pp. 237–238.

58. Hulse, *Forming*, p. 45.

59. V. I. Lenin, *Selected Works*, 3:294; from Theodore Draper, *The Roots of American Communism* (New York, 1957), p. 104. For a discussion of the situation in Finn-

land, where social revolution preceded the formation of the Finnish Communist party, see Lazitch and Drachkovitch, *Lenin and the Comintern*, pp. 90–94.

60. V. I. Lenin, *Collected Works* (London, 1965), 30:91–92.

Chapter III: Between Socialist and Communist Internationals

1. *Unabhängige Sozialdemokratische Partei Deutschlands, Protokoll über die Verhandlungen des ausserordentlichen Parteitages in Leipzig, vom 30. November bis 6. Dezember 1919* (Berlin, 1920), pp. 95–112 (hereafter referred to as *Leipzig Protokoll*): Cf. A. J. Ryder, *The German Revolution of 1918* (Cambridge, 1967), p. 222.

2. Eugen Prager, *Geschichte der USPD* (Berlin, 1922), p. 195.

3. For a full discussion of this congress see Annie Kriegel, *Aux origines du communisme français* (Paris, 1964), pp. 327 ff.

4. Paul Louis, *La crise du socialisme mondiale* (Paris, 1921), 122; Patricia van der Esch, *La Deuxième Internationale, 1889–1923* (Paris, 1957), p. 150.

5. Cf. James W. Hulse, *The Forming of the Communist International* (Stanford, 1964), p. 133.

6. Kriegel, *Aux origines*, pp. 324–325.

7. *La Vie Ouvrière*, July 30, 1919; cited in Hulse, *Forming*, p. 185.

8. Arthur Crispien, "Was war in Luzern?" *Die Freiheit*, Aug. 19, 1919, no. 395, pp. 1–2.

9. L. -O. Frossard, "Deuxième ou Troisième Internationale?" *Le Populaire*, July 15, 1919, p. 1.

10. *Ibid.*

11. Karl Kautsky, "Judas in Luzern," *Die Freiheit*, Aug. 20, 1919, no. 397, p. 1; also A. S., "Das Problem der Internationale," *Die Freiheit*, Oct. 3, 1919, no. 589, pp. 1–2.

12. "Die Reichskonferenz," *ibid.*, Sept. 11, 1919, no. 483, pp. 1–3.

13. See the series of articles by Schwenk entitled "Warum wir für Moskau sind," *ibid.*, Nov. 1–3, nos. 530–533.

14. Genosse, "Il congresso socialista svizzera per la terza interrazionale," *Avanti!*, Aug. 13, 1919, p. 1. Cf. also Andre Donneur, *Histoire d'Union des partis socialistes pour l'union internationale* (Sudbury, Ontario, 1967), *passim*.

15. Hulse, *Forming*, pp. 58–59.

16. "Il saluto dei socialisti svizzeri," *Avanti!*, Oct. 9, 1919, p. 1.

17. "Die Reichskonferenz," *Die Freiheit*, Sept. 11, 1919, no. 438, pp. 1–2.

18. *Leipzig Protokoll*, p. 366.

19. Amadée Dunois, "L'Appel des Indépendents," *Le Populaire*, Sept. 20, 1919, p. 1.

20. *Leipzig Protokoll*, pp. 62–70.

21. These divisions within the reconstructionist movement were perceptively explored by Antonio Coen, "L'Adhésion à la Troisième Internationale," *L'Humanité*, Feb. 2, 1920, p. 2.

22. *Leipzig Protokoll*, p. 80.

23. *Ibid.*, pp. 38–40.

24. *Ibid.*, pp. 319–320.

25. *Ibid.*, pp. 330–331.

26. *Ibid.*, pp. 332.

27. *Ibid.*, pp. 40–41, 348–365.

28. Georg Ledebour, "Zur Abwehr," *Die Freiheit*, Dec. 29, 1919, no. 631, pp. 1–2.

29. *Leipzig Protokoll*, p. 365.

30. *Ibid.*, my italics. The full text of the resolution is on p. 369.

31. *Ibid.*, p. 370.

32. *Ibid.*, p. 372.

33. *Ibid.*, p. 373.

34. *Ibid.*, p. 387.

35. *Ibid.*

36. *Ibid.*, pp. 534–535. The full text of the amendment is as follows: "Sollten die Parteien der anderen Länder nicht gewillt sein, mit uns in die Moskauer Internationale einzutreten, so ist der Anschluss der USPD allein vorzunehmen."

37. The previous paragraph of the new resolution (the last paragraph before the amendment was tacked on), which gave the *Zentrale* authorization to make contact with other revolutionary parties and with the Comintern to arrange for a merger, did mention the necessity of basing negotiations on the USPD program. However, since this had been composed before the amendment was added, it was not clear if it could be taken to mean that the USPD could not join the Comintern alone unless there was basic agreement on program and tactics.

38. *Leipzig Protokoll*, pp. 388–395. USPD voting procedure did not consist of a simple juxtaposition of competing resolutions with a choice to vote for one or the other; rather, each resolution was presented in turn, subject to a "yes" or "no" vote, the one getting the most "yes" votes of course carrying the day. This procedure has confused many observers; cf. Jane Degras, ed., *The Communist International, 1919–1921: Documents* (New York, 1956), pp. 1, 74, who describes the vote as 227 to 54 to leave the Second International and 169 to 114 against joining the Third. The confusion in the SFIO about the Leipzig vote will be discussed in the last section of this chapter.

39. In December, 1918, Kautsky had openly declared that the right wing of the USPD should rejoin the SPD, since the former was so internally divided that it could not seriously be considered a party with coherent goals. Cf. A. J. Ryder, *The German Revolution of 1918* (Cambridge, 1967), p. 183.

40. Kurt Geyer, a leading representative of the extreme left of the USPD, had throughout the fall of 1919 forwarded the idea of uniting with the KPD. But, according to Eugen Prager—a man of the right of the USPD, it should be noted—Geyer was not seriously listened to: *Geschichte der USP* (Berlin, 1922), pp. 203–204. Stoecker had also spoken up for joining hands with the Communists in the summer of 1919, and made contact with the leader of the KPD, Paul Levi; cf. *Leipzig Protokoll*, p. 137.

41. *Leipzig Protokoll*, pp. 255 ff., 348.

42. Georg Ledebour, "Zur Abwehr," *Die Freiheit*, Dec. 29, 1919, no. 631, pp. 1–2.

43. *Ibid.*

44. Richard A. Webster, *The Cross and the Fasces* (Stanford, 1960), p. 54; Jean Alazard, *Communisme et "fascio" en Italie* (Paris, 1922), p. 28.

45. Donald William Urquidi, "The Origins of the Italian Communist Party, 1918–1921" (Ph.D. diss., Columbia University, 1962), p. 107.

46. "XVI Nov., 1919," *Communismo*, Dec. 1–15, 1919, pp. 329–332.

47. *Ibid.*

48. *Ministero dell'Interno, Compendio dei Resultati delle Consultazioni Popolari da 1848 al 1954* (Rome, 1955), 75, 90; from Urquidi, "Origins of Italian Communist Party," p. 121.

49. *Leipzig Protokoll*, pp. 62–70.

50. Arthur Crispien, "Die USPD and die Dritte Internationale," *Die Freiheit*, June 25, 1919, no. 244, p. 5.

51. On Radek's jail-salon, see Otto-Ernst Schüddekopf, "Karl Radek in Berlin," *Archiv für Sozialgeschichte* (Hanover, 1962), 2:87–167.

52. *Die Freiheit*, June 25, 1919, no. 244, p. 5.

53. Text of letter in *ibid.*

54. The Scandinavians had their hands slapped for their initiative. "The Russians flatly refused [to allow a reconstructionist meeting in Scandinavia] and a violent quarrel between party headquarters in Moscow, Stockholm, and Oslo followed." Franz Borkenau, *World Communism* (Ann Arbor, 1962), p. 185. See also *Protokoll über die Verhandlungen des ausserordentlichen Parteitages in Halle, vom 12. bis 17. Okt. 1920* (Berlin, n.d.), p. 19.

55. Amadée Dunois, "L'Appel des Indépendents," *Le Populaire*, Sept. 20, 1919, p. 1.

56. Daniel Renoult, "La Reconstruction de l'Internationale," *Le Populaire*, Dec. 17, 1919, p. 1; Paul Faure, "La Crise des Internationaux," *Le Populaire*, Dec. 23, 1919, p. 1.

57. "Comité de [sic] la Reconstruction," *Le Populaire*, Dec. 30, 1919, p. 1.

58. *Ibid.*

59. L. -O. Frossard, "La Position des Indépendents," *L'Humanité*, Feb. 1, 1920, p. 1; *Parti Socialiste (SFIO), 17e Congrès national, tenu à Strasbourg, Compte rendu sténographique* (Paris, 1920), p. 293 (hereafter referred to as *Strasbourg Compte rendu*).

60. *Strasbourg Compte rendu*, pp. 282 ff., gives a rather detailed account of these conversations. *L'Humanité*, Feb. 1, 1920, p. 1, covers about the same material.

61. *Strasbourg Compte rendu*, p. 285.

62. *Ibid.*, p. 291.

63. *Ibid.*, pp. 291–292; also *L'Humanité*, Feb. 1, 1920, p. 1.

64. It should be noted that the reconstruction of the meeting relies entirely on Frossard's accounts at Strasbourg and in *L'Humanité*. Whether Frossard himself confused the story Crispien gave him or whether he reproduced faithfully a purposely distorted version by Crispien cannot be determined with absolute certainty. It is puzzling that Frossard reported to the congress and was presumably told by Crispien that the new compromise resolution at Leipzig had won by a vote of 170 to 111. This is very close to the 169 "no" to 114 "yes" votes by which *Stoecker's* resolution had been *rejected* at Leipzig before the new compromise resolution had won with 277 "yes" votes to 54 "no." It seems that Crispien gave Frossard the vote that *could* have won with a right-center alliance. The whole matter is doubly puzzling because a letter sent to the SFIO by the USPD, which was read to the Strasbourg delegates before Frossard spoke, gave the *correct* vote; yet no one corrected Frossard. Cf. *Strasbourg Compte rendu*, pp. 203–205.

65. *Strasbourg Compte rendu*, p. 293.

66. Amadée Dunois, "Entretiens avec Graziadei," *L'Humanité*, Jan. 13, 1920, p. 3.

67. Cf. R. Palmer Dutt, *The Two Internationals* (London, 1920), p. 89.

68. L. -O. Frossard, "A Moscou? Comment?" *L'Humanité*, Feb. 13, 1920, p. 1.

69. Cf. Loriot's remarks in *Strasbourg Compte rendu*, p. 404.

70. The resolution can be found in *L'Humanité*, Feb. 6, 1920, p. 2.

71. *Strasbourg Compte rendu*, p. 444.

72. Text in *L'Humanité*, Feb. 4, 1920.

73. *Strasbourg Compte rendu*, pp. 405–408.

74. This was apparently Franz Dahlem, who seems to have been in France illegally; thus his name was kept secret at Strasbourg. Cf. his speech at the USPD's *Reichskonferenz* in September 1920, where he described his activities in France and attacked

Crispien for misrepresenting the USPD. *USPD, Protokoll der Reichskonferenz, vom 1. bis 3. Sept. 1920 zu Berlin* (Berlin, 1920), pp. 95–96.

75. *Strasbourg Compte rendu*, p. 408.

76. Text in "Les motions du Comité de la Troisième Internationale," *L'Humanité*, Feb. 7, 1920, p. 2.

77. Cf. Gilbert Ziebura, *Léon Blum, Theorie und Praxis einer sozialistischen Politik* (Berlin, 1957), 1:199.

78. *Strasbourg Compte rendu*, p. 405.

79. *Ibid.*, p. 458.

80. *Ibid.*, pp. 401–403.

81. *Ibid.*, p. 432.

82. *Ibid.*, p. 438.

83. *Ibid.*, pp. 458–459. Concerning Loriot's patriotic activities at the beginning of the war see Robert Wohl, *French Communism in the Making, 1914–1924* (Stanford, 1966), p. 60. Cf. *Strasbourg Compte rendu*, pp. 350 ff.

85. *Ibid.*, pp. 386 ff. It is puzzling that this letter was known in France by the end of February but, as will be seen, was not given to the USPD until early April. It is doubly puzzling that Dahlem, the USPD delegate secretly at Strasbourg, said nothing to his own party leaders about the letter. It is possible that he was not in the congress hall at the time the letter was read.

86. There was a semiofficial "bureau" in the Norwegian capital, which meant simply that the Christiania communists served the Comintern by relaying messages to the West when other means of communication were slow or unsatisfactory. Cf. Hulse, *Forming*, pp. 74–75.

87. *Strasbourg Compte rendu*, p. 387. Henrietta Roland-Holst, a Comintern representative to Strasbourg, delivered in person a speech which in tone and in its demand that the SFIO rid itself of its right wing paralleled Zinoviev's letter. But the left at Strasbourg paid no more attention to her than they did to the letter. Cf. *ibid.*, pp. 136 ff.

88. Cf. the particularly remarkable speech by Adrien Pressemane, *ibid.*, pp. 331 ff.

89. *Ibid.*, p. 566.

90. *Ibid.*, p. 559.

91. Cf. Marcel Sembat, *La Victoire en déroute* (Paris, 1925), p. 107.

92. *Ibid.* Cf. also Kriegel, *Aux origines*, pp. 340–341.

Chapter IV: Paths to Moscow

1. E. H. Carr, "Radek's 'Political Salon' in Berlin, 1919," *Soviet Studies*, 3 (April, 1952), 411–412.

2. Walter Stoecker was especially insistent on this point. Cf. *Unabhängige Sozialdemokratische Partei Deutschlands, Protokoll über die Verhandlungen des ausserordentlichen Parteitages in Halle, vom 12. bis 17. Okt. 1920* (Berlin, n.d.), p. 19.

3. Arthur Crispien, "Die USPD und die Dritte Internationale," *Die Freiheit*, June 25, 1919, no. 244, p. 5. The account in *Die Freiheit* [a series of articles, later made into a pamphlet, *Die USPD und die Dritte Internationale* (Remscheid, 1920)] is somewhat cryptic at this point. It is not clear why the bolshevik representative could not furnish the USPD leaders with the address of the WES or give more aid in establishing contact with Moscow.

4. Cf. James W. Hulse, *The Forming of the Communist International* (Stanford, 1964), pp. 100–104.

5. The letter was published in the newspaper *Spartakus*, no. 5/6, Ende Januar (date as it appears on the paper), 1920, p. 1; see also the French journal *Bulletin Communiste*, Mar. 1, 1920, pp. 13 ff.

6. Full text in *Manifest, Richtlinien, Beschlüsse des Ersten Kongresses; Aufrufe und offene Schreiben des Exekutivkomitees bis zum Zweiten Kongress* (Hamburg, 1920), pp. 195 ff.; and in a slightly abbreviated form in Jane Degras, ed., *The Communist International, 1919–1921: Documents* (New York, 1956), 2:74 ff.

7. Cf. V. I. Lenin, *Complete Works*, (London, 1965), 30:337–344.

8. Eugen Prager, *Geschichte der USP* (Berlin, 1920), p. 137. Prager's reliability on these matters could be questioned.

9. Borodin was quoted in *Bulletin Communiste*, April 1, 1920, p. 13 as vowing "war to the death against the center." His other comments made it clear that he represented the extreme left wing of the Comintern leadership, although it is unlikely that he had any important role in the formation of policy.

10. Degras, *Communist International*, 2:79.

11. *Ibid.*

12. For a more thorough treatment of this complex strike, see Marjorie Ruth Clark, *A History of the French Labor Movement, 1910–1928* (Berkeley, 1930), pp. 85 ff. For an extremely extensive analysis and narrative, using completely new documents, see Annie Kriegel, *Aux origines du communisme français* (Paris, 1964), pp. 359–521.

13. Paul Faure, "Agir sans délai," *L'Humanité*, March 13, 1920, p. 1.

14. L.-O. Frossard, "La Reconstruction de l'Internationale," *L'Humanité*, May 22, 1920, p. 1.

15. Daniel Renoult, "Le Problème de l'Internationale," *L'Humanité*, May 22, 1920, p. 1.

16. *Ibid.*

17. Frossard, "La Reconstruction."

18. *Independent Labour Party, Report of the 29th Annual Conference* (Southport, March, 1921), p. 12.

19. F. Caussy, "C'est le prolétariat allemand qui a vaincu," *L'Humanité*, March 23, 1920, p. 1. Mistral apparently said nothing of the letter that Grumbach had read at Strasbourg.

20. Renoult, "Le Problème."

21. "Le Cercle des ignorances," *Bulletin Communiste*, June 17, 1920, pp. 1–2.

22. *Le Parti Socialiste et l'Internationale, Rapport sur les négociations conduites à Moscou* (Paris, 1920), pp. 5–6; this document, in an incomplete form, can be found also in the appendix to L.-O. Frossard, *De Jaurès à Lénine, Notes et souvenirs d'un militant* (Paris, 1930), pp. 231 ff. The notes below refer to this much more readily available source.

23. For Renaudel's protests, see Pierre Renaudel, "Voir Clair," *L'Humanité*, June 10, 1920, p. 1; for Frossard's refusal, see "Lettre de Frossard," *L'Humanité*, June 12, 1920, p. 2.

24. L.-O. Frossard, "La Reconstruction de l'Internationale," *L'Humanité*, April 20, 1920, p. 1.

25. *Ibid.*

26. *Ibid.*, p. 239.

27. *Ibid.*, p. 240. Italics in text. Cf. also the extensive treatment of these groups in Kriegel, *Aux origines*, pp. 282–307.

28. Frossard, *De Jaurès*, p. 240.

29. *Ibid.*, pp. 236, 241.

30. V. I. Lenin, *Collected Works* (London, 1965), 30:91–92.

31. *Manifest, Richtlinien*, p. 146.

32. John Cammett, *Antonio Gramsci and the Origins of Italian Communism* (Stanford, 1967), p. 90.

33. *Ibid.*, p. 132. Cf. also Paolo Spriano, *Storia del Partito Communista Italiano* (Turin, 1967), pp. 30–31.

34. Pietro Nenni, *Lo Spettro del Communismo* (Milan, 1921), p. 127.

35. Cammett, *Gramsci*, pp. 132–133.

36. Cf. Spriano, *Storia*, p. 32.

37. "Il Convegno di Milano," *Il Soviet*, May 2, 1920, p. 1.

38. Cf. Niccolini, "La III Internazionale al Partito Socialista Italiano," *Il Soviet*, May 16, 1920, pp. 3–4.

39. At least Serrati later asserted that Niccolini did not bring the question up at this point. Cf. Serrati's speech at Leghorn, *Direzione del Partito Socialista Italiano, Resoconto Stenografica del XVII Congresso Nazionale del Partito Socialista Italiano, Livorno 15–16–17–18–19–20 Gennaio 1921*, (Rome, 1921), p. 311.

40. Helmut König, *Lenin und der italienische Sozialismus, 1915–1921* (Tübingen, 1967), p. 20. Also "Unione o Scissure," *Communismo*, Feb. 15–29, 1920, pp. 689–697.

41. König, *Lenin*, pp. 71–72. Cammett, *Gramsci*, pp. 98 ff. Donald William Urquidi, "The Origins of the Italian Communist Party, 1918–1921," (Ph.D. diss., Columbia University, 1962), pp. 137 ff.

42. Urquidi, "Origins of Italian Communist Party," p. 144.

43. *Ibid.*, pp. 146–147.

44. *Manifest, Richtlinien*, p. 139.

45. *Leninism* (New York, 1963), p. 150.

46. Cf. chap. III, n. 39 and 40.

47. Cf. Richard Lowenthal, "The Bolshevisation of the Spartacus League," in David Footman, ed., *International Communism* (Carbondale, Ill., 1960), *passim*.

48. This point will be more fully discussed in the final section of the last chapter.

49. *Manifest, Richtlinien*, p. 139.

50. Kriegel, *Aux Origines*, pp. 282 ff., thoroughly discusses Péricat and his followers; cf. also Hulse, *Forming*, p. 138.

51. Kriegel, *Aux origines*, p. 347.

52. *Ibid.*, p. 570.

53. *Manifest, Richtlinien*, p. 194.

54. König, *Lenin*, p. 41.

55. *Ibid.*, p. 64.

56. *Ibid.*, p. 65.

57. Luigi Cortesi, *Il Socialismo Italiano tra riforme e rivoluzione* (Bari, 1969), p. 803.

58. "I comitati di fabbrica," pp. 401–407.

59. König, *Lenin*, pp. 69 ff.

60. Abraham Ascher, "Russian Marxism and the German Revolution, 1917–1920," *Archiv für Sozialgeschichte* (Bonn, 1967), 6–7: 424–426.

61. "Oekonomik und Politik in der Epoche der Diktatur des Proletariats," *Die Kommunistische Internationale*, Oct., 1919, no. 6, p. 118.

62. V. I. Lenin, *Left-Wing Communism, An Infantile Disorder* (Moscow, 1947), p. 9.

63. *Der Zweite Kongress der Kommunist. Internationale, Protokoll der Verhandlungen* (Hamburg, 1921), p. 240.

64. For interesting discussion of this whole problem see Stanley Page, *Lenin and World Revolution* (New York, 1959), pp. 138–139.

65. Ascher, "Russian Marxism," pp. 410, 426.

66. Cf. Richard Lowenthal, *World Communism* (New York, 1964), pp. 237–238.

67. *Manifest, Richtlinien*, 145–146; V. I. Lenin, *Collected Works* (Moscow, 1966), 3:90–91.

68. *Ibid.*, 29:565.

69. Cf. Merle Fainsod, *How Russia is Ruled* (Cambridge, Mass., 1954), p. 52; Leonard Schapiro and Peter Reddaway, *Lenin* (London, 1967), pp. 149 ff.

70. Lenin, *Collected Works*, 31:62.

71. *Ibid.*, pp. 62–63.

72. *Ibid.*, p. 63.

73. *Ibid.*, p. 119.

74. Cf. Ascher, "Russian Marxism," pp. 427–32, where the Russian response to the Kapp Putsch is thoroughly explored.

75. Isaac Deutscher, *The Prophet Armed* (New York, 1965), pp. 464–466.

76. Willy Brandt and Richard Lowenthal, *Ernst Reuter* (Munich, 1957), p. 138.

77. Lowenthal, "Bolshevisation," p. 39.

78. Degras, *Communist International*, p. 118.

79. Cf. Henri Guilbeaux, *Du Kremlin au Cherche-Midi*, (Paris, 1933), pp. 43, 241; also Alfred Rosmer, *Moscou sous Lénine* (Paris, 1953), pp. 116–117. Both Guilbeaux and Rosmer were familiar with the inner workings of the ECCI, and both stress Radek's efforts to facilitate an understanding with the USPD and SFIO.

80. Radek's attitude to the KPD and USPD was highly complex and changing. It will be further discussed in the last section of the final chapter.

81. Cf. *Le Parti Socialiste et l'Internationale, rapport sur les négotiations conduites à Moscou* (Paris, 1920), p. 16.

82. The numerous examples of Moscow's interest in a French Communist party that would act as an impediment to counterrevolution are given in Chapter V. Cf. also the similar interest of Jules Humbert-Droz, the Comintern's agent in France in 1921, in his *"L'Oeil de Moscou" à Paris* (Paris, 1964), p. 188.

83. Carr, *Bolshevik Revolution*, 3:76.

84. Frossard soon perceived the particular interest of these three in getting an agreement with him; cf. *Mon Journal de route en Russie des Soviets*, July 15, 1920 (microfilm at Hoover Institution, Stanford, Calif.), n.p.

85. Cf. *Compte rendu de la gestion du Comité Exécutif de l'Internationale Communiste (1920–1921)* (Moscow, 1921), 56; also *Protokoll des III. Kongress der Kommunistischen Internationale, Moskau 22. juni bis 12. juli* (Hamburg, 1921), pp. 149 ff.

86. Cf. Carr, *Bolshevik Revolution*, 1:108–109, 187, 210.

87. Cf. Leon Trotsky, *History of the Russian Revolution* (London, 1966), 2:45.

88. Angelica Balabanoff, *My Life as a Rebel* (New York, 1938), pp. 220–221.

89. Rosmer, *Moscou*, pp. 69–70.

90. Degras, *Communist International*, p. 125.

91. Lenin, *Left-Wing Communism*, pp. 74–75.

92. Cf. "Zum bevorstehenden Kongress der Kommunistischen Internationale," *Kommunistische Internationale* (July–Aug.), no. 12, pp. 56–58, where he attacked the SFIO especially and stressed that the French party should not be compared to the USPD, since the USPD had already split off from the social patriots. Cf. also his vehement denunciation of Longuet and centrism in general, in *The First Five Years of the Communist International* (New York, 1945), pp. 76–83.

93. *Terrorism and Communism* (Ann Arbor, 1963), pp. 190–191 (italics mine).

Chapter V: In the Land of Revolution

1. "Le Cercle des ignorances," *Bulletin Communiste*, June 17, 1920, pp. 1–2.

2. L. -O. Frossard, *De Jaurès à Lénine, notes et souvenirs d'un militant* (Paris, 1930), p. 48.

3. Cf. L. -O. Frossard, *La Décomposition du communisme* (Paris, 1923), p. 17.

4. Frossard, *De Jaurès à Lénine*, p. 45.

5. For some good samples of Cachin's chauvinistic rhetoric, see *L'Humanité*, April 27 and Sept. 21, 1915.

6. Cachin's activities in Italy have been the subject of dispute. Frossard, *Le Jaurès à Lénine*, 45, denies that Cachin was actually the agent to hand over the money to Mussolini. Most of the other sources assert that he was. Cf. Ivone Kirkpatrick, *Mussolini, A Study in Power* (New York, 1964), pp. 61–63; Angelica Balabanoff, *My Life As A Rebel* (New York, 1938), p. 273; Henri Guilbeaux, *La Fin des Soviets* (Paris, 1937), p. 144; Victor Serge, *Memoirs of a Revolutionary* (New York, 1963), p. 104.

7. Guilbeaux, *La Fin*, p. 145.

8. *L'Humanité*, Aug. 24, 1918. Quoted in Annie Kriegel, *Aux origines du communisme français* (Paris, 1964), p. 190.

9. Joseph Paul-Boncour, *Entre deux guerres* (Paris, 1945), p. 60. Poincaré, who stood near Cachin at Strasbourg, made this story widely known; cf. Frossard, *De Jaurès à Lénine*, p. 47. This incident is also described in Guilbeaux, *La Fin*, p. 144.

10. Cf. Serge, *Memoirs*, 167: "He worshipped the party and lived exclusively on his popularity. To keep his reputation going he would strive always to find the strongest current of opinion, which he was quick to smell out."

11. Alfred Rosmer, *Moscou sous Lénine* (Paris, 1953), p. 51.

12. Frossard, *De Jaurès à Lénine*, p. 47. It is significant that this opinion of Cachin was shared by men from the extreme left to the extreme right of socialism: cf. Serge, *Memoirs* (extreme left); Marcel Sembat, *La Victoire en déroute*, (Paris, 1925), p. 107 (moderate); Paul-Boncour, *Entre deux guerres*, pp. 59–60 (extreme right).

13. Dates from G. D. H. Cole, *A History of Socialist Thought: Communism and Social Democracy, 1914–1931* (London, 1958), 4:333.

14. Cf. Frossard, *Décomposition*, pp. 17–18.

15. Frossard, *De Jaurès à Lénine*, p. 47.

16. *Ibid.*, p. 39.

17. *Ibid.*, p. 84.

18. Frossard, *De Jaurès à Lénine*, p. 15.

19. Paul-Boncour, *Entre deux guerres*, p. 61.

20. Cf. Arthur Crispien, "Die USPD und die Dritte Internationale," *Die Freiheit*, June 25, 1920, no. 244, p. 5.

21. This is the series of articles mentioned in chap. IV, section one.

22. Shlyapnikov was the Commissar of Labor in the first Council of People's Commissars and later a leader of the Workers' Opposition. He seems to have favored a more tolerant attitude toward western socialists than did Borodin. Cf. Isaac Deutscher, *Stalin, A Political Biography* (New York, 1960), pp. 177, 222, 309.

23. Arthur Crispien, "Die USPD und die Dritte Internationale," *Die Freiheit*, June 27, 1920, no. 248, p. 5.

24. Jane Degras, ed., *The Communist International, 1919–1921: Documents* (New York, 1956), p. 92.

25. Crispien, *loc. cit.* I have found no evidence of this May 20 publication, which

must have been extremely limited. The insulting hollowness of this excuse stung the bolsheviks when the telegram arrived in Moscow.

26. Degras, *Communist International*, p. 100.

27. The text of the mandate can be found in *U.S.P.D. Protokoll der Reichskonferenz, vom 1. bis 3. Sept. 1920 zu Berlin* (Berlin, 1920), pp. 29–30 (hereafter referred to as *Reichskonferenz Protokoll*). Cf. also the series of articles titled "Antwort an das Executivkomitee," *Die Freiheit*, starting July 11, no. 272, p. 5.

28. J. P. Nettl, *Rosa Luxemburg* (New York, 1966), p. 459.

29. General biographical information on Dittmann can be found in Franz Osterroth, *Biographisches Lexikon des Sozialismus* (Hanover, 1960), vol. 1, 66–67; also Adéodat Compère-Morel, *Grand Dictionnaire Socialiste* (Paris, 1924), p. 223.

30. A. J. Ryder, "The Independent Social Democratic Party and the German Revolution" (Ph.D. diss. London University, 1958), 53. Carl Schorske, *German Social Democracy, 1905–1917* (Cambridge, Mass., 1955), p. 251.

31. Cf. his speech at the congress of Halle, *Protokoll über die Verhandlungen des ausserordentlichen Parteitages in Halle, vom 12. bis 17. Okt. 1920* (Berlin, n.d.), pp. 81–82.

32. Cf. *Kommunistische Internationale*, "Brennende Tagesfragen der internationalen Arbeiterbewegung," no. 11, p. 34. For general biographical information on Crispien, see Osterroth, *Lexicon*, pp. 55–56.

33. V. I. Lenin, *Left-Wing Communism, An Infantile Disorder* (Moscow, 1947), pp. 115–116. Whether Crispien had read these attacks on him before going to Moscow is not possible to say; but once he had arrived there, he was handed a copy of *Left-Wing Communism*, as were all delegates.

34. Ryder, "Independent Social Democratic Party," p. 268. It seems that in his military aspirations as well as in his conception of the role of the *Räte*, Däumig resembled Trotsky.

35. On his turn toward bolshevism, cf. *Reichskonferenz Protokoll*, 129.

36. *Beiträge zur Geschichte der deutschen Arbeiterbewegung* (Berlin, 1968), 4:1057–1071.

37. Cf. *Reichskonferenz Protokoll*, pp. 164, 207 ff., 223. Stoecker vigorously denied the accusations that he had made patriotic statements.

38. *Ibid.*, pp. 69 ff.

39. Helmut König, *Lenin und der italienische Sozialismus, 1915–1921* (Tübingen, 1967), p. 82.

40. Giulio Trevisani, *Piccola Enciclopedia del Socialismo e del Communismo* (Milan, 1958), pp. 656–657.

41. Giuseppi Berti, "Appunti e ricordi, 1919–1926," *Annali* (dell' Istituto Giangiacomo Feltrinelli) VIII (Milan, 1966), pp. 33–34.

42. König, *Lenin*, p. 73.

43. Cf. Pietro Nenni, *Storia di Quattro Anni, 1919–1922* (Rome, 1946), p. 127; also Luigi Ambrosoli, *Nè aderire nè sabotare* (Milan, 1961), p. 293.

44. Berti, "Appunti," *Annali*, p. 29.

45. G. M. Serrati, "Lettera dalla Germania," *Avanti!*, June 17, 1920, p. 1.

46. Vicenzo Vacirca, "Verso la Russia," *Avanti!*, June 17, 1920, p. 3.

47. *Ibid.*

48. A. Graziadei, "I deliberati del Secondo Congresso della Terza Internazionale," *Avanti!*, Aug. 21, 1920, p. 2.

49. E. Colombino, *Tre Mesi nella Russia dei Soviet* (Milan, 1921), p. 7.

50. *Ibid.*

51. Vicenzo Vacirca, *Ciò che ho visto nella Russia Soviettista* (Milan, 1921), p. 72; Angelica Balabanoff, *My Life as a Rebel* (New York, 1938), p. 262.

52. G. M. Serrati, "Missione di Fratellanza," *Avanti!*, May 1, 1920, p. 1.

53. Colombino, *Tre Mesi*, p. 13.

54. *Ibid.*, p. 40.

55. *Ibid.*, pp. 8–9. Cf. also G. M. Serrati, "Petrogrado Rossa," *Avanti!*, July 14, 1920, p. 1.

56. Vincenzo Vacirca, "Instantee moscovite," *Avanti!*, Sept. 23, 1920, p. 3.

57. Colombino, *Tre Mesi*, pp. 40–41.

58. Vacirca, *Russia Soviettista*, pp. 114 ff.

59. *Ibid.*, p. 72.

60. Colombino, *Tre Mesi*, p. 32.

61. The following pages, covering the initial stages of Cachin's and Frossard's journey to Russia, rely heavily on Frossard. Since he composed several sets of memoirs in the years following his trip to Moscow, and since these memoirs vary according to his changed political affiliations, it is possible to do a certain amount of cross-checking. After his arrival in Russia, most of what he says can be checked through other sources.

62. This is at least asserted in an article "Cachin et Frossard seraient rentrés le 1er Juillet" in *Le Populaire*, June 17, 1920, p. 1, although I have found no specific mention in German sources that the USPD and SFIO were to leave together.

63. Cf. L.-O. Frossard, *Mon Journal de route en Russie des Soviets* (Hoover Microfilm), June 5 (n.p.).

64. *Ibid.*

65. *Ibid.*

66. *Ibid.*

67. Cf. *De Jaurès à Lénine*, p. 49.

68. *Ibid.*

69. *Ibid.* It should be noted that in the foreword to his *Mon Journal* (written while still head of the Communist party), Frossard assured his readers that he had published an exact reproduction of the notes he had taken during the voyage, with changes only in literary style.

70. Rosmer, *Moscou*, p. 51. Cf. also Kriegel, *Aux origines*, p. 624.

71. Rosmer, *Moscou*, p. 62.

72. Serge, *Memoirs*, p. 104; cf. also the personal tribute to Rosmer by Albert Camus in the preface to Rosmer's *Moscou sous Lénine*.

73. Rosmer, *Moscou*, p. 51.

74. *Ibid.* This judgment was obviously shaded by Rosmer's knowledge of Frossard's later "journey" from Left to Right.

75. Frossard, *De Jaurès à Lénine*, p. 48.

76. *Ibid.*

77. Frossard, *De Jaurès à Lénine*, p. 244.

78. Frossard, *Mon Journal*, June 14.

79. *Ibid.*

80. Frossard, *De Jaurès à Lénine*, p. 51.

81. Frossard, *Mon Journal*, June 14.

82. Balabanoff, *My Life as a Rebel*, p. 87.

83. König, *Lenin*, p. 82.

84. Colombino, *Tre Mesi*, p. 34.

85. Vacirca, *Russia Soviettista*, p. 119.

86. Colombino, *Tre Mesi*, pp. 35–36.

87. König, *Lenin*, p. 90.

88. Colombino, *Tre Mesi*, p. 36.

89. Vacirca, *Russia Soviettista*, p. 118.

90. Frossard, *Mon Journal*, June 15.

91. *Ibid.*

92. Frossard, *De Jaurès à Lénine*, p. 54.

93. *Ibid.*, p. 53.

94. A summary, though not the text of the telegram, appeared in *Le Populaire*, June 17, 1920.

95. Frossard, *De Jaurès à Lénine*, p. 54.

96. *Ibid.*, p. 55.

97. *Ibid.*, p. 56.

98. "Tagung des All-Russischen Zentral-Executivkomitees der Soviets," *Die Rote Fahne*, July 8, 1920, p. 8. Also "Cachin in Moskau," *Rote Fahne*, July 9, 1920, p. 8.

99. *Ibid.* Frossard's *Mon Journal*, June 16, says about this speech merely that Cachin's eloquence seemed to impress the Bolshevik leaders.

100. Rosmer, *Moscou*, pp. 60–61.

101. *Ibid.*

102. Frossard, *Mon Journal*, June 17.

103. Henri Guilbeaux, *Du Kremlin au Cherche-Midi* (Paris, 1933), p. 241.

104. Frossard, *Mon Journal*, June 17.

105. *Ibid.*, June 18.

106. Frossard, *De Jaurès à Lénine*, pp. 254 ff.

107. *Le Parti Socialiste et l'Internationale, Rapport sur les négotiations conduites à Moscou* (Paris, 1920), p. 16 (hereafter referred to as *Parti Socialiste Rapport*).

108. *Ibid.*

109. Frossard, *Mon Journal*, June 23.

110. *Ibid.*, June 24.

111. Frossard, *Mon Journal*, June 26. A similar conversation occurred later with Rakovsky, who told Cachin and Frossard that revolution would break out first in Germany or Italy, not in France, and then added, "What would the French proletariat be capable of doing in case of the French government's direct intervention [in Italy or Germany]?" Frossard, *Mon Journal*, July 16.

112. *Ibid.*, June 24.

113. *De Jaurès à Lénine*, pp. 105–106.

114. *Parti Socialiste Rapport*, pp. 18–20. All quotations from the speech below are from these pages of the *Rapport*.

115. Cf. *Parti Socialiste (SFIO), 17e Congrès national, tenu à Strasbourg, compte rendu stenographique* (Paris, 1920), pp. 564.

116. Quoted in *Bulletin Communiste*, August 22, 1920, pp. 8–9.

117. Cf. Boris Sokolov, *Voyage de Cachin et Frossard dans la Russie des Soviets* (Paris 1921), pp. 15–16.

118. Colombino, *Tre Mesi*, pp. 41 ff.

119. Sokolov, *Voyage*, pp. 15–16.

120. Frossard, *De Jaurès à Lénine*, p. 79.

121. König, *Lenin*, p. 85.

122. *Reichskonferenz Protokoll*, p. 6.

123. *Ibid.*; *Halle Protokoll*, p. 121.

124. *Ibid.*; Wilhelm Dittmann, "Memoiren" (manuscript at the International Institute for Social History, Amsterdam), XIX, 4.

125. *Reichskonferenz Protokoll*, p. 7. Dittmann, "Memoiren," XIX, 21.

126. *Reichskonferenz Protokoll*, p. 175.

127. Ibid., p. 7.

128. Dittmann, "Memoiren," XIX, 34.

129. *Reichskonferenz Protokoll*, p. 12.

130. A. Crispien, "Die USPD und die Kommunistische Internationale," *Die Freiheit*, Aug. 27, 1920, no. 352, p. 6.

131. *Reichskonferenz Protokoll*, p. 7.

132. *Ibid.*, pp. 7–10.

133. A description of this meeting is also in "Dittmann-Crispien in Moskau und Berlin," *Die Rote Fahne*, Sept. 2, 1920, p. 1.

134. Dittmann, "Memoiren," XIX, 28.

135. *Reichskonferenz Protokoll*, p. 14.

136. Dittmann, "Memoiren," XIX, 28.

137. *Reichskonferenz Protokoll*, p. 14.

Chapter VI: The Second Congress of the Communist Internationale

1. Wilhelm Dittmann, "Memoiren" (manuscript at the International Institute for Social History, Amsterdam), XIX, 8–11.

2. Henri Guilbeaux, *Du Kremlin au Cherche-Midi* (Paris, 1933), p. 242.

3. German was normally the language used in early Comintern meetings. Zinoviev and Bukharin gave their speeches in German, even though they were not fully fluent in it. Usually the most reliable and definitive texts of early Comintern documents are in German. The English version for the Second Congress is garbled in many places, supplies incorrect dates for the sessions, and omits whole sections or places them in improper sequence. The Russian version is apparently a direct translation of the German text.

4. Dittmann, "Memoiren," XIX, 9.

5. *Der Zweite Kongress der Kommunist. Internationale, Protokoll der Verhandlungen* (Hamburg, 1921), p. 36 (hereafter referred to as *Zweite Kongress Protokoll*).

6. *Ibid.*, p. 11.

7. *Ibid.*, p. 12.

8. *Ibid.*, pp. 130–136.

9. James T. Murphy, *New Horizons* (London, 1941), p. 141.

10. *Zweite Kongress Protokoll*, pp. 75 ff.

11. L. -O. Frossard, *Mon Journal* (1921, Microfilm at the Hoover Library, Palo Alto, Calif.), July 15, 1920.

12. L. -O. Frossard, *De Jaurès à Lénine, Notes et Souvenirs d'un Militant* (Paris, 1930), p. 131.

13. Frossard, *Mon Journal*, July 15, 1920; *Le Parti Socialiste et l'Internationale, Rapport sur les négotiations conduites à Moscou* (Paris, 1920), p. 38 (hereafter referred to as *Parti Socialiste Rapport*).

14. Frossard, *Mon Journal*, July 15, 1920.

15. L. -O. Frossard, *La Décomposition du communisme* (Paris, 1923), p. 13; Frossard, *Mon Journal*, July 15, 1920.

16. Frossard, *Mon Journal*, July 15, 1920.

17. Frossard, *De Jaurès à Lénine*, p. 110.

18. *Ibid.*, p. 117.

18. *Ibid.*, p. 145.

20. The article in question was no doubt "L'unité socialiste internationale,"

L'Humanité, June 22, 1920, p. 1. News of Cachin's and Frossard's supposed sudden return had been published five days earlier, "Cachin et Frossard reviendront le 1er juillet," *L'Humanité*, June 17, 1920, p. 3. The dateline on this article, based on information from the Russian news agency *Respublica*, was June 14, which was before the time that Frossard could have sent his telegram. The editors of *L'Humanité* note, however, that the date is probably not reliable.

21. Frossard, *De Jaurès à Lénine*, p. 131.

22. Except where otherwise noted, the following account of the meeting of the Committee on Conditions is based on the extensive account in "Dittmann und Crispien in Moskau," *Die Rote Fahne*, Oct. 10, 1920, pp. 2–5, which is a protocol of the meeting taken from notes of Ernst Meyer, a KPD representative on the committee. Frossard's *Mon Journal*, July 25, refers to this meeting, but the *Rote Fahne* account is by far the more complete. Dittmann, at the USPD Halle congress in November, denied that the *Rote Fahne* account was accurate in all respects, but he did not name any specific inaccuracies. Cf. USPD, *Protokoll über die Verhandlungen des ausserordentlichen Parteitages in Halle vom 12. bis 17.* Okt. 1920 (Berlin, n.d.) p. 122 (hereafter referred to as *Halle Protokoll*).

23. This article appeared also in *Die Kommunistische Internationale*, "Zum bevorstehenden Kongress der Kommunistischen Internationale," n.d., no. 10, pp. 58–59. See also Leon Trotsky, *The First Five Years of the Communist International* (New York, 1945), 88–94. In these later versions there are five basic questions, divided up into numerous subsidiary questions. The fifth question, which was apparently added later and which Cachin did not answer, dealt with exclusions.

24. Frossard, *Mon Journal*, July 25 emphasizes that Cachin said "at this time"; the *Rote Fahne* account does not.

25. The only source for Cachin's reply is the *Rote Fahne* article. It is possible that Meyer exaggerated the extent of Cachin's submission in order to put Crispien's and Dittmann's combativeness in an unfavorable light. It is clear in any case that Cachin did make far-reaching concessions: Crispien later noted that Cachin and Frossard "made penance in sackcloth and ashes" USPD, *Protokoll der Reichskonferenz vom 1. bis 3. Sept. 1920 zu Berlin* (Berlin, 1920), p. 199 (hereafter referred to as *Reichskonferenz Protokoll*); cf. also Raymond Lefebvre "Le parti socialiste français devant la 3e Internationale,'" *Bulletin Communiste*, Dec. 23, 1920, pp. 1–2. In the *Parti Socialiste Rapport*, p. 25 (Cachin's and Frossard's official account of their negotiations in Russia), the impression is given that the French delegation said nothing that went beyond its mandate or party program, and no mention is made of Cachin's concessions and Trotsky's cross-examination.

26. Frossard, *Mon Journal*, July 27, 1920.

27. *Ibid.*, July 25. Frossard reported that Trotsky expressed himself "with great cordiality" at this meeting—hardly the impression given in the *Rote Fahne* account. Trotsky's article also bristles with hostility to the SFIO.

28. Frossard, *Mon Journal*, July 25.

29. *Reichskonferenz Protokoll*, p. 12.

30. *Ibid.* The source for this remark is Dittmann's report at the *Reichskonferenz* in September, 1920; it is thus possible that Zinoviev may not have spoken so strongly against the KPD. The *Rote Fahne* account does not mention any such remark—it could hardly be expected that it would. The whole question of the KPD's actions during the Kapp Putsch was a very sensitive one, since the bolsheviks had also criticized the KPD's actions at this time, although in an extremely confused and contradictory fashion. Cf. Abraham Ascher, "Russian Marxism and the German Revolution, 1917–1920," *Archiv für Sozialgeschichte* (Bonn, 1967), 6–7:427 ff.

31. Frossard, *Mon Journal*, July 25.

32. *Halle Protokoll*, p. 121.

33. Dittmann, "Memoiren," XIX, 13.

34. The above mentioned *Rote Fahne* article, the *Reichskonferenz Protokoll*, p. 12, and Frossard's *Mon Journal*, July 25, all record the sensation caused by Dittmann's remarks.

35. *Halle Protokoll*, p. 121.

36. Frossard, *Mon Journal*, July 25.

37. *Halle Protokoll*, p. 121.

38. *Ibid.*, p. 128.

39. *Reichskonferenz Protokoll*, pp. 12–14.

40. Frossard, *Mon Journal*, July 26.

41. Frossard, *Décomposition*, p. 43.

42. *Parti Socialiste Rapport*, p. 25.

43. Frossard, *De Jaurès à Lénine*, p. 132. Frossard's anger was not mentioned in the official *Rapport*. Alfred Rosmer, in his memoirs, *Moscou sous Lénine* (Paris, 1953), p. 57, notes that he was asked earlier to look over an "open letter" which was "obviously destined to 'prepare' the return of the two emissaries, Cachin and Frossard"— apparently a preliminary draft of the "Answer." He, however, declined, and the job was taken over by Victor Serge.

44. "Notizen über die Verhandlungen der Kommunisten betreffs der Bedingungen zur Aufnahme in die 3. Internationale," *Die Rote Fahne*, Oct. 10, 1920, pp. 5–6; *Reichskonferenz Protokoll*, p. 15.

45. *Die Rote Fahne*, Oct. 10, 1920, pp. 5–6.

46. *Reichskonferenz Protokoll*, pp. 60, 201.

47. In *De Jaurès à Lénine*, p. 132, he says he had definitely decided to break off negotiations and go back to France; in *Mon Journal*, July 26, he says that he was "on the point of breaking off negotiations."

48. Frossard, *De Jaurès à Lénine*, p. 133.

49. Frossard, *Mon Journal*, July 27.

50. Cf. "Per un rinnovamento del partito socialista," *L'Ordine Nuovo*, May 8, 1920, pp. 3–4.

51. Cf. Donald William Urquidi, "The Origins of the Italian Communist Party 1918–1921" (Columbia University, Ph.D. diss. 1962), p. 157.

52. Cf. "Intorno al Congress IC," *Il Soviet*, Oct. 3, 1920, pp. 1–3. Also "Croniche dell' Ordine Nuovo," *L'Ordine Nuovo*, Oct. 9, 1920, p. 129.

53. *Zweite Kongress Protokoll*, p. 655.

54. *Ibid.*, p. 656.

55. Helmut König, *Lenin und der italienische Sozialismus, 1915–1921* (Tübingen, 1967), pp. 95–96.

56. *Ibid.*, p. 86.

57. Alfred G. Meyer, *Leninism* (New York, 1963), p. 119.

58. *Zweite Kongress Protokoll*, p. 317.

59. Graziadei even confided to Frossard that he shared most of Serrati's positions, including the Maximalist leader's opposition to an *immediate* exclusion of Turati and his insistence that the peasantry in the West was completely different from the Russian. But Graziadei chose to keep these differences private and to cultivate friendly relations with the bolsheviks. Cf. Frossard, *Mon Journal*, July 15.

60. "Intorno al Congresso IC," *Il Soviet*, Oct. 3, 1920, pp. 1–3.

61. *Zweite Kongress Protokoll*, p. 81.

62. Frossard, *De Jaurès à Lénine*, pp. 132.

63. Frossard, *Mon Journal,* July 28.

64. Frossard, *De Jaurès à Lénine,* p. 133.

65. *Parti Socialiste Rapport,* p. 25.

66. *Ibid.,* p. 28.

67. *Ibid.,* p. 27.

68. Frossard, *Mon Journal,* July 28.

69. Frossard, *De Jaurès à Lénine,* p. 134.

70. Rosmer, *Moscou,* pp. 112–113.

71. Frossard, *De Jaurès à Lénine,* p. 135.

72. *Zweite Kongress Protokoll,* p. 262.

73. *Parti Socialiste Rapport,* p. 29.

74. Frossard, *Mon Journal,* July 28.

75. *Zweite Kongress Protokoll,* p. 243.

76. *Frossard, Mon Journal,* July 30; Marcel Cachin, *Ecrits et Portraits* (Paris, 1964), pp. 91–98.

77. Frossard, *Mon Journal,* July 29.

78. The latter delegates took little part in the affairs of the Second Congress. They seem to have been impressed with Soviet accomplishments, while still retaining deep reservations about Russia's concept of syndicalism and centralization, and were concerned about the bureaucracy that had arisen under bolshevik leadership. (Cf. Frossard, *Mon Journal,* July 25). All three died in a shipwreck on the way back to France. For personal sketches of the three, see Rosmer, *Moscou,* 132 ff.; also Robert Wohl, "La Révolution ou la Mort: Raymond Lefebvre and the Formation of the French Communist Party," *International Review of Social History,* vii (1962), pp. 177–202.

79. *Zweite Kongress Protokoll,* p. 270.

80. *Ibid.,* pp. 272–273.

81. *Ibid.,* p. 279.

82. *Ibid.,* e.g., pp. 284, 308–309.

83. *Ibid.,* p. 344.

84. *Reichskonferenz Protokoll,* p. 61.

85. Frossard, *De Jaurès à Lénine,* p. 134.

86. *Reichskonferenz Protokoll,* p. 16.

87. *Zweite Kongress Protokoll,* pp. 310–321.

88. *Ibid.,* p. 314.

89. *Ibid.,* pp. 366–378.

90. *Ibid.,* p. 377.

91. *Ibid.,* p. 378.

92. *Ibid.,* p. 385.

93. *Ibid.,* pp. 383–384.

94. *Ibid.,* p. 384.

95. *Reichskonferenz Protokoll,* p. 128.

96. *Ibid.,* p. 28.

97. *Ibid.,* pp. 29–31.

98. *Ibid.,* p. 29; *Die Freiheit,* Aug. 28, 1920, no. 354, p. 1.

99. *Zweite Kongress Protokoll,* p. 286.

100. *Ibid.,* p. 421.

101. *Ibid.,* p. 416.

102. *Ibid.,* p. 429.

103. Dittmann, "Memoiren," XIX, 21. Dittmann mentioned that both Serrati and Graziadei were very friendly to him and it seemed to him that their position was very close to his.

104. *Zweite Kongress Protokoll*, pp. 288 ff.
105. *Ibid.*, p. 658.
106. *Ibid.*, p. 676.
107. *Ibid.*, pp. 690–691.

Chapter VII: The Campaign for Communism

1. "Nos délégués sont arrivés ce matin," *Le Populaire*, Aug. 12, 1920, p. 1.

2. "La dislocation de la majorité," *Bulletin Communiste*, Aug. 5, 1920, p. 3. Italics in text.

3. *Ibid.*

4. Varine, "Leur politique et la nôtre," *Bulletin Communiste*, Aug. 19, 1920, pp. 1–3.

5. "Deux mois en Russie," *Le Populaire*, Aug. 12, 1920, p. 1.

6. "Nos délégués sont arrivés ce matin," *Le Populaire*, Aug. 12, 1920, p. 1

7. "Deux mois en Russie," *Le Populaire*, Aug. 12, 1920, p. 1.

8. "Lettere dalla Francia," *Avanti!*, Aug. 19, 1920. This latter incident was not mentioned in the French newspaper accounts.

9. Gérard Walter, *Histoire du parti communiste français* (Paris, 1948), pp. 30–31.

10. An interesting reversal of roles between the two papers now occurred. During the war *Le Populaire* had been the left-wing journal of protest, while *L'Humanité* was staunchly in favor of the *Union sacrée*. Under the influence of Cachin and Frossard, *L'Humanité* became "revolutionary," while *Le Populaire* voiced the more conservative sentiments within the party.

11. "L'arrivée de Cachin et Frossard," *L'Humanité*, Aug. 12, 1920, p. 1.

12. *Le Parti Socialiste et l'Internationale, Rapport sur les negotiations conduites à Moscou* (Paris, 1920), *passim* (hereafter referred to as *Parti Socialiste Rapport*).

13. The complicated question of the final number and complete text of the conditions for the SFIO is examined below. It should be noted here, however, that even the text of these initial nine conditions varied, contributing to the enormous confusion surrounding the conditions. The USPD first heard that the French had *ten* conditions; Cf. "Die Bedingungen für die französiche Partei," *Die Freiheit*, Sept. 9, 1920, no. 375, 3. Their source was apparently the text given in *Pravda*; cf. André Pierre, *Le Deuxième Congrès de l'Internationale Communiste, compte rendu des débats d'après les journaux de Moscou* (Paris, 1921), pp. 4, 57–68.

14. *Unabhängige Sozialdemokratische Partei Deutschlands, Protokoll der Reichskonferenz vom 1. bis 3. Sept. 1920 zu Berlin* (Berlin, 1920), pp. 156, 192 (hereafter referred to as *Reichskonferenz Protokoll*).

15. *Ibid.*, p. 79.

16. *Ibid.*, p. 80.

17. *Ibid.*, pp. 164, 178.

18. *Ibid.*, pp. 37, 63–64; cf. also *Unabhängige Sozialdemokratische Partei Deutschlands, Protokoll über die Verhandlungen des ausserordentlichen Parteitages in Halle, vom 12. bis 17. Okt. 1920* (Berlin, n.d.), p. 131.

19. Eugen Prager, *Geschichte der USP* (Berlin, 1922), p. 222.

20. *Reichskonferenz Protokoll*, pp. 33–34.

21. *Ibid.*, p. 49.

22. *Ibid.*, pp. 93–95. This delegate was Dahlem, the USPD delegate who was at the Strasbourg congress. He seems to have maintained close contacts with the SFIO.

23. *Ibid.,* p. 60. Dittmann was distorting things somewhat, since the full text of the Twenty-one Conditions had not been formulated before the French delegates' departure. He did, however, have reason for suspicion, since he had given Frossard at least twenty conditions, not nine or ten.

24. *Ibid.,* pp. 123–124, 128.

25. Cf. Helmut König, *Lenin und der italienische Sozialismus, 1915–1921* (Tubingen, 1967), p. 91.

26. "I deliberati del Secondo Congresso della Terza Internazionale," *Avanti!* Aug. 22, 1920, p. 3.

27. Cf. "La 'Lettera agli Italiani,' " *Il Soviet,* Oct. 3, 1920, p. 4.

28. *Die Kommunistische Internationale,* no. 13, p. 287.

29. *Ibid.,* p. 289.

30. V. I. Lenin, *Collected Works* (London, 1965), 31:387.

31. Donald William Urquidi, "The Origins of the Italian Communist Party, 1918–1921" (Ph.D. diss. Columbia University, 1962), p. 342.

32. *Ibid.,* p. 308.

33. Cf. "Polemichette," *Avanti!* Sept. 21, 1920, p. 2; "Non accettiamo lezioni," *Avanti!* Sept. 25, 1920, p. 1.

34. Cf. *Avanti!* articles: "Riunione della Direzione del Partito," Sept. 29, 1920, p. 1; "L'Ampio e profundo debatto sui rapporti interni," Oct. 1, 1920, p. 1; "La Direzione del partito delibera interna alla scissione," Oct. 2, 1920, p. 1.

35. Cf. "Riunione della Direzione del Partito," *Avanti!,* Sept. 29, 1920.

36. Cf. Serrati's articles in *Communismo*: "Filippo Turati ed il massimalismo," Nov. 1–15, 1919, pp. 179–183; "Camillo Prampolini e la dittature proletariata," April 15–May 1, 1920, pp. 1017–1020.

37. Giuseppe Sotgiù, *La Crisi Socialista* (Rome, 1950), p. 50.

38. Cf. Pietro Nenni, *Storia di Quattro Anni, 1919–1922* (Rome, 1946), pp. 175–198.

39. For example, Carlo Niccolini, "Intransigenza di Serrati," *Avanti!,* Oct. 8, 1920, p. 1; "Intransigenza di Serrati, II," *L'Ordine Nuovo,* Oct. 30, 1920, pp. 147–148.

40. G. M. Serrati, "A proposito di Pulcinella," *L'Ordine Nuovo,* Oct. 30, 1920, p. 150.

41. Paulo Spriano, *L'Occupazione delle fabbriche, Settembre 1920* (Turin, 1964), p. 60. The following account follows Spriano.

42. *Ibid.,* p. 81.

43. *Ibid.,* p. 82.

44. *Ibid.,* pp. 104–105.

45. *Ibid.,* p. 123.

46. König, *Lenin,* pp. 129–130.

47. *Direzione del Partito Socialista Italiano, Resoconto Stenografico del XVII Congresso Nazionale del Partito Socialista Italiano, Livorno 15–16–17–18–19–20 Gennaio 1921* (Rome, 1921), p. 361.

48. König, *Lenin.*

49. *Ibid.,* p. 222, n. 32.

50. "Conditions d'admission dans l'Internationale Communiste," *Bulletin Communiste,* Aug. 26, 1920, pp. 16–18; appended to the *Parti Socialiste Rapport* were also eighteen conditions, but it was obvious from the text of the "A tous les prolétaires . . ." document that these eighteen were not intended for France.

51. "Der Bericht über die dritte Internationale," *Die Freiheit,* Aug. 25, 1920, no. 348, p. 3.

52. "Les conditions d'admission dans l'Internationale Communiste," *Le Populaire,* Aug. 30 and Sept. 1, 1920, p. 1.

53. Cited in *ibid.*

54. *Ibid.*

55. These four new conditions have of course already been mentioned in the previous chapter. Condition twelve of the eighteen conditions had been incorporated into the first condition, thus adding up to twenty-one. A twenty-second condition appeared later in the year forbidding Free Masons—that is, Serrati's condition.

56. "Le Parti Socialiste et la C.G.T.," *Le Populaire*, Sept. 3, 1920, p. 1.

57. Mentioned in Paul Faure, "Parlons net," *Le Populaire*, Sept. 3, 1920, p. 1.

58. "Quelques précisions viennent," *Le Populaire*, Sept. 16, 1920, p. 1.

59. André Le Troquer, "Pour la reconstruction de l'Internationale," *Le Populaire*, Sept. 17, 1920, p. 1.

60. L.-O. Frossard, "La reconstruction impossible," *L'Humanité*, Sept. 17, 1920, p. 1.

61. Printed in *Le Populaire*, Oct. 1, 1920, p. 1.

62. In Paul Faure, "Reconstructeurs et destructeurs," *Le Populaire*, Oct. 5, 1920, p. 1.

63. L.-O. Frossard, *De Jaurès à Lénine, Notes et souvenirs d'un militant* (Paris, 1930), p. 148.

64. *Ibid.*, p. 165.

65. L.-O. Frossard, *La Décomposition du communisme* (Paris, 1923), pp. 12–13.

66. Frossard, *De Jaurès à Lénine*, p. 178.

67. Frossard, *Décomposition*, pp. 12–13.

68. "Comité de la reconstruction," *Le Populaire*, Sept. 6, 1920, p. 1.

69. Letter of resignation: "Au Comité de la Reconstruction de l'Internationale," *Le Populaire*, Sept. 25, 1920, p. 1.

70. Ludovico Tarsia, "I Socialisti francesi e la Terza Internazionale," *Il Soviet*, Dec. 23, 1920, p. 1.

71. Urquidi, "Origins of Italian Communist Party," p. 267.

72. "Il Manifesto-Programma della Sinistra del Partito," *Il Soviet*, Oct. 17, 1920, p. 1.

73. König, *Lenin*, pp. 135–136.

74. *Ibid.*, pp. 132–133.

75. *Ibid.*, p. 122.

76. *Ibid.*, pp. 142–143.

77. Cf. "Il Secondo Congresso della Terza Internazionale," *Communismo*, Dec. 15–30, 1920, p. 1621–1627; also Paulo Spriano, *Storia del Partito Comunista Italiano* (Turin, 1967), pp. 30–31.

78. "La relazione sulla Russia dei Soviet al gruppo parlamentare Socialista," *Avanti!*, Oct. 8, 1920, p. 2.

79. "Il Secondo Congresso della Terza Internazionale," *Communismo*, Dec. 15–30, 1920, pp. 1621–1727.

80. *Le Parti Socialiste Italien et l'Internationale Communiste* (Petrograd, 1921), p. 25.

81. *Ibid.*

82. "Il dovere dell'ora presente," *Avanti!*, Oct. 24, 1920, p. 2.

83. Lenin, *Collected Works*, 31:377–396.

84. *Ibid.*, p. 385.

85. *Ibid.*, p. 386.

86. *Parti Socialiste Italien et l'Internationale Communiste*, pp. 80 ff.

87. Giuseppi Berti, "Appunti e ricordi, 1919–1926," *Annali* (dell'Istituto Giangiacomo Feltrinelli) (Milan, 1966), p. 84.

Chapter VIII: The Split in Western Socialism

1. *Unabhängige Sozialdemokratische Partei Deutschlands, Protokoll über die Verhandlungen des ausserordentlichen Parteitages in Halle, vom 12. bis 17. Okt. 1920* (Berlin, n.d.), p. 14 (hereafter referred to as *Halle Protokoll*); "Ein neuer Einmischungs-und Spaltungsversuch," *Die Freiheit*, Sept. 28, 1920, no. 406, p. 2.

2. Eugen Prager, *Geschichte der USP* (Berlin, 1922), pp. 222–223.

3. Fritz Müller, "Berlin-Moskau," *Die Freiheit*, Sept. 12, 1920, no. 380, p. 6.

4. "Der Moskauer Kongress," *Kommunistische Rundschau*, Oct. 1, 1920, pp. 6–11.

5. "Zurückweisung," *Die Freiheit*, Oct. 1, 1920, no. 412, p. 3.

6. "Vor dem Parteitag," *Die Freiheit*, Oct. 12, 1920, no. 430, p. 1.

7. Ossip K. Flechtheim, *Die KPD in der Weimarer Republik* (Offenbach, 1948), 70, says that the difference between this vote and the impression of pro-Comintern weakness at the *Reichskonferenz* was due to the "powerful campaign" of the left; but he ignores the conservative composition of the *Reichskonferenz*.

8. "Die Urwahlen," *Die Freiheit*, Oct. 4, 1920, no. 417, 1; also "Die Urwahlen in Gross-Berlin," *Die Freiheit*, Oct. 5, 1920, no. 418, p. 1.

9. "Die Urwahlen," *Die Freiheit*, Oct. 4, 1920, no. 417, p. 1.

10. Flechtheim, *KPD*, p. 73.

11. Prager, *Geschichte*, p. 223.

12. *Ibid.*; also "Der erste Tag des Parteitags," *Die Freiheit*, Oct. 13, 1920, no. 432, p. 1.

13. For the text of the resolutions, see *Halle Protokoll*, pp. 69–71, 71–73.

14. This began with an article in *Die Freiheit*, "Die Wahrheit über Russland," Sept. 1, 1920, no. 360, p. 1, which was the subject of much bitter comment at the *Reichskonferenz*.

15. Cf. Karl Radek, *Die Masken sind gefallen: eine Antwort an Crispien, Dittmann, und Hilferding* (n.p., 1921), p. 4.

16. *Halle Protokoll*, p. 75.

17. *Unabhängige Sozialdemokratische Partei Deutschlands, Protokoll der Reichskonferenz vom 1. bis 3. Sept. 1920 zu Berlin* (Berlin, 1920), p. 57 (hereafter referred to as *Reichskonferenz Protokoll*).

18. *Ibid.*, pp. 50, 67.

19. *Ibid.*, p. 41 ff.

20. *Ibid.*, pp. 63–64.

21. *Halle Protokoll*, p. 112.

22. *Ibid.*, p. 71.

23. *Ibid.*, p. 41.

24. *Halle Protokoll*, p. 113.

25. *Reichskonferenz Protokoll*, pp. 115 ff.

26. *Halle Protokoll*, p. 75.

27. *Reichskonferenz Protokoll*, pp. 88, 93. It seems clear that the average age of those in favor of affiliation with the Comintern was distinctly lower than that of the antiaffiliation forces. In the 1920s the average age of the KPD leadership in Hamburg was considerably less than that of the SPD leadership; cf. Richard Comfort, *Revolutionary Hamburg* (Stanford, 1966), p. 132 ff.

28. *Halle Protokoll*, pp. 144–179.

29. *Ibid.*, p. 176; the promise was repeated in "Das Exekutivkomitee der Kommunistischen Internationale," *Die Kommunistische Internationale*, Dec., 1920, no. 15, p. 401.

30. *Halle Protokoll*, p. 176.

31. *Ibid.*, pp. 201–202.

32. *Ibid.*, pp. 257–261.

33. Prager, *Geschichte*, p. 226; "Die Spaltung in der Partei," *Die Freiheit*, Oct. 19, 1920, no. 440, p. 1. Prager reported that this final turn of events greatly amused Zinoviev, who smiled broadly as the right made its way out of the hall.

34. *Halle Protokoll*, p. 176.

35. Cf. "Das Exekutivkomitee der Kommunistischen Internationale," *Die Kommunistische Internationale*, Dec., 1920, no. 15, p. 40; cf. also E. H. Carr, *The Russian Revolution* (New York, 1953), 3:330.

36. Ludovico Tarsia, "I Socialisti francesi e la Terza Internazionale," *Il Soviet*, Dec. 23, 1920, p. 1.

37. Cf. Daniel Renoult, "Les leçons de Halle," *L'Humanité*, Oct. 23, 1920, p. 1.

38. Cf. his speech at Halle, *Halle Protokoll*, p. 236.

39. *Ibid.*, 229 ff. "Die Spaltung in der Partei," *Die Freiheit*, Oct. 19, 1920, no. 440, p. 1.

40. Luigi Cortesi, *Il Socialismo italiano tra riforme e rivoluzione* (Bari, 1969), pp. 838–839.

41. Helmut König, *Lenin und der italienische Sozialismus* (Tübingen, 1967), pp. 128–29.

42. Cortesi, *Socialismo*, p. 850.

43. *Ibid.*

44. Text in *Parti Socialiste (SFIO), 18e Congrès national, tenu à Tours, compte rendu sténographique* (Paris, 1921), pp. 563–578 (hereafter referred to as *Tours compte rendu*).

45. *Tours compte rendu*, pp. 580–585.

46. "Etude à reprendre," *Le Populaire*, Nov. 17, 1920, p. 1.

47. Cf. Gilbert Ziebura, *Léon Blum, Theorie und Praxis einer sozialistischen Politik* (Berlin, 1957), 2:206.

48. Text of resolution: *Tours compte rendu*, pp. 586–591.

49. Ziebura, *Blum*, p. 206.

50. In order to reduce repetitiveness, the content of Blum's analysis, largely developed in a series of articles in *L'Humanité*, will be summarized when discussing his famous speech at Tours.

51. "Chez les socialistes parisiens," *Le Populaire*, Nov. 16, 1920, p. 1.

52. "Sinowjew an die französischen Genossen," *Die Internationale*, Nov. 16, 1920, no. 10, p. 3.

53. *Ibid.*

54. Cf. "Ce pistolet de Zinoviev," *Le Populaire*, Nov. 18, 1920, p. 1; "Couteau ou pistolet?" *Le Populaire*, Nov. 19, 1920, p. 1. (A varying translation spoke of a pistol at Longuet's throat.) "Appel aux travailleurs français," *L'Humanité*, Nov. 8, 1920, p. 1.

55. "Nécessité d'une scission," Dec. 2, 1920, pp. 1–3.

56. Jean Longuet, "L'heure décisive," *Le Populaire*, Dec. 4, 1920, p. 1.

57. Jean Longuet, "A la France socialiste," *Le Populaire*, Dec. 16, 1920, p. 1; "Pour l'unité," *Le Populaire*, Dec. 26, 1920, p. 1.

58. Longuet, "A la France socialiste."

59. André Wurmser, *Interdiction de Séjour* (Paris, 1949), 337, cited in Robert Wohl, "The Origins of the French Communist Party, 1914–1920," (Ph.D. diss. Princeton University, 1963), p. 427.

60. Annie Kriegel, *Aux origines du communisme français, 1914–1920* (Paris, 1964), pp. 812–874, has analysed these trends exhaustively.

61. Cf. *Tours compte rendu*, pp. 34, 66, 82.

62. Marcel Sembat, *La Victoire en déroute* (Paris, 1925), p. 105.

63. L. -O. Frossard, *De Jaurès à Lénine, notes et souvenirs d'un militant* (Paris, 1930), pp. 58–59.

64. *Ibid.*, p. 28.

65. *Tours compte rendu*, p. 170.

66. *Ibid.*, p. 171.

67. *Ibid.*, p. 127.

68. *Ibid.*, p. 170, 225, 279 ff.

69. *Ibid.*, p. 145.

70. *Ibid.*, p. 322.

71. *Ibid.*, p. 332.

72. *Ibid.*, pp. 115, 147.

73. *Ibid.*, pp. 243 ff.

74. Cf. the articles entitled "A Moscou?" Oct. 19, Oct. 24, Oct. 31, Nov. 13, 1920.

75. *Tours compte rendu*, p. 252.

76. *Ibid.*, p. 263.

77. *Ibid.*, p. 271; also "Discours de Léon Blum," *L'Humanité*, Dec. 28, 1920, p. 1.

78. *Tours compte rendu*, p. 275; *L'Humanité*, Dec. 28, 1920, p. 1.

79. Frossard, *De Jaurès à Lénine*, p. 227.

80. *Tours compte rendu*, pp. 312–313.

81. *Ibid.*, pp. 315–321.

82. *Ibid.*, pp. 483–488.

83. To the Cachin-Frossard total can be added 44 votes for a "purer" amendment, which avoided hedging on the Twenty-one Conditions and which was proposed by the left wing of the *Comité de la Troisième Internationale*. For the text of the resolutions and the votes they obtained, see *Tours compte rendu*, pp. 563 ff.

84. *Tours compte rendu*, p. 522.

85. *Ibid.*, pp. 522–525.

86. "Alla Soglia del Congresso," *Avanti!*, Jan. 15, 1921, p. 1.

87. Donald William Urquidi, "The Origins of the Italian Communist Party, 1918–1921," (Ph.D. diss. Columbia University, 1962), pp. 347 ff.

88. *Direzione del Partito Socialista Italiano. Resoconto stenografico del XVII Congresso Nazionale del Partito Socialista Italiano, Livorno 15–16–17–18–19 Gennaio 1921* (Rome, 1921), p. 361 (hereafter referred to as *Livorno Resoconto*).

89. *Ibid.*, pp. 390–400.

90. Giuseppe Sotgiù, *La Crisi Socialista* (Rome, 1950), pp. 22 ff.

91. *Ibid.*, 41–42; *Livorno Resoconto*, 238 ff.

92. *Livorno Resoconto*, p. 100.

93. *Ibid.*, p. 101.

94. *Ibid.*, p. 310.

95. Sotgiù, *Crisi*, p. 9.

96. *Livorno Resoconto*, pp. 72 ff.

97. *Ibid.*, pp. 238 ff.

98. Cf. Sotgiù, *Crisi*, pp. 41–42.

99. Cf. *Livorno Resoconto*, p. 374.

100. *Ibid.*, p. 114.

101. *Ibid.*, p. 117.

102. *Ibid.*, p. 106.

103. Sotgiù, *Crisi*, p. 43.

104. G. C., "Saremo bloccati?" *Communismo*, 15–30 Sept., 1920, pp. 1647–1649.

105. Giungi Davide, "Saremo bloccati?" *Communismo*, Dec. 15–30, 1920, pp. 348–350. *Le Parti Socialiste Italien et l'Internationale Communiste* (Petrograd, 1921), p. 79. (This contains excerpts from articles in the Italian and Russian press, including part of Lenin's November article on the "struggle within the Italian Socialist Party."

106. *Livorno Resoconto*, pp. 349 ff., 394 ff.

107. *Ibid.*, pp. 302–303.

108. Sotgiù, *Crisi*, p. 52.

109. *Livorno Resoconto*, p. 260.

110. *Ibid.*, p. 408.

111. Sotgiù, *Crisi*, pp. 71 ff.

112. *Livorno Resoconto*, p. 418.

113. Wilhelm Dittman, "Memoiren," (Manuscript at the International Institute for Social History, Amsterdam), XIX, 44.

114. Charlotte Beradt, *Paul Levi* (Frankfurt am Main, 1969), pp. 20–60.

115. Willy Brandt and Richard Lowenthal, *Ernst Reuter* (Munich, 1957), p. 139.

116. This information was provided by Meyer in a speech at the KPD's congress in November 1920: *Bericht über den 5. Parteitag der KPD (Section der Kommunistischen Internationale), 4–5 Nov. 1920* (Berlin, 1921), p. 27; cf. Richard Lowenthal, "The Bolshevization of the Spartacus League," in David Footman, ed., *International Communism* (Carbondale, Ill., 1960), p. 40.

117. Brandt and Lowenthal, *Reuter*, p. 139.

118. *Bericht über die Verhandlungen des Vereinigungs-parteitages der USPD (linke) und der KPD (Spartakusbund)* (Berlin, 1921), pp. 114–115.

119. Lowenthal, "Bolshevization," p. 44.

120. Paul Levi, "Eine unhaltbare Situation," *Die Rote Fahne*, Dec. 24, 1920, p. 1.

121. Cf. Meyer's account in *Bericht über den 5. Parteitag*, 26–28; also Lowenthal, "Bolshevization," p. 43.

122. Flechtheim, *Die KPD in der Weimarer Republik*, p. 70.

123. Werner Angress, *Stillborn Revolution* (Princeton, 1963), pp. 72–73.

124. *Ibid.*, pp. 90–96.

125. Beradt, *Levi*, pp. 22 ff.

126. Lowenthal, Angress, and Beradt, cited above, are among those who accept this view. In each case their accounts are marred by a lack of familiarity with the situation in the PSI.

127. Cf. Rakosi's speech at the Third Congress, *Protokoll des III. Kongress der Kommunistischen Internationale, Moskau 22 juni bis 12 juli* (Hamburg, 1921), pp. 328–330.

128. *Livorno Resoconto*, p. 16.

129. The text of this article is appended to Kabakschieff, *Die Gründung der Kommunistischen Partei Italiens* (Hamburg, 1921), pp. 49–52.

130. *Ibid.*, 49–50. cf. also Heckert's speech at the Third Congress, *III. Kongress Protokoll*, p. 244.

131. Lowenthal, "Bolshevization," p. 54.

132. *Die Rote Fahne*, Jan. 26, 1921; cited in Lowenthal, "Bolshevization," p. 55.

133. Carr, *The Bolshevik Revolution*, 3:336.

134. Lowenthal, "Bolshevization," pp. 54–56.

135. Angress, *Stillborn Revolution*, pp. 105–196. The following paragraphs owe much to this account.

136. Lowenthal, "Bolshevization," p. 58.

137. Heinrich Ströbel, *Die Deutsche Revolution* (Berlin, 1922), p. 251.

138. Beradt, *Levi*, p. 55.

139. Lowenthal, "Bolshevization," pp. 64–71.

140. Beradt, *Levi*, p. 57.

Epilogue and Conclusion

1. Jules Humbert-Droz, *"L'Oeil de Moscou" à Paris* (Paris, 1964) is an excellent source for the internal developments of the PCI at this time. Also, L. -O Frossard, *La Décomposition du communisme* (Paris, 1923); and Robert Wohl, *French Communism in the Making, 1914–1924* (Stanford, 1966).

2. Alfred Rosmer, *Moscou sous Lénine* (Paris, 1953), pp. 240 ff.

3. Humbert-Droz, *"L'Oeil,"* p. 147.

4. Cf. Helmut König, *Lenin und der italienische Sozialismus, 1915–1921* (Tubingen, 1967), p. 150.

5. John Cammett, *Antonio Gramsci and the Origins of Italian Communism* (Stanford, 1967), pp. 163–165.

6. On this period see Hermann Weber, *Die Wandlung des deutschen Kommunismus* (Frankfurt am Main, 1969).

7. *Ibid.*, pp. 42–43; Werner Angress, *Stillborn Revolution* (Princeton, 1963), *passim*; Ossip Flechtheim, *Die KPD in der Weimarer Republik* (Offenbach, 1948), pp. 173 ff.

8. Weber, *Wandlung*, p. 45.

9. G. D. H. Cole wrote, "It is . . . a matter of history that after the First World War the Comintern . . . deliberately split the working-class movement in every country to which it could extend its influence. . . ." Quoted in C. Wright Mills *The Marxists* (New York, 1962), p. 440. For similar views see, Richard Lowenthal, *World Communism* (New York, 1964); Stanley Page, *Lenin and World Revolution* (New York, 1959).

10. Cf. Walter Tormin, *Zwischen Rätediktatur und sozialer Demokratie* (Dusseldorf, 1954), pp. 111–113; Arthur Rosenberg, *Geschichte der Weimarer Republik* (Karlsbad, 1935), p. 238.

11. An important exception to most of these remarks is Rosmer, who was in his forties at this time, was of proletarian background, had experience in the prewar syndicalist movement, and had kept his head to a remarkable degree at the outbreak of war.

12. Cf. Richard Comfort, *Revolutionary Hamburg* (Stanford, 1966), pp. 131–147; Gerald D. Feldman, *Army, Industry, and Labor in Germany, 1914–1918* (Princeton, 1966), *passim;* Annie Kriegel, *Aux origines du communisme français* (Paris, 1964), pp. 812 ff.

13. Karl Radek, *Soll die VKPD eine Massenpartei der revolutionären Aktion oder eine zentristische Partei des Wartens sein?* (Hamburg, 1921), pp. 15–17. Cf. Richard Lowenthal, "The Bolshevization of the Spartakus League," in David Footman, ed., *International Communism* (Carbondale, Ill., 1960), p. 67.

14. Karl Radek, "Die Krise in der VKPD," *Die Internationale*, III, 3, April 1, 1921, pp. 73–74. Cited in Lowenthal, "Bolshevization," p. 66.

Bibliography

Primary Sources

Documents (Congress reports, public speeches, pamphlets, official publications)

Allgemeiner Kongress der Arbeiter- und Soldatenräte Deutschlands vom 16 bis 21 Dez. 1918 im Abgeordnetenhause zu Berlin. Stenographische Berichte. Berlin, 1919.

Bauer, Otto. *Bolschewismus oder Sozialdemokratie*. Vienna, 1920.

Bericht über die Verhandlungen des Vereinigungsparteitages der USPD (linke) und der KPD (Spartakusbund). Berlin, 1921.

Comité pour la Reprise des Relations Internationales. *Le Parti Socialiste Italien et la Guerre Européenne*. Paris, n.d.

Compte rendu de la gestion du Comité Executif de l'Internationale Communiste (1920–1921). Moscow, 1921.

Crispien, Arthur. *Die Internationale, vom Bund der Kommunisten zur Internationale der Weltrevolution*. Berlin, 1919.

Däumig, Ernst. *Der Aufbau Deutschlands und das Rätesystem*. Berlin, 1919.

Degras, Jane, ed. *The Communist International, 1919–1921: Documents*. New York, 1956.

Der Erste Kongress der Kommunistischen Internationale, Protokoll der Verhandlungen in Moskau von 2. bis 19. März, 1919. Hamburg, 1921.

Direzione del Partito Socialista Italiano. *Resoconto Stenografico del XVI Congresso Nazionale del Partito Socialista Italiano, Bologna 5–6–7–8 Ottobre 1919*. Rome, 1920.

Direzione del Partito Socialista Italiano. *Resoconto Stenografico del XVII Congresso Nazionale del Partito Socialista Italiano, Livorno 15–16–17–18–19–20 Gennaio 1921*. Rome, 1921.

Dokumente und Materialien zur Geschichte der deutschen Arbeiterbewegung. East Berlin, 1958–1966.

Gankin, Olga Hess, and Fischer, H. H. *The Bolsheviks and the World War: The Origins of the Third International*. Stanford, 1940.

Geyer, Kurt. *Sozialismus und Rätesystem*. Leipzig, 1919.

Independent Labour Party, *Report of the 29th Annual Conference*. Southport, March, 1921.

Italyanskaia Sotsialisticheskaia Partiia i Kommunisticheskii Internatsional. Petrograd, 1921.

Kabakschieff, Chr. *Die Gründung der Kommunistischen Partei Italiens.* Hamburg, 1921.

Lenin, V. I. *Collected Works.* Vols. 29, 30, 31, 32, 33. London, 1965.

——. *Left-wing Communism, An Infantile Disorder.* Moscow, 1947.

——. (Spriano, Paolo, ed.) *Sul Movimento operaio italiano.* Rome, 1962.

——. *Über Deutschland und die deutsche Arbeiterbewegung.* Berlin, 1957.

Luxemburg, Rosa. *The Russian Revolution.* Ann Arbor, 1962.

Manifest, Richlinien, Beschlüsse des Ersten Kongresses: Aufrufe und offene Schreiben des Executivkomitees bis zum Zweiten Kongress. Hamburg, 1920.

Parti Communiste (SFIC). *Congrès National de Marseille, Dec. 1921, Un An d'Action Communiste, Rapport du Secrétariat Général, présenté au 19e Congrès National.* Paris, 1921.

Le Parti Socialiste et L'Internationale, Rapport sur les négotiations conduites à Moscou. Paris, 1920.

Le Parti Socialiste Italien et L'Internationale Communiste. Petrograd, 1921.

Parti Socialiste (SFIO). *Congrès national de Strasbourg, Rapport du Secrétariat (la vie du parti, Oct. 1918–Janv. 1920).* Paris, 1920.

Parti Socialiste (SFIO). *18e Congrès national, tenu à Tours, compte rendu sténographique.* Paris, 1921.

Parti Socialiste (SFIO). *17e Congrès national, tenu à Strasbourg, compte rendu sténographique.* Paris, 1920.

Parti Socialiste (SFIO). *Rapports de la CAP, 19e Congrès national, Paris.* Paris, 1921.

Pedone, Franco, ed. *Il Partito Socialista Italiano nei suoi congressi.* Vol. 3, 1917–1926. Milan, 1963.

Piatnitsky, O. *The Twenty-one Conditions of Admission into the Communist International.* New York, 1934.

Pierre, André. *Le Deuxième Congrès de l'Internationale Communiste, compte rendu des débats d'après les journaux de Moscou.* Paris, 1921.

Price, M. Philips. *Capitalist Europe and Socialist Russia.* London, 1919.

Il Primo Anno di Vita del Partito Communista d'Italia. Milan, 1966.

Protokoll des III. Kongress der Kommunistischen Internationale, Moskau 22 juni bis 12 juli. Hamburg, 1921.

Protokoly Kongressov Kommunisticheskogo Internatsionala, Vtoroi Kongress Kominterna. Moscow, 1934.

Radek, Karl. *Die Entwicklung der Weltrevolution und die Taktik der*

Kommunistischen Parteien im Kampfe um die Diktatur des Proletariats. Hamburg, 1921.

————. *Die Masken sind Gefallen: eine Antwort an Crispien, Dittmann, und Hilferding.* N.p., 1921.

————. *Soll die VKPD eine Massenpartei der revolutionären Aktion oder eine zentristische Partei des Wartens sein?* Hamburg, 1921.

Rapports sur le Mouvement Communiste International (présenté au Deuxième Congrès de L'Internationale Communiste). Moscow, 1920.

Im Roten Paradies: Unabhängige und Kommunistische Eingeständisse. Berlin, 1920.

The Second Congress of the Communist International, Proceedings. Moscow, 1920.

Serrati, G. Menotti. *Dalla Seconda alla Terza Internazionale.* Milan, 1920.

Sinowjew, G. *Zwölf Tage in Deutschland.* Hamburg, 1921.

Sokolov, Boris. *Voyage de Cachin et Frossard dans la Russie des Soviets.* Paris, 1921.

Sotgiù, Giuseppe. *La Crisi Socialista.* Rome, 1950.

Stoecker, Walter. *Die Proletarische Internationale (Referat auf der Reichskonferenz der USPD am 10 Sept. 1919).* Berlin, 1919.

Storia della Sinistra Communista. Milan, 1964.

Thèses, Manifestes, et Résolutions, adoptés par les Ier, IIe, IIIe, et IVe Congrès de l'Internationale Communiste (1919–1923). Paris, 1934.

Trotsky, Leon. *The First Five Years of the Communist International.* New York, 1945.

Unabhängige Sozialdemokratische Partei Deutschlands. *Protokoll über die Verhandlungen des ausserordentlichen Parteitages in Leipzig, vom 30. November bis 6. Dezember 1919.* Berlin, 1920.

————. *Protokoll der Reichskonferenz vom 1. bis 3. Sept. 1920 zu Berlin.* Berlin, 1920.

————. *Protokoll über die Verhandlungen des ausserordentlichen Parteitages in Halle, vom 12. bis 17. Okt. 1920.* Berlin, n.d.

Die USPD und die Dritte Internationale (Bericht über die Ausführung des Leipziger Parteitages). Remscheid, 1920.

Weber, Hermann, ed. *Der deutsche Kommunismus, Dokumente.* Cologne, 1963.

Zinoviev, G. *L'Internationale Communiste.* Petrograd, 1920.

Zur Lage in der Kommunistischen Partei Frankreichs. Hamburg, 1922.

Der Zweite Kongress der Kommunist. Internationale, Protokoll der Verhandlungen. Hamburg, 1921.

Der Zweite Weltkongress der Kommunistischen Internationale an das französische Proletariat. [Hamburg?], 1920.

Memoirs and Firsthand Accounts

Bahne, Siegfried, ed. *Archives de Jules Humbert-Droz, I: Origines et débuts des partis communistes des pays latins, 1919–1923*. Dordrecht, 1970.

Balabanoff, Angelica. *Erinnerungen und Erlebnisse*. Berlin, 1927.

———. *Impressions of Lenin*. Ann Arbor, 1964.

———. *My Life as a Rebel*. New York, 1938.

Bianchi, Giuseppi. *Russia Syndicale*. Milan, 1921.

Borghi, Armando. *L'Italia tra due Crispi*. Paris, 1924.

Cachin, Marcel. *Marcel Cachin vous parle*. Paris, 1959.

———. *Ecrits et Portraits*. Paris, 1964.

Colombino, E. *Tre Mesi nella Russia dei Soviet*. Milan, 1921.

Dittmann, Wilhelm. "Memoiren." (Manuscript at the International Institute for Social History, Amsterdam.)

Ferry, Abel. *Les Carnet Secrets d'Abel Ferry*. Paris, 1957.

Frossard, L. -O. *De Jaurès à Lénine, notes et souvenirs d'un militant*. Paris, 1930.

———. *De Jaurès à Léon Blum*. Paris, 1943.

———. *La Décomposition du communisme*. Paris, 1923.

———. *Mon Journal de route en Russie des Soviets*. (Microfilm at the Hoover Library, Stanford, Calif.).

Germanetto, Gionanni. *Memoirs of a Barber*. New York, 1935.

Graziadei, Antonio. *Memorie di Trent'anni (1890–1922)*. Rome, 1950.

Guilbeaux, Henri. *La Fin des Soviets*. Paris, 1937.

———. *Du Kremlin au Cherche-Midi*. Paris, 1933.

———. *Lénine n'était pas communiste*. Paris, 1937.

———. *Mon Crime*. Geneva, 1918.

———. *Le Portrait authentique de V. I. Lénine*. Paris, 1924.

Humbert-Droz, Jules. *"L'Oeil de Moscou" à Paris*. Paris, 1964.

Kautsky, Karl. *Mein Verhältnis zur Unabhängigen Sozialdemokratischen Partei*. Berlin, 1920.

Müller, Richard. *Vom Kaiserreich zur Republik*. 2 vols. Vienna, 1924.

Murphy, James. *New Horizons*. London, 1941.

Nofri, Gregorio, and Pozzani, Fernando. *La Russia com'è*. Florence, 1921.

Parijanine, Maurice. *Des Français en Russie*. Paris, n.d.

Paul-Boncour, Joseph. *Entre deux guerres*. Vols. 1 and 2. Paris, 1945.

Prager, Eugen. *Geschichte der USP*. Berlin, 1922.

Ransome, Arthur. *Russia in 1919*. New York, 1919.

Rosmer, Alfred. *Moscou sous Lénine*. Paris, 1953.

Sembat, Marcel. *La Victoire en déroute*. Paris, 1925.

Serge, Victor. *Memoirs of a Revolutionary*. New York, 1963.

Trotsky, Leon. *My Life*. London, 1930.
―――. *Terrorism and Communism*. Ann Arbor, 1963.
Vacirca, Vicenzo. *Ciò che ho visto nella Russia Soviettista*. Milan, 1921.
Vaillant-Couturier, Paul. *Vers les lendemains qui chantent*. Paris, 1962.
Zetkin, Clara. *Erinnerungen an Lenin*. Berlin, 1957.

Newspapers, Periodicals (consulted for the years 1919–1921)

Der Arbeiter-Rat	*Kommunistische Rundschau*
Avanti!	*L'Ordine Nuovo*
Bulletin Communiste	*Le Populaire*
Communismo	*Rassegna Communista*
Critica Sociale	*Die Rote Fahne*
Die Freiheit	*Spartakus*
L'Humanité	*Il Soviet*
Die Internationale	*Sowjet*
Kommunistische Arbeiterzeitung	*Unser Weg*
Kommunistische Internationale	*La Vie Ouvrière*

Secondary Works

Biographies

Beradt, Charlotte. *Paul Levi*. Frankfurt am Main, 1969.
Brandt, Willy, and Lowenthal, Richard. *Ernst Reuter*. Munich, 1957.
Cammett, John. *Antonio Gramsci and the Origins of Italian Communism*. Stanford, 1967.
Colton, Joel. *Léon Blum, Humanist in Politics*. New York, 1966.
Deutscher, Isaac. *The Prophet Armed*. New York, 1965.
―――. *Stalin, A Political Biography*. New York, 1960.
Fischer, Louis. *The Life of Lenin*. New York, 1964.
Georges, Bernard, and Tintant, Denise. *Léon Jouhaux*. Paris, 1964.
Kirkpatrick, Ivone. *Mussolini, A Study in Power*. New York, 1964.
Nettl, J. P. *Rosa Luxemburg*. 2 vols. New York, 1966.
Schapiro, Leonard, and Reddaway, Peter. *Lenin*. London, 1967.
Valera, Paolo. *Giacinto Menotti Serrati*. Milan, 1920.
Ziebura, Gilbert. *Léon Blum, Theorie und Praxis einer sozialistischen Politik*. Vol. 1. Berlin, 1957.

General Secondary

Alazard, Jean. *Communisme et "fascio" en Italie*. Paris, 1922.
Almanacco Socialista Italiano. Milan, 1919–1922.

Ambrosoli, Luigi. *Nè aderire nè sabotare*. Milan, 1961.

Angress, Werner. *Stillborn Revolution*. Princeton, 1963.

Aquila, Giulio. *Die italienische Sozialistische Partei*. Hamburg, 1922.

Arfè, G. *Storia del socialismo italiano, 1892–1926*. Turin, 1965.

Ascher, Abraham. "Russian Marxism and the German Revolution, 1917–1920." *Archiv für Sozialgeschichte*. Vols. 6–7 Bonn, 1966–67.

Balabanoff, Angelica. *Die Zimmerwalder Bewegung (1914–1919)*. Leipzig, 1928.

Bartelini, Ermanno. *La Rivoluzione in atto, 1919–1924*. Turin, 1925.

Beiträge zur Geschichte der deutschen Arbeiterbewegung. Heft 6. Berlin, 1968.

Berlau, Joseph A. *The German Social Democratic Party, 1914–1921*. New York, 1949.

Berti, Giuseppi. "Appunti e ricordi, 1919–1926." *Annali 1966* (dell' Istituto Giangiacomo Feltrinelli). Milan, 1966.

———. *I primi dieci anni di vita del PCI*. Milan, 1967.

Bilan du communisme. Paris, 1937.

Bonomi, Ivanoe. *From Socialism to Fascism*. London, 1934.

Borkenau, Franz. *World Communism*. Ann Arbor, 1962.

Braunthal, Julius. *Geschichte der Internationale*. Vol. 2. Hanover, 1963.

Brogan, D. W. *France Under the Republic*. New York, 1940.

Carr, E. H. *The Bolshevik Revolution, 1917–1923*. Vols. 1–3. New York, 1953.

———. "Radek's 'Political Salon' in Berlin, 1919." *Soviet Studies*, 3 (1952), 411–430.

Caute, David. *Communism and the French Intellectuals, 1914–1960*. New York, 1964.

Chabod, Federico. *A History of Italian Fascism*. London, 1963.

Chalmers, A. *The Social Democratic Party of Germany*. New Haven, 1964.

Clark, Marjorie Ruth. *A History of the French Labor Movement, 1910–1928*. Berkeley, 1930.

Clough, Shepard. *An Economic History of Modern Italy*. New York, 1964.

Cole, G. D. H. *A History of Socialist Thought: Communism and Social Democracy, 1914–1931*. London, 1958.

Comfort, Richard. *Revolutionary Hamburg*. Stanford, 1966.

Compère-Morel, Adéodat. *Grand Dictionnaire Socialiste*. Paris, 1924.

———. *Socialisme et Communisme*. Paris, 1921.

Coper, Rudolf. *Failure of a Revolution*. Cambridge, 1955.

Cortesi, Luigi. *Il Socialismo italiano tra riforme e rivoluzione*. Bari, 1969.

Delory, G. *Aperçu historique sur la Féderation du Nord du Parti Socialiste.* Lille, 1953.

Dolléans, Edouard. *Histoire du mouvement ouvrier, 1871–1920.* Paris, 1953.

Donneur, André. *Histoire d'Union des partis socialistes pour l'union internationale.* Sudbury, Ontario, 1967.

Drachkovitch, Milorad M. *De Karl Marx à Léon Blum.* Geneva, 1954.

————. *Les socialismes français et allemand et le problème de la guerre, 1870–1914.* Geneva, 1953.

Draper, Theodore. *The Roots of American Communism.* New York, 1957.

Dutt, R. Palme. *The Two Internationals.* London, 1920.

————. *The Internationale.* London, 1964.

Einaudi, Luigi. *La condotta economica e gli effetti sociali della guerra.* Bari, 1933.

Esch, Patricia van der. *La Deuxième Internationale.* Paris, 1957.

Fainsod, Merle. *How Russia is Ruled.* Cambridge, Mass., 1954.

————. *International Socialism and the World War.* Cambridge, Mass., 1935.

Feldman, Gerald D. *Army, Industry, and Labor in Germany, 1914–1918.* Princeton, 1966.

Ferrat, A. *Histoire du Parti communiste français.* Paris, 1931.

Ferri, Franco. "La Rivoluzione d'ottobre e le sue ripercussioni nel movimento operaio italiano." *Società* 14 (1958), 73–262.

Ferro, M. et al. *La Revolution d'Octobre et le mouvement ouvrier européen.* Paris, 1967.

Fiechter, Jean-Jacques. *Le socialisme français: de l'Affair Dreyfus à la Grande Guerre.* Geneva, 1965.

Fischer, Louis. *The Soviets in World Affairs.* Princeton, 1951.

Fischer, Ruth. *Stalin and German Communism.* Cambridge, Mass., 1948.

Flechtheim, Ossip K. *Die KPD in der Weimarer Republik.* Offenbach, 1948.

Florinsky, Michael T. *World Revolution and the USSR.* New York, 1933.

Footman, David, ed. *International Communism.* Carbondale, Ill., 1960.

Fréville, Jean. *Né du Feu.* Paris, 1961.

————. *La nuit finit à Tours.* Paris, 1951.

Galli, Giorgio. *Storia del Partito Communista Italiano.* Milan, 1958.

Gaucher, François. *Contribution à l'histoire du socialisme français.* Paris, 1934.

Gay, Peter. *The Dilemma of Democratic Socialism.* New York, 1952.

Graubard, Stephen Richards. *British Labor and the Russian Revolution, 1917–1924.* Cambridge, Mass., 1956.

Gruber, Helmut. *International Communism in the Era of Lenin.* Ithaca, New York, 1967.

Guilbeaux, Henri. *Le Mouvement socialiste et syndicaliste pendant la guerre.* Petrograd, 1919.

Haimson, Leopold D. *The Russian Marxists and the Origins of Bolshevism.* Cambridge, Mass., 1955.

Halévy, Elie. *Histoire du socialisme européen.* Paris, 1948.

Halperin, William S. *Germany Tried Democracy.* New York, 1946.

Hughes, H. Stuart. *The United States and Italy.* Cambridge, Mass., 1965.

Hulse, James W. *The Forming of the Communist International.* Stanford, 1964.

Hunt, Richard N. *German Social Democracy, 1918–1933.* New Haven, 1964.

Illustrierte Geschichte der deutschen Revolution. Berlin, 1929.

Joll, James. *The Second International, 1889–1914.* New York, 1956.

Kennan, George. *Russia and the West, under Lenin and Stalin.* New York, 1962.

Kolb, Eberhard. *Die Arbeiterräte in der deutschen Innenpolitik, 1918–1919.* Düsseldorf, 1962.

König, Helmut. *Lenin und der italienische Sozialismus, 1915–1921.* Tübingen, 1967.

Kriegel, Annie. *Les internationales ouvrières.* Paris, 1964.

———. *Naissance du Parti communiste français.* Paris, 1964.

———. *Aux origines du communisme français.* 2 vols. Paris, 1964.

Labedz, Leopold. *Revisionism: Essay on the History of Marxist Ideas.* London, 1963.

Landauer, Carl. *European Socialism.* Berkeley, 1959.

Lazitch, Branko. *Lénine et la Troisième Internationale.* Paris, 1951.

Lazitch, Branko, and Drachkovitch, Milorad. *Lenin and the Comintern.* Vol. I. Stanford, 1966.

Lazzeri, Gerolamo. *La Scissione Socialista.* Milan, 1921.

Lefranc, Georges. *Le mouvement socialiste sous la Troisième République.* Paris, 1963.

Lichtheim, George. *Marxism, An Historical and Critical Study.* New York, 1961.

———. *Marxism in Modern France.* New York, 1966.

Ligou, Daniel. *Histoire du socialisme en France.* Paris, 1962.

Lorwin, Val. *The French Labor Movement.* Cambridge, Mass., 1954.

Lösche, Peter. *Der Bolschewismus im Urteil der deutschen Sozialdemokratie, 1903–1920.* Berlin, 1967.

Louis, Paul. *La crise du socialisme mondiale.* Paris, 1921.

――――. *Histoire du socialisme en France.* Paris, 1950.

Lowenthal, Richard. *World Communism.* New York, 1964.

Lübkes, F. P. R. *Die Entwicklung der sozialistischen Bewegung in Frankreich von 1914 bis 1924.* Berlin, 1924.

Mack Smith, Denis. *Italy, A Modern History.* Ann Arbor, 1959.

Malatesta, Alberto. *I socialisti italiani durante la guerra.* Milan, 1926.

Marcuse, Herbert. *Soviet Marxism.* New York, 1958.

Maxe, Jean. *De Zimmerwald au Bolchévisme.* Paris, 1920.

――――. *Anthologie des défaitistes.* 2 vols. Paris, 1920.

Maynard, J. *Russia in Flux.* New York, 1948.

Meyer, Alfred G. *Leninism.* New York, 1963.

Michels, Robert. *Political Parties.* New York, 1962.

Miller, Margaret. *The Economic Development of Russia, 1905–1914.* New York, 1967.

Mills, C. Wright. *The Marxists.* New York, 1962.

Mitchell, Alan. *Revolution in Bavaria, 1918–1919.* Princeton, 1965.

Montreuil, Jean. *Histoire du mouvement ouvrier en France.* Paris, 1946.

Nenni, Pietro. *Lo Spettro del Communismo.* Milan, 1921.

――――. *Storia di Quattro Anni, 1919–1922.* Rome, 1946.

Noland, Aron. *The Founding of the French Socialist Party.* Cambridge, Mass., 1953.

Nollau, Gunther. *International Communism and World Revolution.* New York, 1961.

Osterroth, Franz. *Biographisches Lexicon des Sozialismus.* Hanover, 1960.

Page, Stanley. *Lenin and World Revolution.* New York, 1959.

Prélot, Marcel. *Evolution politique du socialisme français.* Paris, 1959.

Rappoport, Angelo. *Dictionary of Socialism.* London, 1924.

Riboldi, Ezio. *Vicende Socialista.* Milan, 1964.

Ritter, Gerhard A. *Die Arbeiterbewegung im Wilhelminschen Reich.* Berlin, 1963.

Rocher, J. *Lénine et le mouvement zimmerwaldien en France.* Paris, 1934.

Roland-Holst, Henrietta. *Rosa Luxemburg, Ihr Leben und Werken.* Zurich, 1937.

Rosenburg, Arthur. *A History of Bolshevism.* London, 1934.

――――. *Geschichte der Weimarer Republik.* Karlsbad, 1935.

Rosmer, Alfred. *Le mouvement ouvrier pendant la guerre.* 2 vols. Paris, 1936.

Roth, Guenther. *The Social Democrats in Imperial Germany.* Totowa, New Jersey, 1963.

Ryder, A. J. *The German Revolution of 1918.* Cambridge, 1967.

Salone, William. *Italy in the Giolittean Era.* Philadelphia, 1960.

Schapiro, Leonard. *The Communist Party of the Soviet Union*. London, 1960.

Schorske, Carl. *German Social Democracy, 1905–1917*. Cambridge, Mass., 1955.

Schüddekopf, Otto-Ernst. "Karl Radek in Berlin." *Archiv für Sozialgeschichte*. Hanover, 1962. 2, 87–167.

Spriano, Paolo. *L'Occupazione delle fabbriche, Settembre 1920*. Turin, 1964.

———. *Storia del Partito Communista Italiano*. Turin, 1967.

Ströbel, Heinrich. *Die Deutsche Revolution*. Berlin, 1922.

Tasca, Angelo. *Nascita e Avvento del Fascismo*. Florence, 1950.

Thayer, John A. *Italy and the Great War*. Madison, 1964.

Thomson, David. *Democracy in France*. New York, 1964.

Tormin, Walter. *Zwischen Rätediktatur und sozialer Demokratie*. Dusseldorf, 1954.

Trevisani, Giulio. *Piccola Enciclopedia del Socialismo e del Communismo*. Milan, 1958.

Trotsky, Leon. *History of the Russian Revolution*. London, 1966.

Ulam, Adam. *The Bolsheviks*. New York, 1966.

Valiani, Leo. "Il Partito socialista italiano nel periodo della neutralità, 1914–1915." *Annali 1967* (Instituto Giangiacomo Feltrinelli). Milan, 1963. Pp. 260–386.

———. "Il Partito socialista italiano da 1900 al 1918." *Rivista Storica Italiana*, 75, II (1963), 269–326.

———. *Questioni di storia del socialismo*. Turin, 1958.

Vidal, J. *Le mouvement ouvrier en France*. Paris, 1938.

Waldman, Eric. *The Spartacist Uprising of 1919*. Milwaukee, 1958.

Walter, Gérard. *Histoire du Parti communiste français*. Paris, 1948.

Weber, Eugen. *Action Française*. Stanford, 1962.

Weber, Hermann. *Die Wandlung des deutschen Kommunismus*. Frankfurt am Main, 1969.

Webster, Richard A. *The Cross and the Fasces*. Stanford, 1960.

Weill, Georges. *Histoire du mouvement sociale en France, 1852–1924*. Paris, 1924.

Willard, Claude. *Les Guesdistes*. Paris, 1965.

Wohl, Robert. "La Revolution ou la Mort: Raymond Lefebvre and the Formation of the French Communist Party." *International Review of Social History*, 7 (1962), 177–202.

———. *French Communism in the Making, 1914–1924*. Stanford, 1966.

Wolfe, Bertram. *Three Who Made a Revolution*. New York, 1948.

Wright, Gordon. *France in Modern Times*. Chicago, 1960.

———. *Rural Revolution in France*. Stanford, 1964.

Zévaès, Alexandre. *Le Parti socialiste de 1904 à 1923*. Paris, 1926.

Zibordi, Giovanni. *Storia del Partito socialista italiano attraverso i suoi congressi*. Reggio Emilia, n.d.

Unpublished Dissertations

Fainsod, Merle. "The Origins of the Third International, 1914–1919." Harvard University, 1932.

Kieffer, Martin. "French 'Defeatism' in World War I." Columbia University, 1960.

Korey, William. "Zinoviev and the Problem of World Revolution." Columbia University, 1960.

Ryder, A. J. "The Independent Social Democratic Party and the German Revolution, 1917–1920." London University, 1958.

Urquidi, Donald William. "The Origin of the Italian Communist Party, 1918–1921." Columbia University, 1962.

Wohl, Robert. "The Origins of the French Communist Party, 1914–1920." Princeton University, 1963.

Index